Lecture Notes
in Business Information Processing   **314**

More information about this series at http://www.springer.com/series/7911

Juan Garbajosa · Xiaofeng Wang
Ademar Aguiar (Eds.)

Agile Processes in Software Engineering and Extreme Programming

19th International Conference, XP 2018
Porto, Portugal, May 21–25, 2018
Proceedings

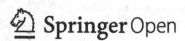

Editors
Juan Garbajosa
Technical University of Madrid
Madrid, Madrid
Spain

Ademar Aguiar
University of Porto
Porto
Portugal

Xiaofeng Wang
Free University of Bozen-Bolzano
Bolzano
Italy

ISSN 1865-1348   ISSN 1865-1356   (electronic)
Lecture Notes in Business Information Processing
ISBN 978-3-319-91601-9   ISBN 978-3-319-91602-6   (eBook)
https://doi.org/10.1007/978-3-319-91602-6

Library of Congress Control Number: 2018944291

Preface

This volume contains the papers presented at XP 2018, the 19th International Conference on Agile Software Development, held during May 21–25, 2018, in Porto, Portugal.

XP is the premier agile software development conference combining research and practice. It is a unique forum where agile researchers, academics, practitioners, thought leaders, coaches, and trainers get together to present and discuss their most recent innovations, research results, experiences, concerns, challenges, and trends. XP conferences have been pushing forward the successful evolution and adoption of agile by teams and organizations, not only in the software industry and academia, but also beyond. Whether you are new to agile or a seasoned agile practitioner, XP 2018 provided a playful and informal environment to learn and trigger discussions around its main theme – make, inspect, adapt.

Submissions of unpublished high-quality research papers related to agile and lean software development were invited for the XP 2018 Research Papers Track. The submissions received addressed the full spectrum of agile software development, broadly on agile, on issues of concern to researchers and practitioners alike. Submissions based on empirical studies and including practitioners and academic collaborations were encouraged. We received 62 submissions for the track. After the first screening by the track chairs, 58 submissions were sent out for single-blinded peer reviews. Each submission received (on average) three reviews from the Program Committee members. The committee decided to accept 21 papers, which are included in these proceedings.

The success of the XP 2018 conference and the Research Papers Track should be attributed to the passionate and hard work of many people. We greatly appreciate the contributions from everyone, especially the authors and presenters of all papers, the Program Committee members, the volunteers, and the sponsors. Last but not least, we would like to express our sincere thanks to the organizing team of XP 2018, for their great and constant support to us.

April 2018

Juan Garbajosa
Xiaofeng Wang
Ademar Aguiar

Preface

Organization

Conference Chair

Ademar Aguiar   Universidade do Porto, Portugal

Research Papers Co-chairs

Juan Garbajosa   Universidad Politécnica de Madrid, Spain
Xiaofeng Wang   Free University of Bozen-Bolzano, Italy

Research Workshops Co-chairs

Stefan Wagner   University of Stuttgart, Germany
Rashina Hoda   The University of Auckland, New Zealand

Research Posters Co-chairs

Hugo Ferreira   Universidade do Porto, Portugal
Davide Taibi   Free University of Bozen-Bolzano, Italy

Doctoral Symposium Co-chairs

Pekka Abrahamsson   University of Jyväskylä, Finland
Casper Lassenius   Aalto University, Finland

Industry and Practice Co-chairs

Jan Coupette   Codecentric, Germany
Nils Wloka   Codecentric, Germany

Experience Reports Co-chairs

Rebecca Wirfs-Brock   Wirfs-Brock Associates, USA
Joseph Yoder   The Refactory, USA

Agile in Education and Training Co-chairs

Craig Anslow   Victoria University of Wellington, New Zealand
Robert Chatley   Imperial College London/Develogical Ltd., UK

Tools and Demos Co-chairs

Seb Rose   Cucumber Limited, UK
Allegra Cooper   IT CTO, The Vanguard Group, Inc., USA

Tutorials and Workshops Co-chairs

Alan O'Callaghan   Emerald Hill Limited, UK
Lachlan Heasman   Independent, Australia

Openspace Chair

Charlie Poole   Poole Consulting, USA

Panels Chair

Steven Fraser   Innoxec, USA

Media Design Chair

Miguel Carvalhais   Universidade do Porto, Portugal

Communication Design

Mafalda Marinho   Freelancer, Portugal
Rita Ribeiro   Freelancer, Portugal

Press and Media Sponsors

Pam Hughes   Agile Alliance, USA

Sponsors Liaison

Philip Brock   Agile Alliance, USA

Student Volunteers Co-chairs

Diogo Amaral   Universidade do Porto, Portugal
André Lago   Universidade do Porto, Portugal

Local Arrangements

Pedro Miguel Silva   Universidade do Porto, Portugal
Esperanza Jurado   Sopeña Badajoz, Spain
Jose Luis Gonzalez   Sopeña Badajoz, Spain

Agile Portugal Liaison

Filipe Correia   Universidade do Porto, Portugal
Catarina Reis   IP Leiria, Portugal

Agile Alliance Liaison

Jutta Eckstein   Independent, Germany

Steering Committee

Juan Garbajosa   Universidad Politécnica de Madrid, Spain
Casper Lassenius   Aalto University, Finland
Erik Lundh   IngenjörsGlädje, Sweden
Hubert Baumeister   Technical University of Denmark, Denmark
Jutta Eckstein   Independent, Germany
Michele Marchesi   DMI - University of Cagliari, Italy
Nils Wloka   Codecentric, Germany
Philip Brock   Agile Alliance, USA
Steven Fraser   Innoxec, USA
Seb Rose   Cucumber Limited, UK

Institutional Partners

Universidade do Porto, Portugal
ScaleUp Porto, Portugal
Agile Portugal, Portugal
Agile Alliance, USA

Program Committee

Pekka Abrahamsson   University of Jyväskylä, Finland
Hubert Baumeister   Technical University of Denmark, Denmark
Jan Bosch   Chalmers University of Technology, Sweden
François Coallier   École de technologie supérieure, Canada
Kieran Conboy   National University of Galway, Ireland
Steve Counsell   Brunel University, UK
Daniela Cruzes   SINTEF, Norway
Torgeir Dingsøyr   Norwegian University of Science and Technology,
                          Norway
Christof Ebert   Vector Consulting Services, Germany
Hakan Erdogmus   Carnegie Mellon University, USA
Michael Felderer   University of Innsbruck, Austria
Brian Fitzgerald   Lero - Irish Software Engineering Research Centre, Ireland
Alfredo Goldman   University of São Paulo, Brazil
Tony Gorschek   Blekinge Institute of Technology, Sweden

Des Greer	Queen's University Belfast, UK
Peggy Gregory	University of Central Lancashire, UK
Eduardo Guerra	National Institute of Space Research, Brazil
Rashina Hoda	The University of Auckland, New Zealand
Helena Holmström Olsson	University of Malmo, Sweden
Sami Hyrynsalmi	Tampere University of Technology, Finland
Andrea Janes	Free University of Bolzano, Italy
Fabio Kon	University of São Paulo, Brazil
Casper Lassenius	Massachusetts Institute of Technology, USA
Lech Madeyski	Wroclaw University of Science and Technology, Poland
Michele Marchesi	DMI - University of Cagliari, Italy
Sabrina Marczak	PUCRS, Brazil
Frank Maurer	University of Calgary, Canada
Claudia Melo	University of Brasília, Brazil
Tommi Mikkonen	University of Helsinki, Finland
Alok Mishra	Atilim University, Turkey
Nils Brede Moe	SINTEF, Norway
Juergen Muench	Reutlingen University, Germany
Daniel Méndez Fernández	Technical University of Munich, Germany
Maria Paasivaara	Helsinki University of Technology, Finland
Kai Petersen	Blekinge Institute of Technology/Ericsson AB, Sweden
Pilar Rodríguez	University of Oulu, Finland
Bernhard Rumpe	RWTH Aachen University, Germany
Hugo Sereno Ferreira	University of Porto, Portugal
Helen Sharp	The Open University, UK
Darja Smite	Blekinge Institute of Technology, Sweden
Roberto Tonelli	University of Cagliari, Italy
Ayse Tosun	Istanbul Technical University, Turkey
Stefan Wagner	University of Stuttgart, Germany
Hironori Washizaki	Waseda University, Japan
Agustin Yague	Universidad Politécnica de Madrid, Spain

Additional Reviewers

Amor, Robert	Dennehy, Denis
Anslow, Craig	Díaz, Jessica
Bajwa, Sohaib Shahid	Edison, Henry
Bordin, Silvia	Gutierrez, Javier
Bruel, Pedro	Hansen, Guido
Carroll, Noel	Khanna, Dron
Correia, Filipe	Klotins, Eriks
Cukier, Daniel	Kropp, Martin
Da Silva, Tiago Silva	Lunesu, Maria Ilaria

Melegati, Jorge
Mikalsen, Marius
Netz, Lukas
Nguyen Duc, Anh
Reis, Catarina I.
Rosa, Thatiane
Schmalzing, David

Serradilla, Francisco
Sibal, Ritu
Solem, Anniken
Stettina, Christoph Johann
Suri, Bharti
Vestues, Kathrine
Wang, Yang

Contents

Agile Requirements

Cosmic User Story Standard. 3
  Miguel Ecar, Fabio Kepler, and João Pablo S. da Silva

Improving Mockup-Based Requirement Specification
with End-User Annotations 19
  *Matias Urbieta, Nahime Torres, José Matias Rivero, Gustavo Rossi,
  and F. J. Dominguez-Mayo*

Agile Testing

Combining STPA and BDD for Safety Analysis and Verification in Agile
Development: A Controlled Experiment. 37
  Yang Wang and Stefan Wagner

Software Tester, We Want to Hire You! an Analysis of the Demand
for Soft Skills. 54
  Raluca Florea and Viktoria Stray

Developers' Initial Perceptions on TDD Practice: A Thematic Analysis
with Distinct Domains and Languages. 68
  Joelma Choma, Eduardo M. Guerra, and Tiago Silva da Silva

Myths and Facts About Static Application Security Testing Tools:
An Action Research at Telenor Digital. 86
  *Tosin Daniel Oyetoyan, Bisera Milosheska, Mari Grini,
  and Daniela Soares Cruzes*

Automated Acceptance Tests as Software Requirements: An Experiment
to Compare the Applicability of *Fit Tables* and *Gherkin Language* 104
  Ernani César dos Santos and Patrícia Vilain

Agile Transformation

Interface Problems of Agile in a Non-agile Environment 123
  Sven Theobald and Philipp Diebold

Enterprise Agility: Why Is Transformation so Hard? 131
  Teemu Karvonen, Helen Sharp, and Leonor Barroca

Technical and Organizational Agile Practices: A Latin-American Survey   146
  Nicolás Paez, Diego Fontdevila, Fernando Gainey,
  and Alejandro Oliveros

Agile Software Development – Adoption and Maturity: An Activity
Theory Perspective   160
  Pritam Chita

Scaling Agile

Do Agile Methods Work for Large Software Projects?.   179
  Magne Jørgensen

Learning in the Large - An Exploratory Study of Retrospectives
in Large-Scale Agile Development   191
  Torgeir Dingsøyr, Marius Mikalsen, Anniken Solem,
  and Kathrine Vestues

Reporting in Agile Portfolio Management: Routines, Metrics and Artefacts
to Maintain an Effective Oversight   199
  Christoph Johann Stettina and Lennard Schoemaker

Inter-team Coordination in Large-Scale Agile Development: A Case Study
of Three Enabling Mechanisms.   216
  Finn Olav Bjørnson, Julia Wijnmaalen, Christoph Johann Stettina,
  and Torgeir Dingsøyr

Supporting Large-Scale Agile Development with Domain-Driven Design   232
  Ömer Uludağ, Matheus Hauder, Martin Kleehaus, Christina Schimpfle,
  and Florian Matthes

Towards Agile Scalability Engineering.   248
  Gunnar Brataas, Geir Kjetil Hanssen, and Georg Ræder

Human-Centric Agile

Stress in Agile Software Development: Practices and Outcomes   259
  Andreas Meier, Martin Kropp, Craig Anslow, and Robert Biddle

Teamwork Quality and Team Performance: Exploring Differences Between
Small and Large Agile Projects.   267
  Yngve Lindsjørn, Gunnar R. Bergersen, Torgeir Dingsøyr,
  and Dag I. K. Sjøberg

Continuous Experimentation

Challenges and Strategies for Undertaking Continuous Experimentation
to Embedded Systems: Industry and Research Perspectives   277
    David Issa Mattos, Jan Bosch, and Helena Holmström Olsson

ICOs Overview: Should Investors Choose an ICO Developed with the Lean
Startup Methodology?   293
    Simona Ibba, Andrea Pinna, Gavina Baralla, and Michele Marchesi

Author Index   309

Agile Requirements

Cosmic User Story Standard

Miguel Ecar[1(✉)], Fabio Kepler[1,2], and João Pablo S. da Silva[1]

[1] Campus Alegrete, Federal University of Pampa,
810 Tiarajú Avenue, Alegrete, RS, Brazil
miguel@ecarsm.com, {fabiokepler,joaosilva}@unipampa.edu.br
[2] Unbabel, Lisbon, Portugal
http://unbabel.com
http://ecarsm.com

Abstract. User Story is a technique widely used in Agile development.
It is characterised as short and high level descriptions of required functionality, written in customer language during the very early requirement
gathering stage and containing just enough information to produce the
estimated implementation effort. The COSMIC method is a second generation technique for function size measurement. The requirement estimation precision in COSMIC is directly proportional to the requirement
detailing level. Current templates for user stories writing might ignore
important information for COSMIC measurement purposes. This paper
introduces a new template for writing user stories which is more expres-
sive in terms of COSMIC size estimation. We performed a qualitative
survey to introduce this new user story template to the COSMIC community, intending to capture the COSMIC users opinion in terms of
expressiveness and how valuable it is. The survey points to promising
results considering the COSMIC users opinion about the new template.
This study contributes to agile requirements from the COSMIC users
point of view. This new template may be a step forward in terms of user
story estimation for COSMIC sizing based projects.

Keywords: COSMIC · Functional Size Measurement · User Story
Agile requirements · Agile development

1 Introduction

The area of Software Requirements is concerned with the elicitation, analysis, specification, and validation of software requirements [1]. There are a large
number of styles and techniques for writing software requirements, including,
for example, requirements list, Use Cases (UC), User Stories (US), and Formal
Specification.

The Extreme Programming (XP) software development framework introduced the idea of User Stories (US), which are basically use cases that concisely
capture functional requirements. Developers usually split it up requirements into

J. Garbajosa et al. (Eds.): XP 2018, LNBIP 314, pp. 3–18, 2018.
https://doi.org/10.1007/978-3-319-91602-6_1

US [2] and typically write user stories on cards to describe each system functionality that the customer desires [3].

User story is one of the most widespread techniques for writing requirements in agile environments. User Stories have gained popularity among agile approaches, being one of the main techniques used when the subject is requirements engineering in agile environments. There is a common template to write user stories, however a number of different extensions have been adding or suppressing information, according to the application context.

Despite this, current requirements specification techniques used in agile software development are customer-oriented and, from the developers point of view, have proven to be insufficient [4]. In other words, there are more information from the customer point of view written in a too high level than from the developers perspective, with some implementation details. Moreover, user stories might reflect in documentation debt [5], which can cause significant impact in terms of maintenance effort and cost in agile software development projects, which drive developers to misunderstanding. Thus, it could be detailed and to continue in high level.

Functional Size Measurement (FSM) was proposed in order to obtain better units of sizing. According to ISO/IEC 14143 [6], FSM was designed to overcome the limitations of earlier methods of software sizing by shifting the focus away from measuring how software is implemented to measuring size in terms of the functions required by the user.

FSM intends to measure software functionality, being independent of technology, platform and individual. Based on defined measurements procedures it is possible to define standard, objective, consistency and comparable results [7].

The Common Software Measurement International Consortium (COSMIC) is a group formed in 1998 which intended to develop the second generation of FSM [8]. The group objective was to develop a method for measuring user requirements in conformity with fundamental software engineering principles and the measurement theory. The method is applicable for measuring business, real-time and infrastructure software [8]. The term COSMIC is used both for the group and the method.

The COSMIC method has been designed to accept extensions for particular domains [9]. A domain for which it has been extended is Agile development. According to [10], the agile guideline has the purpose of providing additional advice beyond the COSMIC Measurement Manual on Agile projects. The COSMIC method is perfectly suited for measuring software evolving through iterations and increments as typically found in Agile development without any adaptation [10].

Sizing software in Agile development requires exactly the same knowledge, principles and rules of the COSMIC Method when used in any other project management method [10].

When sizing user stories using the COSMIC method, Message Sequence Diagrams may be used as shown in Fig. 1. The vertical line represents a functional process and horizontal arrows represent data movements. Entries and Reads are shown as arrows incoming to functional process and Exit and Writes as outgoing arrows, appearing in the required sequence as top-down order [10].

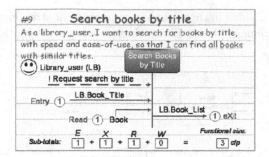

Fig. 1. User Story and Message Sequence Diagram. Source: [10]

As can be seen, sizing user stories using the COSMIC method is not a difficult task. Nevertheless, a precise size estimation is directly proportional to the level of detail a US is written. Thus, based on the example in Fig. 1, some valuable information may by missed, such as connections between data groups and direct user feedback.

This paper introduces a new template for writing user stories which contains more expressiveness in terms of COSMIC size estimation. The proposed template specify possible connections between system data groups and express clearly the presence of user feedback.

We performed a survey to introduce this new user story template to the COSMIC community. The qualitative survey intended to capture COSMIC users opinion in terms of expressiveness and how valuable it was.

The rest of the paper is organized as follows. Section 2 shows the background of the COSMIC method and existing user stories templates. Section 3 presents the proposed template and its details. Section 4 shows the evaluation process conducted via survey with the COSMIC community and its analysis. Finally, Sect. 6 draws some conclusions and future works.

2   Background

In this section we present the COSMIC method in Subsect. 2.1 and an overview of user story templates in Subsect. 2.2.

2.1   COSMIC Method

The COSMIC method was born from the need to measure requirements from systems such as business application, real-time and infrastructure software, and some types of scientific or engineering software [8]. This necessity comes from some IFPUG technique weaknesses. It has become increasingly difficult to map Albrecht's function types to modern ways of modelling software requirements, especially for software as services, real-time domain, and infrastructure software [8].

The method is divided in three phases: measurement strategy phase, mapping phase, and measurement phase. These phases and their definition are shown in Fig. 2.

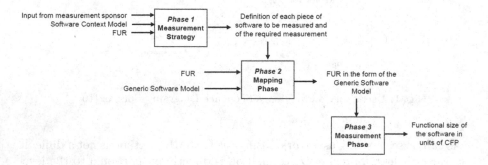

Fig. 2. The COSMIC measurement process [8]

The Measurement Strategy phase defines what will be measured. It must be defined in the functional user perspective, such as humans, hardware devices, or other software which will interact with the software under measurement. First the measurement purpose is defined, which will lead to defining the scope and functional users [8]. There are five key parameters to determine in this phase:

- **Purpose:** helps to determine all the following parameters;
- **Scope:** defines what is included or excluded in the functionality and what are the restrictions;
- **Level of composition:** pieces of software to be measured, for example, the whole application (level 0), or a primary component in a distributed system (level 1), or a re-usable component in a service-oriented software (level 2);
- **Functional users:** must be defined for each piece of software. They are humans or things which will send or receive data to or from the software;
- **Layers:** the software architecture; the piece of software must be confined in one layer.

The Mapping phase consists in creating the functional user requirement COSMIC model, it starts from whatever the artefacts are available. The model is created applying the COSMIC Generic Software Model, which is defined for four principles [8].

The first principle is that a software functionality is composed of functional processes, each functional process corresponds to an event in the functional user world.

The second phase defines that functional processes are consisted of subprocesses, they do only two things, they move and manipulate data. Data movements which move data from functional users into functional processes or viceversa are called **Entries** and **Exits**. Data movements which move data from

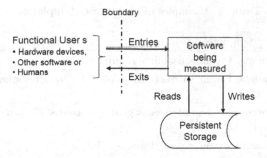

Fig. 3. Data movements [8].

persistence storage and vice-versa are called **Writes** and **Reads**. As may be seen in Fig. 3.

The fourth principle says that each data movement moves a single Data group. Data group is defined as a single object of the functional user interest.

The last principle defines that data manipulation are assumed to be accounted by the associated data movement. Data manipulation are not measured separately.

The Measurement Phase consists in taking account data movements, each data movement is a unit of COSMIC Function Point (CFP). In this phase they are counted and sum over all functional processes. A single functional process must have at least two data movements and there is no upper size limit. When measuring a software enhancement, it must be identified all data movements added, changed and deleted and sum them over all its functional processes. The minimum of any modification is 1 CFP [8].

2.2   User Story Overview

The User Stories technique is widely used in Agile development. They are characterised as short and high level description of the required functionality written in customer language. The traditional story template is: [1]

"As a <role>, I want to <goal/desire>, so that <benefit>".

User Stories are used in the very early stage during requirements gathering. They contain only enough information to estimate the implementation effort. They should be written in customer language before the implementation, for appropriated acceptance [10].

Besides the traditional one, there other User Stories writing templates. The Table 1 shows some examples.

Template US01 [11] only introduces a specific use of user stories to express usability requirements. There is no relevant difference from the traditional template.

The template US02 [12] also, does not present any significant difference. It only makes explicit that the object must be present, which is a natural practice when using the traditional template.

Table 1. Examples of user stories templates.

ID	User story template
US01	"As a <role>, I want <usability requirement>" [11]
US02	"As a <role>, I want to <action> <object>, so that <business value>" [12]
US03	"As a <persona>, I want/need <goal> so that <Nielsen's heuristic> will be met" [13]
US04	"As a <role>, I want <goal/desire>" [14]
US05	"In order to <receive benefit> as a <role>, I want <goal/desire>" [15]
US06	"As <who> <when> <where>, I <what> because <why>." [16]
US07	"As a <role>, I want to <goal/desire>, <non-functional requirement>, so that <benefit>" [10]

Template US03 [13] contributes in terms of usability engineering. The last part, which in traditional template is responsible for expressing feedback or user expectation, is specific for Nielsen's heuristic values, which should be met in the user story.

Template US04 [14] is similar to the traditional template but makes the last part optional. The user story is shorter and does not provide information about feedback or user expectation. It may be useful once maintain only the minimum valuable information.

Template US05 [15] is equivalent to the traditional template but places the benefit first instead of last.

Template US06 [16], also known as "Five Ws", adds more relevant information from the user perspective, namely, "when" and "where", compared to the traditional template.

Template US07 [10] only adds information about non-functional requirements found in the functional process. Considering the counting example presented in [10], this information is not relevant for sizing estimation.

3   COSMIC User Story Standard

Based on the user story templates shown in Table 1, we can observe some weaknesses and limitation.

First of all, none of existent templates provide information about connections between data groups or entities. This information is considerably important in terms of COSMIC estimation, once data movements are detected also considering connections or links present in the functional process.

Furthermore, current templates, besides providing a place for result or user expectation specification, it is not specific for feedback. Thus, it may be used to express user expectation, which might not be related to the functional process, for example, *"As a user, I want to receive by email daily news, so that I am always up to date to the news."*

We propose a template called COSMIC User Story Standard (CUSS). The main improvement is adding information about connections among the data groups manipulated in the functional process. Other improvement is related to user feedback. Some functional processes provide feedback to user, while others may not provide, so it is clearly presented in US.

The CUSS template is the following:

"As a <who/role>, I want to <what>, linked to <connections>; so/then be notified about operation status."
where:

- <who/role> is the Functional User;
- <what> is the verb the represents the action or the functional process;
- <connections> represents other data groups involved in this functional process;
- "so/then be notified about operation status" is optional statement and represents the functional user feedback.

The corresponding "context-free grammar" is presented in Fig. 4. The terminal symbols are As a, As an, As the, I want to, I can, connected to, so,

```
US  -> AS USER I DOT | AS USER I L DOT |
       AS USER I FEED DOT |
       AS USER I L FEED DOT
I   -> IWANT METHOD DG
L   -> LINK PLINK |
       LINK PLINK SLINK TLINK |
       LINK PLINK TLINK

AS    -> As a | As an | As the
IWANT -> COMMA i want to | COMMA i can
LINK  -> COMMA connected to

FEED  -> SEMICOLON so | SEMICOLON then
FBACK -> FEED be informed about operation status

PLINK -> DG
SLINK -> COMMA PLINK | COMMA PLINK SLINK
TLINK -> and DG

DOT       -> .
COMMA     -> ,
SEMICOLON -> ;

USER   -> <list of roles>
METHOD -> <list of verbs/actions>
DG     -> <list of data groups>
```

Fig. 4. Context-free grammar

then, ., ,, ;, and, be informed about operation status, plus any words representing a role, a verb, or a data group. The non-terminal symbols are I, L, AS, IWANT, LINK, FEED, FBACK, PLINK, SLINK, TLINK, DOT, COMMA, SEMICOLON, USER, METHOD, DG. The initial symbol is US.

Examples are presented below.

- As a Manager, I want to remove a book.
- As an user, I can update books; so be notified about operation status.
- As a Manager, I want to add a new book, connected to author.
- As the Manager, I want to save books, connected to author and publishing company.
- As a Manager, I want to create books, connected to author and publishing company; then be notified about operation status.

4   Evaluation

We performed two evaluation strategies. The first one is a survey that was created to raise the COSMIC community opinion about the new template and its advantages and disadvantages. The second evaluation is an example of the size estimation result after decomposing a requirement using the traditional US template and using CUSS template.

4.1   Survey

The survey was created to retrieve the COSMIC community opinion about the proposed US template. The survey is divided in 3 parts. The first part is composed by questions to identify the respondent profile. The second part is composed by open questions about current templates, the proposed template and the impact in the agile aspect. The last part are closed questions in likert scale [17], where 0 is "Disagree Strongly" and 4 is "Agree Strongly" about the same questions from second part.

The survey had 22 responses. The Table 2 shows the respondents relation between certificate holders and years of experience with COSMIC.

Skipping to the third part of the survey, Fig. 5 show the boxplot in likert scale for the three statements, Question 01 is "Current Templates provide enough information in term of COSMIC Sizing." Question 02 is "COSMIC User Story Standard provides greater expressiveness in term of COSMIC Sizing." Question 03 is "COSMIC User Story Standard Template compromises the agility aspect in a process."

Based on this chart, we can observe that concerning to current US templates expressiveness, the concentration is around disagree moderately with an outlier in agree strongly, in other words, we can infer that current US templates do not have good expressiveness in terms of COSMIC sizing.

Moreover, it is observable that regarding to expressiveness increasing in CUSS, the concentration is in agree strongly, based on this, we can conclude that CUSS, is a step forward to have a better US COSMIC size estimation.

Table 2. Respondents distribution into groups.

Experience	Certified	Non certified
1 Year	0	1
2 Years	1	1
3 Years	4	0
4 Years	5	0
5 Years	5	0
6 Years	1	0
8 Years	2	0
10 Years	1	0
15 Years	1	0
	20	2

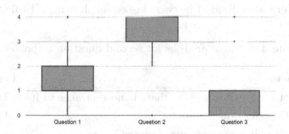

Fig. 5. First statement

Further more, the statement about CUSS to disturb the agile aspect, the chart shows that concentration is around disagree strongly, in other words, we can conclude that there is no heaviness, from agile point of view, in the information added in COSMIC User Story Standard.

Returning to the second part of the survey, we conducted an content analysis to analyse the answers with a deep interpretation.

The first open question is "Do you think that there is a lack of information in current User Story Templates? Please discourse about your answer.", the content analysis is divided in two groups, "Yes" and "No" answers. The "No" answers had not further discourse, so there were no classes in it. The "Yes" answers which had further discourse, were divided in four classes. Table 3 present the content analysis for the first open question. The percentage is over all answers for this question.

Based on answers related to lack of information in current US templates, we can observe that almost 80% of respondents agree that there are gaps in these templates. From this group, around a half of respondents see no problem in this information lack, so, around a half from those ones that agree that there are gaps in current US template see that it could provide more information for COSMIC size estimation.

Table 3. Content analysis for first question responses.

Group	Class	Percent.
No	-	22.7%
Yes	"Yes, but it is inevitable, expected"	13.6%
Yes	"Yes, it is designed to provide basic information"	27.3%
Yes	"Yes, it misses information"	13.6%
Yes	Just Yes	22.7%

The second open question is "In your opinion, Cosmic User Story Standard helps to identify more movements than other templates? Please discourse about your answer." The content analysis, was also, based on "Yes" and "No" answers end their further discourses. The "No" answers were divided in two classes and "Yes" answers were also divided in two classes as shown in Table 4.

Table 4. Content analysis for second question responses.

Group	Class	Percent.
No	"User Story is useless, there is no relevance in it"	13.6%
No	"I prefer other template"	4.5%
Yes	"Yes, it is a major step forward"	18.2%
Yes	"Yes, it is good, great, I like it"	63.6%

Based on the second question content analysis, we can conclude that over 80% agree that CUSS could help to identify more movements. From the percentage, around three-quarter classified it as "good" or "great" and one fourth classified it as "a step forward for US COSMIC sizing". According to this, we can conclude that CUSS may be well received by COSMIC community, and in fact, it may help in early COSMIC size estimation.

The third questions is "Do you think that this addition of information compromises the agile aspect? Please discourse about your answer." Likewise, we considered "Yes" and "No" answers, and classified its discussion. Table 5 presents the content analysis for third question.

Based on Table 5, about 95% of the respondents believe that information added in proposed template does not compromise the agile aspect of user story, in other words, the information added is light weight and the agile aspect is not corrupted.

Considering the first question, we can observe in content analysis that among 65% of the respondents considered that there is information lack in current user story templates, but it is not a problem since user story is designed to express only basic information.

Table 5. Content analysis for third question responses.

Group	Class	Percent.
No	-	31.8%
No	"somehow", "Why?"	27.3%
No	"there is no relation", "agile keeps agile"	27.3%
No	"the addition of information is light weight"	9.1%
Yes	"Certainly"	4.5%

The content analysis for the second question, among 80% consider that the proposed template is a good improvement in terms of COSMIC sizing, almost 20% considered it a major step forward.

For the third question, based on the content analysis among 95% of the respondents considered that the information added in proposed user story template does not compromise the agile aspect. Considering these answers, almost 60% sad just "No" or were not clear about what they think, while among 37% considered that it is not a problem.

4.2 Example

The second evaluation consists in an example that shows how it is different applying the traditional US template versus applying the proposed template when decomposing a requirement written as epic. The main difference can be observed in its value in CFP.

The requirement below is about a simple library system.

– The library system should allow a librarian user maintain authors, books. When a new book is created or edited the author and publisher information should come from the ones registered in the system. The manager user is also able to activate and deactivate registered books. The manager user can also list all booked books per client. The system should allow that client users book and/or rent books. The librarian user can also send emails about new books arrival.

The Table 6 presents the user stories written using the traditional template. The Table 7 shows user stories written using the proposed template.

We can observe that there is a significant difference in the total size of CFP units.

When using the CUSS template the number of CFP counted is 65, when using the traditional template the number of CFP counter is 37. This difference is related to detail level in each template. The proposed template add information which expose more interaction and consequently more movements.

If the estimation is performed based only on the information available in the traditional template, the professional should make assumptions about user

Table 6. Example using traditional template

ID	US	CFP
US01	As a Librarian, I want to register a new book, so that it is available for booking and/or loan	2
US02	As a Librarian, I want to remove books	2
US03	As a Librarian, I want to list all books	3
US04	As a Librarian, I want to update books, so that I can left it up to date	4
US05	As a Librarian, I want to register a new author, so that it can be user for book register	2
US06	As a Librarian, I want to remove an author	2
US07	As a Librarian, I want to list all authors	3
US08	As a Librarian, I want to update an author, so that I can left it up to date	4
US09	As a Manager, I want to activate a book, so that clients can book or rent it	2
US10	As a Manager, I want to deactivate a book, so that clients cannot book or rent it	2
US11	As a Manager, I want to list all booked books	3
US12	As a Client, I can create a new book booking, so that I can rent it	3
US13	As a Client, I can create a new book rental, so that I can rent books	3
US14	As a Librarian, I want to send emails about new books arrival	2
	Total	**37**

feedback and possible connections between data groups. The problem is that these assumption may not be true, so the estimation is over or under precise.

The information added in the proposed template might seem heavy weight, mainly if we are talking about writing US in requirements gathering. But the objective of the CUSS template is to be clear about valuable information in terms of COSMIC sizing.

Moreover, having more information in the very early development stage helps to have a more precise estimation. It is important for managers that have to control and estimate cost, time, team and etc.

5   Threats to Validity

The survey was anonymous and open to community, so anyone could respond it, however, it was published just to COSMIC users and shared via email to specific group of practitioners. Almost 90% of subjects are COSMIC certified, this factor

Table 7. Example using CUSS

ID	US	CFP
US01	As a Librarian, I want to register a new book, connected to author and publisher; then be informed about operation status	7
US02	As a Librarian, I want to remove books; then be informed about operation status	3
US03	As a Librarian, I want to list all books, connected to author and publisher	7
US04	As a Librarian, I want to update books, connected to author and publisher; then be informed about operation status	9
US05	As a Librarian, I want to register a new author; then be informed about operation status	3
US06	As a Librarian, I want to remove an author; then be informed about operation status	3
US07	As a Librarian, I want to list all authors	3
US08	As a Librarian, I want to update an author; then be informed about operation status	5
US09	As a Manager, I want to activate a book; then be informed about operation status	3
US10	As a Manager, I want to deactivate a book; then be informed about operation status	3
US11	As a Manager, I want to list all booked books, connected to clients	5
US12	As a Client, I can create a new book booking, connected to client and book; then be informed about operation status	6
US13	As a Client, I can create a new book rental, connected to client and book; then be informed about operation status	6
US14	As a Librarian, I want to send emails about new books arrival	2
	Total	**65**

increase answers quality and reliability, and even for those ones which are not certified the answers consistency was satisfactory. We considered all answers, due to even non certified may have significant contribution. But even so, all subjects have at least one year of experience with COSMIC in industry.

The survey was conducted comparing well known user story templates to the proposed one. In the first survey step, the subjects could see examples of use and the expressiveness difference between well known templates and the proposed template.

We made a cross validation using two approaches to answer the same questions. So, each question was asked twice via discursive way and likert scale [17]. Based on this double check, was could guarantee consistency between the answers. In other words, we double checked if discursive answers was according to likert [17] answer, finding solid results.

The COSMIC estimation was performed by a junior professional. So, there may be not as precise as an expert certified COSMIC professional estimator.

6   Conclusion and Future Work

This work presented a new template for user story writing. This template is called COSMIC User Story Standard and its purpose is to elevate the user story expressiveness in terms of COSMIC size estimation.

The information added in this template is related to connections among data groups in the estimated system, also there is an improvement related to user feedback. The added information is lightweight and does not make the user story saturated of information.

In order to raise the need to a new user story writing template, we developed a survey with COSMIC community to explore its possibilities and get feedback from potential users. The survey answers were analysed under content analysis. The result is enthusiastic, the template was well received by COSMIC community.

Survey content analysis allows us to realise that the information lack in user story is perceived by COSMIC users, but not necessarily it is seen as a huge problem.

Furthermore, content analysis also allows us to conclude that the proposed template is valuable for COSMIC community being classified as great and as a step forward in terms of COSMIC user story estimation.

Besides, we developed an example of the difference between the estimated size from user stories decomposed from the same epic and written in both, the traditional and the proposed, templates. The difference between the total CFP estimated size using the proposed template and the traditional is huge significant.

As future work, we aims to develop a software based on proposed template for automated grammar validation and verification. Moreover, we have intention to use this template as source to automated COSMIC size estimation of user stories. Furthermore, we pretend to perform empirical evaluation of the proposed template with experiments and case studies.

Acknowledgments. We thank mister Frank Vogelezang who provided insight and expertise that greatly assisted the research.

References

1. Abran, A., Moore, J.W., Bourque, P., Dupuis, R., Tripp, L.L.: Guide to the Software Engineering Body of Knowledge: 2004 Version SWEBOK. IEEE Computer Society, Washington, D.C. (2004)
2. Taibi, D., Lenarduzzi, V., Janes, A., Liukkunen, K., Ahmad, M.O.: Comparing requirements decomposition within the Scrum, Scrum with Kanban, XP, and Banana development processes. In: Baumeister, H., Lichter, H., Riebisch, M. (eds.) XP 2017. LNBIP, vol. 283, pp. 68–83. Springer, Cham (2017). https://doi.org/10.1007/978-3-319-57633-6_5

3. Maurer, F., Martel, S.: Extreme programming. Rapid development for web-based applications. IEEE Internet Comput. **6**(1), 86–90 (2002)
4 Medeiros, J., Vasconcelos, A., Coulão, M., Silva, C., Araújo, J.: An approach based on design practices to specify requirements in agile projects. In: Proceedings of the Symposium on Applied Computing, pp. 1114–1121. ACM (2017)
5. Mendes, T.S., de F Farias, M.A., Mendonça, M., Soares, H.F., Kalinowski, M., Spínola, R.O.: Impacts of agile requirements documentation debt on software projects: a retrospective study. In: Proceedings of the 31st Annual ACM Symposium on Applied Computing, pp. 1290–1295. ACM (2016)
6. ISO: Information technology—software measurement—functional size measurement (2012)
7. Akca, A., Tarhan, A.: Run-time measurement of cosmic functional size for Java business applications: initial results. In: 2012 Joint Conference of the 22nd International Workshop on Software Measurement and the 2012 Seventh International Conference on Software Process and Product Measurement (IWSM-MENSURA), pp. 226–231, October 2012
8. Abran, A., Baklizky, D., Davies, L., Fagg, P., Gencel, C., Lesterhuis, A., Londeix, B., Soubra, H., Symons, C., Villavicencio, M., Vogelezang, F., Woodward, C.: Introduction to the COSMIC method of measuring software. Common Software Measurement International Consortium (2014)
9. Abran, A., Baklizky, D., Desharnais, J.M., Fagg, P., Gencel, C., Symons, C., Ramasubramani, J.K., Lesterhuis, A., Londeix, B., Nagano, S.I., Santillo, L., Soubra, H., Trudel, S., Villavicencio, M., Vogelezang, F., Woodward, C.: COSMIC measurement manual. Common Software Measurement International Consortium (2015)
10. Berardi, E., Buglione, L., Cuadrado-Collego, J., Desharnais, J.M., Gencel, C., Lesterhuis, A., Santillo, L., Symons, C., Trudel, S.: Guideline for the use of COSMIC FSM to manage agile projects. Common Software Measurement International Consortium (2011)
11. Moreno, A.M., Yagüe, A.: Agile user stories enriched with usability. In: Wohlin, C. (ed.) XP 2012. LNBIP, vol. 111, pp. 168–176. Springer, Heidelberg (2012). https://doi.org/10.1007/978-3-642-30350-0_12
12. Zeaaraoui, A., Bougroun, Z., Belkasmi, M.G., Bouchentouf, T.: User stories template for object-oriented applications. In: 2013 Third International Conference on Innovative Computing Technology (INTECH), pp. 407–410. IEEE (2013)
13. Choma, J., Zaina, L.A.M., Beraldo, D.: UserX story: incorporating UX aspects into user stories elaboration. In: Kurosu, M. (ed.) HCI 2016. LNCS, vol. 9731, pp. 131–140. Springer, Cham (2016). https://doi.org/10.1007/978-3-319-39510-4_13
14. Cohn, M.: Advantages of the "as a user, i want" user story template (2008). https://www.mountaingoatsoftware.com/blog/advantages-of-the-as-a-user-i-want-user-story-template. Accessed 9 Sept 2017
15. Matts, C.: Feature injection: three steps to success (2011). https://www.infoq.com/articles/feature-injection-success. Accessed 9 Sept 2017
16. Pupek, D.: Writing user stories the 5 Ws way (2008). http://blog.agilejedi.com/2008/03/writing-user-stories-5-ws-way-writing.html. Accessed 9 Sept 2017
17. Likert, R.: A technique for the measurement of attitudes. Arch. Psychol. **22**, 1–55 (1932)

Improving Mockup-Based Requirement Specification with End-User Annotations

Matias Urbieta[1,2(✉)], Nahime Torres[3], José Matias Rivero[1,2],
Gustavo Rossi[1,2], and F. J. Dominguez-Mayo[4]

[1] LIFIA, Facultad de Informática, UNLP, 50 y 120, La Plata, Argentina
{murbieta, mrivero, gustavo}@lifia.info.unlp.edu.ar
[2] CONICET, Buenos Aires, Argentina
[3] Politecnico di Milano, Piazza Leonardo da Vinci 32, 20133 Milan, Italy
rocionahime.torres@polimit.it
[4] IWT2, Computer Languages and Systems Department, University of Seville,
ETSII, Avda. Reina Mercedes S/N, 41012 Seville, Spain
fjdominguez@us.es

Abstract. Agile approaches, one of the key methodologies used in today's
software projects, often rely on user interface mockups for capturing the goals
that the system must satisfy. Mockups, as any other requirement artifact, may
suffer from ambiguity and contradiction issues when several points of view are
surveyed/elicited by different analysts. This article introduces a novel approach
that enhances mockups with friendly end-user annotations that helps formalizing
the requirements and reducing or identifying conflicts. We present an evaluation
of the approach in order to measure how the use of annotations improves
requirements quality.

Keywords: Requirement · Agile · Documentation · Mockup · Annotation

1 Introduction

Eliciting application requirements implies understanding the needs of one or more
stakeholders even in cases where the business domain may be partially or totally
unknown for the analysts who perform the elicitation. Often, requirements are agreed
by stakeholders in such a way that the semantics and meanings of each used term are
well understood. However, when different points of view [6] of the same business
concept exist, ambiguities and/or inconsistencies may arise being them detrimental to
the software requirement specification. Although the use of agile approaches has
become a key factor in project success[1], the companies practicing these approaches
claim that the minimal documentation provided by user stories is a challenge for the
projects [3]. When the personnel turnover or rapid changes to requirement arises, the
application evolution is severely compromised. Traditionally, conciliation tasks are
performed using meeting-based tools [8] in order to eliminate requirements ambiguity
and inconsistency but in the event of agile approaches the tacit knowledge which is

---

[1] 9th Annual State of Agile Survey - http://stateofagile.versionone.com/.

© The Author(s) 2018
J. Garbajosa et al. (Eds.): XP 2018, LNBIP 314, pp. 19–34, 2018.
https://doi.org/10.1007/978-3-319-91602-6_2

mandatory in this task can be lost on personnel turnover or inaccessibility when the appropriate customer is unavailable. Agile approaches often rely on unit testing for maintaining the alignment of requirements when these suffer changes but large textual descriptions present in documents and the requirement change volatility make it impossible to keep artefacts updated and consistent [1]. When requirement inconsistencies are not detected on time - being this one of the most severe reasons for project cost overrun [21] -, they may become defects in the application. In this context, the effort to correct the faults is several orders of magnitude higher than correcting requirements at the early stages [2].

In practice, agile methodologies reduce the gap between expectations and deliverables by having short development cycles in which a deliverable is released to be confronted with requirements when an iteration ends. This practice often does not focus on documenting the solution (class diagrams, deployment diagrams, etc.) as it is done, for instance, in waterfall or RUP approaches. One of the most important tools for documentation adopted by agile practitioners is the mockup of user interfaces. By using this technique, the way in which business scenarios are instantiated relies on lightweight textual descriptions like User Stories, and wireframes design that easily communicate application behavior to stakeholders.

User Interface mockups are a useful tool for describing scenarios where the real-life data is used for exemplifying the use case instead of abstract descriptions. However, the information they provide is informal and allows misunderstandings by different stakeholders. For example, we could consider a marketplace application showing a product list like the one shown in Fig. 1. For every product, we have an image, a price, a title, a description, a quantity sold, a location, an icon to indicate if the product is new, another to indicate if the seller is premium and one that indicates whether the product has free shipping or not. Although this information is illustrative, it lacks the

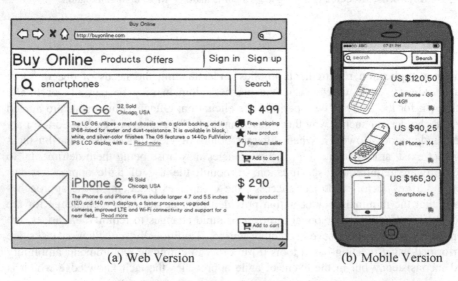

(a) Web Version   (b) Mobile Version

Fig. 1. Mockup of an e-commerce application.

precision to formally describe the requirements expected in the early stages of software development. The mockup's reader is not able to distinguish if the regular price or the Internet price property is intended to be displayed with the label "$499". The team members may interpret different possible behaviors accordingly to their point of view, experience and background. The developers may define by themselves the missing information based on this vague definition where any misconception will be detected later with a costly resolution. This is because the mockup tool is an informal specification which lacks of resources to enumerate abstractions such as variables and entities like UML does.

To make matter worse, as long as new requirements are planned as User Stories in sprints, one or more conflicts can raise. Inconsistencies may also arise from new requirements, which introduce new functionality or enhancements to the application or even from existing requirements that change during the development process. Let's suppose that for the use case exposed on Fig. 1, there is a new slightly different mobile-based user interface. This new mockup is used to describe a new commercial initiative and it has different business rules that cannot be appreciated by only looking at the mockup. Despite of the mobile counterpart may seem to be a legitimate design because much of the shown information is shared by both versions (mobile and web), there are specific details that belong to the mobile version such as promotional discounts or free-shipping benefits that are imperceptible by the reader at first sight.

To cope with the aforementioned problem, we present in this work as novel contribution a colloquial and user-friendly notation to describe data, navigation, business and interaction requirements upon mockups specifications. In order to evaluate the effectiveness of our approach, we include a controlled experiment that assesses the expressiveness improvement of Mockups using this approach.

The rest of this paper is structured as follows. Section 2 presents some related work on requirements validation and model consistency checking. Section 3 describes our approach to annotate mockups using end-user grammar. Section 4 presents an evaluation of our approach. Finally, Sect. 5 concludes this work discussing our main conclusions and some further work on this subject.

2 Related Work

The analysis and detection of conflicts, errors, and mistakes in the requirements phase are the most critical tasks in requirements engineering [7]. In [5], the authors surveyed the way in which Web engineering approaches deal with main tasks: requirements capture, requirements definition and requirements validation and conclude that most approaches use classical requirements techniques to deal with requirements. According to these, there are four main techniques for requirements validation: reviews, audits, traceability matrix and prototypes; in the Web engineering literature, requirements validation is one of the less treated subjects. Besides, none of these techniques offers a systematic approach for detecting conflicts in requirements. Requirements conflicts arise despite the way we document them, for example in [22] they define a framework for quality of user stories and one of the necessary conditions for a US to be of good quality is that it has to be unique and free of conflicts. Additionally, a characterization of conflict in user stories is presented but there is no mention of mockup's conflicts.

Mockups tools are gaining attention in the requirements engineering field since they help to build UI specifications in companion with end-users. Also, they help to discover and define non-UI requirements in a language that is closer to them, as opposed to plain textual specifications [11, 13]. Additionally, mockups have been proven to be an effective method to capture *fluid* requirements [18] – those that are usually expressed orally or informally and are an implicit (and usually lost) part of the elicitation process. The usage of user interfaces prototypes with static structure to define conceptual models has been already shown in [12]. While authors in this work show how E-R models can be derived from structured mockups, their approach is not applicable to informal mockups like the ones that are considered in this work. The ICONIX process [17] proposes to start with Graphical User Interface (GUI) prototypes as a first requirements artifact. While this may provide some initial guideline, in that work the authors do not provide any language or formal guidance to define data requirements. In [14], authors establish a method to work with Use cases and mockups in conjunction, however, Use Cases specification require more effort than a lightweight specification. In [10] the authors explain that sometimes when documenting requirements in agile this is so customer-oriented, that even if the specification is clear for the customer, they might not for the developers, having here conflicts between two actors in software development, and for this they propone Requirement Specification for Developers (RSD); each RSD can have mockups associated, and when a requirement is changed the mockup associated has to be reviewed.

Regarding requirement consistency, last years we have been researching different strategies to capture Web software requirements and validating its consistency and completeness [4, 19]. These approaches were designed to be plugged into "heavy" Model-Driven approaches and do not easily fit in agile development processes. In this work, we aim at introducing tools for the consistency checking of mockups by borrowing concepts from our previous work.

3 Enhancing Mockups with End-User Annotations

After software analysts understand clients' initial needs, they are able to start sketching mockups (with direct stakeholder participation if desired) in order to informally describe how the application will be browsed and will be used later. Mockups can be modelled using any tool in which the analyst has expertise (for instance, Balsamiq[2]). We use as a running example the development and extension of an e-commerce site (Fig. 1).

Mockups are used as a tool for validating requirements' interpretation with stakeholders; they describe how the user interface should look like with illustrative examples belonging to real life scenarios. When using Mockups, analysts take advantages of the fact that the language that they use, user interface widgets, are

---

[2] Balsamiq Mockups - https://balsamiq.com/products/mockups/.

jargon-free (unlike textual requirements artifacts) and represent a common language between the analysts and the stakeholders [11, 15]. However, while mockups allow describing visual and interaction metaphors their solely visual description is not enough for expressing requirements like validation, navigation/activation, business process aspects, etc. Because of this, informal annotations are usually used in companion with mockups to describe those missing aspects. Throughout this section we describe how we formalize these informal descriptions to solve ambiguities.

3.1 Structural User Interface

The approach presented in this paper extends (using an end-user grammar) the MockupDD [15] methodology which provides a metamodel for enhancing mockup widgets with annotations. In the context of MockupDD, mockups are the main, mandatory requirements specification artifacts which, instead of being discarded as in traditional development approaches, are reused as a basis to define more complex software specifications. This reuse is accomplished through (1) the formalization of the mockup structure and widgets, through what it is called a Structural User Interface (SUI) model and (2) the introduction of a set of formal annotations over the structure defined over such model [15]. Every annotation placed over the formalized mockup represents an independent specification related, for instance, to content, navigation, behavior or any other aspect that can be specified over a visual representation of the UI. The semantics defined for every annotation allows formalizing requirements over mockups. Consequently, it allows generating code or actions interpreted at runtime, translating them to semi-textual representations to discuss requirements captured over the mockups with stakeholders. In this case, annotations (called *tags* from now on) are only used to formalize and refine requirements and, eventually, to detect conflicts. Our approach relies on the definition of formal tags which enhance the widgets that composes the UI. For a sake of space, in this work we will omit details of the SUI model since it is not strictly related to the approach – more details about it can be found in [15].

3.2 End-User Grammar Annotations Catalogue

In this section, we introduce the end-user annotation catalogue for enriching the mockup specifications that will be used later in the examples. In order to improve Mockup element description and solve the lack of formality, in this step we use a Domain Specific Language called End User Grammar (EUG) [15] which focuses on describing information source, format and information relationships. Each annotation is a structured colloquial definition which is intelligible to end-users because it does not present any technical concept that would limit its understanding. Next, we introduce annotations patterns and their description.

$$\text{"Mockup Name" view (number)} \tag{1}$$

Defines an ID (number) for a mockup in order to be referenced as a destination for navigation/activation by other tag.

$$a[n] \ [\texttt{list of}] \ \texttt{class} \tag{2}$$

Denotes that an object or a list of objects of class Class is shown or can be manipulated in the UI. For instance, a list in a mockup that shows an index of products.

$$\texttt{Class' attribute [which is a datatype | with options :} \atop \texttt{value}_1,\dots,\texttt{and value}_N] \tag{3}$$

Specifies that the attribute of an object of class Class (called attribute) is shown or can be edited through an underlying graphical widget. Optionally, a datatype can be defined for that attribute (one of Date, String, Integer, Decimal, Boolean, Integer an enumeration or Blob). If no datatype is specified, String is assumed. In the event of an enumeration it is possible to list possible values using "with options $o_1, o_2, \dots, o_N$" clause.

$$\texttt{a Class1 has a[n][optional][list of] Class2, called} \atop \texttt{"aReal-Name"} \tag{4}$$

Denotes that an object of Class2 is shown or can be manipulated through the underlying element in the UI. However, this element is obtained navigating from an association called associationName from another element of class Class1.

$$\texttt{Subclass is a type of Superclass} \tag{5}$$

Denotes that an object of class Subclass is shown or can be manipulated in the User Interface and that the class of this object (Subclass) inherits from another one called Superclass.

$$\texttt{Navigates to <destination>} \tag{6}$$

$$\texttt{Opens a popup <destination>} \tag{7}$$

Denotes that, when executing a default action over the underlying graphical element (e.g., a click) the destination mockup will be shown, navigated to or focused – destination mockup should be tagged with mockupName view (number) and <destination> should reference that number

$$\texttt{Class's attribute is required} \tag{8}$$

Denotes that a non-empty value for attribute attribute of class Class is required.

$$\texttt{Class's attribute min value is minimumValue} \tag{9}$$

$$\text{Class's attribute max value is } \mathtt{maximumValue} \tag{10}$$

$$\text{Class's attribute values must be between } \mathtt{minimumValue} \\ \text{and } \mathtt{maximumValue} \tag{11}$$

Denotes that the values for attribute `attribute` in class `Class` must be less than or equal to a `maximumValue` and/or greater than or equal to a `minimumValue`

$$\text{Class's attribute matches } \mathtt{regularExpresion} \tag{12}$$

The contents of attribute `attribute` of class `Class` must be formatted to match a pattern (`regularExpression`). For instance, phone numbers and ID data have specific formatting constraints.

$$[\mathtt{Saves \mid Deletes}] \text{ a Class} \tag{13}$$

Denotes that, when clicking or triggering a default action over the widget an instance of `Class` (which is being edited) will be created or deleted; respectively.

$$\mathtt{Triggers \ "action \ description"} \tag{14}$$

Denotes that an arbitrary action (described textually) will be invoked when executing the default action over the widget. This construct is used when the expected behavior is not already defined but needs to be pointed out.

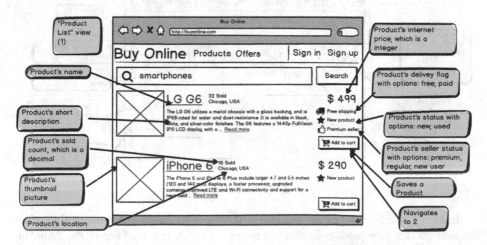

Fig. 2. Descripted mockups using our Colloquial DSL.

3.3   Colloquial Data Description

Mockups often use a real-life scenario defined with illustrative data to describe what User eXperience (UX) the application will provide. During this step, analysts must enrich mockups graphical elements with a template-based colloquial description.

The main advantage of EUG is that it can be easily understood by end-users and also provides the formality required to be processed and, consequently, allows a better validation of requirements. Each description expression must match a specific template with well-defined placeholders that will ease later automate processing.

In Fig. 2, we can see how the mockup presented in Fig. 1a was documented using the tags. For the sake of space, we present in the examples some simple but illustrative sets of annotations that specify the requirements, but the sets of tags can be more exhaustive covering a larger set of elements. In the figure, a mockup built with Balsamiq tool is presented where tags are included using markup capabilities provided by the tool itself. The requirement is first identified with the name "Products list" using Grammar 1 syntax (presented in Sect. 3.2). Then, from the expression "**Product's delivery flag with options: free, paid**" (Grammar 3) we can identify the *Product* business entity that has an attribute called *delivery flag* that has two possible values: *free* and *paid*. Moreover, some behaviors are related to the "Add to cart" button, which creates a new instance of *Product Purchase* object through "**Saves a Product Purchase**" (Grammar 13) and navigates to a Cart view through "**Navigates to 2**" (Grammar 6). The reader should note that the entities considering its attributes and types as well as actions will be used in the consistency analysis of mockups later.

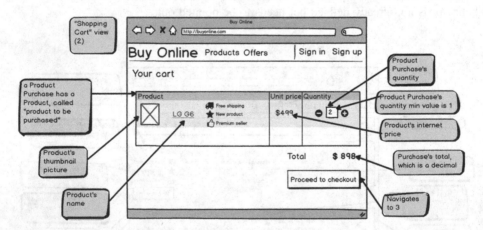

Fig. 3. Checkout mockup

In Fig. 3, the Shopping Cart mockup is shown. This mockup is navigated to after the user adds a new product in their `Product Purchase` clicking in the "Add to cart" button in mockup depicted in Fig. 2, after the Product Purchase is created. The Shopping Cart mockup mostly shows a list of **Product Purchase** and the mockup mostly describes their properties. But, it also features a relationship between the **Product Purchase** and the **Product** - since a **Product Purchase** represents a purchase of specific quantity of an individual **Product** (Grammar 3). This relationship is expressed through the **"Product Purchase has a Product, called 'product to be purchased'"** tag (Grammar 4). Finally, it also includes an annotation `specifying` that the quantity of a **Product Purchase** should be 1 as a minimum (Grammar 9).

3.4   Using End-User Grammar to Identifying Requirement Inconsistencies

A candidate conflict arises when there are syntactic differences between requirements expressed through mockups. These differences may be common mistakes [4]: (a) as consequence of an element absence in one mockup but its presence in the other, (b) the usage of two different widgets for describing the same information which contradict themselves, or (c) a configuration difference in an element such as the properties values of a widget. This situation may arise when two different stakeholders have different views on a single functionality, or when an evolution requirement contradicts an original one. By annotating mockups, we are able to reason over the specification and, both manually or using automatic tools when possible, end-user grammar allows to detect inconsistencies that are not clear with plain mockups – or when using mockups with colloquial, natural language annotations.

A basic conflict detection can be performed by comparing mockups so as to detect the absence of elements or elements' constructions differences. Since Mockups are containers of widgets, we can apply difference operations of set collections in order to detect inconsistencies. For example, currently, it has become common for software products to release both a mobile and a Web version. The arrival of a new mobile version should have the same business goal although it runs in a different platform with different interaction and presentation features. For example, in Fig. 4, a different stakeholder suggests an alternative mockup version to the one presented in Fig. 2. Although their aim is to present the same underlying concept, they have significant differences that would be overlooked without our end-user grammar. In Fig. 2, The Product List mockup defines a Product entity which has Description, Internet Price, Delivery Flag, Thumbnail, Status, Sold Count, and Location attributes. In Fig. 4, a different business entity version also called Product comprises a different set of attributes: Description, Internet Price, Delivery Flag, and Thumbnail. We can appreciate two types of differences: one related to the attribute existence or absence and the other

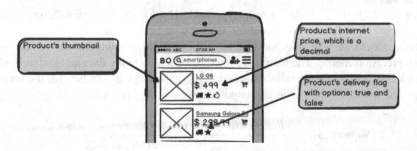

Fig. 4. Annotated Product List mobile version.

related to the attribute configuration. Regarding the former, there are attributes that appear in one figure and not in the other, for example: Status, Sold Count and Location. On the other hand, there are differences related to the type of the attributes, for example in one of its versions a Product has a Delivery Flag as an enumeration and in the other it's a Boolean. Also, the Price is defined as an Integer number in the first version while in its counterpart it's a decimal number (Grammar 3).

Once the inconsistencies are detected, conciliation tasks are performed using meeting-based tools [8] or heuristics [4] to eliminate requirements ambiguity and inconsistence. For the sake of space, we will not provide a throughout discussion of this topic.

4 Evaluation

In this section, we conduct an evaluation of the approach to measure how much it assists in the understanding of mockups following Wohlin et al. guidelines [20]. First, we define the goals, hypotheses and variables of the experiment. Then, we proceed to define metrics and materials considered. After that, we detail subjects, instrumentation, and data collection methods used in the experiment. Then we conduct an analysis of results and their implication. Finally, we consider threats to validity of the evaluation.

4.1 Goals, Hypotheses and Variables

Following the Goal-Question-Metric (GQM) format as is suggested in [20], we define the goal of the experiment in the following way:

Analyze Mockups enhanced with end-user's annotations **for the purpose of** measure how requirements documented with mockups are improved **with respect to** their expressiveness **from the point of view of** researchers **in the context of** software analysts and developers.

After defining the Goal, now we proceed to define the different questions that will allow to answer them. We profit from the precision and recall [9] concepts from information retrieval research field and adapted them to our experiment so as to measure quality of responses.

Our main Research Questions (RQ) are:

RQ1: Do End-user annotations improve the relevancy of the data elements identified in mockups?

For this RQ, we consider as null hypothesis H_0 that there is no difference in the accuracy of identification of involved data by subjects using only mockups and annotated mockups. The relevancy is the response variable which will be measured using a precision metric. The metric is used to assess how many data items identified by the subject in a mockup are relevant accordingly a leading case. In Eq. 15, the formula is depicted where the precision is computed given a subject and a mockup.

$$P\left(Subject_j, M_f\right) = \frac{RelevantResponse\left(M_f\right) \bigcap Response\left(Subject_j\right)}{Response\left(M_f\right)} \tag{15}$$

As alternative hypothesis H_a, we consider there is an improvement in the mean of the response accuracy of subjects using end-user annotations (μ_{EU}) against the basic support of mockups(μ_{MOCK}): $\mu_{MOCK} \leq \mu_{EU}$.

RQ2: Do End-user annotations improve the completeness of the data elements identified in mockups?.

For this RQ, we consider as null hypothesis H_0 that there is no difference in the accuracy of identification of involved data by subjects using only mockups and annotated mockups where the completeness is the response variable. The recall metric is used to assess how many relevant data items are identified by the subjects in a mockup. In Eq. 16, the Recall formula is presented where the precision is computed given a subject and a mockup.

$$R(Subject_j, M_f) = \frac{RelevantResponse(M_f) \cap Response(Subject_j)}{RelevantResponse(M_f)} \tag{16}$$

As alternative hypothesis H_a, we consider there is an improvement in the mean of the response accuracy of subjects using end-user annotations (μ_{EU}) against the basic support of mockups(μ_{MOCK}): $\mu_{MOCK} \leq \mu_{EU}$.

4.2 Experiment Design

In order to answer these questions, we designed a between-subject design experiment where subjects were asked to identify entities and data present in mockups; from now, Experiment Variable (EV). The subjects were randomly divided into two groups for the two alternatives of the approach (the experiment's factor): mockups without any kind of annotations (Control) and mockups with the use of presented end-user annotations (Treatment).

In this experiment, we focused on measuring how the communication of requirement is improved with annotation and we did not consider evaluating the user experience related to the tagging task or comparing the performance against other approach.

4.3 Experimental Unit

The requirement gathering task using mockups requires to document mockups and communicate them, firstly, to stakeholders to validate its definition and later to the developers in order to start its development. For this task, we have modeled use cases using mockups for an e-commerce site – which mockups were similar to the ones depicted in Fig. 1. The main functionalities considered in use cases were system registration and the view of a product's details. Both versions used the same mockups but one of them included the annotations defined in Sect. 4 to enhance their description. Both the modeling and tagging tasks results were validated by senior analysts prior to the experiment.

To evaluate subject's understanding of the requirements, we asked them to fill out a form where they should record each data definition they can extract from the mockups, its expected data type, any kind of validation and the associated widget. Since mockups depict scenarios using examples rather than abstract variables or placeholders, they lack any kind of formalism so the datatype, validations and any other specification is the result of the mockup's reader interpretation. Both the mockup and the form are available online[3].

4.4   Subjects, Instrumentation, and Data Collection

During the experiment, the subjects received a form and a set of mockups. Subjects were 34 developers from different software companies. On average, they were 31 years old, had more than 6 years of programming experience and approximately 3.5 years in requirement analysis tasks. A group of 18 subjects performed the experiment with mockups annotated with end-user grammar meanwhile a group of 16 subjects performed the experiment based on simple mockups. They were motivated and committed to the experiment, as we were sponsored by the CEOs and managers that notified the subjects about the company's commitment to the research experiment.

The experiment protocol was executed in the same way with all the subjects. First of all, they received a brief introduction to the material which had to be used during the experiment. In the case of annotation-based material, the subjects were trained about the end-user grammar usage. Next, participants were asked to complete an expertise survey, read the experiment description, study the mockups, and fill out the questionnaire's form. Each subject performed fully experiment supervised by a researcher who ensured similar facilities layout, infrastructure, and subject isolation conditions. Additionally, the researcher controlled the subject to avoid any answer modification as long as she advanced in the experiment. To achieve the task of processing the collected results, we first processed and digitalized responses. Then, we used different scripts based on Python language (version 3.6.1) and Scipy library (version 0.19.0) to compute Precision and Recall formulas.

4.5   Analysis and Evaluation of Results and Implication

For the analysis of samples, firstly we defined the Relevant Data Elements (RDE) present in the mockups to be used to compute precision and recall metrics. Then, once samples were digitalized, we checked samples against RDE for computing True Positive (TP), and False Positive (FP) elements. That is to say, those elements that a subject correctly reported (TP) when checking whether his response is included in the relevant element set, or erroneously reported (FP). Finally, all samples were processed using Mann–Whitney U test [20], which is a non-parametric statistical hypothesis test technique, considering a standard confidence level (α) of 0.05. This technique can be used with unequal sample size which is the case of this experiment. Additionally, we computed the effect size using Cliff's Delta technique.

The analysis was performed mostly in an automated way using Python-based scripts that resolved the recall and precision calculation, and the hypothesis testing.

In order to answer our research question, we evaluated different possibilities of computing subject's responses and the outcome is presented in Table 1. As we asked

---

[3] https://goo.gl/FMJ6KJ.

subjects to identify abstract data present in UI (the attribute), its data type, and its owner entity, we considered four evaluation strategies for all the possible combinations of evaluating such tuple: (*i*) only the abstract data (attribute) identified in the response, (*ii*) the attribute and its data type, (*iii*) the attribute and its owner entity, and (*iv*) the attribute, its data type and its owner entity tuple. For example, to evaluate whether the tuple birthday, String type, and owned by the entity Person is a valid response or not. For every mentioned evaluation strategy, we calculated Precision (P) and Recall (R) metrics of subject responses when using both mockups without annotations to measure how accurate were their answers. For each metric we reported, in Table 1, the average and standard deviation for each approach (Mockup and Annotation columns respectively), the Cliff's delta value for the effect size, and the p-value resulting from the hypothesis testing that compares the means of both approaches. We can realize how annotated mockups samples excel in performance in all evaluation type. In all cases, the p-value was lower than the alpha level 0,05. Therefore, there is enough evidence to support the alternative hypothesis. That is, the mockup with end-user annotation improves the

To calculate the effect size, we used cliff's delta technique which has as a result value in (−1,1) range. In this case, the values are bigger than 0.474 [16] in all evaluation types depicting a high meaningfulness.

Additionally, we computed the time required for each individual to complete the experiment. It is noteworthy that the subjects extracting information from annotated mockups performed better (requiring less time) than the subjects working on plain-annotated. For annotated mockups 1 and 2, it took to subject on average 297 s and 880 s; respectively. Conversely, for non-annotated mockups, it required 332 s and 947 s.

The recall metric points out that there is an effective understanding of the pieces of data comprised by the mockup. The subjects reported a greater number of relevant elements than those subjects which worked with simple mockups. That means, the subjects were more accurate with the domain element description. The precision was also higher having less irrelevant responses than mockups without annotations. This is another important indication about the responses that they did not combine valid and invalid information reducing the noise in the communication between clients and analysts. For example, without the annotations, subjects defined different irrelevant business entities such Login, User, and Person to compose UI attributes.

Table 1. Sample results

Evaluation	Metric	Mockup 1						Mockup 2					
		Mockup		Annotation		Cliff's delta	P-value	<0.05	Mockup		Annotation		Cliff's delta	P-Value	<0.05
		Avg.	Std.	Avg.	Std.				Avg.	Std.	Avg.	Std.			
(i) Attribute	P	0.48	0.16	0.65	0.19	0.55	0.003	√	0.52	0.10	0.61	0.11	0.43	0.020	√
	R	0.31	0.08	0.45	0.10	0.70	0.000	√	0.44	0.09	0.54	0.07	0.53	0.003	√
(ii) Attribute, Type	P	0.33	0.15	0.55	0.18	0.69	0.000	√	0.50	0.13	0.60	0.12	0.39	0.031	√
	R	0.21	0.09	0.38	0.11	0.77	0.000	√	0.43	0.11	0.52	0.08	0.49	0.005	√
(iii) Attribute, Entity	P	0.00	0.00	0.47	0.29	0.78	0.000	√	0.33	0.23	0.55	0.19	0.57	0.003	√
	R	0.00	0.00	0.35	0.21	0.78	0.000	√	0.29	0.21	0.48	0.16	0.56	0.002	√
(iv) Attribute, Type, Entity	P	0.00	0.00	0.39	0.27	0.72	0.000	√	0.31	0.22	0.53	0.19	0.56	0.004	√
	R	0.00	0.00	0.28	0.19	0.72	0.000	√	0.27	0.21	0.47	0.15	0.58	0.002	√

Summarizing, participants that were subjected to mockups with annotations where more time-efficient and precise in their answers that those that worked with simple mockups and oral clarifications (if required).

4.6 Threats to Validity

There are several threats to validity that were considered during the experiment design. This research presents a preliminary result and for space sake.

Construct Validity. The experiment was designed to measure how the use of end-user annotations improves the communication of requirements. In order to reduce the experiment's complexity and bias introduction possibility, we defined the method (simple mockups or annotated mockups) as the only variable. The reader must note that our approach is not being compared with another approach, and, indeed, it is under evaluation how the annotations extension improves basic mockups.

Internal Validity. To avoid any misunderstanding during the experiment, we presented each material in a brief introduction before subjects performed the experiment and during the experiment, any enquiry related to the sentences was answered without introducing a bias to the sample. The subjects were selected randomly and all of them were working in software companies in Argentina and Spain. The provided material was the same to all subject. We also checked that all the users had basic knowledge in e-commerce application (just a simple users) and had not participated in the development or requirement analysis in any application of this kind.

External Validity. The subjects were software engineers who have played the role of developers and/or analyst during their career. Although their experience levels were different, they are all exposed to the regular responsibilities of any software practitioners: meet with clients, understand requirements, develop the software and honor deadlines for software delivery. A broader experiment considering different subject of different cultures who have worked on different business domains will improve the generality of our claims.

Conclusion Validity. The experiment was based on objective metrics evaluated with all gathered data without any exclusion to guaranty that the outcome of the experiment analysis will be the same and avoiding hypothesis fishing. We used non-parametric tests which have fewer constraints than parametric ones but make it more complex to compute the power and effect size. Therefore, we used well-known guidelines for reporting empirical experiments as checklists for confirming the requirements of the test techniques. Finally, in order to avoid the impact of random irrelevancies on the experiment, we used a large number set of samples that helped the irrelevancies to become diluted.

5 Conclusion and Further Work

We have presented a novel approach for enriching mockups with annotation so that the mockups improve their expressiveness and understandability minimizing the risk of requirement's misunderstanding. The approach is modular, so it can be plugged in any software engineering approach to ensure application consistency, validate require-ments, and save time and effort to detect and solve error in latest software development steps. We have presented some simple examples that illustrate the approach feasibility. Additionally, we present a preliminary evidence highlighting the benefits of our approach, but it is required more validation to support stronger claims.

We are currently working on a tool for the processing of annotations so as to provide a semi-automate syntactic and semantic analysis of inconsistencies. In these lines, some methodologies like Design Sprint [22] are proposing to build realistic prototypes to be validated with final users as soon as possible. Then, these method-ologies propose to see your finished product and customer reactions before making any expensive commitments. Then, it's also necessary to explore in future how to adapt and process these tags notations in general purpose tools like Microsoft PowerPoint and Keynote.

A user experience evaluation for the tagging task will help to identify improve-ments that increase the quality of the requirement specification.

References

1. Bjarnason, E., et al.: Challenges and practices in aligning requirements with verification and validation: a case study of six companies. Empir. Softw. Eng. **19**(6), 1809–1855 (2014)
2. Boehm, B., et al.: Developing groupware for requirements negotiations: lessons learned. IEEE Softw. **18**(3), 46–55 (2001)
3. Cao, L., Ramesh, B.: Agile requirements engineering practices: an empirical study. IEEE Softw. **25**(1), 60–67 (2008)
4. Escalona, M.J., et al.: Detecting Web requirements conflicts and inconsistencies under a model-based perspective. J. Syst. Softw. **86**, 3024–3038 (2013)
5. Escalona, M.J., Koch, N.: Requirements engineering for web applications: a comparative study. J. Web Eng. **2**(3), 193–212 (2003)
6. Kotonya, G., Sommerville, I.: Requirements engineering with viewpoints (1996)
7. Lucassen, G., et al.: Improving agile requirements: the Quality User Story framework and tool. Requir. Eng. **21**(3), 383–403 (2016)
8. De Lucia, A., Qusef, A.: requirements engineering in agile software development (2010)
9. Manning, C.D., et al.: Introduction to Information Retrieval. Cambridge University Press, Cambridge (2008)
10. Medeiros, J., et al.: An approach based on design practices to specify requirements in agile projects. In: Proceedings of the Symposium on Applied Computing - SAC 2017, pp. 1114–1121 (2017)
11. Mukasa, K.S., Kaindl, H.: An integration of requirements and user interface specifications. In: 6th IEEE International Requirements Engineering Conference, pp. 327–328. IEEE Computer Society, Barcelona (2008)

12. Ramdoyal, R., Cleve, A.: From pattern-based user interfaces to conceptual schemas and back. In: Jeusfeld, M., Delcambre, L., Ling, T.-W. (eds.) ER 2011. LNCS, vol. 6998, pp. 247–260. Springer, Heidelberg (2011). https://doi.org/10.1007/978-3-642-24606-7_19
13. Ravid, A., Berry, D.M.: A Method for Extracting and Stating software requirements that a user interface prototype contains. Requir. Eng. 5(4), 225–241 (2000)
14. Reggio, G., et al.: Improving the quality and the comprehension of requirements: disciplined use cases and mockups. In: Proceedings - 40th Euromicro Conference Series on Software Engineering and Advanced Applications, SEAA 2014, pp. 262–266 (2014)
15. Rivero, J.M., et al.: Mockup-driven development: providing agile support for model-driven web engineering. Inf. Softw. Technol. 56(6), 670–687 (2014)
16. Romano, J., et al.: Appropriate statistics for ordinal level data : should we really be using t-test and Cohen's d for evaluating group differences on the NSSE and other surveys? In: Florida Association of Institutional Research Annual Meeting, pp. 1–33 (2006)
17. Rosenberg, D., et al.: Agile Development with ICONIX Process—People, Process, and Pragmatism. A-Press, New York (2005)
18. Schneider, K.: Generating Fast feedback in requirements elicitation. In: Sawyer, P., Paech, B., Heymans, P. (eds.) REFSQ 2007. LNCS, vol. 4542, pp. 160–174. Springer, Heidelberg (2007). https://doi.org/10.1007/978-3-540-73031-6_12
19. Urbieta, M., Escalona, M.J., Robles Luna, E., Rossi, G.: Detecting conflicts and inconsistencies in web application requirements. In: Harth, A., Koch, N. (eds.) ICWE 2011. LNCS, vol. 7059, pp. 278–288. Springer, Heidelberg (2012). https://doi.org/10.1007/978-3-642-27997-3_27
20. Wohlin, C., et al.: Experimentation in software engineering: an introduction. Kluwer Academic Publishers, Norwell (2000)
21. Yang, D., et al.: A survey on software cost estimation in the chinese software industry. In: Proceedings of the Second ACM-IEEE International Symposium on Empirical Software Engineering and Measurement - ESEM 2008, p. 253 (2008)
22. The Design Sprint — GV. http://www.gv.com/sprint/

Agile Testing

Combining STPA and BDD for Safety Analysis and Verification in Agile Development: A Controlled Experiment

Yang Wang$^{(\boxtimes)}$ and Stefan Wagner

University of Stuttgart, Stuttgart, Germany
{yang.wang,stefan.wagner}@informatik.uni-stuttgart.de

Abstract. *Context:* Agile development is in widespread use, even in safety-critical domains. *Motivation:* However, there is a lack of an appropriate safety analysis and verification method in agile development. *Objective:* In this paper, we investigate the use of Behavior Driven Development (BDD) instead of standard User Acceptance Testing (UAT) for safety verification with System-Theoretic Process Analysis (STPA) for safety analysis in agile development. *Method:* We evaluate the effect of this combination in a controlled experiment with 44 students in terms of productivity, test thoroughness, fault detection effectiveness and communication effectiveness. *Results:* The results show that BDD is more effective for safety verification regarding the impact on communication effectiveness than standard UAT, whereas productivity, test thoroughness and fault detection effectiveness show no statistically significant difference in our controlled experiment. *Conclusion:* The combination of BDD and STPA seems promising with an enhancement on communication, but its impact needs more research.

1 Introduction

Agile practices have been widely used in software industries to develop systems on time and within budget with improved software quality and customer satisfaction [1]. The success of agile development has led to a proposed expansion to include safety-critical systems (SCS) [2]. However, to develop SCS in an agile way, a significant challenge exists in the execution of safety analysis and verification [3]. The traditional safety analysis and verification techniques, such as failure mode effect analysis (FMEA) and fault tree analysis (FTA) are difficult to apply within agile development. They need a detailed and stable architecture [4].

In 2016, we proposed to use System-Theoretic Process Analysis (STPA) [6] in agile development for SCS [5]. First, STPA can be started without a detailed and stable architecture. It can guide the design. In agile development, a safety analyst starts with performing STPA on a high-level architecture and derives the relevant safety requirements for further design. Second, Leveson developed STPA based on the systems theoretic accident modeling and processes (STAMP) causality model, which considers safety problems based on system theory rather

© The Author(s) 2018
J. Garbajosa et al. (Eds.): XP 2018, LNBIP 314, pp. 37–53, 2018.
https://doi.org/10.1007/978-3-319-91602-6_3

than reliability theory. In today's complex cyber-physical systems, accidents are rarely caused by single component or function failures but rather by component interactions, cognitively complex human decision-making errors and social, organizational, and management factors [6]. System theory can address this.

The safety requirements derived from STPA need verification. However, there is no congruent safety verification in agile development. Most agile practitioners mix unit test, integration test, field test and user acceptance testing (UAT) to verify safety requirements [2]. In 2016, we proposed using model checking combined with STPA in a Scrum development process [7]. However, using model checking, a suitable model is necessary but usually not available in agile development. In addition, the formal specification increases the difficulties of communication, which should not be neglected when developing SCS [8]. BDD, as an agile technique, is an evolution of test driven development (TDD) and acceptance test driven development (ATDD). The developers repeat coding cycles interleaved with testing. TDD starts with writing a unit test, while ATDD focuses on capturing user stories by implementing automated tests. BDD relies on testing system behavior in scenarios by implementing a template: Given[Context], When[Event], Then[Outcome] [31]. The context describes pre-conditions or system states, the event describes a trigger event, and the outcome is an expected or unexpected system behavior. It could go further into low-level BDD[1]. Yet, it has not been used to verify safety requirements. Leveson said [6]: *"Accidents are the result of a complex process that results in system behavior violating the safety constraints."* Hence, in agile development, we need safety verification to: (1) be able to guide design at an early stage, (2) strengthen communication and (3) focus on verifying system behavior. Thus, we believe that BDD might be suitable for safety verification with STPA for safety analysis in agile development.

Contributions

We propose a possible way to use BDD with STPA for safety verification in agile development. We investigate its effects regarding productivity, test thoroughness, fault detection effectiveness and communication effectiveness by conducting a controlled experiment with the limitation that we execute BDD only in a test-last way. The results show that BDD is able to verify safety requirements based on system theory, and is more effective than UAT regarding communication for safety verification.

2   Related Work

Modern agile development processes for developing safety-critical systems (SCS) advocate a hybrid mode through alignment with standards like IEC 61508, ISO 26262 and DO-178. There have been many considerable successes [9–11]. However, a lack of integrated safety analysis and verification to face the changing architecture through each short iteration is a challenge for using such standards.

---

[1] Low-level BDD is possible to define low-level specifications and interwined with TDD [16].

In 2016, we proposed to use STPA in a Scrum development process [5]. It showed a good capability to ensure agility and safety in a student project [12]. However, we verified the safety requirements only at the end of each sprint by executing UAT together with TDD in development. A lack of integrated safety verification causes some challenges, such as poor verification and communication. The previous research regarding safety verification in agile development suggested using formal methods [13,14]. However, they need models and make intuitive communication harder [7]. In addition, they have not considered specific safety analysis techniques.

Hence, we propose using BDD to verify safety requirements. BDD is specifically for concentrating on behavior testing [15]. It allows automated testing against multiple artifacts throughout the iterative development process [17]. Moreover, it bridges the gap between natural language-based business rules and code language [18]. Okubo et al. [19] mentioned the possibilities of using BDD for security and privacy acceptance criteria. They define the acceptance criteria by creating a threat and countermeasure graph to write attack scenarios. They verify the satisfaction of security requirements by testing the countermeasures, to see whether they can make the attack scenarios or unsecure scenarios fail. Lai et al. [20] combined BDD with iterative and incremental development specifically for security requirements evaluation. They defined the behavioral scenarios by using use case diagram and misuse case diagram. STPA encompasses determining safe or unsafe scenarios. We aim to use BDD verifying these scenarios.

To investigate the effect of using BDD for safety verification, we design a controlled experiment referring to a set of TDD experiments. Erdogmus et al. [23] conducted an experiment with undergraduate students regarding programmer productivity and external quality in an incremental development process. For safety verification in agile development, a high productivity of safety test cases promotes high safety. Madeyski [26] conducted an experiment comparing "test-first" and "test-last" programming practices with regard to test thoroughness and fault detection effectiveness of unit tests. BDD for safety verification covers also low-level tests. Thus, we decided to investigate productivity, test thoroughness and fault detection capability in this experiment. [21,22,28–30] provided evidence of using these three measures. In addition, George and Williams [29] focused on the understandability of TDD from the developer's viewpoint. Using BDD for safety verification, we notice the importance of communication between developers and business analysts. We investigate understandability in the measure of communication effectiveness.

3 STPA Integrated BDD for Safety Analysis and Verification (STPA-BDD)

In this article, we propose STPA-BDD. We mainly focus on safety verification. As we can see in Fig. 1, we have two main parts: STPA safety analysis and

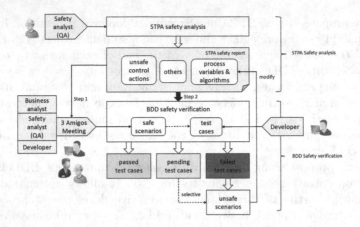

Fig. 1. STPA-BDD concept

BDD safety verification. A safety analyst[2] (QA) starts performing STPA safety analysis with a sufficient amount of code[3]. STPA is executed by firstly identifying potentially hazardous control actions, and secondly determining how unsafe control actions (UCAs) could occur. STPA derives the safety requirements, which constraint the UCAs, as well as system behaviors. Additionally, it explores the causal factors in scenarios for each UCA. The output from the safety analyst (QA) is an STPA safety report with system description, control structure, accidents, hazards, UCAs, corresponding safety requirements, process variables and algorithms.

In BDD safety verification, to generate and test scenarios, the UCAs (in STPA step 1), process variables and algorithms (in STPA step 2) from the STPA safety report are needed. We write other data into "others". BDD safety verification has two steps: In step 1, the business analyst, the safety analyst (QA) and the developer establish a "3 Amigos Meeting" to generate test scenarios. In a BDD test scenario[4], we write the possible trigger event for the UCA in **When [Event]**. The other process variables and algorithms are arranged in **Given [Context]**. **Then [Outcome]** presents the expected behavior - a safe control action. In Fig. 2(a), we present an example. The safety analyst (QA) has provided a UCA as *During auto-parking, the autonomous vehicle does not stop immediately when there is an obstacle upfront.* One of the process variables with relevant algorithms detects the forward distance by using an ultrasonic sensor. The developer considers a possible trigger as the ultrasonic sensor provides the

---

[2] Since we focus on safety in our research, we assign a safety analyst as the QA role in our context.

[3] More descriptions of STPA for safety analysis are given in [7] concerning an example of using STPA in an airbag system and [12] concerning the use of STPA in a Scrum development process.

[4] We illustrate a BDD test scenario using only three basic steps "Given" "When" "Then". More annotations, such as "And", can also be added.

wrong feedback. Thus, a BDD test scenario should test if *the ultrasonic sensor provides the feedback that the forward distance <= threshold (means there is an obstacle upfront)* and whether the vehicle stops. They write this after **When**. The context could be *the autonomous vehicle is auto-parking*. We write them after **Given**. **Then** constraints the safe control action as *the autonomous vehicle stops immediately*. More possible triggers are expected to be generated after **When** to test them. In step 2, after the three amigos discuss and determine the test scenarios, the developer starts generating them into test cases, as shown in Fig. 2(b). BDD test cases use annotations such as **@Given**, **@When**, and **@Then** to connect the aforementioned test scenarios with real code. The developer produces code to fulfill each annotation. We can identify unsafe scenarios when the test cases fail. We correct the trigger event to pass the test cases to satisfy the safety requirement.

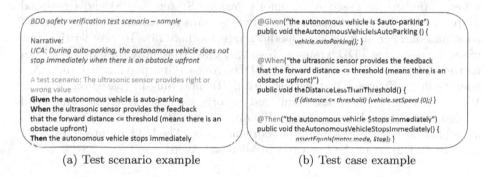

(a) Test scenario example   (b) Test case example

Fig. 2. BDD safety verification example

4   Experiment Design (We follow the guideline by Wohlin et al. [32].)

4.1   Goal

Analyze BDD[5] and UAT[6] for safety verification.
For the purpose of comparing their effect.
With respect to *productivity* by measuring the number of implemented (tested) user stories per minute; *test thoroughness* by measuring line coverage; *fault detection effectiveness* by measuring a mutation score indicator; *communication effectiveness* by conducting a post-questionnaire.
From the point of view of the developers and business analysts.
In the context of B.Sc students majoring in software engineering or other related majors executing acceptance testing.

---

[5] We have a limitation in our experiment that we execute BDD only in a test-last way. More discussion of this issue can be found in Sect. 6.2.

[6] To execute a standard UAT, we mainly refer to [38] with fictional business analysts.

4.2 Context

Participants: The experiment ran off-line in a laboratory setting in an "Introduction to Software Engineering" course at the University of Stuttgart. Since the course includes teaching BDD and UAT technology, the students are suitable subjects for our experiment. We arrange them based on Java programming experiences (not randomly). According to a pre-questionnaire (see footnote 13), 88.6% of the students are majoring in software engineering. We conclude from Table 1 that they have attended relevant lectures and handled practical tasks relating to Java programming, acceptance testing, SCS (with a median value >= 3 on a scale from 1 to 5). The agile techniques show less competency (with a median value of 2 on a scale from 1 to 5). We provide a 1-to-1 training, which lasts 44 h overall, to reduce the weaknesses.

Development environment: We use a simplified Java code with mutants from a Lego Mindstorms based Autonomous Parking System (APS) and Crossroad Stop and Go System (CSGS). These two systems are comparable by lines of code and number of functional modules (see footnote 13). To ease writing test cases, we use a lejo TDD wrapper, Testable Lejos[7] to remove deep dependencies to the embedded environment. The BDD groups (Group A1 and Group A2) operate in an Eclipse IDE together with a JBehave plug-in (based on JUnit)[8]. We use Eclipse log files and JUnit test reports for calculating the number of implemented (tested) user stories. Finally, we use PIT Mutation Testing[9] to assess line coverage and a mutation score indicator. The UAT groups (Group B1 and Group B2) write the test cases in Microsoft Word.

Table 1. Medians of the student's background

Area	Group A1	Group A2	Group B1	Group B2
Java programming	3	3	3	3
Acceptance testing	4	5	3	3
Safety-critical systems	3	4	4	4
Agile techniques	3	3	3	2

Note: The values range from "1" (little experience) to "5" (experienced). Group A1 and Group A2 use BDD, while Group B1 and Group B2 use UAT.

4.3 Hypotheses

We formulate the null hypotheses as:
H_0 $_{PROD}$: There is no difference in productivity between BDD and UAT.
H_0 $_{THOR}$: There is no difference in test thoroughness between BDD and UAT.

[7] http://testablelejos.sourceforge.net/.
[8] http://jbehave.org/eclipse-integration.html.
[9] http://pitest.org/.

H_0 $_{FAUL}$: There is no difference in fault detection effectiveness between BDD and UAT.
H_0 $_{COME}$: There is no difference in communication effectiveness between BDD and UAT.
The alternative hypotheses are:
H_1 $_{PROD}$: BDD is more productive than UAT when producing safety test cases.
H_1 $_{THOR}$: BDD yields better test thoroughness than UAT.
H_1 $_{FAUL}$: BDD is more effective regarding fault detection than UAT.
H_1 $_{COME}$: BDD is more effective regarding communication than UAT.

4.4 Variables

The independent variables are the acceptance testing techniques. The dependent variables are: (1) productivity (PROD). It is defined as output per unit effort [23]. In our experiment, the participants test the user stories in the STPA safety report and produce safety test cases. We assess it via the number of implemented (tested) user stories[10] per minute (NIUS) [23]; (2) test thoroughness (THOR). Code coverage is an important measure for the thoroughness of test suites including safety test suites [27]. Considering a low complexity of our provided systems, line coverage (LC) [26] is more suitable than branch coverage (BC); (3) fault detection effectiveness (FAUL). Mutation testing [25] is powerful and effective to indicate the capability at finding faults [26]. In our experiment, we measure how well a safety test suite is able to find faults at the code level. We assess this via a Mutation Score Indicator (MSI) [26]; (4) communication effectiveness (COME). We assess this via a post-questionnaire with 11 questions for developers covering topics like understandability and 13 questions for business analysts covering topics like confidentiality according to Adzic [35]. The results are in a 5-point scale from −2 (negative) to +2 (positive).

4.5 Pilot Study

Six master students majoring in software engineering took part in a pilot study. We arranged a four-hour training program. The first author observed the operation and concluded as follows: (1) The STPA safety report was too complicated to be used by inexperienced students. We used a comprehensive STPA report by using XSTAMPP[11] in the pilot study. However, a lot of unnecessary data, such as accidents, hazards and safety requirements at the system level, influenced the understanding. It costs too much time to capture the information. Thus, we simplified the STPA report with the process variables, algorithms, and UCAs. (2) We used the original Java code from a previous student project. The complex code affected the quick understanding. After the pilot study, we simplified it. (3) Training is extremely important. In the pilot study, one participant had not

---

[10] In this article, user stories are safety-related user stories.
[11] http://www.xstampp.de/.

taken part in the training program, which led to his experiment being unfinished. We provide a textual tutorial and system description for each participant as a backup. (4) We have only used an experiment report to record the measures. However, the pure numbers sometimes cannot show clear causalities. Thus, we use a screen video recording in parallel with the experiment report.

4.6 Experiment Operation

As we can see in Fig. 3, we divide the 44 participants into 4 groups. We provide 2 systems and evaluate 2 acceptance testing methods. Group A1 uses BDD for system 1. Group A2 uses BDD for system 2. Group B1 uses UAT for system 1. Group B2 uses UAT for system 2. We use two systems to evaluate the communication between developers and business analysts. The developers are the participants in each group, while the fictional business analysts are portrayed by the participants in the other group using various testing methods and systems.

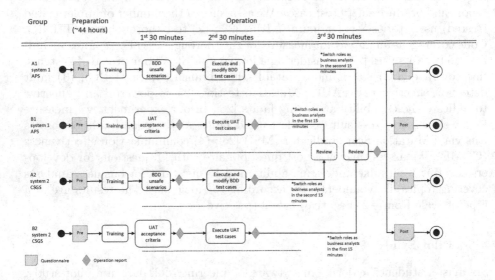

Fig. 3. Experiment operation

The experiment consists of 2 phases: *preparation* and *operation*. The *preparation* was run 2 weeks before the experiment to perform the pre-questionnaire and training. The *operation* consists of three sessions (30 min/session). In the 1st session, four groups write acceptance test cases. Group A1 (BDD) and Group A2 (BDD) write test scenarios in Eclipse with the Jbehave plug-in as a story file. Group B1 (UAT) and Group B2 (UAT) write acceptance criteria in plaintext. We provide 30 unsafe control actions (UCAs) in an STPA safety report. When the students finish all the 30 UCAs in 30 min, they record the time in minutes. After the 1st session, the participants record the NIUS and the time in the operation report. In the 2nd session, Group A1 (BDD) and Group A2 (BDD) write each test scenario into a test case and run the test case. If it fails, they should modify the trigger (code) and pass the test case. Group B1 (UAT) and Group B2 (UAT) review Java code, execute the test cases manually and complete their acceptance test report. At the end of the 2nd session, they run PIT mutation testing. The LC and MSI are generated automatically in the PIT test report. They write down the results in the operation report. In the 3rd session, the participant portrays as a developer for 15 min and a business analyst for 15 min. The developer is expected to explain his/her testing strategy as clearly as possible, while the fictional business analyst should try to question the developer. To this end, they answer a post-questionnaire.

Table 2. Descriptive statistic

Measure	Treatment	Experiment	Mean	St.Dev	Min	Median	Max	95% CI lower	95% CI upper
NIUS	BDD	Group A1	0.52	0.24	0.26	0.45	1.20	0.37	0.66
		Group A2	0.69	0.19	0.42	0.65	1.00	0.58	0.80
	UAT	Group B1	0.58	0.22	0.33	0.57	1.00	0.45	0.71
		Group B2	0.67	0.29	0.27	0.60	1.20	0.50	0.84
LC	BDD	Group A1	0.02	0.01	0.01	0.02	0.05	0.02	0.03
		Group A2	0.02	0.01	0.01	0.02	0.04	0.02	0.03
	UAT	Group B1	0.02	0.01	0.01	0.01	0.03	0.01	0.02
		Group B2	0.02	0.01	0.01	0.01	0.03	0.01	0.02
MSI	BDD	Group A1	0.90	0.38	0.36	1.00	1.33	0.67	1.13
		Group A2	0.93	0.49	0.44	0.83	2.17	0.63	1.22
	UAT	Group B1	0.89	0.36	0.42	0.88	1.56	0.67	1.10
		Group B2	0.85	0.46	0.30	0.65	1.63	0.58	1.12
COME	BDD	Group A1	1.27	0.81	−2.00	**1.50**	2.00	0.79	1.75
		Group A2	1.18	0.70	−1.00	**1.00**	2.00	0.76	1.58
	UAT	Group B1	−0.05	1.20	−2.00	**0.00**	2.00	−0.75	0.66
		Group B2	0.01	1.13	−2.00	**0.50**	2.00	−0.67	0.67

Note: St. Dev means standard deviation; CI means confidence interval. NIUS means number of implemented (tested) user stories per minute. LC means line coverage. MSI means mutation score indicator. COME was assessed via questionnaire with the results in a 5-point scale from −2 (negative) to +2 (positive).

5   Analysis

5.1   Descriptive Analysis

In Table 2, we summarize the descriptive statistics of the gathered measures[12]. To sum up, the results from the two systems in one treatment are almost identical. BDD and UAT have only small differences regarding NIUS and MSI. However,

---

[12] Raw data is available online: https://doi.org/10.5281/zenodo.1154350.

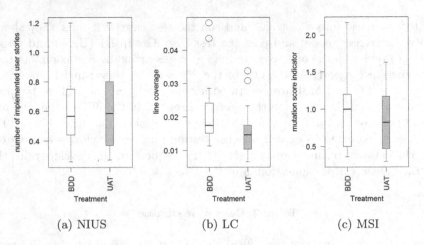

(a) NIUS   (b) LC   (c) MSI

Fig. 4. Boxplot for PROD, THOR and FAUL

COME in BDD (Mean = 1.27, 1.18; Std.Dev = 0.81, 0.70) and UAT (Mean = $-0.05, 0.01$; Std.Dev = 1.20, 1.13) differ more strongly. LC has a small difference. In Fig. 4, we show a clear comparison and can see some outliers concerning LC. In Fig. 5, we use an alluvial diagram to show COME. We can conclude that BDD has a better communication effectiveness than UAT from the perspective of developers and business analysts respectively (depending on the length of black vertical bar on the right side of Fig. 5(a) and (b)). On the left side, we list 24 sub-aspects of assessing the communication effectiveness. The boldness of the colorful lines indicates the degree of impact. A thicker line has a larger impact on each aspect. We can see six noteworthy values from Fig. 5(a) that BDD is better than UAT: (4) Test cases have a clear documentation. (5) They could flush out the functional gaps before development. (6) They have a good understanding of

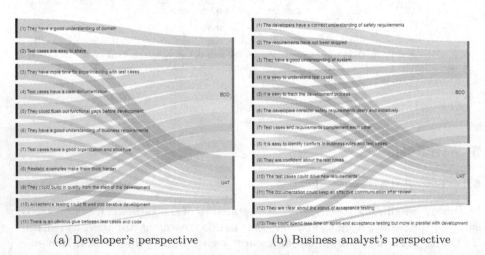

(a) Developer's perspective   (b) Business analyst's perspective

Fig. 5. Alluvial diagram for communication effectiveness

business requirements. (7) Test cases have a good organization and structure. (8) Realistic examples make them think harder. (11) There is an obvious glue between test cases and code. From Fig. 5(b), five noteworthy values show that BDD is better than UAT: (6) The developers consider safety requirements deeply and initially. (8) It is easy to identify conflicts in business rules and test cases. (9) They are confident about the test cases. (12) They are clear about the status of acceptance testing. (13) They could spend less time on sprint-end acceptance testing but more in parallel with development. In addition, the other aspects show also slightly better results when using BDD than UAT.

5.2 Hypothesis Testing

To start with, we evaluate the pre-questionnaire. No statistically significant differences between BDD and UAT groups are found concerning Java programming, acceptance testing, knowledge on SCS and agile techniques (t-test, $\alpha = 0.05$, p > 0.05 for all test parameters). Furthermore, we test the normality of the data distribution with Kolmogorov-Smirnov and Shapiro-Wilk tests at $\alpha = 0.05$. The results show that the data for NIUS in Group A1, for LC in Group A1, A2, B2 and for MSI in Group A1, A2 are not normally distributed. Thus, we use non-parametric tests in the analysis. In addition to the use of p-values for hypotheses testing ($\alpha = 0.05$, one-tailed) from the Mann-Whitney test, Wilcoxon test and ANOVA test, we include the effect size Cohen's d. Since we expect BDD to be better than UAT, we use one-tailed tests. NIUS is not significantly affected by using the BDD or the UAT approach (system 1: p=0.206; system 2: p = 0.359, non-significant). LC is not significantly affected by using BDD or UAT (system 1: p = 0.057; system 2: p = 0.051, non-significant). MSI shows no statistically significant difference between using BDD or UAT (system 1: p = 0.472; system 2: p = 0.359, non-significant). However, COME is significantly different (system 1: p < 0.00001; system 2: p < 0.00001, significant). We accept the alternative hypothesis that BDD shows better communication effectiveness than UAT. Cohen's d shows the values around 0.2, which signifies small effects, around 0.5 stands for medium effects and around 0.8 for large effects. Thus, for COME, system 1 shows a large effect (d = 2.908). For LC we have both medium effects (system 1: d = 0.684; system 2: d = 0.662). The rest of the effects are small.

6 Threats to Validity

6.1 Internal Validity

First, note that we have four groups in our experiment. To avoid a multiple group threat, we prepare a pre-questionnaire to investigate the students' background knowledge. The results of the t-tests show no statistically significant differences among the groups concerning each measure. *Second*, concerning the instrument, UAT is faster to learn than BDD regarding the use of tools. Even though we provide a training to narrow the gap, the *productivity* might have been influenced, since the students have to get familiar with the hierarchy of writing test suites in a BDD tool. The artifacts, such as tutorials and operation report, are designed respectively with the same structure to avoid threats. In addition to the observation, we save the participants' workspaces after the experiment and video recordings for deep analysis. *Third*, the students majoring in software engineering might identify more with the developer role than the business analyst role. Thus, we design two comparable systems. The students in each pair use different systems and test approaches to reduce the influence of prior knowledge. Moreover, we provide a reference [36] on how to perform as a business analyst in an agile project. We also mention their responsibilities in the training.

6.2 Construct Validity

First, the execution of BDD is a variant. BDD should begin with writing tests before coding. However, in our experiment, we use BDD for test-last acceptance testing rather than test-driven design. Thus, we provide source code with mutants. The measures we used could be influenced. In BDD test-first, we write failing test cases first and work on passing all of them to drive coding. According to [39,41], BDD test-first might be as effective as or even more effective than BDD test-last. *Second*, the evaluation concerning productivity, test thoroughness, fault detection effectiveness and communication effectiveness does not seem to be enough. As far as we know, our study is the first controlled experiment on BDD. We can base our measurement (PROD, THOR, FAUL) mainly on TDD controlled experiments and some limited experiments on safety verification. There might be better ways to capture how well safety is handled in testing.

6.3 Conclusion Validity

First, concerning violated assumptions of statistical tests, the Mann-Whitney U-test is robust when the sample size is approximately 20. For each treatment, we have 22 students. Moreover, we use Wilcoxon W test as well as Z to increase the robustness. Nevertheless, under certain conditions, non-parametric rank-based tests can themselves lack robustness [44]. *Second*, concerning random heterogeneity of subjects, we arranged them based on the Java programming experience. According to the pre-questionnaire, the students are from the same course and 88.6% of them are in the same major.

6.4 External Validity

First, the subjects are students. Although there are some skilled students who could perform as well as experts, most of them lack professional experience. This consideration may limit the generalization of the results. To consider this debatable issue in terms of using students as subjects, we refer to [33]. They said: conducting experiments with professionals as a first step should not be encouraged unless high sample sizes are guaranteed. In addition, a long learning cycle and a new technology are two hesitations for using professionals. STPA was developed in 2012, so there is still a lack of experts on the industrial level. BDD has not been used for verifying safety requirements. Thus, we believe that using students as subjects is a suitable way to aggregate contributions in our research area. We also refer to a study by Cleland-Huang and Rahimi, which successfully ran an SCS project with graduate students [2]. *Second*, the simplicity of the tasks poses a threat. We expect to keep the difficulty of the tasks in accordance with the capability of students. Nevertheless, the settings are not fully representative of a real-world project.

7   Discussion and Conclusion

The main benefit of our research is that we propose a possible way to use BDD for safety verification with STPA for safety analysis in agile development. We validate the combination in a controlled experiment with the limitation that we used BDD only in a test-last way. The experiment shows some remarkable results. The *productivity* has no statistically significant difference between BDD and UAT. That contradicts our original expectation. We would expect BDD, as an automated testing method, to be more productive than manual UAT. Yet, as the students are not experts in our experiment, they need considerable time to get familiar with the BDD tool. The students use Jbehave to write BDD test cases in our experiment, which has strict constraints on hierarchy and naming conventions to connect test scenarios with test cases. UAT should be easier to learn. We therefore analyzed our video recordings and found that BDD developers use nearly 25% to 50% of their time to construct the hierarchy and naming. Scanniello et al. [37] also mentioned this difficulty when students apply TDD. In the future, we plan to use skilled professionals in test automation to replicate this study. This could lead to different results. The *test thoroughness* and *fault detection effectiveness* show a non-significant difference between BDD and UAT. We could imagine that our provided Java code is too simplified to show a significant difference. The mutants are easily found with a review. These aspects need further research.

The *communication effectiveness* shows better results by using BDD than UAT on 24 aspects. We highlight 11 significant aspects. The *developers* found that: **BDD has a clear documentation.** A clear documentation of acceptance test cases is important for communication [42]. The scenarios are written in plain English with no hidden test instrumentation. The given-when-then format is clear for describing test scenarios for safety verification based on system theory. **The developers using BDD could flush out functional gaps before development.** The communication concerning safety could happen at the beginning of the development. They discuss safety requirements with the business analysts and spot the detailed challenges or edge cases before functional development. UAT happens mostly at the end of the development. It makes the rework expensive and is easy to be cut in safety-critical systems. **The developers using BDD have a good understanding of the business**

requirements. A good understanding of safety requirements helps an effective communication. They could build a shared understanding in the "3 Amigos Meeting" to ensure that their ideas about the safety requirements are consistent with the business analysts. The developers using UAT might understand safety requirements with a possible bias. **BDD test cases have a good organization and structure.** This makes the test cases easy to understand, especially during maintenance. They include strict naming conventions and a clear hierarchy to manage test scenarios and test cases. **Realistic examples in BDD make the developers think harder.** The safety requirements are abstract with possibly cognitive diversity, which leave a lot of space for ambiguity and misunderstanding. That negatively influences effective communication. Realistic examples give us a much better way to explain how safe scenarios really work than pure safety requirements do. **There is an obvious glue between BDD test cases and code.** There is glue code in BDD safety verification, which allows an effective separation between safety requirements and implementation details. This glue code supports the understanding and even communication between business analysts and developers. In addition, it ensures the bidirectional traceability between safety requirements and test cases. The *business analysts* thought that: **The developers using BDD consider the safety requirements deeply and initiatively.** The collaboration promotes a sense of ownership of the deliverable products. That increases an initiative communication. Instead of passively reading the documents, the developers participate in the discussion about writing test scenarios and are more committed to them. **The business analysts are more confident about the BDD test cases.** Confidence promotes effective communication [43]. The business analysts could give a big picture with safety goals to the developers. Feedback from developers and their realistic unsafe scenarios give the business analysts confidence that the developers understand the safety goals correctly. **It is easy to identify conflicts in business rules and test cases when using BDD.** BDD has a set of readable test scenarios focusing on business rules (safety requirements). Each test scenario and test case are directly connected to the code. The business analysts can pull out test cases related to a particular business rule. This helps communication, especially when there is a changing request. **The business analysts are clear about the status of acceptance testing when using BDD.** It promotes a state-of-art communication. That can be attributed to the automated test suites, which might be connected with a continuous integration server and a project management tool to receive a verification report automatically. **The business analysts could spend less time on sprint-end acceptance tests but more in parallel with development.** They can verify the safety requirements periodically and therefore enhance communication throughout the project.

In conclusion, to some extent, BDD is an effective method for verifying safety requirements in agile development. As this is the first experiment investigating BDD for safety verification, further empirical research is needed to check our results. We invite replications of this experiment using our replication package[13].

---

[13] https://doi.org/10.5281/zenodo.846976.

References

1. Dybå, T., Dingsøyr, T.: Empirical studies of agile software development. A systematic review. Inf. Softw. Technol. **50**(9–10), 833–859 (2008)
2. Cleland-Huang, J., Rahimi, M.: A case study: injecting safety-critical thinking into graduate software engineering projects. In: Proceedings of the 39th International Conference on Software Engineering: Software Engineering and Education Track. IEEE (2017)
3. Arthur, J.D., Dabney, J.B.: Applying standard independent verification and validation (IV&V) techniques within an Agile framework: is there a compatibility issue? In: Proceedings of Systems Conference. IEEE (2017)
4. Fleming, C.: Safety-driven early concept analysis and development. Dissertation. Massachusetts Institute of Technology (2015)
5. Wang, Y., Wagner, S.: Toward integrating a system theoretic safety analysis in an agile development process. In: Proceedings of Software Engineering, Workshop on Continuous Software Engineering (2016)
6. Leveson, N.: Engineering a Safer World: Systems Thinking Applied to Safety. MIT Press, Cambridge (2011)
7. Wang, Y., Wagner, S.: Towards applying a safety analysis and verification method based on STPA to agile software development. In: IEEE/ACM International Workshop on Continuous Software Evolution and Delivery. IEEE (2016)
8. Martins, L.E., Gorschek, T.: Requirements engineering for safety-critical systems: overview and challenges. IEEE Softw. **34**(4), 49–57 (2017)
9. Vuori, M.: Agile development of safety-critical software. Tampere University of Technology, Department of Software Systems (2011)
10. Stålhane, T., Myklebust, T., Hanssen, G.K.: The application of Safe Scrum to IEC 61508 certifiable software. In: Proceedings of the 11th International Probabilistic Safety Assessment and Management Conference and the Annual European Safety and Reliability Conference (2012)
11. Ge, X., Paige, R.F., McDermid, J.A.: An iterative approach for development of safety-critical software and safety arguments. In: Proceedings of Agile Conference. IEEE (2010)
12. Wang, Y., Ramadani, J., Wagner, S.: An exploratory study of applying a Scrum development process for safety-critical systems. In: Proceedings of the 18th International Conference on Product-Focused Software Process Improvement (2017)
13. Eleftherakis, G., Cowling, A.J.: An agile formal development methodology. In: Proceedings of the 1st South-East European Workshop on Formal Methods (2003)
14. Ghezzi, C., et al.: On requirements verification for model refinements. In: Proceedings of Requirements Engineering Conference. IEEE (2013)
15. Wynne, M., Hellesoy, A.: The Cucumber Book: Behaviour-Driven Development for Testers and Developers. Pragmatic Bookshelf, Dallas (2012)
16. Smart, J.F.: BDD in Action: Behavior-Driven Development for the Whole Software Lifecycle. Manning, New York (2015)
17. Silva, T.R., Hak, J.L., Winckler, M.: A behavior-based ontology for supporting automated assessment of interactive systems. In: Proceedings of the 11th International Conference on Semantic Computing. IEEE (2017)
18. Hummel, M., Rosenkranz, C., Holten, R.: The role of communication in agile systems development. Bus. Inf. Syst. Eng. **5**(5), 343–355 (2013)
19. Okubo, T., et al.: Security and privacy behavior definition for behavior driven development. In: Proceedings of the 15th International Conference on Product-Focused Software Process Improvement (2014)

20. Lai, S.T., Leu, F.Y., Chu, W.: Combining IID with BDD to enhance the critical quality of security functional requirements. In: Proceedings of the 9th International Conference on Broadband and Wireless Computing, Communication and Applications. IEEE (2014)
21. Fucci, D., Turhan, B.: A replicated experiment on the effectiveness of test-first development. In: Proceedings of the International Symposium on Empirical Software Engineering and Measurement. IEEE (2013)
22. Fucci, D., et al.: A dissection of test-driven development: does it really matter to test-first or to test-last? IEEE Trans. Software Eng. **43**(7), 597–614 (2017)
23. Erdogmus, H., Morisio, M., Torchiano, M.: On the effectiveness of the test-first approach to programming. IEEE Trans. Software Eng. **31**(3), 226–237 (2005)
24. Kollanus, S., Isomöttönen, V.: Understanding TDD in academic environment: experiences from two experiments. In: Proceedings of the 8th International Conference on Computing Education Research. ACM (2008)
25. Hamlet, R.G.: Testing programs with the aid of a compiler. IEEE Trans. Software Eng. **4**, 279–290 (1977)
26. Madeyski, L.: The impact of test-first programming on branch coverage and mutation score indicator of unit tests: an experiment. Inf. Softw. Technol. **52**(2), 169–184 (2010)
27. Marick, B.: How to misuse code coverage. In: Proceedings of the 16th International Conference on Testing Computer Software (1999)
28. Pančur, M., Ciglarič, M.: Impact of test-driven development on productivity, code and tests: a controlled experiment. Inf. Softw. Technol. **53**(6), 557–573 (2011)
29. George, B., Williams, L.: A structured experiment of test-driven development. Inf. Softw. Technol. **46**(5), 337–342 (2004)
30. Siniaalto, M., Abrahamsson, P.: A comparative case study on the impact of test-driven development on program design and test coverage. In: Proceedings of 1st International Symposium on Empirical Software Engineering and Measurement (2007)
31. North, D.: JBehave. A framework for behaviour driven development (2012)
32. Wohlin, C., et al.: Experimentation in Software Engineering. Springer, Heidelberg (2012). https://doi.org/10.1007/978-3-642-29044-2
33. Falessi, D., et al.: Empirical software engineering experts on the use of students and professionals in experiments. Empirical Softw. Eng. **23**(1), 452–489 (2018)
34. Enoiu, E.P., et al.: A controlled experiment in testing of safety-critical embedded software. In: Proceedings of the International Conference on Software Testing, Verification and Validation. IEEE (2016)
35. Adzic, G.: Bridging the Communication Gap: Specification by Example and Agile Acceptance Testing. Neuri Limited, London (2009)
36. Gregorio, D.: How the business analyst supports and encourages collaboration on agile projects. In: Proceedings of International Systems Conference. IEEE (2012)
37. Scanniello, G., et al.: Students' and professionals' perceptions of test-driven development: a focus group study. In: Proceedings of the 31st Annual Symposium on Applied Computing. ACM (2016)
38. Crispin, L., Gregory, J.: Agile Testing: A Practical Guide for Testers and Agile Teams. Pearson Education, Boston (2009)
39. Huang, L., Holcombe, M.: Empirical investigation towards the effectiveness of Test First programming. Inf. Softw. Technol. **51**(1), 182–194 (2009)
40. Madeyski, L.: Impact of pair programming on thoroughness and fault detection effectiveness of unit test suites. Softw. Process: Improv. Pract. **13**(3), 281–295 (2008)

41. Rafique, Y., Mišić, V.B.: The effects of test-driven development on external quality and productivity: a meta-analysis. IEEE Trans. Software Eng. **39**(6), 835–856 (2013)
42. Haugset, B., Stålhane, T.: Automated acceptance testing as an agile requirements engineering practice. In: Proceedings of the 45th Hawaii International Conference on System Science. IEEE (2012)
43. Adler, R.B.: Confidence in Communication: A Guide to Assertive and Social Skills. Harcourt School (1977)
44. Kitchenham, B., et al.: Robust statistical methods for empirical software engineering. Empirical Softw. Eng. **22**(2), 579–630 (2017)

Software Tester, We Want to Hire You! an Analysis of the Demand for Soft Skills

Raluca Florea$^{(\boxtimes)}$ and Viktoria Stray

University of Oslo, Gaustadalléen 23 B, 0373 Oslo, Norway
{ralucamf, stray}@ifi.uio.no

Abstract. One important discussion in the software development field is related to the skills that people need to have to build successful software products. This debate is generated on one hand by a large number of failures and delays of software projects. On the other hand, the debate is triggered by the need to build even better-quality software in a rapidly changing world. We will examine to which extent soft skills are relevant when hiring software testers and if there are any specific skills required for agile testers.

We analyzed 400 job advertisements for testers from 33 countries, out of which 64% ask for soft skills. Of the advertisements asking for soft skills, there is, on average, a request for 5 soft skills, 11 testing skills, and 5 technical skills. Only 30% of the companies ask explicitly for agile testers. However, our analysis shows no notable differences in skill demands for agile testers and the rest.

Software companies want to hire testers who can communicate well and have analytical and problem-solving skills. There is a significant increase in the need for openness and adaptability, independent-working and team-playing since 2012. In addition, there are new categories of soft skills identified, such as having work ethics, customer-focus and the ability to work under pressure.

Keywords: Soft skills · Competency requirements
Software tester competence · Software testing · Agile software development
Industrial needs

1 Introduction

Software testing is a complex activity that implies mastering both technical and soft skills. To be a productive software tester, one needs to understand business requirements from customers and to communicate them to the developers. Testers need to be organized, efficient and able to prioritize their work. Furthermore, they have to bear the pressure of finishing their job as soon as possible, so that the product can be released [1]. It is essential that they learn fast and master many kinds of responsibilities [2]. Testers need to be especially flexible because they face stress [3] and changes [4] throughout the development process.

It may also be that testers need soft skills additional to the ones required for developers or managers [5, 6]. Because of the nature of their job combining different domains and perspectives, it may be that user focus [7] and critical thinking [8] have to

© The Author(s) 2018
J. Garbajosa et al. (Eds.): XP 2018, LNBIP 314, pp. 54–67, 2018.
https://doi.org/10.1007/978-3-319-91602-6_4

be traits of efficient software testers. Moreover, the user-centered design and agile development are already common practices in companies, and the results look promising. But there are hinders to these practices such as communication breakdowns or the lack of acknowledgement of user involvement [9], issues deeply connected to soft skills.

Rivera-Ibarra et al. [10] found that the quality and innovation of software products strongly depends on the knowledge, abilities, and talent of all the people developing software. Technical and hard skills have been a long-time focus point for research in the software development field [11]. Soft skills, human factors, and intrinsic motivation have recently begun to gain attention, but with a focus on the software developer role [12]. However, the role of software tester has not been given the same attention. It can constitute a drawback since building software is a teamwork and essentially a human activity [13] shaped by the human skills of all contributors into bringing software to live. Systematic literature reviews in software testing show relevant testing areas or methods of testing [14], but we did not find information about the soft skills in the testing world. Other research has looked at soft skills depending on various phases of development, from requirements engineering to design, implementation and testing [15]. But this approach does not look at testing as an on-going activity, involved in all phases of developing software [16]. Nor does it comprise the role of tester as a sum of all these activities [17].

Soft skills are defined by Lippman et al. [18] as: "The competencies, behaviors, attitudes, and personal qualities that enable people to effectively navigate their environment, work well with others, perform well, and achieve their goals." It refers to a combination of people skills, social skills, character traits and attitudes and complement other skills such as technical and academic skills [18]. We wanted to investigate: what do companies look for in software testers? What are the soft skills they ask for? How do these needs evolve? What is specifically required of agile testers? In this study, we aim to answer the following research questions:

RQ1: What is the trend for soft skills requirements for testers?
RQ2: Are there specific soft-skill requirements for testers in agile projects?

To answer the first research question, we use a categorization of soft skills proposed in a study by Ahmed et al. [19], where the authors analyzed 500 job advertisements in IT positions (developers, designers, system analysts and software testers). By comparing with the result of the analysis specifically for software testers from 2012 [19], we were able to look at the skills requirement trend in the last 5 years. Moreover, to answer the second research questions, we analyze specifically the ads mentioning agile methods. Additionally, we make a preliminary analysis of job advertisements not asking for any soft skills.

This paper is structured as follows: Sect. 2 discusses the way we have collected and analyzed data. Section 3 presents the results of our findings. We discuss and interpret the results in Sect. 4 and present the limitations of our study in Sect. 5. In Sect. 6 we present implications and in Sect. 7 we draw the conclusion and discuss future work.

2 Data Collection and Analysis

We collected job advertisements from 33 countries on five continents. The majority of the ads were collected from the USA, Canada and Norway, see Table 1 for the details. We chose to use online job-search engines to collect the raw job advertisements. We decided to use such tools instead of going to specific hiring companies because we consider the search engines to be an efficient way of including in our analysis a large number of hiring companies, a great diversity of companies and large visibility to job-seekers. We investigated which were the most significant job-search engines by two dimensions: the number of users and the number of jobs posted. According to commercial web traffic data and analytics services provided by Alexa(Amazon)[1] and SymilarWeb[2], we chose the five most popular job-search engines, namely Indeed.com, Monster.com, GlassDoor.com, CareerBuilder.com, and SimplyHired.com.

To obtain a 95% confidence level with a confidence interval of $\pm 5\%$ we needed a minimum of 384 job ads [20]. We thus decided to study 400 job ads. We only selected the jobs that referred to the role of software testers. We have included therefore jobs such as testers, QAs, technical testers, usability testers, performance testers, game testers and financial-system testers. We have not considered jobs referring to other roles within a software development team, such as developers, architects, technical writers, or UX designers.

We collected job ads posted in multiple national languages because we consider it to be relevant to include countries that are important actors in the software development industry, whose language is not English. We gathered job ads posted in 20 different languages. We collected 226 job ads that were posted directly in English and 174 job ads that we translated into English. To make sure we translated the advertisements correctly, we used two independent online translation tools from Google[3] and DeepL Translator[4], respectively Etranslator[5], to translate and to cross-check the coherence of the translations. We included only the job ads where the results of translations were the same. Using in parallel translation tools and comparing the results worked well because most of the job advertisements were posted in plain language, using standard terms. However, we still triple-checked with a fluent software professional or native speaker the translations to English from French, Italian, Spanish, German, Hindi, Vietnamese and all Scandinavian languages and the translation results provided by the tools were confirmed.

As a last point, it is worth mentioning that the job advertisements were collected from both in-house software developers, as well as consultancy companies. Both the public sector and private sectors were represented. For example, Amazon, Norges Bank, Expedia, Nasdaq, Texas Instruments, Verizon, Motorola Solutions, Fujitsu, VISA, IBM, Nokia, New South Wales Government, National Bank of Canada, Accenture, Sogeti and Sopra Steria.

---

[1] https://www.alexa.com/.
[2] https://www.similarweb.com/.
[3] https://translate.google.com/.
[4] https://www.deepl.com/translator/.
[5] http://www.etranslator.ro/.

Table 1. Job advertisements collected from each country

Country	No. of ads	% of the total ads
USA	96	24,0%
Canada	65	16,3%
Norway	22	5,5%
UK	20	5,0%
Argentina	17	4,3%
France	17	4,3%
Mexico	15	3,8%
South Africa	14	3,5%
China	14	3,5%
Vietnam	13	3,3%
Greece	13	3,3%
India	12	3,0%
Sweden	10	2,5%
Portugal	10	2,5%
Australia	10	2,5%
Spain	9	2,3%
Italy	8	2,0%
Germany	8	2,0%
Other countries	27	6,8%
	400	**100,0%**

2.1 Coding of Soft Skills

In this paper, we examine which categories of soft skills are in most demand from employers. We determine which categories of soft skills are most popular for tester roles, compare them with the existing studies and interpret the findings.

We chose to manually analyze the data because the ads have different structures: some of the job-search engines allow job advertisers to post in their specific format, but also various job-search engines use different formats for job ads. Last but not least, not all advertisers have the same understanding of the information that has to be filled-in an ad. Therefore, we found soft skills in the sections dedicated to requirements, job attributes, duties. We went manually through each of the job ads and looked for soft skills requirements. We copied the content of the ads into the following categories:

- Country
- Job title
- Job description
- Responsibilities and tasks
- Job requirements
- Education needed
- Other certification needed
- Minimum prior experience required
- Nice to have

Table 2. Definition of the soft skills categories

Skill category	Definition based on [19]
Communication skills	The ability to convey information so that it is well received and understood
Interpersonal skills	The ability to deal with other people through social communication and interactions
Analytical and problem-solving skills	The ability to understand, articulate and solve complex problems and make sensible decisions based on available information
Team player	The ability to work effectively in a team environment and contribute toward the desired goal
Organizational skills	The ability to efficiently manage various tasks and to remain on schedule without wasting resources
Fast learner	The ability to learn new concepts, methodologies, and technologies in a comparatively short timeframe
Ability to work independently	The ability to carry out tasks with minimal supervision
Innovative	The ability to come up with new and creative solutions
Open and adaptable to changes	The ability to accept and adapt to changes when carrying out a task without showing resistance
Others	Soft skills that do not fit any of the above categories

To map the soft skills, we used the categories defined in an earlier study of job advertisements in software development [19], as our coding scheme, see Table 2. Moreover, we added the tenth category: "Other soft skills", where we coded soft skills that did not fit any of the other categories, for example, "good sense of humor", "multitasking", "ability to work under pressure" and "customer focus". We considered both the soft skills that were required imperatively (mandatory requirements) and the soft skills that were considered a plus for getting hired (nice to have). We did not distinguish between different strengths of the same skills. For instance, "strong communication skills" and "excellent communication skills".

3   Results

Of the 400 ads, 257 ask for soft skills (64,2%). We identified in all ads a total of 1.218 of soft skills, which leads us to an average of 4,73 soft skills per advertisement that demands soft skills. In comparison, the same ads ask for an average of 11,3 testing skills, 5,27 technical skills, and 0,7 domain-specific skills. Table 3 shows examples of soft skills requirements asked for in the ads.

In order to analyse the trend, we use [19] as a proxy for the skills demands in 2012. Figure 1 shows the results of comparing the soft skills demands in [19] and all the ads in our study. Focusing on the ranking, in both studies the most important category of skills is communication. Second, comes analytical and problem-solving skills. We see similar results for four types of skills: interpersonal, analytical and problem-solving, organizational and innovation: in [19] and in our research, they are demanded in

Table 3. Examples of categorized soft skills

Category name	Extracts
Communication skills	"Excellent communication skills with team members and business contacts"
Interpersonal skills	"Is able to interact with system developers, business analysts and others"
Analytical and problem-solving skills	"Demonstrated ability to analyze and solve technical issues"
Team player	"Values teamwork"
Organizational skills	"You must be well-organized with the ability to work to deadlines"
Fast learner	"A passion for learning and testing"
Ability to work independently	"Must be able to work with minimal or no supervision on extra-large and multiple concurrent projects and coordinate the work of others in this environment"
Innovative	"An ability to think creatively"
Open and adaptable to changes	"Ability to work in a rapidly changing environment"
Others	"Customer-service orientation"

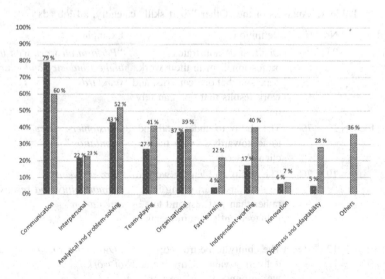

Fig. 1. Comparative analysis of soft skills requirements

approximatively the same measure. However, the demand for communication skills has decreased by 19%. The need for team-playing skills have increased by 14%, fast-learning skills have increased by 18%, independent-working skills by 23% and openness and adaptability skills have increased by a spectacular 25%.

The category named "Others" contains 121 ads and 161 skills that did not fit into the predefined categories in [19], see Table 4. When we analyzed these skills, we found that the first and most important was having work ethics. Here we included skills such as integrity, trustworthiness, ethical behavior, honesty, respectability, credibility. The other large categories of other skills were customer focus, proactivity and responsibility.

Out of the 400 analyzed jobs, 120 specify that the role is for an agile working environment. That is, there is mentioned "agile, Scrum, Kanban or Lean" in the advertisement. To see if there were particular requirements for agile software testers, we analyzed the 120 ads in more detail. We found that 91 ads ask for a total of 429 soft skills, which leads to an average of 4,71 soft skills per job ad. There are 64,2% of all ads asking soft skills and 75.8% agile ads asking for soft skills. The average number of skills is, however, similar. Referring to the "Others" category, most ads ask for work ethics (8%), customer focus (7%) and be proactive (5%).

The analysis shows that 257 ads out of 400 are asking for soft skills. The percentage is good (64,2%), in the sense that more than half of the job advertisers recognize the need for soft skills from their testers and verbalize the need in their job advertisements. However, 144 job ads do not ask for soft skills. Job ads coming from Canada and the USA ask in the biggest proportion of soft skills: Canada with 80% and the USA with 74%. China, Vietnam and Portugal have a moderate number of job ads not asking for soft skills (around 30% each). The rest of the studied countries have less than half of their ads mentioning soft skills.

Table 4. Analysis of the "Others" soft skills category, all job ads

Other skills	No	%	Definition	Example
Work ethic	24	9%	One that demonstrates professionalism in their work. A person that one can trust and work results that one can rely on	*"Perform all work with the highest industry and ethical standards"*
Customer focus	20	7%	The ability to understand and to act towards serving the clients' needs	*"Customer-service orientation"*
Proactive	19	7%	The ability to identify work to be done and start doing it, rather than just respond to management's requirements to complete work tasks	*"Pro-activeness, accountability and results orientation"*
Responsible	12	4%	The ability to be trusted; delivering valid, definitive and well-grounded work results	*"Ownership and responsibility of work"*
Works under pressure	12	4%	The ability to perform job duties under the mental distress of multiple matters requiring immediate attention	*"Ability to multi-task under tight deadlines and report status"*

(continued)

Table 4. (*continued*)

Other skills	No	%	Definition	Example
Critical-thinking	8	3%	The ability to understand information in order to identify, construct and evaluate arguments	*"Critical thinking: use logic and reasoning to identify strengths and weaknesses of alternative solutions"*
Motivated	8	3%	One that has a reason for doing something	*"Thrive in self-motivated innovation-driven environments"*
Detail-oriented	6	2%	One that pays attention to details and makes a conscious effort to understand causes instead of just effects	*"Detail-oriented and analytical individual"*
Quality-oriented	6	2%	One that understands the product's ability to satisfy the customers' needs	*"With a focus on improving development team productivity and enhancing product quality."*
Committed	6	2%	The ability to give time and energy to something one believes in	*"The successful candidate will be a self-motivated and committed individual"*
	121	36%		

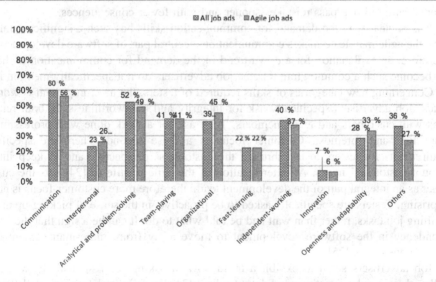

Fig. 2. Soft skills particularities for agile testers

4 Discussion

Our findings show that while more than half of the advertisers ask for soft skills, the percentage is smaller than the ones asking for testing skills or technical skills. Therefore, even though the human factors contribute the most to the success of software projects [21], the demand for soft skills still lags significantly behind the demand for testing and technical skills. The results are however is in line with the findings in [22], which underlines this paradox when hiring in the software industry.

To answer our first research question: *What is the trend for soft skills requirements for testers?* we compared the result of our analysis with a similar study from 2012 [19]. In the set of findings [19], by analysing the trends in requirements for soft skills, we observe that there is a stronger need for team-playing skills, fast-learning skills, independent-work skills and openness and adaptability skills. Agile software development puts an emphasis on teamwork having a central role in software development, therefore, being a team-player is essential. There is little literature on fast-learning skills. However, we can assume that, given the rapidly changing tasks and requirements, testers have to learn fast concepts, tools or even whole new domains, such as accounting or statistics to perform their work.

We know that independent-working skills are directly related to how much activity is required of the learner. If one can work independently, then the burden of supervision, control, and feedback for the individual learner or the team is decreased [23]. Therefore, independent-learning is a desirable skill, in order to decrease the burden on the team.

Both openness and adaptability are traits that need to be fostered within development teams, and the explanation is it makes it easier for team members to admit their own mistakes, to negotiate, listen and facilitate [6]. Therefore, it is explainable that the request for these skills has increased, as a consequence of the desire of software companies to go overpass mistakes sooner and with fewer consequences.

It is unclear why the demand for communication skills has such a significant fall. Even the agile manifesto makes communication a central part of software development. Therefore, an explanation for a down-trend in the demand for communication is that has become such a common trait that the job advertisers do not specifically mention it.

Concerning new categories of skills required of testers, the most important is work ethics. Job advertisers specifically ask for integrity and trustworthiness, in both relations with customers and team members. They ask for a work done with professionalism first and foremost. Customer focus is a close second. There are specific requirements for testers to test through the customers' perspective and to keep into account customers' needs. An interpretation of the agile manifesto [24] sets the customer as an integral part of the development team; therefore more customer-focus is not surprising. Testers are specifically asked to be proactive, in the sense of picking-up and fulfilling job tasks, rather than wait and be told what to do. It can be a sign that there is a tendency in the software development to move away from micro-management to autonomous teams [25].

Job advertisers seem to exhibit a trend now in asking for responsibility-related skills; they emphasize the candidate to be able to deliver definitive work and well-grounded work results. We can translate this requirement by that work half-done is not accepted. One has to finish their job, and one has to prove that their work results are correct. Other notable new demands are the ability to work under pressure, the ability of critical-thinking, be motivated, committed, detail-oriented and quality-oriented. We consider it to be a positive signal the small number of requests for multitasking (4%), as this practice, especially inter-projects, is often associated with a loss of effectiveness [26].

Our second research question was *"Are there specific soft-skill requirements for testers in agile projects?"*. Only 30% of the companies mentioned agile in the advertisement. Since a recent study found that at least 70% of developers work in agile projects [27], we would expect the number of agile testing ads to be higher. One explanation for the low number is that nowadays so many projects work with agile methods, that employers do not specify it anymore in the job ads.

The agile ads are slightly more oriented towards interpersonal skills, organizational skills and openness and adaptability skills. It is explicable from the perspective of agile development, where the focus is on people talking to each other, self-organizing teams and facing changes at a faster pace. Regarding particular requests for agile testers, it seems that more ads are asking for soft skills. It can be that in an agile environment the need for soft skills is more visible, therefore the demand for soft skills is more often expressed. The results show that there are no significantly different requirements for the agile testers: the soft skills requirements are relatively similar.

5   Limitations

The time span of the data collected is 2 months, December 2016 – January 2017. We have made a choice not to look at job ads in printed newspapers because the majority of job-ads in the software industry are published online. We have decided to choose a confidence level of 95% with a confidence interval of ±5%, which we consider to be satisfactory enough. If we were to have selected a confidence level of 99% with an interval of ±1%, we would have had to analyze over 16.600 jobs.

A limitation of the study can be the fact that two categories of skills, as grouped by Ahmed et al. [19], contain a combination of two skills. These categories are "analytical and problem-solving" and "openness and adaptability". We have adopted that way of grouping the soft skills because we aimed at a comparative analysis with [19].

Last, a limitation is that the number of the job ads we have collected per country does not reflect directly the importance the country has in software development. This limitation comes from the fact that we do not have figures for how many jobs in software development or testing exist for the majority of countries.

6   Implications

Practitioners can use our results to identify which soft skills they should practice or enhance. Based on our findings, companies can identify their gaps in soft skills requirements. An analysis from 2009 shows that IT executives prefer soft skills and competencies for their employees [28] and that companies seek for more rounded practitioners with well-developed soft skills [29]. Soft skills, an essential factor in the way people collaborate, play a major part in team norms, in the sense of shared expectations of how to behave and interact with team members. Team norms have an important role in affecting team performance in software teams [30]. Therefore, teams having more insight regarding their team members' soft skills can have a positive influence on the team performance.

Soft skills have a strong influence on certain parts of the test activities. While soft skills might not affect unit or integration testing, it is likely that the soft skills shape the way testers conceive and perform the kinds of tests having the user at their center, i.e. user experience and accessibility testing [31].

The Computer Science and Information Systems universities can have a significant contribution to practicing and shaping students' soft skills. We notice that indifferent of the environment in which software testers work, the demand for and the importance of soft skills stay the same. Therefore, universities should aim to train all categories of skills identified in our study. While categories such as communication, analytical and problem-solving, organizational, individual-working, and work under pressure skills are partly addressed through the way students are trained and evaluated in the courses they attend, it is important for universities to include in the tasks for the students to train their interpersonal, innovation, fast-learning or team-playing skills. Also, universities and colleges can include in their teaching examples regarding work ethics, customer-focus, well-grounded work results. It would also be a valuable addition for to students to be able to practice, through exercises, their attention to detail, mindfulness towards quality, critical thinking. The universities could encourage the students to be pro-active and committed. The reason is that soft skills are often seen by practitioners more important than hard skills in new graduates, therefore the need to introduce soft skills in the curriculum [32].

7 Conclusion and Future Work

Given the fact that more than half of the job advertisements ask explicitly for soft skills, we can conclude that employers consider them as qualities that affect the job performance of software testers. The most important soft skill for software testers is having good communication skills. The demand for soft skills seems to be stable over the years. However, we found that the trends in these demands are changing. There is an increase in the skills requirements regarding being a team-player, fast-learner, independent-working and having openness and adaptability skills. The trend could point to an increase in the number of responsibilities for testers. It may be that software testers now have to be involved in more aspects of the development pipeline: from creating software to managing it, quality-check it, building it and releasing it. It could also mean that projects themselves have changed the structure, becoming smaller and more open to changes, and people working on them must adapt to this new way of developing software.

Additionally, we identified new skills that employers want software testers to have: work ethics, customer focus, pro-activeness, responsibility, ability to work under pressure, focus on details, focus on quality and commitment. Exhibiting professionalism in one's work, delivering finished work and trustable results get more into the focus of employers.

We expected that testers working in agile environments are requested for significantly more team-playing, communication, interpersonal and fast learning skills. But the results show that these requirements are the same for all kinds of job ads. A possible explanation is that nowadays so many projects work in an agile manner, that they do not specify it anymore in the job ads. But we can also say that, indifferent of the development model adopted, the relevant soft skills for testers remain unchanged.

Future work should get a better insight into the soft skills required in agile projects by interviewing agile project members. Other possible questions are: how will the trends in soft-skills requirements evolve in the next years? Will the agile tester be required for more specialized soft skills? Will the new categories of soft skills gain even more importance? What are the new trends in soft skills requested from developers: do they correspond to the new categories of soft skills asked from software testers? Future work should also investigate why some employers do not ask for any soft skills in their advertisements for software testers.

References

1. Cohen, C.F., Birkin, S.J., Garfield, M.J., Webb, H.W.: Managing conflict in software testing. Commun. ACM **47**(1), 76 81 (2004)
2. Joseph, D., Ang, S., Chang, R.H., Slaughter, S.A.: Practical intelligence in IT: assessing soft skills of IT professionals. Commun. ACM **53**(2), 149–154 (2010)
3. Humble, J., Farley, D.: Continuous Delivery: Reliable Software Releases through Build, Test, and Deployment Automation (Adobe Reader). Pearson Education, London (2010)
4. Nurmuliani, N., Zowghi, D., Powell, S.: Analysis of requirements volatility during software development life cycle. In: Proceedings of the 2004 Australian Software Engineering Conference. IEEE (2004)
5. Kumar, S., Hsiao, J.K.: Engineers learn "soft skills the hard way": planting a seed of leadership in engineering classes. Leadersh. Manag. Eng. **7**(1), 18–23 (2007)
6. Sukhoo, A., Barnard, A., Eloff, M.M., Van der Poll, J.A., Motah, M.: Accommodating soft skills in software project management. Issues Inform. Sci. Inform. Technol. (IISIT) **2**, 691–703 (2005)
7. Black, R.: Pragmatic Software Testing: Becoming An Effective and Efficient Test Professional. Wiley, Hoboken (2007)
8. Halpern, D.F.: Teaching critical thinking for transfer across domains: disposition, skills, structure training, and metacognitive monitoring. Am. Psychol. **53**(4), 449 (1998)
9. Bordin, S., De Angeli, A.: Focal points for a more user-centred agile development. In: Sharp, H., Hall, T. (eds.) XP 2016. LNBIP, vol. 251, pp. 3–15. Springer, Cham (2016). https://doi.org/10.1007/978-3-319-33515-5_1
10. Rivera-Ibarra, J.G., Rodríguez-Jacobo, J., Serrano-Vargas, M.A.: Competency framework for software engineers. In: 2010 23rd IEEE Conference on Software Engineering Education and Training (CSEE&T). IEEE (2010)
11. Mayer, R.E., Dyck, J.L., Vilberg, W.: Learning to program and learning to think: what's the connection? Commun. ACM **29**(7), 605–610 (1986)
12. Kuusinen, K., Petrie, H., Fagerholm, F., Mikkonen, T.: Flow, intrinsic motivation, and developer experience in software engineering. In: Sharp, H., Hall, T. (eds.) XP 2016. LNBIP, vol. 251, pp. 104–117. Springer, Cham (2016). https://doi.org/10.1007/978-3-319-33515-5_9
13. Storey, M.-A.D., Čubranić, D., German, D.M.: On the use of visualization to support awareness of human activities in software development: a survey and a framework. In: Proceedings of the 2005 ACM symposium on Software visualization. ACM (2005)

14. Garousi, V., Mäntylä, M.V.: A systematic literature review of literature reviews in software testing. Inform. Softw. Technol. **80**, 195–216 (2016)
15. Holtkamp, P., Jokinen, J.P., Pawlowski, J.M.: Soft competency requirements in requirements engineering, software design, implementation, and testing. J. Syst. Softw. **101**, 136–146 (2015)
16. Graham, D., Van Veenendaal, E., Evans, I.: Foundations of Software Testing: ISTQB Certification. Cengage Learning EMEA, Boston (2008)
17. Dustin, E.: Effective Software Testing: 50 Ways to Improve Your Software Testing. Addison-Wesley Longman Publishing Co., Inc., Boston (2002)
18. Lippman, L.H., Ryberg, R., Carney, R., Moore, K.A.: Workforce Connections: Key "Soft Skills" That Foster Youth Workforce Success: Toward A Consensus Across Fields. Child Trends, Washington, DC (2015)
19. Ahmed, F., Capretz, L.F., Campbell, P.: Evaluating the demand for soft skills in software development. IT Prof. **14**(1), 44–49 (2012)
20. Cohen, J.: Statistical power analysis. Curr. Dir. Psychol. Sci. **1**(3), 98–101 (1992)
21. Brooks Jr., F.P.: The Mythical Man-Month: Essays on Software Engineering, Anniversary, 2nd edn. Pearson Education, London (1995)
22. Litecky, C.R., Arnett, K.P., Prabhakar, B.: The paradox of soft skills versus technical skills in IS hiring. J. Comput. Inform. Syst. **45**(1), 69–76 (2004)
23. van Hout-Wolters, B., Simons, R.J., Volet, S.: Active learning: self-directed learning and independent work. In: Simons, R.J., van der Linden, J., Duffy, T. (eds.) New Learning, pp. 21–36. Springer, Dordrecht (2000). https://doi.org/10.1007/0-306-47614-2_2
24. Beck, K., Beedle, M., Van Bennekum, A., Cockburn, A., Cunningham, W., Fowler, M., Grenning, J., Highsmith, J., Hunt, A., Jeffries, R.: Manifesto for Agile Software Development (2001)
25. Kirkman, B.L., Rosen, B.: Beyond self-management: antecedents and consequences of team empowerment. Acad. Manag. J. **42**(1), 58–74 (1999)
26. Stettina, C.J., Smit, M.N.W.: Team portfolio scrum: an action research on multitasking in multi-project scrum teams. In: Sharp, H., Hall, T. (eds.) XP 2016. LNBIP, vol. 251, pp. 79–91. Springer, Cham (2016). https://doi.org/10.1007/978-3-319-33515-5_7
27. Stray, V., Moe, N.B., Bergersen, G.R.: Are daily stand-up meetings valuable? A survey of developers in software teams. In: Baumeister, H., Lichter, H., Riebisch, M. (eds.) XP 2017. LNBIP, vol. 283, pp. 274–281. Springer, Cham (2017). https://doi.org/10.1007/978-3-319-57633-6_20
28. Stevenson, D.H., Starkweather, J.A.: PM critical competency index: IT execs prefer soft skills. Int. J. Proj. Manag. **28**(7), 663–671 (2010)
29. Turner, R., Lowry, G.: Towards a profession of information systems and technology: the relative importance of "hard" and "soft" skills for IT practitioners. In: Issues and Trends of Information Technology Management in Contemporary Organizations, pp. 676–678 (2002)
30. Stray, V., Fægri, T.E., Moe, N.B.: Exploring norms in agile software teams. In: Abrahamsson, P., Jedlitschka, A., Nguyen Duc, A., Felderer, M., Amasaki, S., Mikkonen, T. (eds.) PROFES 2016. LNCS, vol. 10027, pp. 458–467. Springer, Cham (2016). https://doi.org/10.1007/978-3-319-49094-6_31
31. Bai, A., Mork, H.C., Stray, V.: A cost-benefit analysis of accessibility testing in agile software development results from a multiple case study. Int. J. Adv. Softw. **10**(1 & 2), 2017 (2017)
32. Turner, R., Lowry, G.: The third dimension of the IS curriculum: the importance of soft skills for IT practitioners. In: Proceedings of ACIS 2001, p. 62 (2001)

Developers' Initial Perceptions on TDD Practice: A Thematic Analysis with Distinct Domains and Languages

Joelma Choma[1(✉)], Eduardo M. Guerra[1(✉)], and Tiago Silva da Silva[2(✉)]

[1] National Institute for Space Research, São José dos Campos, Brazil
jh.choma@hotmail.com, guerraem@gmail.com
[2] Federal University of São Paulo, São José dos Campos, Brazil
silvadasilva@gmail.com

Abstract. Test-Driven Development (TDD) is one of the most popular agile practices among software developers. To investigate the software developers' initial perceptions when applying TDD, we have performed an exploratory study. This study was carried out with participants who had about ten years of professional experience (on average), the majority of whom with no experience using TDD. The study is in the context of an agile project course at the postgraduate level of a research institute. Participants individually developed medium size projects addressed to different domains and using different programming languages. Through a structured questionnaire with open and semi-open questions, we collected information on TDD effects such as the perceived benefits, encountered difficulties, and developer's opinion about the quality improvement of the software. Afterward, we conducted a thematic analysis of the qualitative data. Most participants noticed improvements in code quality, but few have a more comprehensive view of the effects of TDD on software design. Our findings suggest that after overcoming the initial difficulties to understand where to start, and know how to create a test for a feature that does not yet exist, participants gain greater confidence to implement new features and make changes due to broad test coverage.

Keywords: Test-driven development · Test-first programming
TDD · Qualitative study · Thematic analysis

1 Introduction

Test-driven development (TDD) [3] is a technique for designing and developing software widely adopted by agile software development teams. TDD was proposed by Kent Beck in the late 1990s as a practice of the Extreme Programming. Motivating the programmer to think about many aspects of the feature before coding it, this technique suggests an incremental development in short cycles by first writing unit tests and then writing enough code to satisfy them [14]. TDD consists of small iterations by following three steps: (1) write a test for

© The Author(s) 2018
J. Garbajosa et al. (Eds.): XP 2018, LNBIP 314, pp. 68–85, 2018.
https://doi.org/10.1007/978-3-319-91602-6_5

the next bit of functionality you want to add; (2) write the functional code until the test passes; and (3) refactor both new and old code to make it well-structured [3]. TDD focuses on unit tests to ensure the system works correctly [8]. By following this method of testing before coding, the software can be incrementally developed without a need for detailed designing it upfront [15].

Many studies have highlighted the benefits of TDD in software quality by comparing it with other software development approaches. Other studies sought to understand how TDD is addressed as design and development practice by software developers. As a result of this type of investigation, some studies point out that programmers experienced in TDD report that this practice increases the confidence in the result of their work and ensures a good design and fewer defects in code [7]. As a consequence, these factors collaborate to increase the quality of software [22].

Nevertheless, programmers considered novices to the TDD might experience difficulties when applying this practice for the first time. As an effect of these initial challenges, programmers can become unmotivated because they do not feel productive using TDD [2]. Understanding the purpose of testing is one of the main difficulties reported by developers [9]. Despite the difficulties, most of them recognize that when traditionally developing software – i.e., testing only at the end – they are subject to spending more time searching for bugs and trying to evolve the software.

In this paper, we present the results of an exploratory study involving software developers, many of them with many years of professional experience, but that had never tried programming using TDD. This study was carried out in the context of an agile project course at the postgraduate level of a research institute. Our goal is to gain insights into the initial perceptions of developers regarding the TDD effects on design and development practice.

Unlike many studies that usually propose simpler activities to evaluate the use of TDD involving, for example, the coding of a single class or function; our study offered to the participants to develop projects with complete features. Thus, participants developed medium size projects (i) addressed to different domains and (ii) using different programming languages. From the participants' projects, we collected information about their perceptions concerning the perceived benefits, encountered difficulties, and their opinion about the quality improvement of the software attributed to the use of TDD.

The remainder of this paper is organized as follows. In Sect. 2 we review related work. In Sect. 3 we describe the empirical study. In Sect. 4 we present the results of the thematic analysis. In Sect. 5 we discuss our findings. Finally, Sect. 6 presents the conclusions, limitations, and future work.

2   Related Work

A growing number of empirical studies have been conducted both in academic or industrial settings to investigate the effects of TDD over the software quality (internal and external), productivity, and test quality [9,18,23].

Gupta and Jalote [15], in an academic setting, evaluated the impact of TDD on activities like designing, coding, and testing. By comparing it with the conventional code development, their results suggest that TDD can be more efficient regarding development efforts and developer's productivity. However, the study participants reported higher confidence in code design for traditional approach than needed for the TDD approach.

Janzen and Saiedian [17] conducted some experiments to compare the effects of TDD against Test-Last-Development (TLD) approach, involving students in undergraduate courses (early programmers) and professional training courses (mature developers). Their study revealed that mature developers are much more willing to adopt TDD than early programmers. However, they identified confounding factors between the two groups which may have interfered in their results – such as project size, TDD exposure time, programming language, and individual and paired programming style.

In an industrial setting, George and Williams [13] complemented a study about efficiency and quality of test cases with a survey to gather perceptions from 24 professional pair-programmers about their experiences using TDD. On average, the survey results indicate that 80% of professional programmers consider TDD an effective practice; and 78% claimed that practice improves programmers' productivity. Also, their results indicated that the practice of TDD facilitates a more straightforward design, and the lack of initial design is not an obstacle. However, for some of the programmers, they found that the transition to the TDD mindset is the most significant difficulty.

In an experiment involving teams composed of 3–6 undergraduate students, Huang and Holcombe [16] evaluated TDD effectiveness focusing on aspects related to productivity, coding effort, testing effort, and external quality. One result of the comparative study is that TDD programmers spent a higher percentage of time on testing and a lower portion of time on coding than TLD programmers. Moreover, they found that, statistically, TDD programmers neither delivered software of higher quality nor were more productive, although their productivity was on average 70% higher than that of TLD. In this study, they used external clients' assessment as a measure of quality rather than defect rate.

Vu et al. [24] also examined the TDD effects on both the internal and external quality of the software and the programmers' perception of the methodology. They carried out an experiment with 14 upper-level undergraduate and graduate students, who were divided into three teams. Two of the three teams utilized TDD while the remaining team utilized a TLD. In contrast to several previous studies, their results indicated that the TDD did not outperform TLD in many of the measures; and concerning the programmer's perception, although were not significant, the results indicated a preference for TDD.

Aniche and Gerosa [1] carried out a qualitative study with 25 software practitioners, aiming mainly to investigate developers' perceptions of how the practice of TDD influences class design. Most of the interviewees were professionally experienced and had some practice in TDD. As a result, they found that the constant need of writing a unit test for each piece of the software forces developers to create testable classes. For this reason, developers agreed that the practice of TDD helps them to improve their class design.

Scanniello et al. [21] also conducted a qualitative investigation on practical aspects related to TDD and its application with focus groups, in which 13 master students and five professional software developers discussed their experience in the programming using TDD. Among the findings, they reported that applying TDD can be tricky without the knowledge of advanced unit testing techniques – e.g., mock objects; and that participants admit that refactoring is often neglected. When TDD is compared to TLD, they found that novices believed that TDD improves productivity, whereas professionals consider that TDD decreases productivity in developing software. Romano et al. [20] conducted an ethnographically-informed study with 14 graduate students and six professionals software developers, to understand the values, beliefs, and assumptions of TDD. From their observations, they found that, in most cases, developers wrote production code in a quick-and-dirty way to pass the tests, and often ignored refactoring.

In analyzing the studies mentioned above, we have noted that most of them compare the effects of TDD to a test-last approach. Nevertheless, there is no consensus on their results, since each experience involves different contexts and other potential influence factors, as observed by Janzen and Saiedian [17]. In our study, we are not directly comparing TDD with any other approach, but we are taking into account the participants' prior experience with traditional approaches (e.g., TLD). Notably, there are few qualitative investigations exploring the TDD effects from the viewpoint of the developers [20, 21]. In this study, we also are interested in exploring and knowing the opinion of the developers about the use of TDD, its effects and other factors that imply in its application. However, we intend to capture perceptions and draw conclusions regardless of the programming language or application domain.

3   Empirical Study

This section first describes the study context and participants' profile recruited. Secondly, we present some characteristics of the projects implemented by the participants using TDD. Finally, we outline the methods of collection and analysis employed in this study.

Subjects and context. The 19 subjects involved in this study were recruited in the context of the postgraduate course of Agile Projects from the National Institute for Space Research in Brazil, in the third period of 2015 and 2016. Participants were experienced professionals – had about ten years on average of experience in software development.

During the course, all subjects received the same training about TDD based on Java programming language and JUnit framework. The training consisted of face-to-face classes and practical exercises applied in Java. However, the concepts have been taught to be applied using any language. Based on these concepts and practical exercises, the subjects had to develop an application using TDD individually. We have established that each subject was responsible for defining the type and goal of the application, and for choosing the programming language, the IDE and the unit test tools. This variability of projects would allow us to mitigate a bias observed in other studies, and to bring the implemented software closer to real needs. The subjects had around two months to develop the application in their work environment. After the development period, the participants were asked about their experience using TDD. However, it is important to point out that neither the answers nor the software delivered was considered for evaluation, to allow the participants greater freedom of speech.

As shown in the Table 1, subjects had at least two years of experience in programming. However, most of them had between 5 and 22 years of experience and good skill with the language of programming chosen for the project. For analysis, we have considered more experienced those subjects with more than five years of experience. There were only five subjects with shallow knowledge about the language used in their projects. Regarding experience with TDD, only

Table 1. Projects characterization

#	Project	Programming language	Programmers' experience (years)
S1	System for decoding avionics data bus	Python	2
S2	Model-based Testing Tool	Java	3
S3	Annotation Validation System	Java	5
S4	System for E-Commerce	Java	5
S5	Implementation of parametric curves	C++	5
S6	System for generation of geospatial data	C++	15
S7	Management system for coffee shop	C++	9
S8	Extraction of historical software metrics	JavaScript	13
S9	Web service for conversion of XML models	Java	10
S10	Implementation of training algorithm	Java	14
S11	System for weather forecast data gathering	PHP	12
S12	Drawing application for digraphs	Java	12
S13	API for mathematical calculus	Java	22
S14	Framework for gamification	Java	2
S15	API for searching of code-annotations	Java	5
S16	Metadata-based framework	Java	7
S17	Classification of remote sensing images	C++	11
S18	Framework for Adaptive Object Models	Java	19
S19	API for mining of software dependencies	Java	10

two subjects had previously used TDD but had minimal experience of it in their practice.

Projects characterization. The participants had defined their projects with different purposes, i.e., all projects were different from each other. Table 1 shows a brief description of each project. As displayed in Table 1, many of them were focused on applications for the field of space science and technology. As for the programming language, 12 projects were developed in Java; and the other languages used were C++ (4), Python (1), PHP (1) and JavaScript (1). About the type of project, 12 participants reported that their projects were part of their academic research; 3 participants developed part of the real projects that they had been developing in the industry, and other 3 participants developed personal projects. Of all the projects, twelve of them used as their starting point an existing code, while the others seven were built from scratch.

Data gathering and analysis. In this field study, a structured questionnaire with open, semi-open and closed-ended questions was used as the principal means of data collection from the software projects carried out by the study participants. For the open and semi-open questions, in particular, we have using a thematic analysis technique [4], through which we looked for themes/patterns across qualitative data to capture the critical points about developers' perceptions regarding the TDD practice.

Thematic analysis (TA), such as proposed by Braun and Clarke [5], is a theoretically flexible approach to analyzing qualitative data widely used to arrange and describe a data set in rich detail, and also to interpreter various aspects of the research topic. According to them, this approach can be used as a realist method to reports experiences, meanings and the reality of participants; or as a constructionist method to examine how events, realities, meanings, experiences are the effects of a range of discourses and behaviors.

Further, TA can be used to analyze different types of data; to work with large or small data-sets, and to produce data-driven or theory-driven analyses [6]. Thus, to accomplish the analysis of the participants' answers, we carried out a thematic analysis following the six steps proposed by Braun and Clarke [5]: (i) familiarizing with the data; (ii) generating initial codes; (iii) searching for themes; (iv) themes review and refinement; (v) defining and naming themes; and (vi) writing the final report. The first author performed the thematic analysis, and then the other two authors reviewed the themes and helped in refining them.

4   Findings

In this section, we first present some information about the projects developed by the study participants, and then we describe the results of the thematic analysis grouped into five topics related to the questionnaire: (i) difficulties in applying TDD; (ii) test failures and unexpected situations; (iii) key benefits of TDD, (iv) software design; and (v) mock objects. The results of the thematic analysis are presented in tables. The questions asked the participants are under the headings of each table. For each question, we present the themes and sub-themes that have emerged from participants' answers. Alongside each theme and sub-theme, we included the number of participants who mentioned something about them. Also, we included some participants' quotations. Such quotations, originally in Portuguese, were translated into English by the authors.

Projects size and test coverage. Once the applications had different purposes (see Table 1), our intention was not to compare the projects with each other. However, we collected some software metrics, which have been provided to us by the participants, to obtain information on the size of the applications, and on the coverage of tests. Table 2 presents the metrics related to: (i) total of hours spent in implementation; (ii) number of lines of code; (iii) number of classes (or functions, or modules); (iv) number of methods; (v) number of lines in the test code; (vi) number of classes (or files) in the test code; and (vii) number of methods in the test code. Additionally, Table 2 also shows the percentage of test coverage, and the tools used to support programmers in the unit tests.

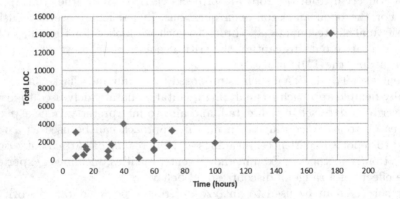

Fig. 1. Development time and total lines of code

Regarding development time, about 84% of the projects took in the range of 9 to 72 h to be implemented considering the production code and the unit tests (see Fig. 1). The amount of LOC of production ranged from 103 to 11,316; while the number of LOC of tests ranged from 101 to 4,588. Given the total number of LOC (production and testing), almost half of the projects (47%) range from 1,000 to 2,000 lines of code. As for the code coverage, 12 projects (about 63%) reached over 80% coverage. We point out that testing coverage is evidence that reinforces the use of TDD by participants.

Difficulties in applying TDD. Analyzing the participants' answers, we identified four themes on difficulties encountered by developers when developing the software through TDD: (i) the lack of culture and skill; (ii) difficulties related to unit testing; (iii) difficulties related to using TDD for software design; and (iv) difficulties with mock objects. There were other difficulties mentioned by

Table 2. Software metrics

#	TIME	LOC	NOC	NOM	t-LOC	t-NOC	t-NOM	Coverage %	Tool
S1	30	132	5	17	246	5	20	100.0	PyUnit
S2	9	2669	11	42	400	1	8	96.2	JUnit
S3	50	103	7	27	136	6	52	85.3	JUnit
S4	60	1214	47	236	959	19	55	95.8	JUnit
S5	30	359	9	125	603	8	41	96.7	GTest
S6	72	1627	38	296	1,619	12	49	75.7	Gtest
S7	176	11,316	146	2,320	2,762	1	38	80.0	QTestLib
S8	15	830	6	85	654	4	44	98.7	Mocha
S9	16	843	9	27	307	2	25	87.2	JUnit
S10	9	285	4	28	140	3	11	98.4	JUnit
S11	14	463	9	32	101	3	11	71.4	PHPUnit
S12	32	1,109	26	108	579	3	43	57.6	JUnit
S13	60	809	19	62	376	13	58	85.1	JUnit
S14	30	3,231	41	169	4,588	14	237	79.1	JUnit
S15	100	1,442	8	63	428	1	21	58.8	JUnit
S16	70	1,228	69	256	390	163	144	83.0	JUnit
S17	60	547	2	14	544	3	24	100.0	GTest
S18	40	2,000	3	10	2,000	3	10	78.5	JUnit
S19	140	1,674	56	415	536	7	69	49.0	JUnit

TIME - Total of spent hours in implementation; LOC - Number of lines of code;
NOC - Number of classes (or functions, or modules); NOM - Number of methods;
t-LOC - Number of lines in the test code; t-NOC - Number of classes in the test code;
t-NOM - Number of methods in the test code

the participants, which were more related to other technical problems than to
the development method itself. Table 3 presents the themes and sub-themes that
emerged from our analysis of difficulties reported by participants. There was only
one participant who mentioned that he had no difficulty in applying TDD.

Test failures and unexpected situations. During the tests, participants had
to deal with some sort of unexpected situation. As an answer to this question,
we found that 42.1% of participants (8 of 19) pointed out that such situations
occurred when a new test passed when it should have failed; for 68.4% of participants (13 of 19) when a previous test failed unexpectedly when a new feature
was being introduced; for 57.9% of participants (11 of 19) when a code refactoring generated failure in some test; and for 78.9% of participants (15 of 19) when
an error discovered in another way motivated them to add a new automated
test. Table 4 presents the themes and sub-themes related to the test failures and
unexpected situations reported by participants. In this case, the sub-themes refer
to the facts leading to the unexpected situations.

Table 3. Difficulties in applying TDD

Question: What major difficulties did you have in the development?		
Themes	Sub themes	Quotes
Lack of culture and skill (n = 14)	create test first (n = 6)	"The biggest difficulty was thinking about the test before having the functionality, that is, I don't know how to get started." [S3]
	control on the size of steps (n = 3)	"To follow the steps, instead I wanted to implement the main functionality as soon as possible." [S5]
	low productivity(n = 3)	"Due to lack of knowledge of TDD, in the beginning, it was required more time to get the job done." [S16]
	keep pace (n = 2)	"... keep pace with TDD (write test / red bar / feature / green bar / refactor); sometimes I got caught "unconsciously" jumping phases." [S8]
Unit testing (n = 10)	test quality (n = 8)	"To define the scope of the tests: some tests required implementation of more than one function." [S8]
	support tool (n = 2)	"In the case of Java IDE, there is a lot of support, but in languages like PHP, I found it harder because of IDE did not give me so much support." [S4]
Software design (n = 3)	how to design using TDD (n = 3)	"To think about how the API will behave before you design it." [S14]
Mock objects (n = 2)	use or not use (n = 2)	"In this way, many "mock objects" would need to be created to isolate the behavior that is carried out by my study, being that this mining code is very repetitive, but it is very small and very little would be effectively tested." [S19]

Key benefits of TDD. Concerning the perceived benefits of TDD, we identified four themes: (i) testing coverage, (ii) code quality, (iii) software design, and (iv) baby steps. Table 5 presents the themes and sub-themes that emerged from our analysis of benefits reported by participants. The most benefits are related to what the test coverage provides the developer, such as a safe refactoring, confidence to evolve and change the code, bug prevention, and consistency of code working correctly. The quality of the code is another benefit much-mentioned and perceived by almost all participants. Curiously, one of the developers reported that he could not identify improvements in code quality using TDD compared to Test Last. Instead, he mentioned only a greater comfort in implementing new features since the tests were in place, and a reduction in time to identify flaws introduced in the code. Software design and baby steps were two topics identified, but in fact were little mentioned.

Table 4. Test failures and unexpected situations

Question: Tell us about unexpected situations that occurred during testing.		
Themes	Sub themes	Quotes
New test passes unexpectedly (n = 8)	implementation errors (n = 4)	"Upon verification, I noticed errors in the implementation that were later corrected." [S17]
	bad writing test (n = 3)	"In some cases, the tests needed more manipulation, in others of better-elaborated assertions." [S19]
	incomplete method (n = 1)	"I did not realize that one of the methods was still incomplete." [S2]
A previous test failed unexpectedly (n = 11)	insertion of new rules (n = 6)	"Faced with a new functionality, part of the implementation that previously passed the test, stopped working, because it became necessary to implement more functional rules." [S12]
	in the integration (n = 5)	"The tests failed during the integration of the two frameworks." [S16]
Refactoring generates failures (n = 8)	changing methods (n = 2)	"It happened several times, after moving some method or changing the operation of some method." [S1]
	implementation failure (n = 3)	"Thus, it was necessary to adjust these tests to the new situation, and in other cases fix the implementation." [S12]
	data structures (n = 2)	"It occurred mainly when data structures were changed." [S6]
	addition of a new pattern (n = 1)	"Some tests failed when a new pattern (responsibility chain) was added." [S3]
New test for new discovered bugs (n = 15)	unthought cases (n = 11)	"Changing some tests to reject, I realized that it was the case to add one more test to cover that situation." [S1]
	artifact errors (n = 2)	"The encoding of the imported file did not match the header encoding declaration." [S11]
	mock objects (n = 1)	"I discovered the error by performing tests using mocks objects." [S16]
	in the integration (n = 1)	"It happened during the integration of the class that makes the requisitions." [S8]

Table 5. Key benefits of TDD

Question: What are the key benefits you noticed when using TDD?		
Themes	Sub themes	Quotes
Test coverage (n = 31)	safe refactoring (n = 10)	"The code can be refactored with minimal impact." [S13]
	confidence (n = 9)	"Due to the increased coverage afforded by TDD usage, the changes become easier and safer." [S17]
	preventing bugs (n = 9)	"By validating the code in small parts from the beginning of development, it ends up reducing greatly the appearance of bugs and failures." [S10]
	consistency (n = 3)	"The tests previously created ensure the structure and consistency of the code, i.e. the code that was working kept working." [S2]
Code quality (n = 21)	clean, clear, and simpler (n = 11)	"TDD has helped me to improve the code making it more readable." [S16]
	lean programming (n = 7)	"I coded only what was needed, avoiding to treat every imaginable situation." [S6]
	maintainability (n = 3)	"TDD allows greater maintainability." [S1]
Software design (n = 4)	less coupled classes (n = 3)	"The classes were less coupled, so I was able to understand the behavior of the class without depending on the total execution of the system." [S4]
	less complicated integration (n = 1)	"Integration of separately created modules was performed in a less complicated way." [S2]
Baby steps (n = 3)	thinking in a simpler way (n = 3)	"Because of the baby steps, I was forced to think in a simpler way, which ended up reducing the complexity of what I had envisioned." [S4]

Software design. When asked if participants had used TDD for software design, we found three types of situations. In the first situation, 42.1% of participants (8 of 10) defined the software design through TDD. In the second situation, 31.6% of participants (6 of 19) already had part of their classes and methods defined. Thus they used TDD only for the development and internal design of the classes. Moreover, in the third situation, 26.3% participants (5 of 19) defined during the TDD only the methods and the interaction issues since the classes already were defined. Table 6 presents the themes and sub-themes that emerged on software design.

Mock objects. Mock objects allow developers to write the code under test as if it had everything it needs from its environment, guiding interface design by the services that an object requires, not just those it provides [11]. In our study, we found that nine participants (47.4%) used this expedient, while other ten participants (52.6%) did not use it. Table 7 presents the themes and sub-themes

Table 6. TDD for software design

Question: How did you use TDD for software design activity?		
Themes	Sub themes	Quotes
For entire software design (n = 11)	bottom-up development (n = 7)	"After the test possibilities were exhausted for first created class, I thought of the next class and created a test file for it. I was creating new tests, always generating classes associated with the other classes with tests previously created." [S5]
	lots of refactoring (n = 2)	"The process required a lot of refactoring, changes in the name of modules and methods, extraction of functionalities and so on." [S8]
	slow, but efficient (n = 1)	"This insecurity made the whole process very slow, but I practically did not have to change any tests - in relation to the purpose of the test." [S10]
	mock objects (n = 1)	"In the file search module in the file system, the tests were directed to use the Observer pattern, including the use of mock." [S6]

(continued)

Table 6. (*continued*)

Question: How did you use TDD for software design activity?		
Themes	Sub themes	Quotes
For the internal design of the classes (n = 6)	new functionalities (n = 1)	"I decided to apply the TDD for the implementation of the new functionalities of the software." [S3]
	decoupled objects (n = 1)	"By using TDD, I needed to develop decoupled objects." [S4]
	methods validation (n = 1)	"The unit tests served to validate the operation of the methods." [S7]
	patterns and refactoring (n = 3)	"The class layout is equaled to the interfaces." [S16]
For methods design (n = 5)	integration problems (n = 1)	"At the time of integration, I saw interface problems between classes that required, for example, changes in method returns." [S1]
	previous sketching of classes (n = 4)	"I listed of the activities my software could perform in increasing order of complexity; and for each of these activities would, in principle, correspond to a test." [S2]

about the use of mock objects by participants. For participants who used mock, the sub-themes highlight what purpose they were used for. As mentioned earlier, one of the difficulties of the participants was deciding whether or not to use mocks in their projects. Then, nine participants decided that it was unnecessary, and one participant was able to conclude that it would be an effort without effect.

5   Discussion

TDD requires a new mindset because it recommends some practices which are not common among developers, such as test-first, baby steps, and continuous improvement of the design via refactoring. Like George and Williams [13], we also found that transitioning to the TDD mindset is difficult. Developers are slow to get pace because they take time to know where to start, and how to create a test case for something that does not yet exist.

If, on the one hand, thinking about the test before implementing the code – without having a design up front – can cause insecurity to the developer; on the

Table 7. Use of mock objects

Question: Have you used mock objects in your project?		
Themes	Sub themes	Quotes
Using mocks (n = 10)	behavior simulation (n = 6)	"I found it essential to simulate the behavior of other classes and to verify if the iteration between the objects was done as expected." [S4]
	isolating classes (n = 2)	"It helped me to verify what kind of dependency I would need to use between classes." [S10]
	external components (n = 2)	"It was very useful for testing a class that interacts with an external component." [S6]
Not using mocks (n = 10)	unnecessary (n = 9)	"Maybe I could create a mock for the graphical interface but I found it unnecessary since the manipulation of the classes could be done without it." [S12]
	without effect (n = 1)	"The case where I could have used to isolate the tested behaviors, I would not have the expected result." [S19]

other hand, a more considerable effort to create the tests before implementation can be offset by less spent time in the bug fixes. There is little empirical evidence showing if TDD, in fact, increases or decreases productivity [19]. In our study, we can infer that the lack of practice surely is one of the aspects that can impact productivity. Moreover, for this reason, developers often do not feel productive when using TDD for the first time.

As suggested by Kent Beck [3], baby steps consist of to write tests for the least possible functionality, simplest code to pass the test, and always do only one refactoring at a time. This practice encourages developers to evolve the software through small steps. According to Fucci et al. [12], an incremental test-last and TDD "could be substitutes and equally effective provided that they are performed at the same level of granularity and uniformity". Thus, they suggested that the quality assurance might not be tied to its test-first nature, but on granularity effect.

Although baby steps are a key factor, we found that various developers initially have difficulty setting the size of the steps. In particular, we noticed that the less experienced developers struggle more against the anxiety because they want to implement the requirements as soon as possible. On the other hand, more experienced developers know to assess when baby steps are the best option. Some participants realized that baby steps could help to reduce the complexity of the design. Also, in the developers' perception, problems including failures and bugs tend to be easier to solve when they are discovered because of development in small steps.

Once they overcome the initial difficulties, the participants gain greater confidence to implement new features and make changes, since everything built so far was already tested. Therefore, the test coverage is the most significant benefit perceived by them – bringing a safety in refactoring (less traumatic) and helping to prevent bugs [18]. These effects encourage the continuous improvement of the code. But, this is not always done at every step, as recommended in TDD. In line with the Scanniello et al.'s [21] findings, we also noticed that, sometimes, refactoring was only performed after a set of tests and implemented features. We underline how important is this issue to be addressed in the TDD training and coaching, and focusing more on realistic situations.

The quality of the code regarding readability and simplicity is also one of the forces of TDD perceived by developers – providing a leaner programming and better software maintainability. By writing tests before code, programmers would be "forced" to make better design decisions during development [9]. According to Turhan et al. [23], incremental and straightforward design are expected to emerge when using the TDD. Although some developers mentioned less-coupled classes, few developers realize the influence of TDD on design activity. This probably happened because the effect over software design is considered an indirect consequence, as pointed out by Aniche and Gerosa [1]. For instance, one participant claimed that decoupling was an effect of the use of mock objects.

Developers can gain a broad understanding of the requirements, since before writing the tests they need to think about how features should work. Furthermore, the test cases can be used to explain the code itself [13]. A better understanding of the code certainly helps in its maintenance. However, we noticed that few developers directly perceive a positive effect of TDD on software maintainability. Nevertheless, we believe that such benefit seems to be better perceived in the long run, or by more experienced developers, as pointed out by Dogša and Batič [10].

6   Conclusion, Limitations and Future Work

The major concern of existing studies has been to evaluate the effects of TDD compared to other development approaches; however, few studies seek to understand such effects more deeply from the viewpoint of developers. This study contributes empirical evidence on the use of TDD from developer's perspective. Unlike other studies, the design of this study involved a variability of projects with different sizes and purposes, and using different programming languages and support tools. Our findings are in agreement with the results of several related studies.

We have found that, in the participant's vision, the adoption of TDD happens slowly due learning curve and change of mindset. But, like any new practice that involves non-routine, knowledge work, this is an issue already expected. For them, in the beginning, the main difficulties are to know where to start, and then to know how to create a test for a feature that does not yet exist. Regarding perceived benefits, we found that participants gain greater confidence to implement new features and make changes due to broad test coverage. Most participants noticed improvements in code quality, but few have a broader view of the effects of TDD on software design. Less experienced developers have difficulty applying baby steps because tend to be more eager to view the all features implemented. Many of them cannot assess when using mock objects is appropriate to the project.

Regarding the limitations of this study, we have to consider that generalizability of qualitative research findings is usually not an expected attribute, since qualitative research studies are meant to study a specific issue or phenomenon, involving a certain population, and focused in a particular context. In our study, for example, although the study participants have different profiles and personal experiences, some traits of culture can be typical of the Brazilian developers. Therefore, we can not assume that our results apply outside the specific setting in which it was run. Besides, the number of participants in this study may not be sufficient to generalize the results.

Another validity concern is the possibility of researcher's influence on the qualitative data analysis. To mitigate this threat, we have adopted the thematic analysis as a systematic method following a pre-established protocol. Also, the results of the analysis were reviewed by the other two authors. Regarding study participant's, despite most developers had no previous experience with TDD, it may be that one's personal experience has influenced their particular opinions and perceptions. In future work, this issue can be better analyzed.

Acknowledgements. We would like to thank the support granted by Brazilian funding agencies CAPES and FAPESP (grant 2014/16236-6, São Paulo Research Foundation).

References

1. Aniche, M., Gerosa, M.A.: Does test-driven development improve class design? a qualitative study on developers' perceptions. J. Braz. Comput. Soc. **21**(1), 15 (2015)
2. Aniche, M.F., Ferreira, T.M., Gerosa, M.A.: What concerns beginner test-driven development practitioners: a qualitative analysis of opinions in an agile conference. In: 2nd Brazilian Workshop on Agile Methods (2011)
3. Beck, K.: Test-Driven Development: By Example. Addison-Wesley Professional, Reading (2003)
4. Boyatzis, R.E.: Transforming Qualitative Information: Thematic Analysis and Code Development. Sage, Thousand Oaks (1998)
5. Braun, V., Clarke, V.: Using thematic analysis in psychology. Qual. Res. Psychol. **3**(2), 77–101 (2006)

6. Clarke, V., Braun, V.: Teaching thematic analysis: overcoming challenges and developing strategies for effective learning. Psychologist **26**(2), 120–123 (2013)
7. Crispin, L.: Driving software quality: how test-driven development impacts software quality. IEEE Softw. **23**(6), 70–71 (2006)
8. Deng, C., Wilson, P., Maurer, F.: FitClipse: a fit-based eclipse plug-in for executable acceptance test driven development. In: Concas, G., Damiani, E., Scotto, M., Succi, G. (eds.) XP 2007. LNCS, vol. 4536, pp. 93–100. Springer, Heidelberg (2007). https://doi.org/10.1007/978-3-540-73101-6_13
9. Desai, C., Janzen, D., Savage, K.: A survey of evidence for test-driven development in academia. ACM SIGCSE Bull. **40**(2), 97–101 (2008)
10. Dogša, T., Batič, D.: The effectiveness of test-driven development: an industrial case study. Softw. Qual. J. **19**(4), 643–661 (2011)
11. Freeman, S., Mackinnon, T., Pryce, N., Walnes, J.: Mock roles, objects. In: Companion to the 19th Annual ACM SIGPLAN Conference on Object-Oriented Programming Systems, Languages, and Applications, pp. 236–246. ACM (2004)
12. Fucci, D., Erdogmus, H., Turhan, B., Oivo, M., Juristo, N.: A dissection of the test-driven development process: does it really matter to test-first or to test-last? IEEE Trans. Softw. Eng. **43**(7), 597–614 (2017)
13. George, B., Williams, L.: A structured experiment of test-driven development. Inf. Softw. Technol. **46**(5), 337–342 (2004)
14. Guerra, E., Aniche, M.: Achieving quality on software design through test-driven development. In: Software Quality Assurance: In Large Scale and Complex Software-Intensive Systems, p. 201 (2015)
15. Gupta, A., Jalote, P.: An experimental evaluation of the effectiveness and efficiency of the test driven development. In: Proceedings of the First International Symposium on Empirical Software Engineering and Measurement, ESEM 2007, pp. 285–294. IEEE Computer Society, Washington, DC (2007). https://doi.org/10.1109/ESEM.2007.20
16. Huang, L., Holcombe, M.: Empirical investigation towards the effectiveness of test first programming. Inf. Softw. Technol. **51**, 182–194 (2009)
17. Janzen, D.S., Saiedian, H.: A leveled examination of test-driven development acceptance. In: 29th International Conference on Software Engineering (ICSE 2007), pp. 719–722. IEEE (2007)
18. Jeffries, R., Melnik, G.: Guest editors' introduction: TDD-the art of fearless programming. IEEE Softw. **24**(3), 24–30 (2007)
19. Pančur, M., Ciglarič, M.: Impact of test-driven development on productivity, code and tests: a controlled experiment. Inf. Softw. Technol. **53**(6), 557–573 (2011)
20. Romano, S., Fucci, D., Scanniello, G., Turhan, B., Juristo, N.: Results from an ethnographically-informed study in the context of test driven development. In: Proceedings of the 20th International Conference on Evaluation and Assessment in Software Engineering, p. 10. ACM (2016)
21. Scanniello, G., Romano, S., Fucci, D., Turhan, B., Juristo, N.: Students' and professionals' perceptions of test-driven development: a focus group study. In: Proceedings of the 31st Annual ACM Symposium on Applied Computing, pp. 1422–1427. ACM (2016)
22. Shull, F., Melnik, G., Turhan, B., Layman, L., Diep, M., Erdogmus, H.: What do we know about test-driven development? IEEE Softw. **27**(6), 16–19 (2010)

23. Turhan, B., Layman, L., Diep, M., Erdogmus, H., Shull, F.: How effective is test-driven development. In: Making Software: What Really Works, and Why We Believe It, pp. 207–217 (2010)
24. Vu, J.H., Frojd, N., Shenkel-Therolf, C., Janzen, D.S.: Evaluating test-driven development in an industry-sponsored capstone project. In: 2009 Sixth International Conference on Information Technology: New Generations, ITNG 2009, pp. 229–234. IEEE (2009)

Myths and Facts About Static Application Security Testing Tools: An Action Research at Telenor Digital

Tosin Daniel Oyetoyan[1]([⊠]), Bisera Milosheska[2], Mari Grini[2],
and Daniela Soares Cruzes[1]

[1] Department of Software Engineering, Safety and Security,
SINTEF Digital, Trondheim, Norway
{tosin.oyetoyan,danielac}@sintef.no
[2] Telenor Digital, Oslo, Norway
{bisera.milosheska,mari}@telenordigital.com

Abstract. It is claimed that integrating agile and security in practice is challenging. There is the notion that security is a heavy process, requires expertise, and consumes developers' time. These contrast with the agile vision. Regardless of these challenges, it is important for organizations to address security within their agile processes since critical assets must be protected against attacks. One way is to integrate tools that could help to identify security weaknesses during implementation and suggest methods to refactor them. We used quantitative and qualitative approaches to investigate the efficiency of the tools and what they mean to the actual users (i.e. developers) at Telenor Digital. Our findings, although not surprising, show that several barriers exist both in terms of tool's performance and developers' perceptions. We suggest practical ways for improvement.

Keywords: Security defects · Agile · Static analysis
Static application security testing · Software security

1 Introduction

The need and urgency for quality software is higher than any other time in our history because of the rate of interconnection and dependence on software. Society, systems, and businesses are driven by software systems that are integrated into a complex system of systems (e.g. automation systems, business systems, Internet of Things, mobile devices). This is changing the threat landscape continuously. Unfortunately, the rise in consumer software technologies and methodologies for delivering them are not matched with an increase in security investment. This is evidenced in large-scale vulnerability reports and regular breaches [1].

Information gathering, exploits and hacking tools [e.g. Kali Linux] are now easily accessible and the ability for an attacker to cause serious damage is more

© The Author(s) 2018
J. Garbajosa et al. (Eds.): XP 2018, LNBIP 314, pp. 86–103, 2018.
https://doi.org/10.1007/978-3-319-91602-6_6

real than ever. On the other side, developers do not code with the mindset of an attacker because they care more about delivering functionalities. Common coding mistakes and inadvertent programming errors are weaknesses that often evolve into exploitable vulnerabilities[1]. It is claimed that, about 70-percent of reported attacks are performed at the application layer rather than the network layer [12].

Integrating static analysis tool could be envisaged to help developers code defensively [26]. Tools are important in agile development that values continuous delivery [21]. Static analysis tools (SATs) play important role to ensure product meets the quality requirements. SATs exercise application source code and check them for violations [8]. With respect to security, the decision to implement static analysis tools has to be guided. Using a static analysis tool does not imply an automatic improvement in the security of the code. For instance, teams may use such tools for checking styles, method quality, and maintenance related issues (e.g. duplicated code). These do not translate directly to security, as elegant code can still be vulnerable to attacks [20].

The security group at Telenor Digital is focused on integrating security activities in their agile teams. Telenor Digital is a community within Telenor Group, a Norwegian based international telecom operator, working to position Telenor as a digital service provider. As a result, the community researches into new possibilities and develops the next-generation digital solutions for Telenor customers transnationally. Telenor Digital is distributed in Oslo, Trondheim, and Bangkok. Each team has autonomy in its processes and leverages agile development methodologies.

One of the steps the security group has taken is to collaborate with the SoS-Agile project[2], which investigates how to meaningfully integrate software security into agile software development activities. The method of choice for the project is Action Research [16]. The combination of scientific and practical objectives align with the basic tenet of action research, which is to merge theory and practice in a way that real-world problems are solved by theoretically informed actions in collaboration between researchers and practitioners [16]. Therefore, the approach taken has considered the usefulness of the results both for the companies and for research.

Since traditional security engineering process is often associated with additional development efforts and as a result often invokes resentment among agile development teams [5]. It is thus important for the security group to approach development teams in a way that guarantees successful integration. This paper investigates the efficiency and developers' perceptions of static application security testing (SAST) tool within the agile teams at Telenor Digital. Our findings have implications for both practice and research. They show the challenges faced by developers, enumerate practical improvement approaches, and contribute to the body of knowledge about the performance of static analysis tools.

---

[1] https://cwe.mitre.org/.
[2] http://www.sintef.no/sos-agile.

The rest of this paper is structured as follows: In Sect. 2, we present the background to the study and our research questions. In Sect. 3, we describe our case study and present the results. Section 4 discusses the implications of the study for both practice and research. We present the limitations to the study in Sect. 5 and conclude in Sect. 6.

2 Background

Different studies have investigated why developers do not use static analysis tool to find bugs e.g. [18] or how developers interact with such tools when diagnosing potential security vulnerabilities e.g. [23]. Findings show that false positives and the way warnings are presented are barriers to use. Similarly, deep interaction by developers with tool's result and several questions they asked highlight another challenge of cognitively demanding tasks that could threaten the use of such tool [23]. Baca et al. [4] evaluated the use of a commercial static analysis tool to improve security in an industrial settings. They found that, although the tool reported some relevant warnings, it was hard for developers to classify them. In addition, developers corrected false positive warnings, which created vulnerabilities in previously safe code. Hofer [17] has used some other metrics to guide tools' selection such as installation, configuration, support, reports, errors found, and whether the tools can handle a whole project rather than parsing single files.

Other researchers have also performed independent quantitative evaluation of static analysis tools with regards to their performances to detect security weaknesses. The Center for Assured Software (CAS) [19] developed a benchmark testsuite with "good code" and "flawed code" across different languages to evaluate the performance of static analysis tools. They assessed 5 commercial tools and reported the highest recall of 0.67 and highest precision of 0.45. Goseva-Popstojanova and Perhinschi [15] investigated the capabilities of 3 commercial tools. Their findings showed that the capability of the tools to detect vulnerabilities was close to or worse than average. Díaz and Bermejo [10] compared the performance of nine tools mostly commercial tools using the SAMATE security benchmark test suites. They found an average recall of 0.527 and average precision of 0.7. They found also that the tools detected different kinds of weaknesses. Charest [7] compared 4 tools against 4 out of the 112 CWEs in the SAMATE Juliet test case. The best average performance in terms of recall was 0.46 for CWE89 with an average precision of 0.21.

The methodology employed by the security group and the SoS-Agile research team combined both the qualitative and quantitative approaches. Although, we could learn from the reported studies in the literature, we could not directly apply these results to the organization's case because of context issue. First, the set of tools that are to be evaluated against the benchmark of our choice are mostly not within the set reported in the literature and in many cases the names of the tools are not disclosed. Second, tools' evolution over time is also a context factor that makes it reasonable to re-evaluate them even if they have been previously evaluated. Third, the developers in the organization could express specific challenges that might not have been mentioned in the literature but would be important if the security team wants to succeed with introducing a static analysis tool.

Therefore, there are 2 research questions that are of interest to the security group at Telenor Digital and the SoS-Agile research team with regards to integrating SAST tools in the organization:

RQ1. What are the capabilities of the SAST tools in order to make informed decision for the development team? Implementing SAST tools in a meaningful and useful ways requires evaluating various tools independently in order to make informed decision. We disregard statements from vendors as they can overrate the capability of their tools. We do not distinguish between open source and commercial tools because implementing inefficient tools irrespective of license type has implications with respect to cost, time, and long-term perception/future adoption.

Furthermore, different classes of weaknesses are of interest. For instance, how does a SAST tool perform with regards to authentication and authorization weaknesses or with regards to control flow management weaknesses. Such understanding is crucial to know the strengths and weaknesses so that even if a tool is adopted, our knowledge of its strengths would prevents overestimation and a false sense of security and our knowledge of its weaknesses would guide further testing activities later in the development lifecycle.

RQ2. How do developers perceive static analysis tools with respect to successful implementation and long-term adoption by teams? Understanding the desired features in SAST tools that could increase the chance of adoption would be important. Likewise, understanding the challenges and developers' fears regarding new security tools that could lessen the chance of adoption would also be useful. By using this complimentary information, managements have better possibility to improve the chance of adoption by the team.

3   Case Study

We have used quantitative and qualitative approaches to investigate our research questions. For RQ1, we performed an independent evaluation using a benchmarking approach [2,19] of open source SAST tools and a commercial SAST tool being considered for adoption at the organization. For RQ2, we interviewed 6 developers in one of the teams regarding their perceptions about SAST tool.

3.1   Evaluating Static Analysis Tools

Our approach to evaluate SAST tools includes the selection of benchmark testsuites, selection of static analysis tools, running the analysis tools on the testsuites, and presenting the results using performance metrics. Evaluating tools using natural code is very challenging [14]. One challenge is reviewing each result of the tool to determine whether it is correct or not. This is a time consuming activity with no guarantee of correctness. Another is the difficulty to compare results from different tools since they report differently. We thus decided to use an artificial benchmark test suite.

Benchmark for Evaluating SAST Tools: Different benchmark test suites exist for testing security tools. Common examples are the OWASP Benchmark [2] and the NIST test suites [19]. We decided for NIST dataset because it is not only limited to top 10 vulnerabilities unlike OWASP benchmark test dataset. In addition, NIST dataset is designed for all range of weaknesses and not only limited to web-based weaknesses like OWASP.

NIST Test Suite: The National Institute of Standards and Technology (NIST) Software Assurance Reference Dataset (SARD) Project [19] provides a collection of test suites intended to evaluate the performance of different SAST tools. The test suite uses the common weaknesses and enumeration (CWE) dictionary by MITRE (see footnote 1) and contains artificial bad and good files/methods. The bad file/method contains the actual weakness to be tested by the tool. The good file/method contains no exploitable weakness. Figure 1 shows an example of a test case that is vulnerable to cross-site scripting (XSS) attack since the user-supplied value stored in the variable "data" is not properly sanitized before being displayed. However, Fig. 2 shows a fix by using a hardcoded value for "data" (trusted input). Although, the sink still contains the weakness that could lead to XSS attack, no user-supplied value is passed to the variable "data". Therefore, this weakness cannot be exploited. This simple design is valuable to differentiate between tools that only perform string pattern matching against those that use more sophisticated approaches (e.g. control/data-flow analysis). We have used the Juliet Test Suite v1.2 with a total of 26,120 test cases covering 112 different weaknesses (CWEs). In order to compare the tools at a higher granularity level, the CWEs are aggregated into 13 categories as shown in Table 1.

```
/* uses badsource and badsink */
public void bad(HttpServletRequest request, HttpServletResponse response)
        throws Throwable
{
    String data;

    /* POTENTIAL FLAW: Read data from a
     * querystring using getParameter
     */
    data = request.getParameter("name");

    if (data != null)
    {
        /* POTENTIAL FLAW: Display of data in web page
         * after using replaceAll() to remove script
         * tags, which will still allow XSS with strings
         * like <scr<script>ipt> (CWE 182: Collapse
         * of Data into Unsafe Value)
         */
        response.getWriter().println("<br>bad(): data = "
            + data.replaceAll("(<script>)", ""));
    }

}
```

Fig. 1. Bad source and bad sink method for XSS - CWE80

```
/* goodG2B() - uses goodsource and badsink */
private void goodG2B(HttpServletRequest request, HttpServletResponse response)
        throws Throwable
{
    String data;

    /* FIX: Use a hardcoded string */
    data = "foo";

    if (data != null)
    {
        /* POTENTIAL FLAW: Display of data in web page
         *  after using replaceAll() to remove script
         * tags, which will still allow XSS with strings
         * like <scr<script>ipt> (CWE 182: Collapse
         * of Data into Unsafe Value)
         */
        response.getWriter().println("<br>bad(): data = "
        + data.replaceAll("(<script>)", ""));
    }

}
```

Fig. 2. Good source and bad sink method for XSS - CWE80

Selected Static Analysis Tools: We have evaluated 5 open source tools (Find-Bugs, FindSecBugs, SonarQube, JLint, and Lapse+) and a mainstream commercial tool. Commercial tools use proprietary license and are thus challenging for research purposes. The open source tools are selected based on language support, ease of installation and that they can be used to find security flaws. Additionally, FindBugs, FindSecBugs, and SonarQube are widely adopted. The commercial static analysis tool is being considered for adoption at Telenor Digital.

Automated Analysis and Comparison: Tools report results in different formats and thus makes the comparison of tools a somewhat cumbersome process. We need to create a uniform format to compare the results from the tools. We adopted the approach by Wagner and Sametinger [24] and transformed each report into a CSV file, where each line contains details about each detected flaw, such as: name of the scanner (tool), abbreviation of the flaw reported by the scanner, name of the file and line number where the flaw was located, as well as the message reported by the scanner. To map the reported flaws from each scanner to their possible CWE codes, we used the CWE XML-mapping file as shown in Fig. 3 for each scanner (tool). This file contains the tool's code for a reported flaw and their possible CWE equivalent. Where vendors do not provide this information, we look for the best possible matching from the CWE database. The flaws reported in the CSV reports for each tool are then mapped to CWE numbers using the scanner's CWE XML-mapping files.

We automate some parts of the process and manually process the other parts due to how the tools can be configured and accessed (e.g. through a command line, user interface or integrated development environment) and the different operating systems they support. For example, only FindBugs, FindSecBugs, and SonarQube could be executed via command line on OS X platform. JLint is only compatible with Windows OS and for Lapse+, we have to generate the result through the IDE.

We have used the tool in [24] for tools accessible via command line. The tool did not perform recursive scanning of files in subfolders and thus missed several

Table 1. Weakness categories [13]

Weakness class	Description	Examples
Authentication and Access Control	Testing for unauthorized access to a system	CWE-620: Unverified Password Change
Code Quality	Issues not typically security related but could lead to performance and maintenance issues	CWE-478: Omitted Default Case in a Switch
Control Flow Management	Timing and synchronization issues	CWE-362: Race Condition
Encryption and Randomness	Weak or wrong encryption algorithms	CWE-328: Reversible One-Way Hash
Error Handling	Failure to handle errors properly that could lead to unexpected consequences	CWE-252: Unchecked Return Value
File Handling	Checks for proper file handling during read and write operations to a file on the hard-disk	CWE-23: Relative Path Traversal
Information Leaks	Unintended leakage of sensitive information	CWE-534: Information Leak Through Debug Log Files
Initialization and Shutdown	Checks for proper initializing and shutting down of resources	CWE-415: Double Free
Injection	Input validation weaknesses	CWE-89: SQL Injection
Malicious Logic	Implementation of a program that performs an unauthorized or harmful action (e.g. worms, backdoors)	CWE-506: Embedded Malicious Code
Miscellaneous	Other weaknesses types not in the defined categories	CWE-482: Comparing instead of Assigning
Number Handling	Incorrect calculations, number storage, and conversion weaknesses	CWE-369: Divide by Zero
Pointer and Reference Handling	Proper pointer and reference handling	CWE-476: Null Pointer Dereference

of the test suite files. We fixed this serious bug and provided an extension of the tool[3]. For Lapse+ and Commercial tool, we processed the reports separately and converted them to the uniform CSV format because of platform differences.

---

[3] Bisera Milosheska and Tosin Daniel Oyetoyan. Analyzetoolextended. https://github.com/biseram/AnalyzeToolExtended.

```xml
<mappings scanner="SonarQube">
    <scannerCode desc="Credentials should not be hard-coded" name="S2068">
        <cwe id="259" />
        <cwe id="798" />
    </scannerCode>
    <scannerCode desc="Security constraints should be defined" name="S3369">
        <cwe id="284" />
    </scannerCode>
</mappings>
```

Fig. 3. XML mapping of tools to CWE

Lastly, we developed additional Java tool to compute the performance metrics to fit the metrics originally defined by CAS [13].

3.2 Performance Metrics

We use the following performance metrics [13].

Truc Positive (TP): The number of cases where the tool correctly reports the flaw that is the target of the test case.

False Positive (FP): The number of cases where tool reports a flaw with a type that is the target of the test case, but the flaw is reported in non-flawed code.

False Negative (FN): This is not a tool result. A false negative result is added for each test case for which there is no true positive.

Discrimination: The number of cases where tool correctly reports the flaw and does not report the non-flaw (i.e. TP = 1 and FP = 0). The discrimination rate is usually equal or lower than the TP rate (Recall).

Blank (Incidental flaws): This represents tool's result where none of the types above apply. More specifically, either the tool's result is not in a test case file or the tool's result is not associated with the test case in which it is reported.

- $Recall = \frac{TP}{TP+FN}$
- $Precision = \frac{TP}{TP+FP}$
- $DiscriminationRate = \frac{\#Discriminations}{TP+FN}$

It is possible to have both TP and FP in the same file as shown in Fig. 2. In this case, the tool is not sophisticated enough to discriminate for instance when data source is hardcoded and therefore does not need to be sanitized. When we compute discrimination, we are only concerned with cases when the tool reports TP. We set the discrimination to 1 if it does not report FP on the same file.

We adopt the "strict" metrics defined by CAS [13] as they truly reflect real-world situation. For instance, Wagner and Sametinger [24] modified this metrics by accepting tools' detection in the "non-flaw" part of the code as valid as long as they are reported in the target CWE file. While this modification may make a tool's performance look better, in the true sense, it does not reflect how developers interact with tool's report. Precision of reported issue in a file is important otherwise it might lead to confusion and cognitive stress when developers try to make sense of it.

3.3   Results of Tools' Evaluation

We report the evaluation results of the 6 tools on Juliet Test Suite v1.2. As shown in Table 2 and Fig. 4, FindSecBugs records the highest recall of 18.4% with approximately 90% precision. It also has the highest discrimination rate, which is slightly lower than its recall. Lapse+ follows with a detection rate of 9.76% but with poor discrimination rate of 0.41%. However, when we break down the result into different weakness categories, this number was found only in "File Handling" and "Injection" weaknesses. The results from the Commercial tool is not as competitive as it ranked third. However, results in the categories revealed certain areas where the tool could be ahead of others.

The tools reported several other warnings, which are recorded under "incidental flaws". These warnings are not the target of the test but they indicate the "noise" levels of the tools. Many of the warnings could be categorized as "trivial" when compared with security issues. An example is warning about code styling.

We made the following observations under each weakness category (see Table 3):

Authentication and Authorization: FindSecBugs has the best detection rate of 57.20% and followed by "Commercial" tool with 29.39%. The discrimination rate is as good as the detection rate for all the tools. Both JLint and Lapse+ did not detect any weakness in this category.

Number Handling: None of the tools could detect the weaknesses under this category. The tools report different issues in the "Number Handling" CWE files,

Table 2. Number of identified weaknesses by tools from a total of 26120 flaws

Tool	TP	FP	#Discrimination	Incidental flaws
SonarQube	1292	1275	200	237845
Commercial	2038	3834	1085	360212
FindSecBugs	4811	604	4338	41637
Lapse+	2550	2736	108	18950
JLint	125	26	104	586
FindBugs	426	98	341	22245

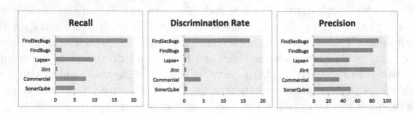

Fig. 4. Overall performance results from the tools

Table 3. Performance of tools against weakness categories

CWE Class	#Flaws	SonarQube Recall	Disc.Rate	Precision	Commercial Recall	Disc.Rate	Precision	Lapse+ Recall	Disc.Rate	Precision	FindBugs Recall	Disc.Rate	Precision	Jlint Recall	Disc.Rate	Precision	FindSecBugs Recall	Disc.Rate	Precision
Authentication and Access Control	701	0.43	0.43	100.00	29.39	22.97	45.78	0.00	0.00	0.00	0.14	0.14	100.00	0.00	0.00	0.00	57.20	54.35	92.61
Code Quality	500	0.40	0.40	66.67	5.20	4.00	16.77	0.00	0.00	0.00	6.80	6.80	94.44	0.80	0.80	100.00	6.80	6.80	94.44
Control Flow Management	599	0.00	0.00	0.00	0.50	0.50	3.49	0.00	0.00	0.00	5.68	5.68	100.00	0.00	0.00	0.00	5.68	5.68	100.00
Encryption and Randomness	622	16.40	7.88	65.8	1.93	0.96	7.55	0.00	0.00	0.00	0.00	0.00	0.00	0.00	0.00	0.00	22.83	2.73	52.01
Error Handling	142	25.35	11.97	65.45	0.00	0.00	0.00	0.00	0.00	0.00	11.97	11.97	100.00	0.00	0.00	0.00	0.00	0.00	0.00
File Handling	946	0.00	0.00	0.00	0.00	0.00	0.00	58.35	2.54	48.94	3.59	3.59	97.14	0.00	0.00	0.00	3.59	3.59	97.14
Information Leaks	188	0.00	0.00	0.00	9.57	9.57	26.47	0.00	0.00	0.00	0.00	0.00	0.00	0.00	0.00	0.00	0.00	0.00	0.00
Initialization and Shutdown	3175	0.54	0.35	73.91	0.03	0.03	5.00	0.00	0.00	0.00	0.57	0.57	94.74	0.00	0.00	0.00	0.57	0.57	100.00
Injection	10602	9.68	0.88	47.99	16.07	7.91	37.27	18.85	0.79	48.05	1.16	1.16	96.09	0.00	0.00	0.00	38.00	34.91	90.19
Malicious Logic	408	0.00	0.00	0.00	1.23	0.74	9.26	0.00	0.00	0.00	0.00	0.00	0.00	0.00	0.00	0.00	4.17	4.17	100.00
Miscellaneous	88	0.00	0.00	0.00	9.09	9.09	40.00	0.00	0.00	0.00	8.09	8.09	100.00	19.32	19.32	100.00	0.00	0.00	0.00
Number Handling	7626	0.00	0.00	0.00	0.00	0.00	0.00	0.00	0.00	0.00	0.00	0.00	0.00	0.00	0.00	0.00	0.00	0.00	0.00
Pointer and Reference Handling	523	20.27	4.78	55.78	10.52	4.97	20.30	0.00	0.00	0.00	24.28	8.03	58.80	20.08	16.06	80.15	19.50	19.50	100.00

which are not the actual weaknesses. This was alarming and indicates that manual code review in addition to automatic analysis by tool should be performed for number handling weaknesses (e.g. division by zero).

File Handling: Lapse+ produced the best detection rate of 58.35%. However, only 2.54% (discrimination rate) is correctly identified without flagging warning simultaneously in the "bad code" construct. Apart from Lapse+, only FindBugs and FindSecBugs could detect weaknesses in this category with a detection rate of 3.59%.

Miscellaneous: JLint recorded the best performance under miscellaneous (e.g. CWE-482: Comparing instead of Assigning) category with a recall and discrimination rate of 19.32%. Commercial tool and FindBugs have detection rates of 9.09% and 8.09% respectively. SonarQube, Lapse+ and FindSecBugs did not detect any weakness in this category.

Code Quality: The tools' performance is surprisingly low in this category. The highest recall of 6.8% were recorded by FindSecBugs and FindBugs.

Control Flow Management: FindBugs, FindSecBugs, and Commercial tool detected some issues in this category. However, FindSecBugs and FindBugs detection rate is 11.36 times better than the commercial tool.

Encryption and Randomness: FindSecBugs has the highest detection rate of 22.83% but with very low discrimination rate of 2.73%. SonarQube detected 16.40% issues, while Commercial tool detected 1.93% issues. The remaining 3 tools did not find any issue in this category.

Error Handling: Only SonarQube and FindBugs detected weaknesses in this category. SonarQube has a detection rate of 25.35% and FindBugs has 11.97% detection rate.

Information Leaks: Only the Commercial tool detected weaknesses in this category with a detection rate of 9.57%

Initialization and Shutdown: The performances of the tools are very poor in this category. Four tools (SonarQube, Commercial, FindBugs, and FindSecBugs) detected some weaknesses with the highest detection rate of 0.57%.

Injection: JLint did not find any issue in this category. FindSecBugs has the highest detection rate of 38%, followed by Lapse+ at 18.85% but with poor discrimination rate of 0.79% and Commercial tool with 16.07%.

Malicious Logic: Only Commercial tool and FindSecBugs detected weaknesses under this category. The highest detection rate is 4.17% by FindSecBugs while commercial tool only detected 1.23% of the weaknesses.

Pointer and Reference Handling: Lapse+ did not detect any weakness in this category. FindBugs, SonarQube, FindSecBugs, and JLint have relatively similar detection rate of about 20%. However, only FindSecBugs showed the best discrimination power of 19.5%. Commercial tool detection rate is 50% lower than the rest of the tools.

3.4   Interview

We have interviewed 6 out of the 8 developers in the selected team. The interview was divided into 5 sections. The first part covered the professional background such as job title, years of programming experience, and whether they had security related experiences. The second part covered personal opinion on their expectations and challenges with implementing SAST tools. It also included questions about their current practices. The third covered their development approaches. For instance software development methodology, release cycles, and refactoring practices. The fourth part concerned questions about development environments and the last part covered team's quality assurance and security practices.

3.5   Practices and Demography

The team is composed of developers that specialize in separate functionalities, such as business support, system integration, hosting, setup and infrastructure. They use a combination of Scrum and Kanban and perform sprint review every two weeks.

The goals of the review are to: keep track of project objectives, define the scope of the next sprint, define a set of tasks that should be included in the next iteration, and perform time estimation for those tasks. From privacy and information security point of view, the developers mentioned that they store sensitive personal data; such as personal messages and voice conversations and these assets are the most critical part of their software. Any security weakness that leads to an unauthorized disclosure or modification of the customers' highly sensitive information can be damaging to the customers and their business.

Quality assurance is performed in multiple phases starting from the design phase of the software development life-cycle (SDLC), when the team discusses potential issues. The team codes mainly in Java and uses common coding standards for Java and additional standards proposed at Telenor Digital. They perform code review, unit and acceptance testing. Lastly they perform continuous refactoring of their code.

Despite all these practices, there is no specific focus on security testing of the products. Potential security threats are discussed during the design phase of the SDLC and bad practices are avoided while coding. The team is, however, aware of some design issues they have to fix, such as securing confidential and sensitive logs and as a result, they desire to have automatic security analysis on a regular basis. The developers are free to choose the development software platform they are most comfortable with. Therefore, they develop on all the three major OS platforms: OS X, Windows and Linux. They use various integrated development environments (IDEs), such as IntelliJ, NetBeans, Emacs, Eclipse, and Sublime. Their software is mostly written in Java, but they also develop parts of it in JavaScript, shell script and Python. Jenkins[4] is used as a build server for continuous integration.

3.6   Experience with Static Analysis Tools and Security

The team is composed of developers with 4 to 37 years of development experience (see Table 4). The developers mentioned that they have used a static analysis tool called sonar before. However, this tool was used for checking code quality such as styling, standards, and large methods. One developer said: "... We use something called Sonar, ..., It's good for finding complexity in software, like referential loops ..., Bad style, non-conformance to coding standard, methods that are large or complex, ... ". The developers stated not to have used the tool to find specific security weaknesses. Although they are somehow familiar with vulnerabilities, nearly all indicated little experience with using static analysis tools specifically for security audits.

Table 4. Professional background and experiences

Title	Programming experience (years)	Familiarity with security vulnerabilities (scale: 1–5)
Software engineer	4	2
Senior software engineer	18	3
Senior software engineer	37	3
Senior software engineer	20	3–4
Senior software engineer	20	3
Software engineer	6	4

---

[4] Jenkins is a self-contained, open source automation server, which can be used to automate all sorts of tasks such as building, testing, and deploying software.

3.7   Perceptions of the Developers About SAST Tools

Setting Up the Tool and Getting it to Work. The developers fear the effort to setup a third party SAST tool and get it to work seamlessly in their development and build environments. One of the developers who has experience with previous tool said: *"... Making the things actually work, that usually is the worst thing. The hassle-factor is not to be underestimated..."*. Both Emanuelsson and Nilsson [11] and Hofer [17] report on installation as a seemingly important metric when choosing a static analysis tool.

Invasiveness and Disruption to Regular Workflow. Alerts may distract and interrupt the developer's flow and can also be a time consuming activity. The developers are clear about the fact that acting on the issues reported from the tool would depend on whether it does not overburden them. They fear that the tool may disrupt the flow of their work. One of the developers said: *"... It depends a lot on the tool and how easy it is to use and how it flows into your regular workflow,..."*

False Positives or Trivial Issues. The developers were unanimous about their concerns with false positives. They are concerned about the tool reporting high number of trivial or unnecessary issues. For instance, one of the developers said: *"... At least from my experience with the Sonar tool is that it sometimes complains about issues that are not really issues..."*

Cognitive Effort to Understand Tool's Messages. This is a concern to the developers. They would want to use the tool with minimum amount of cognitive effort. It should not be very difficult to understand the message or vocabulary used by the tool. A developer said: *"... What I fear is if they make it necessary to engage mentally a lot in the tool, as to the messages it uses then I would be reluctant to use it..."*

Broad Range of Programming Languages. The developers point out the challenge of supporting several programming languages. They develop using several languages and foresee that it might be challenging to generate static analysis warnings for each of the languages. A developer said: *"... We have several software languages that we write in. Predominantly Java and Javascript. But also some C++ as well. So to target each of those different languages would be an issue..."*

Huge Technical Debts. One of the challenges expressed is having a huge technical debt after running an implemented static analysis tool. The team rushed their products into the market the previous year and thus fears the possibility that the tool would flag many issues for refactoring. A developer says: *"... and the problem is that when you set it up at this stage of the project we have a huge design debt, because I guess things were implemented quickly, rushed before summer last year..."*

4   Discussions and Implications

Based on the results from the interview and independent tools evaluation, we discuss the implications of our findings.

One Tool Is Not Enough: We found that using one SAST tool is not enough to cover the whole range of security weaknesses at the implementation phase. This is synonymous with the findings by Austin and Williams [3] that compares different techniques across implementation and verification stages. It becomes obvious that developers have to tradeoff on some of their requirements. For instance, full language support might not be covered by one single tool and a single tool that covers many languages might suffer from low performances in many of them. Future research should focus on how to harmonize results from different tools for maximum performance.

Tools' Capability Is Low: The capability of the tools is generally low with regards to detecting security weaknesses in the Juliet Java code. The commercial tool, although highly rated in the market is not an exception. This is very challenging for developers, as they need to focus on important security warnings and disregard the noise. One helpful way we found is to filter the results by using the CWE tag provided by some of the tools. For example, FindSecBugs, SonarQube and the Commercial tool provide support for this feature.

Static Analysis Results Are Non-functional Requirements: Developers have hidden bias when it comes to fixing issues reported by static analysis tools. Statements such as: *"... if you are just looking for functionality and spend a lot of time on making your system secure or safe and doing things that you are not getting paid for or the customers are not willing to pay for... "* and *"... And of course in itself is not productive, nobody gives you a hug after fixing SonarQube reports,... "* demonstrate the challenges and need for making security as part of the development process and in a seamless manner. It shows a need for a top down approach where product owners (POs) are able to prioritize security and include it in the developers' workflow. Since static analysis reports are non-functional requirements and not features, they never become user story in many cases in agile settings. However, it is possible to adopt the approach in Rindell et al. [22] by moving relevant tool's report into the product backlog.

Do Not Underestimate Integration Effort: Developers are wary of tools that take lots of effort to integrate. This is understandable, as it has cost implication both at the present and in the future. For instance, it would require increased effort to upgrade such tool if something breaks in it. An approach taken by Telenor Digital is to dedicate a resource person as responsible for tools' implementations, configurations, and maintenance. This is beneficial as it prevents the *"hassle-factor"* and allows the agile team to focus squarely on business delivery.

Developers Are Positive to Have a SAST Tool: On the other hand, the developers agree that implementing a SAST tool would improve the security of their product. Some are very enthusiastic to learn new things and to get immediate feedback when mistakes are made and learn more about language and platform internals. These would be possible if the tools are able to point out real issues, if it is possible to mark part of the code that should not be scanned, if it is automated and easy to use, if it is not cognitively demanding to interact with the tool, and if the tools report in a way that developers understand.

Collaboration Between Researchers and Practitioners: Practitioners sometimes view research-oriented studies to be costly and time consuming. As a result, practitioners could be skeptical to collaborate. However, collaboration between researchers and practitioners can be important and useful drivers to meaningfully improve security in practice. From the perspective of the security group at Telenor Digital, the study was valuable to provide insights both qualitatively and quantitatively and to also drive future decisions. The statement by the head of the security team confirmed this: *"... But I have in particular now noted that it might not be sufficient with only one tool and that it might be more important than we anticipated before this study to understand strengths and weaknesses of the different available tools for static analysis. I also noticed that several open source tools seem to have strengths worthwhile taking into account...."*

Advice for Future Integrators: One major challenge with integrating security activities in agile is the dichotomy between the security professionals and developers [6]. Security activities are often perceived by developers to be time consuming. While the traditional assurance practice dictates to maintain independence between security professionals and developers in order to be objective and neutral [25]. This is confirmed through the use of third-party consultants by some of the teams at Telenor Digital to perform penetration testing for their applications [9]. The security team at Telenor Digital has similar challenges with bridging this gap. The approach used in this study was helpful to allow the security team understands how the developers perceive security activities and what are the important factors that could motivate to adopt them.

It is also important to warn that there is a cost for implementing inefficient tools. If there is no benefit from the tool, developers would not use it and this may also affect future possibility to adopt new tool. It is very important to let developers become aware of the strengths and weaknesses of the tools early so that they can have a realistic expectation. It is obvious that today's SAST tools still need lots of improvements to become better with catching implementation security bugs. However, it is very helpful when developers are part of the decision making such that they know the capability of the tools. This collective "ownership" culture of agile method [6, 25] is the approach undertaken at Telenor Digital to introduce and implement a new static application security testing tool for their agile teams.

5   Limitations

Size and Subjectivity: Interview subjects are few with different experiences and perceptions about static analysis tools. We can therefore not generalize the results.

Type of Benchmark: We have used artificial Java code for our evaluation, it is thus possible that real-code and different languages produce different results.

Size of Tools: We have used a few number of tools including a very popular commercial tool, however, other tools may present different results to what we have reported.

Size/Type of Organization: The organization where this study is carried out is medium-sized and as a result, stakeholders in smaller organizations or startups may express different perceptions.

Literature Review: Our pre-study review was conducted informally and not systematically.

6   Conclusion

We have investigated developers' perceptions and efficiency of static analysis tools for finding security bugs. We found several barriers exist for adoption by teams such as tools' low performance, technical debts when implemented late, non-functional nature of security bugs, and the need for many tools. However, teams are positive to use SAST tool to reduce security bugs. We recommend onboarding development teams to learn about the capability of prospective tools and to create synergy between them and the security team.

Acknowledgements. The work in this paper was carried out at Telenor Digital with support by the SoS-Agile team. The SoS-Agile project is supported by the Research Council of Norway through the project SoS-Agile: Science of Security in Agile Software Development (247678/O70).

References

1. Bugtraq mailing list. http://seclists.org/bugtraq/. Accessed 10 May 2017
2. Owasp. benchmark. https://www.owasp.org/index.php/Benchmark. Accessed 20 Oct 2016
3. Austin, A., Williams, L.: One technique is not enough: a comparison of vulnerability discovery techniques. In: 2011 International Symposium on Empirical Software Engineering and Measurement (ESEM), pp. 97–106. IEEE (2011)
4. Baca, D., Carlsson, B., Petersen, K., Lundberg, L.: Improving software security with static automated code analysis in an industry setting. Softw. Pract. Exp. **43**(3), 259–279 (2013)
5. ben Othmane, L., Angin, P., Welters, H., Bhargava, B.: Extending the agile development process to develop acceptably secure software. IEEE Trans. Dependable Secur. Comput. **11**(6), 497–509 (2014)

6. Beznosov, K., Kruchten, P.: Towards agile security assurance. In: Proceedings of the 2004 Workshop on New Security Paradigms, pp. 47–54. ACM (2004)
7. Charest, N.R.T., Wu, Y.: Comparison of static analysis tools for Java using the Juliet test suite. In: 11th International Conference on Cyber Warfare and Security, pp. 431–438 (2016)
8. Chess, B., McGraw, G.: Static analysis for security. IEEE Secur. Privacy **2**(6), 76–79 (2004)
9. Soares Cruzes, D., Felderer, M., Oyetoyan, T.D., Gander, M., Pekaric, I.: How is security testing done in agile teams? A cross-case analysis of four software teams. In: Baumeister, H., Lichter, H., Riebisch, M. (eds.) XP 2017. LNBIP, vol. 283, pp. 201–216. Springer, Cham (2017). https://doi.org/10.1007/978-3-319-57633-6_13
10. Díaz, G., Bermejo, J.R.: Static analysis of source code security: assessment of tools against samate tests. Inf. Softw. Technol. **55**(8), 1462–1476 (2013)
11. Emanuelsson, P., Nilsson, U.: A comparative study of industrial static analysis tools. Electron. Notes Theor. Comput. Sci. **217**, 5–21 (2008)
12. Fong, E., Okun, V.: Web application scanners: definitions and functions. In: 40th Annual Hawaii International Conference on System Sciences, 2007, HICSS 2007, pp. 280b–280b. IEEE (2007)
13. Center for Assured Software. CAS static analysis tool study - methodology. https://samate.nist.gov/docs/CAS%202012%20Static%20Analysis%20Tool%20Study%20Methodology.pdf. Accessed 20 Oct 2016
14. Center for Assured Software. Juliet test suite v1.2 for c/c++ user guide. https://samate.nist.gov/SRD/resources/Juliet_Test_Suite_v1.2_for_C_Cpp_-_User_Guide.pdf. Accessed 20 Oct 2016
15. Goseva-Popstojanova, K., Perhinschi, A.: On the capability of static code analysis to detect security vulnerabilities. Inf. Softw. Technol. **68**, 18–33 (2015)
16. Greenwood, D.J., Levin, M.: Introduction to Action Research: Social Research for Social Change. SAGE Publications, Thousand Oaks (2006)
17. Hofer, T.: Evaluating static source code analysis tools. Technical report (2010)
18. Johnson, B., Song, Y., Murphy-Hill, E., Bowdidge, R.: Why don't software developers use static analysis tools to find bugs? In: 2013 35th International Conference on Software Engineering (ICSE), pp. 672–681. IEEE (2013)
19. Okun, V., Delaitre, A., Black, P.E.: NIST SAMATE: static analysis tool exposition (sate) iv, March 2012. https://samate.nist.gov/SATE.html
20. Oyetoyan, T.D., Soares Cruzes, D., Jaatun, M.G.: An empirical study on the relationship between software security skills, usage and training needs in agile settings. In: 2016 11th International Conference on Availability, Reliability and Security (ARES), pp. 548–555. IEEE (2016)
21. Phillips, A., Sens, M., de Jonge, A., van Holsteijn, M.: The IT Managers Guide to Continuous Delivery: Delivering Software in Days. BookBaby, Pennsauken (2014)
22. Rindell, K., Hyrynsalmi, S., Leppänen, V.: Case study of security development in an agile environment: building identity management for a government agency. In: 2016 11th International Conference on Availability, Reliability and Security (ARES), pp. 556–563. IEEE (2016)
23. Smith, J., Johnson, B., Murphy-Hill, E., Chu, B., Lipford, H.R.: Questions developers ask while diagnosing potential security vulnerabilities with static analysis. In: Proceedings of the 2015 10th Joint Meeting on Foundations of Software Engineering, pp. 248–259. ACM (2015)
24. Wagner, A., Sametinger, J.: Using the Juliet test suite to compare static security scanners. In: 2014 11th International Conference on Security and Cryptography (SECRYPT), pp. 1–9. IEEE (2014)

25. Wäyrynen, J., Bodén, M., Boström, G.: Security engineering and extreme programming: an impossible marriage? In: Zannier, C., Erdogmus, H., Lindstrom, L. (eds.) XP/Agile Universe 2004. LNCS, vol. 3134, pp. 117–128. Springer, Heidelberg (2004). https://doi.org/10.1007/978-3-540-27777-4_12
26. Zheng, J., Williams, L., Nagappan, N., Snipes, W., Hudepohl, J.P., Vouk, M.A.: On the value of static analysis for fault detection in software. IEEE Trans. Softw. Eng. **32**(4), 240–253 (2006)

Automated Acceptance Tests as Software Requirements: An Experiment to Compare the Applicability of *Fit Tables* and *Gherkin Language*

Ernani César dos Santos[(✉)] and Patrícia Vilain[(✉)]

Federal University of Santa Catarina, Florianópolis, Santa Catarina, Brazil
ernani.santos@posgrad.ufsc.br,
patricia.vilain@ufsc.br

Abstract. It is estimated that 85% of the defects in the developed software are originated from ambiguous, incomplete and wishful thinking software requirements. Natural language is often used to write software requirements specifications as well as user requirements. However, natural language specifications can be confusing and hard to understand. Some agile methodologists consider that acceptance tests are more precise and accurate sources of information about the customer's needs than descriptions in natural language. Several studies have addressed the use of acceptance tests as software requirements specification. Therefore, none of the previous studies has performed experiments to compare the applicability of different acceptance testing techniques in order to support an organization in the selection of one technique over another. This paper addresses this problem reporting an experiment conducted with undergraduate students in Computer Science. This experiment compares the applicability of two acceptance testing techniques (Fit tables and Gherkin language) as software requirements specification. This research tries to answer three questions: (a) Which technique is the easiest to learn in order to specify acceptance test scenarios? (b) Which technique requires less effort to specify acceptance tests? (c) Which technique is the best one to communicate software requirements? The results show that there is no sufficient evidence to affirm that one technique is easier to specify test scenarios or better to communicate software requirements. Whereas, the comparison of effort in terms of time to specify acceptance testing shows that the mean time to specify test scenarios using Gherkin language is lower than Fit tables.

Keywords: Acceptance testing · Software requirements · Fit tables
Gherkin language · FitNesse · Cucumber · TDD · ATDD · BDD

1 Introduction

Software system functionalities are specified through requirements engineering artifacts, which are a valuable starting point for the software development [1]. Natural language is often used to write system requirements specifications as well as user

J. Garbajosa et al. (Eds.): XP 2018, LNBIP 314, pp. 104–119, 2018.
https://doi.org/10.1007/978-3-319-91602-6_7

requirements [2]. According to [1], most of the software requirements specifications are written in natural language.

However, natural language specifications can be confusing and hard to understand. Various problems can arise when requirements are written in natural language, for example, readers and writers can use the same word for different concepts, or even, it is possible to express the same concept in completely different ways [2]. In addition, it is estimated that 85% of the defects in the developed software are originated from ambiguous, incomplete, and wishful thinking software requirements [3].

Some agile methodologists utilize acceptance tests as a way to specify software requirements [3–6] instead of using more common artifacts based on natural language. They consider that acceptance tests are more precise and accurate sources of information about the customer's needs than descriptions in natural language [7].

Besides the improvement over requirements specification expressed in natural language, acceptance tests also collaborate to the requirements gathering process, because they promote integration between stakeholders and software engineers during the writing of test scenarios of the application to be developed.

Several studies have addressed the use of acceptance tests as software requirements specification. However, none of the previous studies has performed experiments using more than one technique to compare the applicability of them as software requirements in the same project in order to support organizations in the selection of one technique over another. This paper addresses this problem reporting an experiment conducted with undergraduate students of the Computer Science program at the Federal University of Santa Catarina to compare the use of a tabular notation for acceptance test scenarios versus a textual scenario notation, which are Fit tables and Gherkin language, respectively.

The rest of this paper is organized as follows. Section 2 presents the related works. Section 3 presents an overview of the main concepts related to this paper. Section 4 defines the design of our experimentation and the research questions. In Sect. 5 we propose answers for each research question and discuss the results. Section 6 presents the threats to the validity. Section 7 presents the conclusion and future works.

2 Related Works

In [4] two experiments were conducted using the tables of the Framework for Integrated Test (Fit). The results show that when software requirements are written in natural language and complemented by Fit tables, they become four times easier to understand by developers than when Fit tables are not used. However, the authors claim that Fit tables do not replace textual requirements, but rather, they suggest that these tables bridge the gaps of software requirements specification which are written exclusively using natural language, reducing the ambiguity and misinterpretation of them.

In [5] an experiment with master students was performed. The experiment aims to verify the use of executable Fit acceptance test scenarios as software requirements in maintenance and evolution tasks. The results indicate that Fit tables help developers to perform the maintenance tasks correctly and they also show that these tables may be used to perform regression tests.

Melnik et al. [7] have performed an experiment to show that non-technical users, working together with software engineers, can use acceptance test scenarios as a way to communicate and to validate software business requirements. The acceptance testing technique used in this experimentation was the Fit tables. Although the experimentation concludes that non-technical users can specify clearly software requirements using Fit tables, it points out that users have difficulty in learning how to specify test scenarios using this notation. Additionally, this study shows that some non-technical users do not approve the use of Fit tables as an artifact to specify requirements.

A user-centered language called BehaviorMap is proposed in [8]. This language is based on behavior models written in Gherkin language that aims to specify behavioral user scenarios in a cognitive way. In this study, an experiment was conducted with 15 individuals to verify the understandability of the BehaviorMap. The results show that BehaviorMap scenarios are easier to understand in relation to textual scenarios, especially when considering scenarios with higher complexity.

The use of acceptance test scenarios as an artifact to specify software requirements were also analyzed in [9], which performed an experiment to verify the capability of non-technical users in creating user scenarios of a puzzle game using acceptance testing. The acceptance testing technique used in this experimentation was the User Scenario through User Interaction Diagram (US-UID). The experimentation has pointed out that non-technical users could create US-UID scenarios of the application correctly with a few hours of training.

These previous studies have focused on verifying the applicability of acceptance tests as an artifact to clarify software requirements specifications written in natural language or have checked their applicability as software requirements specifications rather than using artifacts such as user stories or use cases. However, none of them compared the applicability of two different notations to express acceptance tests and their adherence to communicate software requirements. This study compares the use of a tabular notation, Fit tables, versus a textual scenario notation, Gherkin language, in terms of: ease of learning, ease of use, effort required to specify acceptance tests scenarios, and capability to communicate software requirements.

3 Background

Test-driven development (TDD) is a software development approach which tests are written before beginning the development of the SUT, this practice becomes widely established after 1999 by Kent Beck. This practice is performed in five steps, as follows [13]:

1. Write a new test case.
2. Run all test cases and see the new one fails.
3. Write just enough code to make the test pass.
4. Re-run the test cases and see them all pass.
5. Refactor code to remove duplication.

In 2002, Ward Cunningham introduced the concept of Fit Tables. In this approach, users write acceptance tests using Fit tables, and programmers write fixtures (glue code) to connect these tables with the future source code of the SUT. The remaining process of this approach is equivalent to steps 2 through 5 of the TDD. This process is called Acceptance test-driven development (ATDD) because acceptance tests are written before the SUT [14].

Acceptance testing is a black box testing that aims to determine if a software system meets customer requirements from user's point of view [3, 7, 9]. As defined in the IEEE Standard 1012-1986 [10], acceptance testing is a "formal testing conducted to determine whether or not a system satisfies its acceptance criteria and to enable the customer to determine whether or not to accept the system".

Fit is an example of framework to express acceptance test scenarios. Using this framework, the acceptance tests are written in the form of tables, which are called Fit tables. Besides Fit tables are used to represent test scenarios, they are also used for reporting the results of tests [11]. Figure 1 shows an example of Fit report table, which was used to perform several tests in a functionality to calculate discount over an amount. The first column of this table, named amount, represents an input, whereas, the second columns, which name is followed by parenthesis, represent the expected output. When a test fails, the expected and actual output values are showed to the user [11].

CalculateDiscount	
amount	discount()
999.00	0.00
1000.00	0.00 *expected* 50.0 *actual*
1010.00	50.50
1200.00	60.00

Fig. 1. Fit table report sample [11].

Behavior-driven development (BDD) is an agile software development approach that enhances the paradigm of TDD for acceptance testing. In the BDD approach, the behavior of the SUT is described through user stories and acceptance tests before beginning its development. Scenarios representing the user stories are described using BDD languages, such as Gherkin language [12].

Gherkin language is a domain specific language (DSL) that can express the behavior and the expected outcome of the SUT [12]. It uses some words as commands, such as Given, When and Then. The word *Given* expresses the inputs or pre-conditions to perform a test, the word *When* expresses conditions or specified behavior, and the word *Then* expresses expected outputs or expected changes due to the specified behavior. As with the Fit tables, Gherkin language also needs a glue code to connect

the features (a set of test scenarios) with the source code of the SUT [12]. An example
of the syntax of this language is as follows:

```
Scenario: Pop element
Given a non-empty Stack
When a stack has N elements
And element E is on top of the stack
Then a pop operation returns E
And the new size of the stack is N-1
```

4 Experiment Definition

In this section, we report the experiment definition, design, and planning, following the
guidelines proposed in [15, 16], as well the experiments conducted in [3, 4]. The
objective of this experimentation is to compare the applicability of Fit tables and
Gherkin language to communicate requirements in a software development process
regarding specification effort and requirements consistency. The perspective is to adopt
Fit tables or Gherkin language to express software system requirements in outsourcing
contracts for software development. The context of the experiment consists of undergraduate students (subjects) and a Java application (object). The participants (subjects)
involved in the experiment are undergraduate students in the last years of the Computer
Science program. The object of this study is a human resource (HR) management
application named HRS, which supports functionalities such as compliance, payroll,
personnel files, and benefits administration.

4.1 Experiment Participants

The participants were 18 students from a course called Special Topics in Technology
Applications I, in the last years of the bachelor's degree in Computer Science at UFSC.
The students have already attended courses on software programming and software
engineering, and they had a medium knowledge and expertise level in programming
and software engineering topics. The most of them have been taking part of trainee
programs. The participants have never taken any course or professional experience in
Fit or Gherkin language. Although the experiment was conducted as a mandatory
activity of the course, the students were not graded based on the artifacts produced, but
rather, they were graded based on their participation. Also, students were advised that
the activities were parts of an experiment to compare the applicability of two acceptance testing techniques as artifacts to communicate software requirements.

4.2 Experiment Material

The experiment was performed on a set of four requirements for the HRS application.
We granted access permission for each participant to access a web directory that
contains a textual description of the application, instructions to set up the application
project (download the zipped Java project and import it into the Eclipse IDE), a time

sheet and a questionnaire. The timesheet was used by the participants to take note of the time spent in each task of the experiment. The questionnaire is a set of 24 questions to investigate the background of the participants and to perform a qualitative analysis of the performed tasks. The answers for these questions are five-point scales, such as 1 = Strongly agree, 2 = Agree, 3 = Not certain, 4 = Disagree, 5 = Strongly disagree.

The development environment was set up by the participants, who received a tutorial to guide this activity. The tutorial content is:

- Installation and configuration of Java Enterprise;
- Installation and configuration of the standalone version of Fit wiki and its dependencies;
- Installation and configuration of Eclipse IDE with the Cucumber plugin;
- Quick-start examples to validate all development environments.

4.3 Hypothesis Definition

Considering Fit tables and Gherkin language as available acceptance testing techniques, this experiment addresses the following research questions:

- **RQ1.** Which of these acceptance tests techniques is easier to learn?
- **RQ2.** Which of these acceptance tests techniques requires less effort (in time) to specify acceptance test scenarios?
- **RQ3.** Which of these acceptance tests techniques is the best one to communicate software requirements, as a form of expressing consistent requirements?

Once the research questions are formulated, it is possible to turn it into null hypotheses to be tested in the experiment:

- **H_{0a}** the correctness of acceptance test scenarios specified by participants who attended a three-hour lecture about Fit tables and Gherkin language is the same for both acceptance testing techniques.
- **H_{0b}** the effort to specify acceptance test scenarios is the same for both techniques.
- **H_{0c}** the correctness of software functionalities specified using Fit tables and Gherkin language and implemented by the participants is the same using both acceptance testing techniques.

On the other hand, the alternative hypotheses are:

- **H_{1a}** the correctness of acceptance test scenarios specified by participants who attended a three-hour lecture about Fit tables and Gherkin language is different when both acceptance testing techniques are used.
- **H_{1b}** the effort to specify acceptance test scenarios using Fit tables is not the same when Gherkin language is used.
- **H_{1c}** the correctness of software functionalities implemented by the participants is different when both acceptance testing techniques are used.

The dependent variables of our study are:

- **ATS#.** Acceptance tests of requirement # were specified: {correctly, incorrectly};
- **ATST#.** The participants need {?} minutes to specify acceptance test scenarios of requirement #;
- **AR#.** The delivered source code implemented based on the acceptance test scenarios of requirement # is executable and it was accepted by the business stakeholder: {yes, no};

Where the symbol "#" represents a change software requirement identified from SR1 to SR4 in Table 1, and the symbol "?" represents an integer value.

Table 1. Objects of the experiment

Id	Requirement
SR1	Rectification of personnel profile information
SR2	Calculation of salary bonus per person
SR3	Exclusion of personnel profile information
SR4	Calculation the average of salary bonus per position

The number of acceptance test scenarios that were specified correctly (*ATS#*) was obtained from the evaluation of artifacts delivery by participants. This evaluation was performed by a researcher who is expert in acceptance tests and he does not have any connection with the experimentation. The time needed to specify acceptance test scenarios of each requirement (*ATST#*) has been measured by asking participants to fill it in the timesheet. The number of requirements correctly coded (*AR#*) was obtained from the evaluation of executable source code delivered by participants. This evaluation was conducted by a business stakeholder, who accepted or not the delivered functionality through black box testing. If the business stakeholder accepts the delivered functionality, the coded requirement is considered correct. Otherwise, it is considered incorrect. This person has not been involved with the specification of acceptance test scenarios that were used by participants to develop the set of required software changes.

4.4   Experiment Design

We divided the experiment into two parts. Part 1 addresses the specification of acceptance test scenarios. Part 2 addresses the implementation of new requirements for the HRS application using the acceptance test scenarios to represent the requirements.

In both parts, we have four objects and two treatments. The objects are the new requirements of the HRS application, as shown in Table 2. The treatments are the following:

- **(F)** Software requirements specified as acceptance test scenarios using Fit Tables.
- **(G)** Software requirements specified as acceptance test scenarios using Gherkin language.

The participants were split into two groups, which were identified by the letters A and B. In Part 1, the group A specified two software requirements as acceptance test scenarios using Fit tables, meanwhile, the group B specified two software requirements as acceptance test scenarios using Gherkin language. Table 2 shows, for each group, which treatment was used to specify which software requirement.

Table 2. Experiment design of Part 1 – Specification of acceptance test scenarios. At the top of this table, SR1, SR2, SR3, and SR4 are abbreviations to the objects listed in Table 1.

Participants	Objects and treatments			
	SR1	*SR2*	*SR3*	*SR4*
Group A	(F)	(F)	–	–
Group B	–	–	(G)	(G)

In Part 2 of this experiment, the set of software requirements specified by group A were send to group B, and vice versa. Then, as shown in Table 3, the group A developed requirements SR3 and SR4, which were specified by group B using Gherkin language, whereas, the group B developed requirements SR1 and SR2, which were specified by group A using Fit tables. Before performing this exchange of acceptance test scenarios between the groups, an expert verified the correctness and conciseness of each scenario. Test scenarios that presented problems were replaced by others, which were correct and express the same set of requirements. This intervention was necessary to prevent false negatives in the analysis of capability of executable acceptance tests to communicate software requirements.

Table 3. Experiment design of Part 2 – implementation of new requirements.

Participants	Objects and treatments			
	SR1	*SR2*	*SR3*	*SR4*
Group A	–	–	(G)	(G)
Group B	(F)	(F)	–	–

4.5   Training

Participants have been trained in meaning and usage of the following subjects:

- a half-hour lecture about acceptance testing, TDD, ATDD, and BDD;
- one-and-a-half-hour lecture about Fit tables and FitNesse, including how to configure this framework and practice exercises;
- one-and-a-half-hour lecture about Gherkin language and Cucumber, including how to configure this framework and practice exercises.

4.6 Experiment Procedure

The experimentation was carried out as explained in the following. First, the participants were given a short introduction to the experimentation, then they were randomly assigned to one of the two groups. After this, they received the timesheet and the questionnaire, described in Sect. 4.2.

Then, the experiment was conduct according to the following steps:

- (1) Participants had 20 min to check if their environment to specify acceptance tests, which was previously set up in the training section, was working. In this step, they also answered the six first questions of the questionnaire.
- (2) Participants read an overview of the HRS application and received a document with the description of two new requirements for this application.
- (3) For each requirement:
- (3.a) Participants filled the start time in their time sheets.
- (3.b) Participants had to understand the requirements; if they had any doubt a business stakeholder was available to clarify them.
- (3.c) Participants had to specify the requirement using the acceptance testing technique assign to them.
- (3.d) When finished, participants had to mark the stop time on their time sheet.
- (4) Then, participants had to answer the next eight questions of the questionnaire and to send the produced artifact to a web repository. The artifacts were identified by a random numeric id and only the researchers knew who uploaded them.
- (5) An expert in acceptance testing evaluated all uploaded artifacts and marked the ones that were inconsistent or incomplete. This mark was visible only to the researchers.
- (6) In the sixth step, the second part of our experiment was started. Participants had 20 min to check if their environment to develop the next tasks was working. After this, they had to download acceptance tests artifacts produced by a participant of the other group.
- (7) Then, participants had to answer two questions in the questionnaire related to their view about the downloaded artifacts.
- (8) The researchers had to verify which participants downloaded acceptance tests that, according to the expert evaluation, were incorrect. Then, they exchanged the incorrect acceptance tests by correct tests that express the same requirements using the same acceptance testing technique.
- (9) Then, for each acceptance test scenario (requirement):
- (9.a) Participants had to fill the start time in their time sheets.
- (9.b) Participants had to understand by themselves the acceptance test.
- (9.c) Participants had to develop the new requirement of the HRS application expressed by the acceptance tests.
- (9.d) When finished, participants had to mark the stop time on their time sheet.
- (10) Then, participants had to answer the next eight questions of the questionnaire and to send the produced source code to a web repository. The artifacts were identified by a random numeric id, and only researchers knew who uploaded them.

This procedure was carried out in two sections. The first with three and a half-hour of duration and the second one with two hours of duration.

5   Results and Data Analysis

In this Section, we show and discuss the results achieved from the experiment. The experiment data and charts are available at www.leb.inf.ufsc.br/index.php/xp2018/.

5.1   Consistency and Correctness of the Acceptance Test Scenarios

Table 4 is the contingency table for the dependents variables (see Sect. 4.3) from ATS*SR1* to ATS*SR4*. The first line of this table shows the number of tasks performed using Fit tables as acceptance testing technique: 17 tasks were completed, and only one task failed. The second line shows the number of tasks performed using Gherkin language as acceptance testing technique: 13 tasks were completed, and five tasks failed. The tasks performed by the same participant were considered as independent measures.

We applied the Fisher's test in the data presented in Table 4. This test returned a p-value of 0.1774. The result is not significant at $p < 0.05$. Thus, H_{0a} is accepted, there is no statistically significant influence of the treatment on the acceptance test scenarios specification.

Table 4. Contingency table for correct specifications of acceptance tests

Treatment	Acceptance test scenarios were specified:	
	Correctly	Incorrectly
Fit Tables (T)	17	1
Gherkin Language (G)	13	5

Although we cannot obtain the answer of RQ1 with Fisher's test, we suppose that extra training sections and practical exercises could decrease the number of incorrect specification around zero because the errors identified in the test scenarios specified by participants in both techniques are basic mistakes. Thus, we found that the complexity to learn both acceptance testing techniques by software developers is the same.

5.2   Time to Complete Acceptance Test Scenarios Specifications

Table 5 presents the time, in minutes, spent by participants to complete the specification task of each requirement. The underlined time values in this table refer to test scenarios that were specified incorrectly by participants. The tasks performed by the same participant were considered as independent measures, and the distribution of requirements and treatments were conducted as shown in Table 2.

We used the Shapiro-Wilk normality test to check if the data collected from the experiment for the two treatments have a normal distribution. Then, we performed a

Table 5. A list of time spent to develop new software requirements in the HRS application.

Treatment	Time list (in minutes)
Fit tables (F)	{20, 21, 21, 23, 35, 36, 40, 45, 50, 65, 66, 77, 79, 88, 108, 120, 126, 135}
Gherkin Language (G)	{15, 16, 17, 15, 39, 30, 30, 30, 45, 35, 60, 28, 40, 40, 70, 57, 84, 75}

t-test that returned a p-value of 0.0291. We also performed the same test excluding the underlined values and we obtained a p-value of 0.0334. The results are significant at p < 0.05. Thus, in both tests H_{0b} is rejected and the alternative hypotheses are accepted. Therefore, there is a difference, in terms of the mean time spent to specify acceptance tests, between Fit tables and Gherkin language.

Answering the RQ2, we found that the effort, in terms of the meantime, to specify acceptance tests using Gherkin language (40 min) is lower than using Fit Tables (64 min).

5.3 Applicability of Acceptance Test Scenarios to Communicate Software Requirements

Table 6 is the contingency table for the dependents variables (see Sect. 4.3) from ARSR1 to ARSR4. The first line of this table shows the number of tasks implemented based on the requirements specified using Fit tables: 13 tasks were successfully completed, and five tasks failed. The second line shows the number of tasks using Gherkin Language: 10 tasks were successfully completed, and eight tasks failed.

We applied the Fisher's test in the data presented in Table 6. This test returned a p-value of 0.4887. The result is not significant at p < 0.05. Thus, H0c is accepted, therefore, there is no statistically significant influence of the treatment on the development of software requirements expressed by acceptance test scenarios using both techniques.

Table 6. Contingency table for correct development of software requirements expressed by acceptance tests

Treatment	The delivered source code implemented based on the acceptance test scenarios is executable and it was accepted by the business stakeholder:	
	Yes	No
Fit Tables (T)	13	5
Gherkin Language (G)	10	8

Then, addressing the RQ3, we cannot assume based on the Fisher's test result that a technique is better than another to communicate requirements. In addition, in the same way that we suppose that extra training could improve acceptance test scenarios specification, it also could improve requirements communication. However, despite these experimentation evidences, we claim that Gherkin language scenarios communicate requirements better than Fit tables because we observe that tables are weak in details and depending on the software requirement a complementary textual description is required to communicate a requirement completely, whereas, in Gherkin language the acceptance test scenarios are complemented on default by a textual description.

5.4   Experiment Questionnaire

In this section, we discuss six questions of the questionnaire that we applied in the experiment. The questions were answered on a five-point scale, where one maps to Strongly agree, two maps to Agree, three maps to Not certain, four maps to Disagree, and five maps to Strongly disagree. Question 1 (Q1) and question 3 (Q3) were applied to group A, whereas question 2 (Q2) and question 4 (Q4) were applied to group B. Questions 5 (Q5) and 6 (Q6) were applied to both groups.

Q1. I experienced no difficulty in specifying acceptance test scenarios using Fit tables. Half of the participants strongly agree (22.22%) or agree (27.78%) with this statement and 22.22% are not certain, whereas, the rest of the participants disagree (5.56%) or strongly disagree (22.22%).

Although the results presented in Sect. 5.1 shows that the major part of the acceptance tests was specified correctly, we observed, through this questionnaire, that participants had difficulty to specify the acceptance tests. So, we realized that in a next experiment we should dedicate more time performing training lectures intending to decrease the time spent by participants to specify acceptance tests and to increase the quality of acceptance test scenarios using Fit tables.

Q2. I experienced no difficulty in specifying acceptance test scenarios using Gherkin language. This result was different than we expected. The percentage of participants who answered that they strongly disagree (16.67%) or disagree (16.67%) with this statement is greater than the percentage of who answered that strongly agree (5.56%) or agree (16.67%). The rest of participants (44.44%) are not certain about this statement.

Our initial belief was that participants who used Gherkin language had experimented less difficulty to create acceptance test scenarios than ones that used Fit tables because Gherkin language is similar to English spoken language. However, the results obtained from the questionnaire tend to be the opposite. As concluded in Q1, the participants should spend more time with the lecture and exercises to improve their experience with Gherkin Language.

Q3. I experienced no difficulty in implementing new requirements in the HRS application, which specification were expressed as acceptance test scenarios writing through Fit tables. The major part of participants reported that they had difficulty in the implementation tasks, 55.56% answered that strongly disagree

(27.78%) and disagree (27.78%) with this assertion, whereas 38.89% of the participants are not certain, 5.56% agree and 0.00% strongly agree with this assertion.

Q4. I experienced no difficulty in implementing new requirements in the HRS application, which specification were expressed as acceptance test scenarios writing through Gherkin Language. The major part of participants reported that they had difficulty in the implementation tasks, 27.78% and 33.33% answered respectively that strongly disagree and disagree with this assertion, whereas, 27.78% of the participants are not certain, 5.56% agree and 5.56% strongly agree with this assertion.

Although only a few participants agree or strongly agree with this assertion, the percentage is two times bigger than the percentage of the same group in Q3. We assign this to the fact that acceptance test scenarios written in Gherkin language are more verbose than tables, which becomes Gherkin language easier to understand than Fit tables. However, as presented in Sect. 5.3, there is no evidence that one technique is better than another to communicate software requirements.

Q5. I will use acceptance testing to validate software in future projects. The number of participants (27.78%) that agree with this assertion is greater than the number of participants that disagree (11.11%) or strongly disagree (11.11%). However, 50.00% are in doubt about using acceptance testing to validate software.

Q6. I will use acceptance test scenarios to communicate requirements for future projects. 33.33% of the participants did not approve the use of acceptance tests as requirements and they would not like to take part in projects that use this approach. 38.89% of the participants are not certain about this assertion, the rest of the participants, 27.78%, agree with this assertion.

In both Q5 and Q6, the number of participants that are in doubt about using acceptance testing to validate software or to communicate requirements is greater than the number of participants that are certainly that will use or will not use it in the future. We think that the high number of participants that are in doubt is due to the inexperience in acceptance testing, which is in agreement with the background questionnaire where 100% of participants answered they had never seen it before.

6 Threats to the Validity

Although we assigned different requirements to groups A and B in the same part of our experiment, we choose requirements that have similar business logic and complexity. However, the complexity of the requirements could affect results, mainly regarding time.

An expert in acceptance testing verified the artifacts produced by participants in part 1 and a business stakeholder verified the artifacts produced in part 2. These two individuals had an important role in our experimentation because they decided what is or not correct. However, we could carry out our experiment without these individuals in a different way:

- using the acceptance tests specified by an expert as input for part 2, avoiding that some mistakes in the acceptance test scenarios created by other participants were unnoticed by the expert;
- using automated acceptance tests, or even JUnit tests, to validate if the code implemented by the participants meets the user needs.

However, we choose this approach to approximate our experiment to a real-world scenario, where there is a variation on the style of acceptance tests scenarios written, such as vocabulary, idioms, and level of details.

Another issue is the time sheets. It is very difficult to ensure that all participants are marking the time spent in each task. During the experiment, we checked if the forms have been filled correctly and asked the participants to fill out the forms very carefully. Finally, the small sample size may limit the capability of statistical tests. In this study, the time was compared using t-test, and for contingency tables, we used Fisher's exact test.

7 Conclusion

In this study, we have experimented to compare the applicability of acceptance tests, which were written using Fit tables and Gherkin language, as software requirements. The results show that there is no sufficient evidence to affirm that one technique is easier to use than another or one technique communicates software requirements better than another. Whereas, the comparison of effort regarding time to specify acceptance testing shows that the mean time to specify test scenarios using Gherkin Language is lower than using Fit tables.

Additionally, the questionnaire applied shows that participants had difficulty to specify and understand acceptance tests writing in both techniques. We assign this difficulty because neither of the participants had used Fit tables and Gherkin language before. Despite only a few participants answered that is easy to understand requirements expressed by acceptance tests, they have pointed out Gherkin language scenarios as easier to understand than Fit tables.

Finally, the number of participants who agreed with the possibility of using these acceptance testing techniques as software requirements in future projects is very similar to the numbers of those participants who disagree with this possibility. We assign this result to the participants' inexperience in acceptance testing, which resulted in a poor impression about the application of these techniques in real-world projects. As future works, we intend to improve our experimental design to carry it out with others acceptance testing techniques and include other personas like non-technical users and software engineers.

References

1. Sarmiento, E., Leite, J.C.S.P., Almentero, E.: C&L: Generating model-based test cases from natural language requirements descriptions. In: 2014 IEEE 1st International Workshop on Requirements Engineering and Testing (RET), pp. 32–38 (2014)
2. Sommerville, I.: Software Engineering. 9th edn. Pearson Education, Boston (2015)
3. Torchiano, M., Ricca, F., Penta, M.D.: "Talking tests": a preliminary experimental study on fit user acceptance tests. In: First International Symposium on Empirical Software Engineering and Measurement (ESEM 2007), pp. 464–466 (2007)
4. Ricca, F., Torchiano, M., Penta, M.D., Ceccato, M., Tonella, P.: Using acceptance tests as a support for clarifying requirements: A series of experiments. Inf. Softw. Technol. **51**, 270–283 (2009)
5. Ricca, F., Torchiano, M., Penta, M.D., Ceccato, M., Tonella, P.: On the use of executable fit tables to support maintenance and evolution tasks. In: Third International ERCIM Symposium on Software Evolution, pp. 83–92 (2007)
6. Clerissi, D., Leotta, M., Reggio, G., Ricca, F.: A lightweight semi-automated acceptance test-driven development approach for web applications. In: Bozzon, A., Cudre-Maroux, P., Pautasso, C. (eds.) ICWE 2016. LNCS, vol. 9671, pp. 593–597. Springer, Cham (2016). https://doi.org/10.1007/978-3-319-38791-8_55
7. Melnik, G., Maurer, F.: The practice of specifying requirements using executable acceptance tests in computer science courses. In: Companion to the 20th Annual ACM SIGPLAN Conference on Object-oriented Programming, Systems, Languages, and Applications, pp. 365–370. ACM, San Diego (2005)
8. Wanderley, F., Silva, A., Araújo, J.: Evaluation of BehaviorMap: a user-centered behavior language. In: 2015 IEEE 9th International Conference on Research Challenges in Information Science (RCIS), pp. 309–320 (2015)
9. Longo, D.H., Vilain P.: Creating user scenarios through user interaction diagrams by non-technical customers. In: Proceedings of the International Conference on Software Engineering and Knowledge Engineering, SEKE, pp. 330–335 (2015)
10. IEEE: IEEE Standard for Software Verification and Validation Plans. IEEE Std 1012-1986. IEEE (1986)
11. Mugridge, R., Cunningham, W.: Fit for Developing Software: Framework for Integrated Tests. Pearson Education, Upper Saddle River (2005)
12. Rose, S., Wynne, M., Hellesøy, A.: The Cucumber for Java Book: Behaviour-Driven Development for Testers and Developers. 1st edn. Pragmatic Bookshelf (2015)
13. Beck, K.: Test-Driven Development: By Example. Addison-Wesley Professional, Boston (2003)
14. Deng, C., Wilson, P., Maurer, F.: FitClipse: a fit-based eclipse plug-in for executable acceptance test driven development. In: Concas, G., Damiani, E., Scotto, M., Succi, G. (eds.) XP 2007. LNCS, vol. 4536, pp. 93–100. Springer, Heidelberg (2007). https://doi.org/10.1007/978-3-540-73101-6_13
15. Wohlin, C., Runeson, P., Höst, M., Ohlsson, M.C., Regnell, B., Wesslén, A.: Experimentation in Software Engineering – An Introduction. Springer, Heidelberg (2012)
16. Juristo, N., Moreno, A.: Basics of Software Engineering Experimentation. Kluwer Academic Publishers, Boston (2001)

Agile Transformation

Interface Problems of Agile in a Non-agile Environment

Environment

Sven Theobald and Philipp Diebold[✉]

Fraunhofer Institute for Experimental Software Engineering (IESE),
Fraunhofer-Platz 1, 67663 Kaiserslautern, Germany
{sven.theobald, philipp.diebold}@iese.fraunhofer.de

Abstract. Agile is the widespread software development approach. But many projects are still working with traditional methods. In addition, non-technical business units continue working in traditional ways. Thus, problems arise on the interface of agile and traditional due to their fundamental differences. To prevent potential problems, one must be aware of the existing interfaces and common pitfalls. Based on a literature search and workshops, we identified existing interfaces, collected and grouped problems. We present the identified problems and propose a matrix that facilitates classification of interface problems. This matrix can be used to identify and classify more problems as well as understanding and preventing problems on the interface of agile and traditional.

Keywords: Agile · Traditional · Plan-based · Non-agile environment
Hybrid organization · Interface · Problems · Challenges · Classification
Agile transition

1 Introduction

Agile is widespread, especially on team level [1]. But other studies show that complete agile enterprises are quite rare. This is mainly the case because at least the supporting functions, such as marketing or human resources, are still operating in their established ways. Thus, the agile parts of an organization do have at least those interfaces to these traditional environments. Alignment between agile and traditional approaches is challenging [2]. There is a lack of guidance for problems at those interfaces, although many practitioners confirmed that these problems exist. Understanding and addressing them is viable to make use of the benefits provided by agile, and to support agile initiatives to progress towards an agile organization. This work discusses which interfaces exist, presents the problem fields and proposes a problem classification.

2 Related Work

An interface problem is a (potential) problem or challenge occurring on the interface of agile and traditional approaches, e.g., caused by the conflicting underlying principles, culture, or processes. There exists literature reporting problems with agile, e.g., [1, 3], or [4]. Interface problems are already mentioned, but the borders to other organizational

© The Author(s) 2018
J. Garbajosa et al. (Eds.): XP 2018, LNBIP 314, pp. 123–130, 2018.
https://doi.org/10.1007/978-3-319-91602-6_8

internal or external entities surrounding the agile team are not explicitly considered. The following literature focused on interface problems.

In interviews with 21 agile practitioners, two problem categories resulted [5]: Increased IT landscape complexity, caused by concurrent development streams, separated layer development and different processes. The other one was lack of business involvement, caused by a centralized it department and a traditional project organization. Mitigation strategies were proposed to address the identified challenges.

Based on interviews with seven German practitioners, problems in agile projects within traditionally organized corporations were identified [6]. The study is limited to the viewpoint of agile teams, especially on global software engineering. Among the 8 identified problems, 3 had an non-agile environment: "wrong application of agile", "lack of acceptance of agile principles" and "difficulties in translating agile […] into their non-agile counterparts." Further interface problems are mentioned, such as "fragmented documentation in agile" or "combined usage of paper and electronic media".

With the aim of analyzing how agile and lean approaches are adopted at scale, a literature review was conducted focusing on challenges and success factors [7] considering interfaces to other organizational units. We identified 17 of their challenges as interface problems. The groups with the highest number of interface problems were "integrating non-development functions", "hierarchical management and organizational boundaries" and "coordination challenges in multi-team environment".

Kusters et al. [8] identified challenges and risks that appear in hybrid organizations. The focus was on project and program level issues that impact the coordination and cooperation. 22 issues were classified in six groups: Organization and structure, business processes and control, culture and management style, development and testing, involvement of stakeholders, documentation and communication.

Motivation has to be considered when interfacing with non-agile surroundings [9]. Agile team members might get frustrated by missing or unsynchronized feedback from traditional stakeholders, or when having to work in a traditional way after experienced agile projects. More interface problems were mentioned, such as a fixed budget and project plan at the project start or having to adapt to the surrounding stage-gate process.

Kuusinen et al. [10] already went one step further and identified strategies to mitigate such problems. The information was collected from a survey and a workshop. The themes were grouped in two categories, one for organizational themes and one for change themes. Most strategies are generic and can be applied at different interfaces.

3   Research Method

Our overall research goal is described in the GQM-goal-template [11] as following: Identify and analyze *common existing problems on the interface of agile in a non-agile environment* in order to *create a classification* in the context of *organizations developing software or systems* from the perspective of *research and practice*. Because this goal covers several different aspects, we needed to refine it into several research questions (RQs). For this reason, these are the RQs refining our study goal: **RQ1** - Which interfaces of agile entities to a non-agile environment exist? **RQ2** - Which problems do appear on the identified interfaces? **RQ3** - How to classify and group these problems?

The research procedure contained the following steps: (1) We started with a brief research on the state of the art in existent literature. (2) Second, we performed a workshop with five IESE employees, all experienced in agile and some in systems engineering. (3) Third, we had the possibility to discuss this topic at the Automotive Agile PEP-Conference. We were able to collect further problems from practitioners and discuss most important problems to identify concrete solutions. (4) Afterwards, an initial classification was developed. (5) Finally, this classification was used to categorize the identified problems on specific interfaces according to the dimensions of the classification.

4   Results

The results are presented along the RQs. Thus, we first present the different interfaces, where problems might arise. Then we present an overview over the problems, identified and categorized into different problem fields. Finally, a matrix that supports classification of interface problems and solutions is presented and discussed.

4.1   Existing Interfaces (RQ1)

The first step was to identify all possible situations where agile approaches could interface with traditional development. The identified interfaces can be categorized into company-internal (I) and external (E) interfaces, see Table 1:

Table 1. Presenting the interfaces (name, external/internal interface, description/example)

Name	E/I	Description/Example
Project–Team	I	The coordination between agile and non-agile teams in large projects appears to be a challenge, e.g. the synchronization between agile software teams and hardware teams
Organization - Project	I	In larger organizations, projects collaborate with different organizational units, e.g. the line management demanding traditional reporting or synchronization with other organizational parts like human resources or operations. Agile projects have a different mind-set and information demands than traditional organizational units
To Customer	E	Successful collaboration with customers and other stakeholders is important, e.g. for requirements clarification or meetings. Working with traditional customers is challenging for an agile project
To Subcontractor	E	Traditional subcontractors slow down the agile process and complicate synchronization. Also, agile subcontractors of traditional teams might cause issue
To Reg. authority	E	The requirements posed by regulatory authorities have to be considered. Regulated organizations have to provide evidences for the fulfillment of regulations, leading to a focus on documentation

4.2   Existing Problem Fields (RQ2)

In total, 169 problems were assigned to various interfaces during our data collection. Different categories emerged when grouping similar problems into the so called problem fields. Example problems will be given either in the description of the problem fields or in the problem classification (cf. Sect. 4.3).

Project Planning. Traditional plans are specified upfront, e.g. in detailed milestone- or Gantt-charts and only updated when necessary. Thus, it is difficult to synchronize with agile plans which are only detailed for a short period of time and which are adapted each iteration. Traditional project managers perceive Agile as lacking the right amount of risk management, traceability, requirements management and quality assurance. Breaking down dependencies between agile and traditional teams is challenging.

Controlling, Reporting & Approval. Similarly, traditional project managers demand a different kind of reporting and expect different artifacts than delivered by agile. This leads to effort for a second report or the transformation of agile reports. The regular reprioritization and de-scoping done by agile teams is perceived as lack of control. There might be differences between the formal approval of delivered artifacts, especially concerning safety aspects in system development. KPIs might differ, e.g., individual performance is measured while often team productivity is measured in Agile.

Contracting & Budgeting. Contracting between a traditional customer and agile projects is a common challenge. The customer usually expects to have certainty of time, scope and budget at the beginning of the project. The approval of the product depends on the contractually defined features from the start of the project, even if the scope was changed to optimize business value. Traditional customers are often not able to provide the team with a representative who collaborates with the team on a daily basis and is knowledgeable enough to take over product responsibility.

Process Requirements. Especially regulated domains have to stick to standards and regulations prescribing how their process has to look like. Original Equipment Manufacturers demand certain development approaches by their suppliers. Regulations demand upfront planning, heavyweight documentation of requirements or proofs of risk management. Standards like Automotive SPICE or ISO 26262 are relevant in the automotive context, and it is still not clear how agile processes cover these standards.

Tooling & Infrastructure. Traditional and agile teams have different needs for tools and infrastructure. Some projects are forced to use the organizational tool chains, although these might not fit to agile. The agile way of using paper-based media like a whiteboard, physical task boards or burn charts is a problem in distributed projects.

Coordination & Integration. Dependencies and integration of products developed by several teams need to be synchronized. It is a challenge to coordinate agile iterations with the stage-gate process of traditional (system) development. The communication needs of agile teams are often not met by other non-agile business units (e.g., marketing, sales, operations, customer service) who are not used to direct involvement. Therefore, long reaction time slows down the agile teams. For distributed teams, especially over time zones, agile collaboration creates more challenges due to the regular collaboration and feedback loops. From the technical point of view, dependencies in the architecture of several teams might become a problem, since agile architectures emerge during the project, while traditional architectures are extensively planned upfront and expected not to change. Also, dependencies between fast software and slower hardware development have to be tackled, as well as collaboration with dedicated quality assurance teams.

Staffing. The typical traditional organizational structure is functional, hence the knowledge is distributed in silos. An agile team contains all roles necessary to conduct the project, so there are no borders between different functional teams handing over products or artifacts to another silo. Traditional teams are overfilled with team members, each one working only partially on the project. Agile suggests that team members are dedicated to only one product, and teams are only as big as they have to be. There is a change in role profiles, since agile demands different skills from team members as well as from managers. Developers in agile teams are expected to be T-shaped, having expertise in a specific field while being able to collaborate with other disciplines.

4.3 Problem Classification (RQ3)

Using the concepts of interfaces and problem fields allows classifying existing problems along two dimensions: Which interface does the problem occur at? Which problem field does the problem belong to?

Some of the identified problems might occur on several interfaces and it might be possible that one problem fits to several problem fields, because some problem fields have borders to each other. Based on the resulting classification matrix, each problem (and solution) can be related to one (or more) cells of the following classification matrix (cf. Table 2). As an example for the classification, synchronization between an agile software team and a traditional system development project happens in the problem field Coordination & Integration on the interface Project – Team.

A comparison of the number of problems occurring on the different interfaces helps to assess which interfaces are more relevant, since they contain the most problems. Especially the interface Organization - Project contains a wide range of problems (n = 64), since multiple organizational units have to cooperate with a software team, e.g., human resources, sales, operations, marketing, etc. Thus, there are many instances of the organizational unit, therefore more possibilities to find problems. The high number of problems on the Project - Team interface (n = 50) is understandable, since this is where most organizations currently are [1]. Some pilot teams are already agile, but have to work with traditional teams to deliver a common product. Although the interface To Customer is very specific, surprisingly many problems were found (n = 28). This shows that many customers still lack the understanding of agile and have to learn how to collaborate with agile teams. There are also quite many problems on the interface To Subcontractor (n = 27). None were identified yet on the interface To Regulatory Authorities.

Regarding the problem fields, a comparison of the amount of problems in each problem field might show which field is causing the most problems. Coordination & Integration is the biggest problem field (n = 39), potentially because it is very broad

and many things can be classified as the very general term collaboration. Contract &
Budgeting (n = 31) and Project Planning (n = 27) were also two problem fields with a
high amount of problems, followed by Staffing (=23) and Controlling, Reporting &
Approval (n = 20). Process Requirements (n = 15) and Tooling & Infrastructure
(n = 14) were the problem fields with the smallest number of problems.

Some combinations of problem fields and interfaces are more common. That means
that certain problem fields are more likely to cause problems on a certain interface.
Coordination & Integration problems happen most often on the interface Project –
Team. Staffing issues are most likely to occur on the interface Organization & Project,
often with the human resource department representing the organization. Contracting
problems occur mainly on the interface To Customer or To Subcontractor. Controlling
is challenging on the interface Organization – Project. Further, Project Planning is
relevant for both Organization - Project and Project – Team interfaces. Tooling
problems are most likely to occur on the interface between a Team and the overall
Project.

Table 2. Matrix presenting the two dimensions and the total number of identified problems
(from literature, from IESE, from conference workshop).

Problem fields	Interfaces				
	Organization-Project	Project - Team	To Customer/ Stakeholders	To Reg. Authority	To Subcontractor
Project Planning	11 (8, 3, 0)	10 (6, 2, 2)	4 (1, 2, 1)		2 (0, 2, 0)
Controlling, Reporting & Approval	10 (8, 1, 1)	5 (3, 2, 0)	4 (2, 2, 0)		1 (0, 1, 0)
Contract & Budgeting	7 (0, 2, 5)	1 (1, 0, 0)	12 (3, 3, 6)		11 (1, 1, 9)
Process Requirements	8 (3, 1, 4)	4 (3, 1, 0)	2 (0, 2, 0)		1 (0, 1, 0)
Tooling & Infrastructure	3 (2, 1, 0)	6 (2, 2, 2)	1 (0, 1, 0)		4 (0, 2, 2)
Coordination & Integration	9 (8, 1, 0)	21 (11, 4, 6)	4 (2, 2, 0)		5 (1, 1, 3)
Staffing	16 (11, 3, 2)	3 (0, 3, 0)	1 (0, 1, 0)		3 (0, 3, 0)

4.4   Limitations

Except for the data from literature, data is mostly representing the automotive domain.
IESE experiences are based on agile projects often conducted with automotive companies or suppliers and the participants of the workshop were mainly from this domain.
This poses a threat to the generalization of results to other domains. The literature
review was not conducted as a systematic literature review, and did only consider a few
of the first sources that were identified. This led to a limited amount of identified

problems, which limits the validity of the classification matrix and the possibility to analyze which problem fields or interfaces cause the most problems.

5   Conclusion and Future Work

Although general problems with agile are covered by research, there is few related work investigating problems on the interface of agile and traditional approaches. We collected those interface problems with a literature review and within workshops, categorized them into problem fields, and finally suggested a classification matrix. The results support practitioners in considering and mitigating potential problems, and help researchers align their research efforts on the most common and important problems. Of course, the classification matrix has to be refined, evaluated and improved with the help of further data. This data will be identified in interviews with practitioners or from reviewing literature.

References

1. VersionOne: 11th Annual State of Agile Report. https://www.versionone.com/
2. Thamhain, H.J.: Can we manage agile in traditional project environments? In: 2014 Portland International Conference on Management of Engineering & Technology (PICMET), pp. 2497–2505. IEEE, July 2014
3. Nerur, S., Mahapatra, R., Mangalaraj, G.: Challenges of migrating to agile methodologies. Commun. ACM **48**(5), 72–78 (2005)
4. Gregory, P., Barroca, L., Sharp, H., Deshpande, A., Taylor, K.: The challenges that challenge: engaging with agile practitioners' concerns. IST **77**, 92–104 (2016)
5. Van Waardenburg, G., Van Vliet, H.: When agile meets the enterprise. IST **55**(12), 2154–2171 (2013)
6. Richter, I., Raith, F., Weber, M.: Problems in agile global software engineering projects especially within traditionally organised corporations. In: Proceedings of International C* Conference on Computer Science & Software Engineering, pp. 33–43. ACM, July 2016
7. Dikert, K., Paasivaara, M., Lassenius, C.: Challenges and success factors for large-scale agile transformations: a systematic literature review. JSS **119**, 87–108 (2016)
8. Kusters, R., van de Leur, Y., Rutten, W., Trienekens, J.: When agile meets waterfall - investigating risks and problems on the interface between agile and traditional software development in a hybrid development organization, pp. 271–278 (2017)
9. Gren, L., Torkar, R., Feldt, R.: Work motivational challenges regarding the interface between agile teams and a non-agile surrounding organization: a case study. In: Agile Conference, 2014, pp. 11–15. IEEE, July 2014
10. Kuusinen, K., Gregory, P., Sharp, H., Barroca, L.: Strategies for doing agile in a non-agile environment. In: Proceedings of ESEM, p. 5. ACM, September 2016
11. Basili, V., Caldiera, G., Rombach, D.: The goal question metric approach. In: Encyclopedia of Software Engineering, vol. 2, pp. 528–532 (1994)

Enterprise Agility: Why Is Transformation so Hard?

Teemu Karvonen$^{(\boxtimes)}$, Helen Sharp, and Leonor Barroca

The Open University, Walton Hall, Milton Keynes MK7 6AA, UK
{teemu.karvonen, helen.sharp,
leonor.barroca}@open.ac.uk

Abstract. Enterprise agility requires capabilities to transform, sense and seize new business opportunities more quickly than competitors. However, acquiring those capabilities, such as continuous delivery and scaling agility to product programmes, portfolios and business models, is challenging in many organisations. This paper introduces definitions of enterprise agility involving business management and cultural lenses for analysing large-scale agile transformation. The case organisation, in the higher education domain, leverages collaborative discovery sprints and an experimental programme to enable a bottom-up approach to transformation. Meanwhile the prevalence of bureaucracy and organisational silos are often contradictory to agile principles and values. The case study results identify transformation challenges based on observations from a five-month research period. Initial findings indicate that increased focus on organisational culture and leveraging of both bottom-up innovation and supportive top-down leadership activities, could enhance the likelihood of a successful transformation.

Keywords: Enterprise agility · Enterprise agile · Organisational transformation
Organisational culture · Leadership

1 Introduction

Empirical studies of large-scale agile have instigated academic debate regarding transformation challenges and agile principles applicability in a large-scale context [1–3]. Studies of Continuous Software Engineering and DevOps [4, 5] are also prime examples of how the software development domain is approaching aspects of agility beyond software development teams. Continuous activities related to budgeting, product management and business-value-related decisions are made in shorter cycles to enable research and development (R&D) capability for rapid delivery and customer experimentation [5].

Meanwhile, agility (i.e. organisational adaptability and flexibility [6, 7]) is impacting contemporary business strategies and practices for managing product programmes and business portfolios also in a non-IT context. Strategic business management [6] views agility as an organisational capability related to management under deep uncertainty, resource fluidity and continuous business model renewal.

© The Author(s) 2018
J. Garbajosa et al. (Eds.): XP 2018, LNBIP 314, pp. 131–145, 2018.
https://doi.org/10.1007/978-3-319-91602-6_9

Large-scale agile development [1, 2] and enterprise agility [6, 8] can be viewed through multiple lenses. These lenses may include but are not limited to agile budgeting, agile manufacturing, agile production, agile strategic management, agile business models, agile culture and organisational theories related to agility. While many principles of enterprise agility can be found in the literature (e.g. Beyond Budgeting [9], Lean Enterprise [10] etc.), empirical studies [1–3, 11, 12] have indicated that it is still rather challenging for most organisations to perform such a holistic and sustainable transformation. Why is transformation so hard? Given that enterprise agility involves not just software development, but the whole organisation, investigations of enterprise agility must address several aspects related to business, development and operations [4]. Leadership and cultural aspects have especially been identified as key challenges in earlier studies of large-scale agile transformations, e.g. [2, 3]. This paper explores enterprise agility by investigating transformation activities in a large organisation in the higher education domain. For this investigation, we focus particularly on transformation, leadership and cultural aspects related to enterprise agility. We apply the Competing Values Framework (CVF) [13] to analyse characteristics of organisational culture and its implications to enterprise agility transformation. As the investigated case organisation operates in the higher education domain, this work contributes to understanding how agile methods and principles are interpreted and adapted in non-IT domains. One of the key contributions of this paper therefore is that it provides empirical evidence of challenges in non-IT agile transformation. Another key contribution is to introduce ideas and concepts from strategic management into the debate around non-IT agile transformation.

2 Background and Related Work

Large-scale agile development is becoming increasingly relevant to projects and product programmes in many industrial domains. Recent studies of adopting agile principles in large organisational contexts have indicated both organisational challenges and success factors related to organisational transformation towards agile [2, 3]. However, investigations of large-scale agile transformation are often focused on aspects of software development projects. Many studies of large-scale agile development focus on agile development activities that involve multiple teams (typically more than two teams). According to Dingsøyr et al. [1], 'enterprise agile' is more than simply considering multiple teams and requires a more comprehensive view of the business.

This paper aims to study agility from this more comprehensive point of view. It applies business management and organisational culture definitions and models to analyse enterprise agility. Enterprise agility views agility beyond software i.e. as a holistic 'transformation of organisations', including business, operations and cultural aspects. Several authors have suggested 'lean thinking' [4, 14] as a useful lens for analysing enterprise agility. Lean production principles, made famous by Toyota Motor Company, have inspired also many agile software development researchers. Recent studies on 'continuous delivery', 'DevOps' and 'experimentation-driven development' [4, 5, 14] have provided more evidence on how business, development and operations can benefit from establishing continuous integrative activities throughout a value stream.

The research in this paper is largely motivated by an increased understanding of commonly addressed agile practitioner's challenges related to people's 'mindsets' and 'organisational culture'. However, research in this area is also considered to be very challenging, due to its multidisciplinary aspects. Challenges are also related to empirical validation of enduring (sustainable) agile transformation, rather than a short-term transient phase of transformation. In practice, understanding organisational agile transformation requires a comprehensive investigation of organisational culture, business strategies, technologies and architectures, organisational structure and processes, business models and how they can be efficiently integrated and synchronised into contextually relevant continuous incremental cycles.

Agile frameworks, such as AgilePfM [15], SAFe [16] and LeSS [17] are nowadays increasingly adopted in large-scale software-intensive product development. These frameworks can provide a useful baseline for coordinating large-scale development and delivery cycles. Large-scale transformations, however, typically involve many contextual and cultural variations that have to be addressed by local change management activities. Moreover, different industry domains, such as public sector and non-IT businesses may have to adapt framework terminology and principles that originate from the software development context. Consequently, some organisations are increasingly leveraging aspects of bottom-up innovation, communities of practice and experimentations related to agile transformation [3].

The benefits of understanding organisational culture have been addressed by many authors in the business management discipline [13, 18, 19]. Cultural characteristics may either accelerate or hinder transformation towards enterprise agility. Meanwhile, the 'ability to change organisational culture' has been identified as one of the key factors related to large-scale agile development [2]. A recent trend of adapting agile and lean principles to large-scale projects and organisational level e.g. 'enterprise agile' [8] and 'Continuous *' [4] (i.e. 'BizDev' and 'DevOps' activities) clearly necessitates a deeper understanding of the cultural change required, and learning new ways to lead transformation.

2.1 Defining Enterprise Agility

In terms of being able to analyse challenges related to transformation, we first need to define 'the goal of agile transformation', i.e. what are the organisational characteristics that are associated with enterprise agility. The agile software development literature has indicated various interpretations of agility in software development. Laanti et al.'s [20] review of definitions indicated that there is currently no uniform definition for agility in agile software development nor in agile project management. Consequently, they state that it is increasingly important that researchers and practitioners themselves carefully specify what they mean by agile. Since our research is conducted in a non-IT context we focus primarily on how the management discipline has defined agility (Table 1). Moreover, we believe that incorporating business management definitions is useful in investigations related to large-scale software development. However, there is no uniform definition for agility in business management either.

Enterprise agility as a research topic has been debated in management literature for at least three decades, although it is also referred to nowadays as 'flexibility' to

Table 1. Dimensions of enterprise agility

Author	Dimensions of enterprise agility
Teece et al. [6]	Dynamic capabilities: *Sensing* - Identification, development, co-development, and assessment of technological opportunities (and threats) in relation to customer needs (the "sensing" of unknown futures) *Seizing* - Mobilization of resources to address needs and opportunities and capture value from doing so ("seizing") *Transforming* - Continued renewal ("transforming" or "shifting")
Overby et al. [8]	Sensing and responding capabilities: *Sensing environmental change* – competitive market opportunities; evolving conditions; environmental change AND *Responding Readily* – seize with speed and surprise; respond efficiently and effectively
Doz et al. [7]	Strategic meta-capabilities: *Strategic sensitivity:* the sharpness of perception of, and the intensity of awareness of and attention to, strategic development. Anticipating, experimenting, distancing, abstracting, reframing *Leadership unity:* the ability of the top team to make bold, fast decisions, without being bogged down in top-level 'win-lose' politics. Dialoguing, revealing, integrating, aligning, caring *Resource fluidity:* the internal capability to reconfigure capabilities and redeploy resources rapidly. Decoupling, modularizing, dissociating, switching, grafting
Beyond Budgeting [22]	Leadership principles: *Purpose* – Engage and inspire people around bold and noble causes; not around short-term financial targets *Values* – Govern through shared values and sound judgement: not through detailed rules and regulations *Transparency* – Make information open for self-regulation, innovation, learning and control: don't restrict it *Organisation* – Cultivate a strong sense of belonging and organize around accountable teams; avoid hierarchical control and bureaucracy *Autonomy* – Trust people with freedom to act: don't punish everyone if someone should abuse it *Customers* – Connect everyone's work with customer needs; avoid conflicts of interest Management processes: *Rhythm* – Organise management processes dynamically around business rhythms and events; not around the calendar year only *Targets* – Set directional, ambitious and relative goals: avoid fixed and cascaded targets *Plans and forecasts* – Make planning and forecasting lean and unbiased processes: not rigid and political exercises *Resource allocation* – Foster a cost-conscious mindset and make resources available as needed; not through detailed annual budget allocations *Performance evaluation* – Evaluate performance holistically and with peer feedback for learning and development; not based on measurement only and not for rewards only *Rewards* – Reward shared success against competition; not against fixed performance contracts

distinguish it from the rise of the 'agility' terminology [6]. Consequently, in this paper we use those two terms interchangeably, and when referring to agile software development specifically then we are explicit about it. The business management literature identifies four dimensions of agility: economic, organisational, operational and strategic [21]. We consider these dimensions to be complementary and useful viewpoints for analysing enterprise agility. The economic agility viewpoint has been addressed, for example, in conjunction with theories for management of financial buffers against demand uncertainties or external market shocks. The operational agility viewpoint deals with aspects of manufacturing system flexibility, e.g. ability to adapt the manufacturing system to different environmental conditions and a variety of product features. Agile software development literature referenced by Laanti [20] captures especially operational agility aspects related to software component development, e.g. management of rapidly changing business requirements and iterative delivery practices. The organisational agility viewpoint deals with models of organisation (e.g. organisation of individuals and teams) and labour flexibility in rapidly changing environment [21].

Business management literature views strategic agility through culture [19], leadership [7] and dynamic capabilities [6] that enable an organisation to sense and seize opportunities, manage deep business uncertainty and to be able to perform rapid changes in the business environment. According to Toni et al. [21] strategic flexibility (or agility) consists of four distinct categories: (1) speed and variation of the competitive priorities, (2) range of strategic options, (3) rapidity of movement from one business to another, and (4) variety of the possible new businesses.

Continuous business model renewal [7] and continuous business model 'stress testing' [23] are considered as important elements of leadership processes related to enabling enterprise agility. In addition to continuous evaluation of risks and uncertainties related to the business model, Bowman et al. [23], Doz et al. [7] and Teece et al. [6] have addressed the leadership role in conjunction with business model innovation and ability to continuously evaluate opportunistically alternatives related to elements of a business model [24]. Table 1 summarises their viewpoints on dimensions of agile capabilities and leadership activities for enabling enterprise agility.

2.2   Organisational Culture

Schein [19] and Cameron et al. [13] have both addressed the impact of leadership in conjunction with the evolution of an organisational culture. According to Schein [19] leadership impacts largely on existing culture and is the key element for shaping the new culture. Relationships between agile methods and culture have been investigated also in various case studies [25, 26].

In this study we apply the Competing Values Framework (CVF) [13] to identify the characteristics of agile culture, and to represent the existing organisational culture of the case organisation. Figure 1 illustrates the CVF dimensions and four major culture types: (1) the hierarchy culture, (2) the market culture, (3) the clan culture, and (4) the adhocracy culture. According to Cameron et al. [13] most organisations have one or two most dominating culture types and CVF allows the diagnosis of an organisation's cultural profile.

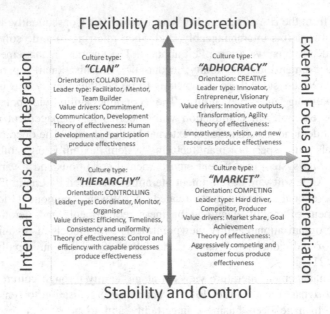

Fig. 1. Competing Values Framework [13]

Based on our brief review of papers that have applied CVF in agile software development [27, 28], agility is typically associated with the 'adhocracy' culture, the top-right quadrant of the CVF model [27] in Fig. 1. However, as far as we know, there is no single preferred or idealistic profile for agile culture, because different organisations and business situations require multiple different cultural traits to exist in parallel for the organisation to be effective [26].

Organisational values, closely related to organisational culture, have often been addressed in conjunction with agile methods. For example Beck and Andres [29] stated that introducing Extreme Programming (XP) in organisations with values such as "secrecy, isolation, complexity, timidity, and disrespect" is ineffective and moreover, "will cause trouble rather than improvements". Consequently, transformation towards agile necessitates understanding of organisational values that are part of the organisational culture. Organisational culture has often been identified as one of the main challenges in adoption of agile values and principles. Consequently, organisations may benefit from analysing the existing organisational culture even before they decide to start their transformation journey towards agile [18].

2.3   Summary of Approaches for Achieving Enterprise Agility

This section summarises approaches for achieving large-scale enterprise agility as described in related literature. Approaches are not exclusive and they may co-exist in organisations.

Scaled Framework-Driven Approach (Incremental Diffusion of Operational Agility). The scaled framework-driven approach achieves agility through incremental adoption of agile methods and frameworks e.g. agile maturity models [30], agile management frameworks and agile development methods (DSDM, AgilePM, SAFe, Scrum, LeSS, Kanban, Scrumban etc.). These frameworks focus often on describing operational aspects of the organisation, e.g. how to orchestrate development functions, optimising flow value stream, and re-organising value creation activities and delivery cycles. Olsson et al. [31] stated that software enterprise transformation is typically initiated by individual R&D teams, that start exploring agile methods usage in team-level activities. The next steps in transformation are characterised by increased integration, and activities and interactions between verification and validation, programme management and customer. Frameworks such as AgilePfM [15], SAFe [16] and LeSS [17] aim to provide guidance on how to manage portfolios, projects and the collaboration of multiple agile software development teams. However, as pointed out by Paasivaara et al. [3] and Dikert et al. [2], empirical evidence on the validity of these frameworks is largely missing.

Business-Driven Approach (Strategic Orientation Towards Agility). The business-driven approach takes a business level viewpoint such as business model stress testing [23] and continuous business model renewal [7, 32]. This could mean for example strategic orientation towards leveraging state-of-the-art digital services and architectures for doing business and/or continuously evaluating alternative revenue streams and channels for deploying customer value. The main difference between this and the 'scaled framework-driven approach' is that rather than focusing on better-faster-cheaper development i.e. 'doing the thing right', the business-driven approach views agility more broadly through organisational strategy and business model flexibility i.e. 'doing the right thing'. Doz et al. [7] pointed out that "many companies fail, not because they do something wrong or mediocre, but because they keep doing what used to be the right thing for too long, and fall victim to the rigidity of their business model". This viewpoint of agility is valid in particular for organisations in highly competitive, non-regulated and global markets.

Sustainable Agility Approach (Cultural Orientation Towards Agility). The sustainable agility approach addresses agility through a cultural understanding and orientation in adoption of agile values for sustainable operational excellence. The link between sustainable operational excellence, culture and agility has been addressed by Carvalho et al. [18]. Continuous and sustainable aspects of transformation, have been addressed also in conjunction with lean principles [14]. This approach focuses on orientation towards a holistic viewpoint, sustainability and long-term objectives in transformation. Organisational culture is seen as the main point of interest in planning and orchestrating transformation activities. While this approach may leverage also business- and framework-driven approaches in transformation they are seen as secondary to, for example, people's behaviours and values that are appreciated in all transactions for example with customers and between internal stakeholders. This approach can be characterised by the notion that enduring enterprise agility is achieved as a result of culturally aligned, highly motivated, and empowered people working together towards a common cause, rather than as a result of business model renewal or adoption of an agile method or framework. Continuous business model renewal and adoption of an agile framework are outcomes of transformation rather than causes of enterprise agility.

3   Case Organisation and Study Design

The case organisation is large and distributed; it has approximately 9000 employees. Organisational change in the case organisation involves many areas, such a new strategy and various change programmes that are characterised by organisational adaptability, agility and operational efficiency. In this paper, we focus on change related to the design and development of curriculum elements (text, video, books etc.). We define the unit of analysis as the module production process. Module production activities involve multiple organisational units and stakeholders from academic faculties to media production functions. Module production can be considered as the primary channel for delivering value to the organisation's internal and external stakeholders.

Data collection was carried out in a five-month period in 2017–2018, and included meetings with managers in charge of module production and participation in team-work sessions referred to as 'agile discovery sprints'. In addition, internal reports and plans were available, which provided a broader understanding of the research context and evidence of the organisational strategy, culture, transformation actions and objectives of the organisational transformation.

'Agile discovery sprints' work sessions took place between November and December 2017. Agile discovery sprints involved 37 people from various module production roles who had volunteered to study and experiment with agile methods use in the organisation. Volunteers were assigned to five teams to explore how agile development methods and principles could be applied in the module design and production process. Teams were following the Google design sprints [33] for planning and demoing findings within and between teams. Each team had a predefined theme/topic related to agile methods and principles. Topics were: (1) AgilePM, (2) Scrumban, (3) Kanban, (4) Agile Principles & Values, and (5) Agile Teams and Organisation. People in these teams were empowered to make decisions related to how they worked and what aspects they considered most interesting, e.g. most challenging or most prominent approaches for increasing agility in the organisation.

Discovery sprints were facilitated by two agile change agents i.e. facilitators that organised and coordinated agile discovery sprint activities, including inviting volunteers to participate, assignment of people in teams, and definition of topics for each team. Facilitators were involved in each team's sessions throughout the increment. Facilitators made sure that teams were able to progress in their assigned themes and they acted as agile coaches providing answers to questions related to agile methods and principles. The chosen facilitators were also experts in module design and production, and hence, they had good understanding of existing processes, organisational structures and the main constraints. One of the facilitators was interviewed after the first two-month increment. The semi-structured interview (of about an hour) focused on understanding the key impacts and results, challenges and lessons learned during the discovery sprints.

Researchers (authors of this paper) participated altogether in 16 discovery sprint sessions (each session lasted 1–2 h) and made field notes and took pictures and videos that were further used in qualitative analysis [34]. Researchers also participated in team activities and discussions both online and face-to-face. Hence, the researchers impacted the outcomes of the working sessions. Each team used a Trello board for coordination of the team's tasks, communication and consolidation of working material, documents, discussions and so on. All material in the Trello boards (such as cards and attachments) were also used in the data analysis.

Thematic analysis [34] was applied in relation to the research question 'What are the challenges related to agile transformation in this case organisation?' The analysis proceeded in phases. After data collection, the first author of this paper performed a consistent reading of all collected data and identified the main patterns related to transformation challenges. These patterns (themes) were further validated by discussing with other authors who also participated in data collection. CVF culture types (Fig. 1) definitions were used as a lens for analysing aspects of organisational culture in the case organisation and possible implications related to transformation challenges. In addition to our empirical data, this analysis also drew on an internal report that had been commissioned to characterise the organisation's culture[1].

4   Findings

The case organisation had recently launched a new strategy that emphasised 'organisational adaptability' and 'customer orientation'. Transformation urgency was justified by increased competition and operational efficiency. A key part of the latter motivation was a reduction in costs associated with module production. Hence, the enterprise agility changes we investigated were focused mainly on internal operational agility improvement (e.g. 'doing the thing right') rather than strategic orientation towards sensing and seizing new business opportunities and threats (e.g. 'doing the right thing').

Considering the organisation's culture, a complex organisational structure and multiple management layers had created siloes and barriers between people working in different units. Organisational culture was also characterised by 'tribes' that sometimes had difficult and suspicious relationships. In this study organisational barriers could be identified between the module production unit and content providers (one production manager commented that "we worry about the buy-in from module teams... people choose to attend or not"). Module design and production requires close collaboration between curriculum content creation (e.g. learning modules) and colleagues whose role it is to prepare materials for presentation, e.g. editing books, website design and maintenance, processing of digital media content and management of budget and quality of the production process. Facilitators' and sprint volunteers' comments

---

[1] Internal report on characteristics of the case organisation's culture. Report was made by external consultants and it was based on data collected from staff surveys, and focus groups held between 2013–2015.

throughout the collected data emphasised the organisation as 'highly hierarchical'. Hence, we consider the most dominant existing culture in the case organisation currently to be the hierarchy culture, i.e. bottom left in Fig. 1. Hierarchy culture was most clearly manifested by existing strong reliance on defined processes, bureaucratic management practices and organisational structures. The internal report on organisational culture had also indicated that many elements of bureaucratic processes characterise the way of working in the case organisation.

Although the dominant culture was hierarchical, the culture report indicated the existence of the 'clan' culture (top left in Fig. 1). Employees often bypassed formal procedures and used their personal networks to get tasks done, which could indicate the existence of underlying elements of the clan culture. Both clan and hierarchy cultures indicate that the case organisation currently values stability, internal focus and integration more than external focus and flexibility. Although not part of the module production process, several team members mentioned that some sub-units in the wider organisation, such as IT, had already adopted elements of market and adhocracy culture. Consequently, although we could not find any concrete evidence of market and adhocracy culture in our study, they might exist as sub-cultures in smaller units and teams. Problems may however arise when these agile teams have to collaborate with less agile hierarchical organisational units. We elaborate more on this problem in the next section that focuses on transformation challenges.

4.1   Transformation Challenges

The most commonly-encountered transformation challenges referred to by team members and facilitators are consolidated into four themes that we elaborate in this section. The main challenge as we perceived in this study is related to the prevailing hierarchical culture. A need for organisational transformation towards 'adaptive organisation and culture' had been communicated the year before our study was conducted, as one of the strategic objectives. Consequently, it has been largely initiated as a top-down organisational activity. We could already see multiple top-down activities such as transformation programmes and people nominated in change management positions. This is an indication of 'command and control' i.e. a prevalent top-down approach for coordinating transformation. However, challenges related to Theme 1 (below) indicated that currently these top-down activities were not properly aligned and coordinated.

The discovery sprint activity that we studied was a clear indication of an initiative to enable also bottom-up activity for agile transformation. In CVF terms this would indicate a transition towards an adhocracy culture. The main challenge, however, focuses on how to enable a sustainable bottom-up activity in a prevalent hierarchy culture. We believe that transformation towards an adhocracy culture would have to demonstrate quickly both tangible improvements and a positive atmosphere among employees and managers in all levels of the organisation. In addition, as highlighted by one of the facilitators there is an urgent need for establishing an 'organisational brain' i.e. a learning repository - a community and body of knowledge that is able to keep a record of innovations and best practices related to agile transformation: "When you talk to people, tacitly there is loads and loads of knowledge there, but we are not leveraging it".

Online tools and communities were considered as important enablers for establishing this kind of activity. We identified the following challenges related to organisational transformation in the case organisation:

Theme 1: Synchronising Separate Change Programmes and Activities. Although the case organisation had already launched multiple activities related to new tools and processes that would help it to become more agile, these activities needed a stronger top-down effort for synchronisation, alignment and continuous sharing of learnings and best-practices. "Current organisation has not been ready for the way we orchestrate change activities to work together. The governance has not been in place".

Theme 2: Leveraging Incrementally Both a Bottom-Up Approach and Knowledge from Local Experts in the Transformation. 'Experimental test and learn' and 'scale up incremental' approaches were considered to be important in order to enable the transformation to have a sustainable change effect in the organisation. However, as noted in our data, senior management was expecting a faster schedule and action plan, that would indicate a hastier 'big bang' approach in transformation. Consequently, one of the main challenges is to align the top-down (hasty) and bottom-up (slow) transformation approaches.

Theme 3: Establishing Long-Lasting Module Production Team Structures, Agile Roles and Empowerment of Teams. Discovery sprint session results indicated that the current organisational structure was based largely on functional siloes i.e. different production specialists, content providers, infrastructure and support units were all operating rather independently. Module design and production requires a co-operation between multiple units. Hence, current ways of working were considered to have multiple operational disadvantages such as waiting, bureaucracy and overproduction of the content. Cross-functional longer-lived team structures were considered as a potential solution for the problem. Agile methods such as AgilePM, Scrum, Kanban and Scrumban outline guidelines, however adapting their practices and terminology to non-IT module production was considered to be challenging. The most acute problems were related to which agile method to adopt, how to form teams, how to redefine old roles and define new roles and how to ensure empowerment of teams. A prevailing hierarchical culture also caused challenges to enable empowerment of people and teams.

Theme 4: Adoption of the Mentality for Continuous Product Improvements and Minimum Marketable Products in Module Design and Production. Several discovery sprint team results indicated that the existing way of working was considered to emphasise effort and resources that were used for creating the first version of the module, i.e. maintenance and change beyond the initial version was difficult. This approach was considered to be generally too slow and expensive. Transformation towards an agile organisation was considered to require shorter increments and faster delivery that would leverage module experimentation and increased use of customer feedback. In addition, content structure would have to increasingly support modularity and re-use. Challenges were identified in the definition of quality criteria, referred to also as 'good enough', in order for the 'cheaper and faster' operational target to not jeopardise quality of the modules and customer experience.

5 Limitations and Future Work

The main limitation of our current study is that the level of understanding of this organisation's transformation and culture is focused on the module production process. As this is the unit of analysis, we have so far not identified activities related to business model renewal; this is for a later stage in the project. Such a study may require several years to provide a reliable and accurate picture of the case organisation. On the other hand, agile transformation could be a long-term journey that has multiple phases and stages of adoption. We intend to continue the study by using elements of an ethnographic research approach [35]. In addition we are planning to use the Organisational Culture Assessment Instrument (OCAI) [13] for diagnosing the organisational culture profiles of CVF with different sub-units and roles in the organisation.

A second limitation of this study is that we have not yet captured senior level management viewpoints in this investigation. Consequently, it could be highly appropriate to investigate how senior management perceives the transformation and the organisational culture. Earlier studies by Cameron et al. [13] have indicated that sometimes the top management team has different perceptions of the culture. Moreover, understanding how top management perceives the ideal future culture would provide further insight.

In terms of the reliability of the findings we consider that our findings are still preliminary. The current number of actors ($\sim$40 people) who participated in this research is rather moderate. Consequently, we aim to extend the research by incorporating semi-structured interviews from different sub-units and roles. We consider that preliminary findings reported in this paper are a useful baseline for planning the ongoing investigation.

6 Discussion and Conclusion

Our research objective was to explore challenges related to transformation towards enterprise agility. Our empirical findings indicated especially change coordination as a main challenge in the case organisation. As suggested by related earlier studies [36], successful large-scale transformation necessitates coordination as well as unanimous buy-in from leaders in top- and middle levels of the organisation. As part of data collection, we participated in discovery sprint sessions that aimed to enable experimental, bottom-up aspects of transformation. Paasivaara et al.'s [3] case study indicated that the experimental transformation approach was applied also in Ericsson's agile transformation. Based on our findings, we believe that consistent use of agile discovery sprints practice can help the case organisation significantly to change staff mindsets and organisational culture. Moreover, an 'agile way of implementing agile', as suggested by earlier studies [2, 3], can increase the likelihood of a successful and sustainable transformation. However, in parallel, organisations must also sustain a certain level of control and coordination, so that bottom-up innovation and creativity are not only tacit but commonly shared knowledge that can benefit other units in the organisation.

In addition, we reviewed definitions of enterprise agility from management literature and summarised approaches for achieving organisational agility. Our brief literature review has indicated that definitions of enterprise agility can involve multiple different viewpoints that may be useful from an empirical research point of view (e.g. economic, strategic, organisational and operational). In addition, we've noticed that enterprise agility transformation journeys can take multiple different routes and have multiple different goals. We believe that future research, especially on large-scale agile software development, could use these particular lenses for analysing transformation activities. Earlier studies on agile methodologies and frameworks have largely focused on describing operational aspects of agility such as product development and delivery processes. Existing empirical studies [2] of large-scale agile have indicated challenges related to lack of strategic investments and an inability to change culture and leadership behaviour. Consequently, we believe that focusing on, for example, organisational culture and strategic agility lenses could provide more in-depth knowledge on how to mitigate and overcome these challenges and how to evaluate risks associated with large-scale transformation.

To summarise our findings for practitioners, there are multiple dimensions related to enterprise agility as well as various ways to transform. Agile change can focus on operational, strategic or cultural aspects of agility, however, holistic transformation towards enterprise agility necessitates a very sophisticated and unique interplay of all of these elements. Hence, existing recommendations (i.e. practices, models, tools and frameworks) related to effective change management, such as [37, 38] need to be supplemented for an agile transformation context.

This paper has addressed contemporary challenges related to transformation to 'enterprise agility' in a large organisation in the higher education domain. Enterprise agility transformation is so hard because it requires many different considerations (lenses) to be applied all at once. Moreover, the size of the organisation increases the difficulty of the transformation. Our challenges relate to leadership, organisational culture, and integration of the different perspectives that have to be taken into account. We suggest that current enterprise agility frameworks need to look towards aspects of these other lenses if successful transformation is to be achieved. In our experience, organisational culture frameworks such as CVF can help researchers and practitioners to articulate cultural traits and define transformation direction and objectives related to adoption of agile values and mindset.

Acknowledgements. We would like to thank all our collaborators. This work was supported by The Agile Business Consortium (www.agilebusiness.org).

References

1. Dingsøyr, T., Moe, N.B., Fægri, T.E., Seim, E.A.: Exploring software development at the very large-scale: a revelatory case study and research agenda for agile method adaptation. Empir. Softw. Eng. **23**, 490–520 (2017)
2. Dikert, K., Paasivaara, M., Lassenius, C.: Challenges and success factors for large-scale agile transformations: a systematic literature review. J. Syst. Softw. **119**, 87–108 (2016)
3. Paasivaara, M., Behm, B., Lassenius, C., Hallikainen, M.: Large-scale agile transformation at Ericsson: a case study. Empir. Softw. Eng. 1–47 (2018)

4. Fitzgerald, B., Stol, K.J.: Continuous software engineering: a roadmap and agenda. J. Syst. Softw. **123**, 176–189 (2017)
5. Bosch, J.: Continuous software engineering: an introduction. In: Bosch, J. (ed.) Continuous Software Engineering, pp. 3–13. Springer, Cham (2014). https://doi.org/10.1007/978-3-319-11283-1_1
6. Teece, D., Peteraf, M., Leih, S.: Dynamic capabilities and organizational agility: risk, uncertainty, and strategy in the innovation economy. Calif. Manag. Rev. **58**, 13–35 (2016)
7. Doz, Y.L., Kosonen, M.: Embedding strategic agility: a leadership agenda for accelerating business model renewal. Long Range Plann. **43**, 370–382 (2010)
8. Overby, E., Bharadwaj, A., Sambamurthy, V.: Enterprise agility and the enabling role of information technology. Eur. J. Inf. Syst. **15**, 120–131 (2006)
9. Beyond Budgeting Institute: Beyond Budgeting Institute - the adaptive management model. https://bbrt.org/
10. Humble, J., Molesky, J., O'Reilly, B.: Lean Enterprise: How High Performance Organizations Innovate at Scale. O'Reilly Media, Inc., Sebastopol (2015)
11. Paasivaara, M., Lassenius, C.: Scaling scrum in a large globally distributed organization: a case study. In: 2016 IEEE 11th International Conference on Global Software Engineering (ICGSE), pp. 74–83. IEEE (2016)
12. Maples, C.: Enterprise agile transformation: the two-year wall. In: 2009 Agile Conference, pp. 90–95. IEEE (2009)
13. Cameron, K.S., Quinn, R.E.: Diagnosing and Changing Organizational Culture: Based on the Competing Values Framework. Jossey-Bass, San Francisco (2011)
14. Poppendieck, M., Cusumano, M.A.: Lean software development: a tutorial. IEEE Softw. **29**, 26–32 (2012)
15. Agile Business Consortium: Agile Portfolio Management. Agile Business Consortium Limited, Ashford (2017)
16. Scaled Agile Inc.: Scaled Agile Framework – SAFe for Lean Enterprises. http://www.scaledagileframework.com/
17. The LeSS Company B.V.: Overview - Large Scale Scrum (LeSS). https://less.works/
18. Carvalho, A.M., Sampaio, P., Rebentisch, E., Carvalho, J.Á., Saraiva, P.: Operational excellence, organisational culture and agility: the missing link? Total Qual. Manag. Bus. Excell. 1–20 (2017)
19. Schein, E.H.: Organizational Culture and Leadership. Jossey-Bass, San Francisco (2010)
20. Laanti, M., Similä, J., Abrahamsson, P.: Definitions of agile software development and agility. In: McCaffery, F., O'Connor, R.V., Messnarz, R. (eds.) EuroSPI 2013. CCIS, vol. 364, pp. 247–258. Springer, Heidelberg (2013). https://doi.org/10.1007/978-3-642-39179-8_22
21. Toni, D.A., Tonchia, S.: Definitions and linkages between operational and strategic flexibilities. Omega **33**, 525–540 (2005)
22. Beyond Budgeting Institute: The 12 Beyond Budgeting principles - see the list here. https://bbrt.org/the-beyond-budgeting-principles/
23. Bouwman, H., Heikkilä, J., Heikkilä, M., Leopold, C., Haaker, T.: Achieving agility using business model stress testing. Electron. Mark. 1–14 (2017)
24. Teece, D.: Business models, business strategy and innovation. Long Range Plann. **43**, 172–194 (2010)
25. Strode, D.E., Huff, S.L., Tretiakov, A.: The impact of organizational culture on agile method use. In: 2009 42nd Hawaii International Conference on System Sciences, pp. 1–9. IEEE (2009)
26. Robinson, H., Sharp, H.: Organisational culture and XP: three case studies. In: Agile Development Conference (ADC 2005), pp. 49–58. IEEE Computer Society (2005)

27. Iivari, J., Iivari, N.: The relationship between organizational culture and the deployment of agile methods. Inf. Softw. Technol. **53**, 509–520 (2011)
28. Muller, S.D., Ulrich, F.: The competing values of hackers: the culture profile that spawned the computer revolution. In: 2015 48th Hawaii International Conference on System Sciences, pp. 3434–3443. IEEE (2015)
29. Beck, K., Andres, C.: Extreme Programming Explained: Embrace Change. The XP Series, 2nd edn. Addison-Wesley, Boston (2004)
30. Wendler, R.: Development of the organizational agility maturity model. In: Proceedings of the 2014 Federated Conference on Computer Science and Information Systems, pp. 1197–1206 (2014)
31. Olsson, H.H., Alahyari, H., Bosch, J.: Climbing the "Stairway to heaven" - a mulitiple-case study exploring barriers in the transition from agile development towards continuous deployment of software. In: 2012 38th EUROMICRO Conference on IEEE Software Engineering and Advanced Applications (SEAA), pp. 392–399 (2012)
32. Helaakoski, H., Iskanius, P., Peltomaa, I., Kipina, J.: Agile business model in the steel product industry sector. In: 2006 IEEE International Conference on Management of Innovation and Technology, pp. 1010–1014. IEEE (2006)
33. Google: The Design Sprint — GV. http://www.gv.com/sprint/
34. Braun, V., Clarke, V.: Using thematic analysis in psychology. Qual. Res. Psychol. **3**, 77–101 (2006)
35. Sharp, H., Dittrich, Y., de Souza, C.R.B.: The role of ethnographic studies in empirical software engineering. IEEE Trans. Softw. Eng. **42**, 786–804 (2016)
36. Nightingale, D.J., Srinivasan, J.: Beyond the Lean Revolution Achieving Successful and Sustainable Enterprise Transformation. American Management Association, New York (2011)
37. Kotter, J.P.: Sense of Urgency. Harvard Business Press, Boston (2008)
38. Manns, M.L., Rising, L.: Fearless Change: Patterns for Introducing New Ideas. Addison-Wesley, Boston (2005)

Technical and Organizational Agile Practices:
A Latin-American Survey

Nicolás Paez(✉) ⓘ, Diego Fontdevila ⓘ, Fernando Gainey ⓘ,
and Alejandro Oliveros ⓘ

Universidad Nacional de Tres de Febrero, Caseros, Argentina
nicopaez@computer.org,
{dfontevila, fgainey, aoliveros}@untref.edu.ar

Abstract. *Background:* Agile Software Development is widely used nowadays
and to measure its real usage we need to analyze how its practices are used.
These practices have been categorized by several authors and some practitioners
have suggested that technical practices have a lower usage level than organizational practices. *Objective:* In this study we aim to understand the actual usage
of technical and organizational agile practices in the Latin-American Agile
community. *Method:* We conducted a three-stage survey in conferences of the
Latin-American Agile Community. *Results:* Organizational practices are much
more used than technical ones. The number of practices used is a direct function
of organization experience using agile. The difference between technical and
organizational practices reduces with the experience of the organization using
agile. Team size and project duration seem to have no effect in the number of
practices used.

Keywords: Agile practices · Practices categories · Practices usage

1 Introduction

Agile Software Development is now mainstream and as usual with mainstream there is
so much marketing and buzzwords around it that it is not easy to understand what is
really happening. There is so many people talking and writing about agile, but what is
really happening? what are practitioners really doing?. Agile is a mindset and like any
mindset is abstract and sometimes difficult to understand. So to have a usage measure
we focus our study on practices since they are a concrete way to obtain evidence about
the actual way software development is performed.

In the context of software development, practices can be categorized into technical
and organizational. This categorization has been applied by researchers and practitioners, although it takes slightly different forms: Meyer uses technical and
organizational/managerial [1] while Pantiuchina *et al.* use speed and quality [2]. A right
balance between technical and organizational practices seems reasonable, given that
technical practices support product quality and effectiveness, while organizational
practices in general affect cost, schedule and team sustainability. Projects severely
lacking in any of these two aspects are more likely to fail (Chow *et al.* identify
engineering practices as one of the three main success factors in agile projects [3]).

© The Author(s) 2018
J. Garbajosa et al. (Eds.): XP 2018, LNBIP 314, pp. 146–159, 2018.
https://doi.org/10.1007/978-3-319-91602-6_10

Furthermore, cost-effectiveness might probably depend heavily on a balanced approach taking into account costs, quality and productivity. Popular approaches like CMMI and Scrum promote adoption paths that start with organizational practices. CMMI Level 2 focuses on project management, while Level 3 brings in more technical process areas, such as Product integration, Technical solution, Validation and Verification [4]. Scrum does not include any technical practices, but Scrum teams are encouraged to add technical practices as they evolve their process. This approach makes sense from an organic maturation perspective, but risks incomplete implementations. We believe that is why some technical practices, like Software Configuration Management, are considered hygienic and non-negotiable by mature teams (in CMMI SCM is a Level 2 Process Area).

Some authors suggest that in companies that claim to be agile, organizational practices are more used than technical practices. In 2009 Martin Fowler coined the term Flaccid Scrum [5] to refer to those projects that embrace Scrum but without paying attention to technical practices, which after a while turns their code base into a mess.

More recently Joshua Kerievsky described a similar situation: adoption of agile practices leaving out technical practices [6]. Our motivation for this study is based on our own experience as practitioners and the preceding discussions about the perception that technical practices are not widely used.

The overall research questions that guide our study are:

- Q1: What is the usage rate of practices in actual software development projects?
- Q2: Is there any difference between the usage rate of technical and organizational practices?

By usage rate we mean the number of projects that make regular use of a practice over the total number of projects. We focused on projects developed by practitioners in the Latin-American Agile community, because our own experiences as members of this community motivated us to better understand it, and because it allowed us to reach industry practitioners.

The rest of the paper is organized in the following way: Sect. 2 mentions related work, Sect. 3 explains how we carried our study, Sect. 4 presents our results and findings, Sect. 5 lists the possible threats to the validity and finally Sect. 6 presents conclusions and future work.

2 Related Work

There are several studies focused on agile practices and their actual adoption in industry, and studies that focus on methods but also assess practices. We explicitly exclude studies dealing with the specifics of each practice, since that is beyond the scope of this work. The advantage of practice-focused research is that it allows finer grained study of actual software development processes beyond the overall process framework or method. For example, the HELENA Survey is an initiative that focuses on hybrid development methods, i.e. it mixes agile and non-agile practices, and as such, it covers a wide spectrum of practices, from full agile to traditional approaches [7, 8].

Diebold *et al.* have studied what practitioners vary when using Scrum [9], their results show that very few, only one out of ten of the companies studied, actually perform most of the practices that make up Scrum "by the book". This resonates with our experience and results, since Scrum is a simple framework with few practices and still not all its practices have the same level of adoption. The authors note that the daily scrums are more widely used than retrospectives.

There are several studies on regional agile communities of practice. A study of the Spanish agile community, also conducted during an Open Space agile conference, produced results very similar to our own, and it also included a comparison with the state of practice of several European organizations [10]. The study involved approximately 100 participants.

In Brazil, a more general study on the historical evolution of the agile community included both academia and industry, but did not analyze specific practices [11]. Also in Brazil, Melo *et al.* have published a technical report with the results of a survey on agile methods that includes information on practices usage, but the list of practices covered is different from ours [12].

Kropp *et al.* [13] have conducted the Swiss Agile Survey for several years, and their results show that agile practice adoption grows with agile experience, which is consistent with our own results [14, 15].

Industry surveys also show significant differences in practice adoption [16–18]. For example, Ambler's online survey, based on 123 online responses, shows TDD as the hardest to implement agile practice [16], which is consistent with its very low level of adoption in our studies.

Several studies have also focused on practice categorization. Bertrand Meyer categorizes agile practices in technical and organizational in his extensive review of agile [1]. Pantiuchina *et al.* distinguish between speed and quality practices, roughly matching our categorization of organizational and technical practices [2]. Kropp *et al.* distinguish between technical and collaborative practices (they also differentiate a few advanced practices, like limited work in progress and BDD) [13]. Their categorization also roughly matches our own, with their collaborative category corresponding to our organizational one.

Some practices are consistently categorized across studies, but some are categorized differently by different researchers. For example, Meyer considers Continuous Integration to be organizational, while we regard it as technical, same as Kropp *et al.* On the other hand, Kropp *et al.* consider the Burndown chart to be a technical practice, while we would consider it organizational. In general, there is no explicit criteria set forth by authors for practice categorization (Table 1).

Considering empirical studies on success factors, Van Kelle *et al.* found that the level of practice adoption, value congruence and transformational leadership were the most significant predictors of project success [19]. Chow *et al.* have identified agile software engineering techniques, delivery strategy and team capability as the top three critical success factors [3]. Aldahmash *et al.* have used technical and organizational (and also people and process) as categories for critical success factors in agile software development [20].

Finally, the partial results of the first two stages of our work were presented in the Argentinean National Congress of Systems Engineering [14, 15].

Table 1. Practice categorization overview.

Categories	Meyer	Kropp	Pantiuchina
Technical	Technical	Technical	Quality
Non-technical	Organizational (Managerial)	Collaborative	Speed

3 Methodology

In this section we present the methodology applied, the study description, our working definition of the technical and organizational categories, and the criteria applied to categorize practices.

3.1 Technical and Organizational Categorization

As we have discussed, the distinction between technical and organizational practices and the hypothesis of their different rates of adoption were the initial drivers of our research.

To classify practices, we have applied the following criterion: is a given practice specific to software projects or could it potentially be used in other contexts? Accordingly, we can distinguish between those practices that are specific to software projects, regarded as "technical practices", and those that are not specific to software projects and that can be used in other kinds of projects, regarded as "organizational practices". We called the latter group "organizational" because they deal with how people organize and coordinate their activities. By applying these criteria, the following classification emerged:

- Technical Practices: Continuous Integration, Emergent Design, Pair Programming, Test Automation and Test-Driven Development.
- Organizational Practices: Frequent Release, Iterative Process, Retrospectives, Collective Ownership and Self-Organization.

In most cases, the criterion allowed us to assign a category without ambiguity, but in the case of Collective Ownership, also known as Collective Code Ownership, the reference to "code" presented a challenge. It deals with code ownership (i.e. who can modify which parts of the code), not with the actual modification of the code. The purpose of the practice is to reduce the concentration of knowledge about certain components, thus making the team more robust and less dependent on any single person (a popular informal metric, the team's "truck number" or "truck factor" highlights this purpose). This led us to a corollary criterion: when in doubt, focus on the practice's purpose over form. Table 2 shows the rationale for our categorization.

Table 2. Practice categorization and rationale.

Practice	Category	Rationale
Continuous integration	Tech	Continuously integrated software version is verified automatically, by tests and static analysis
Emergent design	Tech	Design decisions about the product are software specific
Pair programming	Tech	Programmers write and review software in pairs with the purpose of improving code quality and shared knowledge
Test automation	Tech	Automated tests are software created to verify other software under test
Test-driven development	Tech	Is a very precise method for developing software
Collective ownership	Org	Determines that any developer may modify any part of the code base, promoting team robustness. The goal is to ensure that no one person becomes a bottleneck for changes
Frequent release	Org	Completed work is frequently delivered to end users to obtain feedback and maximize value
Iterative process	Org	The final product is created by successive refinements
Retrospectives	Org	The team meets periodically with the purpose of reflecting and committing to improving the process
Self-organization	Org	Team members are responsible for assigning themselves tasks and managing their process

3.2 Study Description

We organized our study in three stages. In each stage we followed the same methodology, that is: we identified a set of practices to study, we designed a questionnaire to survey practices' usage and we ran the survey in a conference organized by the agile community. In each stage we extended the number of practices under study and based on that we updated the questionnaire to include new questions and also the feedback obtained in the previous stage.

We focused our study on core agile practices. To identify those practices, we considered 4 main sources: the agile manifesto [21], the book Agile! by Bertrand Meyer [1], the work of Alistair Cockburn [22] and our own experience. Alistair Cockburn is one of the authors of the agile manifesto and is very involved in the agile community. On the other hand, Meyer is a well-known academic and engineer with an extensive experience far beyond agile. We consider this mix of sources a good balance in order to develop an objective analysis.

In Stage 1 we selected six practices: Continuous Integration, Frequent Release, Iterative Process, Retrospectives, Test Automation and Test-Driven Development.

In Stage 2 we extended the list of practices to eight by adding: Coding Standards and Self-Organization.

Finally, in Stage 3 we extended the list to ten practices: we added Pair-Programming, Emergent Design and we removed Coding Standards because we consider it to be a very common practice nowadays even beyond agile contexts and we added Collective Ownership, which we consider a more significant practice and more aligned with agile principles like shared responsibility and self-organization.

In this article we present the results of the final and third stage of our study. In this stage we ran our survey in the context of Ágiles 2017, the Latin-American Agile Conference [23]. Table 3 shows the contextual information of each stage of our study.

Table 3. Comparison of the 3 stages of the study.

Property	Stage 1	Stage 2	Stage 3
Conference	Agile Open Camp 2016	Agile Open Camp 2017	Ágiles 2017
Location	Bariloche, Argentina	Cajón del Maipo, Chile	Santiago de Chile, Chile
Data points collected after depuration	44	49	107
Date	March 2016	May 2017	October 2017
Participants in the Conference	98	79	~800
Number of practices under study	6	8	10

In every case we ran the survey in person, that is: we attended the conference and asked each person to complete the survey. When asking someone to complete the survey we explained that all answers should be based on one project that met that following criteria:

- The project should be representative of the organization
- It should be a project in which the person had been actively involved
- It should be a recent project, that means the project should have been completed within the past year

We implemented the questionnaire simultaneously in paper and online (using Google forms) allowing the respondents to pick the format they preferred. In order to simplify the processing of the answers, once the conference was over we loaded all the answers through the online questionnaire. Once we had all the answers in the online questionnaire we exported them to a spreadsheet to continue with the data analysis.

In this third stage we distributed 150 paper copies of the questionnaire, many of which we waited around for people to complete. We obtained 80 responses out of these paper questionnaires, 2 of which were incomplete and were excluded. We also promoted around the conference a link to the online questionnaire. We obtained only 31 online responses, but 2 of them were discarded when we confirmed they belonged to duplicated projects. The resulting total number of valid responses was 107.

In all cases the questionnaire was divided into 2 main sections: the first one targeting demographic information and the second one targeting practices. For each practice under study we included 2 questions: a direct question and a validation question.

Figure 1 shows the direct question for the retrospective practice while Fig. 2 shows the corresponding validation question.

Do you do Retrospectives?
• Yes
• No
• No, but we have another mechanism to detect improvement opportunities
• Don't know / don't answer

Fig. 1. Direct question

How frequently do you do Retrospectives?
• We don't do retrospectives
• Everyday
• Every week
• Every 2 weeks
• At the end of each phase of the project
• At the end of the project
• Other (please specify):

Fig. 2. Validation question

It is worth mentioning that although the questions shown in Figs. 1 and 2 are in English, the whole survey was written in Spanish.

4   Results and Findings

In this section we present the study results and relevant findings.

4.1   Demographics

In Fig. 3 we can observe that there is a balanced mix of technical and non-technical people. We consider technical roles to be those of developer, architect and tester. We consider non-technical roles to be those of product owner, scrum master, agile coach, project leader, analyst and manager.

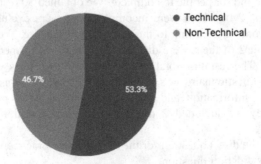

Fig. 3. Roles of respondents

Figure 4 shows personal and organizational experience using agile. It is worth mentioning that over 40% of respondents belong to organizations with more than 3 years of experience with agile while over 50% belong to organizations with less than 3 years. Regarding personal experience, 50.4% of respondents report more than 3 years of experience with agile. The coincidence between personal and organizational experience suggests that many respondents were motivated change agents (they attended an agile conference) and promoted agile in their organizations from the beginning.

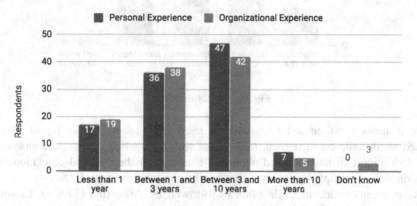

Fig. 4. Experience using agile

For project characteristics, Figs. 5 and 6 show team size and project duration information, in both cases the responses are varied and most of them are consistent with standard agile recommendations.

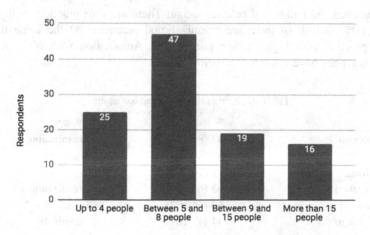

Fig. 5. Team size

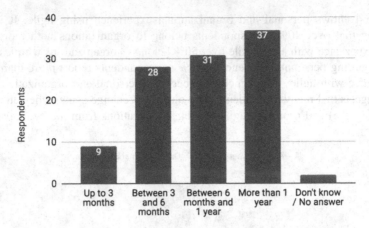

Fig. 6. Project duration

As sources for their agile knowledge, most respondents (86%) report to have learned about agile on their own, 63% report to have learned in private courses, and only 15% report to have learned about agile as part of their formal education. This question was a multiple-option one, that is why the total exceeds 100%.

Respondents reside in Chile (48.6%) followed by Argentina (17.8%), Colombia (12.1%), Peru (8.4%), Ecuador (4.7%), México (3.7%), Uruguay (2.8) and others (1.9%).

Regarding the reference method, Scrum is the most used one (60%), followed by Scrum in combination with Extreme Programming (17.8%), Kanban (9.3%), Extreme Programming (2.8%) and others combinations (10.1%).

4.2 Ranking of Practices

Table 4 presents the ranking of practice usage. There are four practices with a usage rate over 60% and all of them are organizational practices. At the same time, the technical practice with higher usage rate is Test Automation with 60%. All other technical practices have a usage rate below 50%.

Table 4. Raw ranking of practice usage.

Practice	% usage	Category
Iterative process	83 (89/107)	Organizational
Frequent release	83 (89/107)	Organizational
Retrospectives	71 (76/107)	Organizational
Self-organization	63 (67/107)	Organizational
Test automation	60 (64/107)	Technical
Emergent design	44 (47/107)	Technical
Continuous integration	38 (40/107)	Technical
Collective ownership	38 (40/107)	Organizational
Pair programming	35 (37/107)	Technical
Test-driven development	20 (21/107)	Technical

When doing the calculation to create the ranking of practice usage we found interesting situations worth mentioning here:

- Test-Driven Development is the least used practice with just 20%, but there is an additional 28% of respondents that reported that "someone in their teams does Test-Driven Development". We didn't consider these answers when calculating the ranking because our unit of study is the project and having someone in the project practicing Test-Driven Development is not enough for us to consider Test-Driven Development a project practice.
- Iterative process is one of the top practices in our ranking with 83% of usage. In most cases (74.8%) the iteration length is 2 weeks.
- Test Automation is used by 60% of respondents but it is interesting to note that there is an additional 22% of respondents that reported to have outdated automated tests. That is: they have automated tests that are rarely updated when the features under test are changed. We didn't consider these cases for the calculation of the ranking because outdated tests do not add value.
- Collective Ownership is used by 38% of respondents, but we found that an additional 28% answered "No" or "Don't know/Don't answer" when asked "Does your team use the Collective Ownership practice?". At the same time that same group reported that any team member was able to modify any part of the code of the project, which is the core idea of the Collective Ownership practice. This situation leads us to think that this portion of respondents may be using the practice even though they do not know it by name. This additional 28% would round the total usage of Collective Ownership to 66% which would position this practice in the top section of the ranking together with the rest of the organizational practices.
- Retrospectives are used by 71% of respondents, but an additional 12% answered that they performed retrospectives "At the end of each project phase". Given that a phase can be an arbitrary long period, we cannot establish cadence so we did not consider these answers as following the standard practice. It is interesting that including these answers would rank Retrospectives at 83%, the same usage rate as the top ranked practices, Iterative Process and Frequent Release.

4.3 Quartile Analysis

The average number of practices used when considering the whole sample is 5.5, but when performing a drill-down analysis considering the different quartiles we observed some interesting findings. The higher the number of practices used, the more balanced the relationship between technical and organizational ones. In the first quartile this relationship is 1 to 4.4, that is, 1 technical practice is used every 4 organizational practices. The same relationship decreases to 1.2 in the fourth quartile (Table 5).

Table 5. Quartile analysis.

Quartile	Avg practices used	Avg org practices used	Avg tech practices used	Org/tech practices used
1	2.9	2.6	0.59	4.41
2	4.7	3.4	1.2	2.83
3	6.0	3.7	2.3	1.61
4	8.3	4.5	3.7	1.22

4.4 Factors Influencing Practice Adoption

In order to understand the factors influencing the adoption of practices we consider 4 items: organizational experience using agile, team size, project duration and reference methods used.

We didn't observe any relationship when analyzing the number of practices used and the team size and project duration.

We did find a possible relationship between the count of practices in use and the organizational experience. As shown in Table 6 the count of practices tends to increase with the organizational experience with Agile. This result is consistent with some other studies [13, 14].

Table 6. Average practice usage vs organizational agile experience.

Organizational experience using agile	Average practices used
Less than 1 year	4.4
Between 1 and 3 years	5.1
Between 3 and 10 years	6.0
More than 10 years	7.0

We also found a possible relationship between the count of practices and the reference method used. Those projects based on Scrum in combination with XP use in average 6.5 practices while those using just Scrum, use 5. This situation can be explained because of the set of practices under study and the focus of each method. Scrum is a purely organizational process framework, whereas XP is a balanced technical/organizational method. Also, in our set of practices, 4 out of 10 (all organizational) practices are described in Scrum, while 9 out of 10 practices are described in XP.

When analyzing the respondents using Test-Driven Development, the least used practice, we see that the average number of practices is 7.5. At the same time, when doing the same analysis for Frequent Release and Iterative Process, the most used practices, we see that the average number of practices are 5.7 and 5.8 respectively. This situation suggests that Test-Driven Development could be considered a "late adoption practice" while Frequent Release and Iterative Process could be considered as "early adoption practices". Another possible interpretation could be that Frequent Release and Iterative Process represent a better benefit/cost relation than Test-Driven Development.

Frequent Release and Iterative Process are easier to implement than Test-Driven Development and at the same time are more visible and with greater/direct impact than Test-Driven Development.

5 Threats to Validity

Our study of the Latin-American Agile Community is based on a survey filled by practitioners that attended a conference, it is the most important conference of the community but entrance is open so the attendants may not be strict representatives of the community.

The gathered information is based on the perception of the respondents about the projects they were involved in.

The sample was not random, we asked attendants to complete the survey in person in the opening of some sessions.

From a regional perspective we lack data points covering the Brazilian community.

The categorization has been performed by other authors in the past with different results, that is, there is no agreed upon criteria for practice categorization.

6 Conclusions and Future Work

Organizational practices show a much higher rate of usage than technical practices. This situation has been confirmed in the three stages of our study [14, 15]. Also, as the number of used practices increases, the relationship between technical and organizational practice usage becomes more balanced.

The number of practices used is a direct function of organization experience. At the same time the difference between the technical and organizational practices decreases with organization experience. Team size and project duration seem to have no effect. This is consistent with the generalized community perception that agile, although apparently simple at first sight and appealing for many organizations, requires long term commitment to improvement.

In future work we will explore the reasons for this difference in the usage rate of technical vs organizational practices. We suspect there may be some factors related to formal education since the percentage of respondents with formal agile education is very low (15%). We also tend to see technical practices ignored in agile training sought by customers and adoption programs in industry. We recommend more balanced approaches, with simpler technical practices like continuous integration as good candidates for initial adoption.

This research is conducted as part of a larger research project on process and practice usability. We consider processes and practices as tools that people use to organize and define their activities, and usability characterizes good interactions between people and their tools. Future research could analyze if usability factors may be influencing the rate of usage for each practice [24]

This study has focused on core/traditional agile practices and it could be interesting to study if the findings of this work apply also to newer practices like continuous delivery and specification by example.

References

1. Meyer, B.: Agile!: The Good, the Hype and the Ugly. Springer, New York (2014). https://doi.org/10.1007/978-3-319-05155-0
2. Pantiuchina, J., Mondini, M., Khanna, D., Wang, X., Abrahamsson, P.: Are software startups applying agile practices? The state of the practice from a large survey. In: Baumeister, H., Lichter, H., Riebisch, M. (eds.) XP 2017. LNBIP, vol. 283, pp. 167–183. Springer, Cham (2017). https://doi.org/10.1007/978-3-319-57633-6_11
3. Chow, T., Cao, D.B.: A survey study of critical success factors in agile software projects. J. Syst. Softw. **81**(6), 961–971 (2008). https://doi.org/10.1016/j.jss.2007.08.020
4. Chrissis, M.B., Konrad, M., Shrum, S.: CMMI® for Development, Version 1.3. Addison-Wesley Professional (2011)
5. Fowler, M.: Flaccid Scrum. https://martinfowler.com/bliki/FlaccidScrum.html. Accessed 18 Jan 2018
6. Kerievsky, J.: Stop Calling them Technical Practices. https://www.linkedin.com/pulse/stop-calling-them-technical-practices-joshua-kerievsky/?published=t. Accessed 18 Jan 2018
7. Kuhrmann, M., Münch, J., Diebold, P., Linssen, O., Prause, C.: On the use of hybrid development approaches in software and systems development. In: Proceedings of the Annual Special Interest Group Meeting Projektmanagement und Vorgehensmodelle (PVM) Lecture Notes in Informatics (LNI), vol. 263 (2016)
8. Paez, N., Fontdevila, D., Oliveros, A.: HELENA study: Initial observations of software development practices in Argentina. In: Felderer, M., Méndez Fernández, D., Turhan, B., Kalinowski, M., Sarro, F., Winkler, D. (eds.) PROFES 2017. LNCS, vol. 10611, pp. 443–449. Springer, Cham (2017). https://doi.org/10.1007/978-3-319-69926-4_34
9. Diebold, P., Ostberg, J.-P., Wagner, S., Zendler, U.: What do practitioners vary in using Scrum? In: Lassenius, C., Dingsøyr, T., Paasivaara, M. (eds.) XP 2015. LNBIP, vol. 212, pp. 40–51. Springer, Cham (2015). https://doi.org/10.1007/978-3-319-18612-2_4
10. Rodriguez, P., Musat Salvador, D., Yagüe Panadero, A., Turhan, B., Rohunnen, A., Kuvaja, P., Oivo, M.: Adopción de Metodologías Ágiles: un estudio comparativo entre España y Europa. Revista Española en Innovación, Calidad e Ingeniería del Software **6**(4), 6–28 (2010). ISSN 1885-4486
11. Melo, O., Santos, C.V., Katayama, E.: The evolution of agile software development in Brazil. J. Braz. Comput. Soc. **19**(4), 523–552 (2013)
12. Melo, O., Santos, C.V., Corbucci, H., Katayama, E., Goldman, A., Kon, F.: Métodos ágeis no Brasil: estado da prática em times e organizações. Relatório Técnico RT-MAC-2012-03. Departamento de Ciência da Computação. IME-USP, May 2012. http://www.agilcoop.org.br/files/metodos_ageis_brasil_estado_da_pratica_em_times_e_organizacoes.pdf. Accessed 12 Mar 2018
13. Kropp, M., Meier, A., Biddle, R.: Agile practices, collaboration and experience. In: Abrahamsson, P., Jedlitschka, A., Nguyen Duc, A., Felderer, M., Amasaki, S., Mikkonen, T. (eds.) PROFES 2016. LNCS, vol. 10027, pp. 416–431. Springer, Cham (2016). https://doi.org/10.1007/978-3-319-49094-6_28
14. Paez, N., Fontdevila, D., Oliveros, A.: Characterizing technical and organizational practices in the Agile Community. In: Proceedings of CONAIISI, Salta, Argentina, (2016)

15. Paez, N., Gainey, F., Oliveros, A., Fontdevila, D.: An empirical study on the usage of technical and organizational practices in the Agile Community. In: Proceedings of CONAIISI, Santa Fe, Argentina (2017)
16. Ambler, S.: Agile Practices Survey Results, July 2009. http://www.ambysoft.com/surveys/practices2009.html. Accessed 19 Jan 2018
17. Version One: State of Agile Development Survey, Version One (2016)
18. Scrum Alliance: The 2015 State of Scrum Report, Scrum Alliance (2015)
19. Van Kelle, E., Visser, J., Plaat, A., Van Der Wijst, P.: An empirical study into social success factors for agile software development. In: Proceedings of the 8th International Workshop on Cooperative and Human Aspects of Software Engineering, CHASE 2015, pp. 77–80 (2015)
20. Aldahmash, A., Gravell, A.M., Howard, Y.: A review on the critical success factors of agile software development. In: Stolfa, J., Stolfa, S., O'Connor, R.V., Messnarz, R. (eds.) EuroSPI 2017. CCIS, vol. 748, pp. 504–512. Springer, Cham (2017). https://doi.org/10.1007/978-3-319-64218-5_41
21. Beck, K., et al.: Manifesto for Agile Software Development (2001). http://agilemanifesto.org/
22. Cockburn, A.: Crystal Clear: A Human-Powered Methodology for Small Teams. Addison-Wesley Professional, Boston (2004)
23. Ágiles Conference Homepage. http://www.agiles.org/agiles-20xx. Accessed 19 Jan 2018
24. Fontdevila, D., Genero, M., Oliveros, A.: Towards a usability model for software development process and practice. In: Felderer, M., Méndez Fernández, D., Turhan, B., Kalinowski, M., Sarro, F., Winkler, D. (eds.) PROFES 2017. LNCS, vol. 10611, pp. 137–145. Springer, Cham (2017). https://doi.org/10.1007/978-3-319-69926-4_11

Agile Software Development – Adoption and Maturity: An Activity Theory Perspective

Pritam Chita[(✉)]

Edinburgh Napier University, Edinburgh, UK
p.chita@napier.ac.uk

Abstract. This paper suggests that Activity Theory is a useful lens for examining aspects of agile software development adoption and maturity. Implementing agile approaches is influenced by many factors and attention is focused on individual and collective software development activity within an organisation's socially constructed environment. The research aim is to examine specific organisational, historical, cultural and social hindrances and facilitators that impact individual and collective learning opportunities and subsequent implementation of agile practices. This paper reports on the initial stages of research that consisted of a series of interviews and a survey. The results indicate that socially constructed hindrances and tensions are wide spread and vary in the levels at which they occur. They also correlate with many of the factors that influence agile maturity that have already been identified within the literature. This study contributes to research by integrating elements of learning theory and agile software development practice.

Keywords: Agile · Maturity · Learning · Activity theory · Expansive learning

1 Introduction

Much of the literature regarding Agile approaches identifies success factors and challenges at different levels that impact on the transition to and development of agile practices [14, 15]. They don't however provide detailed accounts of the different social and environmental causal factors & tensions behind these challenges and the behavioural, historical and learning elements that influence, impede or facilitate them. Many of these studies do draw attention to the need for further research in this area as well as the lack of suitable analytical techniques. Vijaysarathy and Turk [66] dialectical perspective provides insights into the role of detracting factors and their interactions with enablers and they stress the need to examine these factors at work and the dialectical interplay between them.

Dennehy and Conboy [12] point to multiple studies that highlight the critical role of culture and team dynamics and the need to study software development within the environment within which it is to be implemented. Given the inter-related and complex nature of the environment faced by organisations undertaking Agile approaches, this study draws on Engestrom's Activity Theory (AT) framework [16] as a wide-ranging integrative analytical tool. Derived from Cultural-Historical Analytical Theory (CHAT), the framework facilitates the examination of multiple aspects of work practice

© The Author(s) 2018
J. Garbajosa et al. (Eds.): XP 2018, LNBIP 314, pp. 160–176, 2018.
https://doi.org/10.1007/978-3-319-91602-6_11

including the tensions, contradictions and friction that can arise when new initiatives and practices are developed. Activity Theory has a focus on expansive learning [16] which starts with questioning the existing practice, then proceeds to actions of analyzing its contradictions and modelling a vision for a new approach and then to actions of examining and implementing the new model into practice.

Importantly the resolution of these contradictions can be viewed as drivers of change and an opportunity to reflect and learn as well as identifying new ways of structuring activities [12]. Therefore this study identifies the occurrences of contradictions and tensions as organisations seek to implement agile approaches and this focus provides a means of understanding change and action [18, 38].

This paper is organised as follows. Section 2 links learning with maturity and addresses issues regards agile maturity. Section 3 introduces Activity Theory and Expansive learning and the notion of contradictions within activities. Section 4 discusses the application of Activity Theory to the Agile software development domain and discusses the findings of the research conducted to date. Finally, Sect. 5 discusses planned future research and concludes the paper.

2 Agile Maturity

The Capability Maturity Model integration (CMMi) is probably the most well-known maturity model which Meyer [47] indicates is a collection of best practices that are specified precisely to facilitate an assessment of compliance so that organisations can reach identified goals, He identifies that the three elements of Goals, Practices & Assessment are at the centre of the maturity model approach. CMMi is predominantly an American approach whilst the ISO/IEC 15504 SPICE (Software Process Improvement & Capability Determination) is a European equivalent focused specifically at software development elements. As indicated by Paulk [57] an organisation with these well-defined processes is much more likely to produce software that consistently meets user's requirements. Therefore there appears to be a sound rationale to attempt to link agile practices to traditional maturity model.

However as Meyer [47] also points out, this is in marked contrast to the general perception of agile advocates who view the two as incompatible and this has given rise to a substantial number of agile maturity models [44]. Fritzsche and Keil [23] attempted to determine which CMMi processes are supported by agile methods with some adjustments and which processes are in conflict. They indicate that CMMi level 2 can be obtained by agile methods (Scrum & XP). Apart from two process areas, agile methods can achieve Level 3. However levels 4 & 5 are not possible without adopting additional practices [64] or "without making changes to the methods that contradict agility" [23].

A recent review of Agile maturity models [32] identified that the agile maturity model literature was predominantly divided into two major groups. The first was concerned with the co-existence of agile methods in an environment where CMMi was present [45] and the second related to improving agile implementations without the consideration of other process improvement frameworks. In this latter group the intent is to provide an equivalent maturity model for agile implementations [55, 56, 63].

This rise in the number of agile maturity models has been critiqued by Gren et al. [28] who advocate instead more effort to validate existing ones to facilitate their use by practitioners. They also question the idea of separate maturity models for Agile methods and indeed the whole notion of maturity and state that

"We generally do not believe a hierarchical model of practice is a good model for agility in organisations. For example, why would technical excellence be on the highest level and collaborative planning on the lowest? We do not believe it makes sense to state that collaborative planning is a prerequisite for technical excellence" [28].

Fontana et al. [21] point to another issue with the use of agile maturity models. They note that agile practices are customized for specific contexts where teams adopted different practices based on different circumstances. These circumstances do not lend themselves to the prescriptive practices & processes of maturity models and their associated requirements. Instead they proposed a generic checklist ("Agile Compass") that could be used to assess maturity without specifying practices and where "teams achieve maturity via an evolutionary pursuit of specific outcomes" [22].

Consequently there is a growing appreciation of the factors involved in agile maturity that go beyond sets of practices to consider some form of cultural assessment that might also be included as part of the assessment process [28]. The literature varies from academic articles with large lists of personnel and human resource success factors for adopting agile [9, 14] to industry surveys of the State of Agile [65]. These articles do identify a wide range of cultural, organisational and people factors as key elements of the transition process. In particular Nerur et al. [50] examined the challenges of migrating to agile methods and emphasized that culture exerts considerable influence on decision-making processes, problem-solving strategies, innovative practices and social negotiations. Of interest is their indication that neither culture nor mind-sets can easily be changed pointing out that facilitating this shift will require the "right blend of autonomy and cooperation".

In addition to the shift in emphasis to cultural and human factors is another recent consideration of transitioning to agile and the development of agile practices in a more incremental and responsive manner. Heidenberg et al. [31] developed a method based on multiple case studies in a large organisation that helps to pilot agile. They indicate that systematic piloting can be used to build experience and assist in the deployment of agile approaches. Ganesh and Thangasamy [25] indicate that a general guiding principle for implementation should be to maintain the facility to respond to changing requirements rather than following a specific set of practices. Gandomani and Nafchi [24] pick up this principle and propose a framework for Agile transformation and adoption loosely based on the PDCA (Plan, Do, Check, Act) or later PDSA (Plan, Do, Study, Act) approach also known as the Deming wheel [11] which is itself a form of the scientific method "Hypothesis – experiment – evaluate".

This approach closely aligns with the agile philosophy of incremental and iterative development and involves continuous learning on the part of all stakeholders. The authors indicate that "the outcome of the iterations are adopted practices and not deliverable product elements" [24]. This is contrasted with other adoption and transition frameworks which the authors claim are too complex and inflexible and require significant organisational overhead.

2.1 Agile Maturity and Learning

Several articles particularly stress the important role of an organisation's ability to nurture learning, team work, personal empowerment and self-organisation [51, 62]. Misra et al. [48] undertake a large survey focused on success factors rather than "challenges" in adopting agile software development. In particular the identification of a "Learning & Training" factor is interesting as it was assessed by the authors by examining the "willingness to continuously learn from one another and train the team members through mentoring and professionally guided discussions" [48].

There is an emphasis on continuous learning from participating individuals and these "challenges" and "success factors" are typical of a number of studies in this area. Maier et al. [46] review agile maturity models and agile improvement and adoption frameworks/grids on the basis of work orientation, mode of assessment and intent. They also query what it is that actually makes organisational capabilities mature and they identify "Emphasis on Learning" as one of four elements that are typical. Maier et al. [46] draw on Argyris and Schon's [1] concepts of single & double loop learning to discriminate between different levels of maturity.

Korsaa et al. [40] support this focus on the people & learning aspects in amongst all the process and practice improvement focus of CMMi and SPICE initiatives. They assert that improving software processes does depend upon the organisation's ability to support empowered individuals through a learning environment. This is key as it recognizes the importance of individuals being empowered to learn as a means of achieving improvements in the delivery of software. They recognize that the human aspect is crucial for process improvement as it is entirely dependent upon the individual's motivation to change the way they work. Korsaa et al. [40] also compare the work of Michael Hammer [29] and Jacobsen et al. [33] and conclude that both perspectives place the individual central in process analysis making individuals responsible for changes and improvements. This is most likely to take place within a learning organisation culture that supports continuous improvement.

Boehm [4] points out that as agile projects do not put the emphasis on documentation then the implication is that much of the project knowledge will not be held explicitly and will be held tacitly within individual's minds. Following a survey of agile professionals, Rejab et al. [59] identify five approaches to distributing (sharing) knowledge and expertise within agile teams from hands-on learning to apprentice– master models and coaching & mentoring. In terms of facilitating this knowledge sharing, Kahkonen [35] advocates that Agile project management approaches need to incorporate practices that lead to the creation of Communities of Practice (CoPs) and has found them to be useful in aspects of Agile methods as well as ultimately assisting with the agility of the organisation.

Similarly, Jugdev and Mathur [34] identify Project Reviews and Communities of Practice as vehicles for gathering and sharing project learning and more recently there has been a significant focus on CoPs with Paasivaara and Lassenius [53] and Paasivaara and Lassenius [54] identifying the existence of multiple examples of the adoption of Communities of Practice within a large distributed Agile project management environment (Ericsson). They identified varied examples of Communities of Practice occurring including Coaching CoPs, Development CoPs and specific feature driven

CoPs. The authors conclude that these CoPs supported the process of implementing Agile Project Management and were central to easing the problems of the Agile transformation process. From an organisational perspective it would be prudent to encourage the development of these CoPs but there is some concern that they can be formally fostered although Kahkonen [35] is confident that although such ad hoc situated learning approaches arise naturally, organisations can nevertheless influence their development and this view is also supported by Wenger et al. [68].

Newell and David [52] examined learning in IT projects and the influence of situated practice learning compared to the use of formal project management methodologies. They contend that social processes distort the traditional project management elements such as plans and visions but that this distortion is not necessarily negative and in fact may realize greater benefits than simply focusing on effective work practices. They note that this is not poor management but a realisation that ad-hoc processes can be the norm and will influence and modify formal processes as people will learn & modify new practices & approaches in their own way [52].

Continuing the ad-hoc processes premise, Gherardi [26] proposes a similar approach of "learning-in-organisations" which is essentially constructivist - whereby people will construct their own understanding and knowledge of the world through experience and on reflecting on those experiences. Anything new that is experienced has to be reconciled with past experiences therefore individuals are actively creating their own knowledge. Gherardi [27] makes the following points.

- Learning occurs through practice (a domain of knowing and doing) where a network is socially woven around a domain of knowledge. The knowledge, the subject (person), the object (what is being done such as software development) are produced together within a situated practice.
- The locus of knowledge and learning is situated in practice (which connects knowing with doing). This is distinct from Communities of Practice which emphasize the collaboration and social and situated aspects of learning [42].

Given the emphasis on individuals within the agile approach [21] it is suggested that agile improvements and maturity will have much to do with an individual's learning opportunities which in itself will be a function of their work practices (both historical & current), interactions & collaborative activities and the organisational and social elements and infrastructure that impacts on these aspects. Gherardi [27] notes that the use of Activity Theory within a situated practice context could help understand where knowledge is socially constructed and how it is constructed both actively and passively.

3   Activity Theory (AT)

Instead of solely focusing on mental processes, Activity Theory (AT) considers the relevance of actually undertaking the activity and the important influence of the environmental mix such as culture, language, peers, teachers and artifacts. The Activity Theory perspective of Vygotsky [67] and Leont'ev [43] was extended by Engestrom [16] beyond the single activity and whereas Leont'ev regards the subject of the activity as an individual, Engestrom sees the unit of analysis as collective activity rather than as individual activity [36] and the object (motive) is shared by a group or a community. Bodker [6] does clarify this somewhat and indicates that although these activities are regarded as collective, each activity is conducted through the actions of individuals directed towards an object.

Engestrom [16] argues that the collective perspective is a useful tool for studying organisational change and this gives rise to the well-known triangular diagram illustrated in Fig. 1 below which has been adapted to represent software delivery activity. It is this collective directed activity perspective that is utilized in this study to examine learning within agile teams as they pursue improvements in agile approaches and gives rise to increasing "agile maturity".

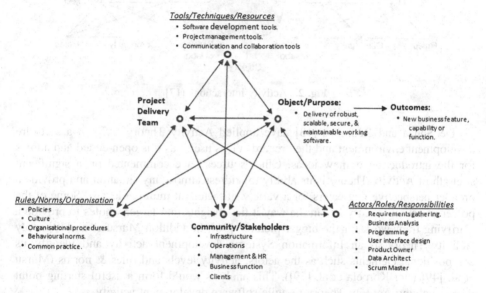

Fig. 1. Example project delivery activity (after Engestrom [17])

The main focus of attention is the line through the middle of the triangle from the Project Delivery Team node to the Object/Purpose node that represents the focus or purpose of the activity/work. In addition, activities both mediate and are mediated (affected/influenced) by the node representing Tools/Techniques/Resources that are used as part of the activity as well as by the Community/Stakeholders context node within which the activity takes place. For example the software development activity is mediated by the tools used such as Kanban Boards or conformance with a planned work package specification. Similarly the software development activity is mediated by the community & social group context such as whether clients are closely involved within the development activity.

This perspective has a further dimension where the relationship between the Project Delivery Team node and the Community/Stakeholders node is mediated by the node representing Rules/Norms/Organisation. Similarly the relationship between the

Community/Stakeholders node and the Object/Purpose is mediated by the Actor/Roles/Responsibilities node that reflects how work & responsibilities are divided and & allocated.

This can be developed further to include multiple perspectives and networks of interacting activities and Fig. 2 below shows the interaction of two neighbouring activities which for instance could be the activity of a development team in an IT department interacting with the activity of a client in another organisational function.

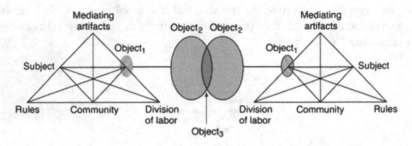

Fig. 2. Activity interactions [17]

De Souza and Redmiles [13] have applied Activity Theory (AT) to a software development environment and they regard AT as useful as it is open-ended and allows for the introduction of new ideas. Other sources have commented on a significant strength of Activity Theory is its ability to address almost any situation and provide a broader perspective that caters for a variety of factors at multiple levels "Some of the power of activity theory lies in the way it ties insights into larger wholes to provide a clarifying framework for the bigger picture" [36]. In addition Mursu et al. [49] apply Activity Theory to an Information Systems development activity and identify its compositional elements such as the actors, activity levels and rules & norms (Mursu et al. [49] after Korpela et al. [39]). This analysis would form a useful starting point when applying Activity Theory to agile software development activity

In their Activity Theory based study of software development environments, Barthelmess and Anderson [7] focus on improving support for collaboration and conclude that each situation will be different and individuals will do things their own way. Perhaps this perspective sheds some light on why often cited lists of success factors [14] prove effective in one environment but are ineffective in another. It also might be indicative as to why there are so many different and varied agile maturity models and perspectives on what constitutes agile maturity and such points have been made extensively elsewhere [22, 52]. What an Activity Theory perspective does facilitate is a more detailed examination of the socially constructed environmental mix within which each individual organisation's context contributes to and enables the practice and activity of collaborative software development.

Korsaa et al. [40] point to another complication in the difference between the process that may be prescribed by an organisation and the process that is actually applied and followed by the performers. This causes difficulty in translating successful processes to other teams as the prescribed process will vary from that which is actually followed by the successful team. This further suggests a deeper level of analysis is required of actual practices at a collective and individual activity levels.

3.1 Activity Theory and Expansive Learning

Engestrom [18] indicates that the subjects of learning are contained within these activities and they are inter-connected. Activities have their own internal contradictions and resolutions that will result in learning taking place and also there will be contradictions between activities as teams and organisations adapt and learn new practices and processes.

According to Engestrom [16] the introduction of a new technology, work practice or system can impact a collaborative activity and initiate a new process of learning by giving rise to new questions tensions and contradictions that lead to expansive learning where the object and the motive of the activity are re-conceptualized to embrace a radically wider horizon of possibilities than previously envisaged which he terms "expansive learning".

Engestrom identifies a problem with traditional approaches to learning that pre-suppose that the knowledge or skill to be learnt is itself well known, well-defined and stable [16]. Engestrom [18] indicates that learning in modern organisations doesn't correlate with this view and that people are continually learning something that is new, undefined and not stable.

> "In important transformations of our personal lives and organisational practices we must learn new forms of activity which are not yet there. They are literally learned as they are created. There is no competent teacher. Standard learning theories have little to offer if one wants to understand these processes" [18].

For example with reference to a learning approach based on Communities of Practice (CoPs), Engestrom [19] indicates that the motivation comes from participation in culturally valued collaborative practices where something useful is produced. Engestrom's view is that this works well for novices in a field transiting to valued experts in stable practices but argues that the motivations for risky expansive learning associated with major transformation is not well explained by mere participation and the gradual acquisition of mastery [19].

It is suggested that it is exactly this kind of situation and learning processes that occur during the implementation and development of Agile practices where individuals and organisations are faced with highly variable approaches and perspectives that are not easily described or evaluated [5]. Due to the necessary emphasis on human and cultural elements within Agile practices unlike traditional maturity models (CMMi) where the emphasis is on clearly specified processes and practices [21] in Engestrom's terms these new Agile practices to be learned "are not yet there" [18].

Engestrom indicates that learning new practices comes from identifying and understanding contradictions and conflicts within existing activities [17] and follow a cycle of expansive learning as illustrated in Fig. 3 below.

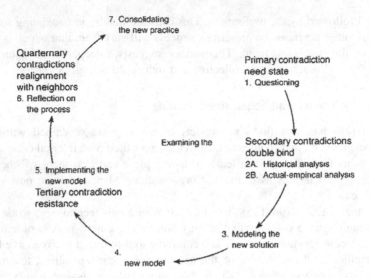

Fig. 3. Strategic learning actions and corresponding contradictions in the cycle of expansive learning [18].

This is described more fully as follows:

1. **Questioning:** This is the important trigger point in expansive learning where there is a conflicting contradiction/tension that leads to the questioning of existing standard practice. A *Primary Contradiction* will emerge from within a node of an activity system.
2. *Secondary Contradictions*: This step leads to deeper analysis and more detailed questioning of the historical and cultural aspects. This is likely to emerge between two or more nodes within an activity system.
3. **Modeling:** This is where a new solution (activity/practice) is modelled.
4. **New Model**: This is where the new model (activity/practice) is validated.
5. **Implementation model**: This is likely to give rise to a new set of contradictions between the old and the new activity. *Tertiary Contradictions* will emerge between a new system and a previous instance.
6. **Reflection on the process and alignment** with neighbouring activities. *Quaternary Contradictions* emerge between a new re-organised activity and its neighbouring activities
7. **Consolidating new Practice**: The activity/practice previously unknown is now consolidated and becomes the norm.

Barab et al. [2] explain that as tensions enter the activity they are the driving forces behind the contradictions and disturbances which lead to the activity/practice changing and developing. These contradictions are best understood as tensions amongst the different elements of the activity system. Through understanding the interplay within these dualities, researchers can better understand and support the development and innovation & learning within the activity system. Barab et al. [3] indicate that contradictions within an activity/practice are potential opportunities for intervention and improvement. They see contradictions as providing elements or functions of a growing & expanding activity system and can be viewed as a "gap-analysis" exercise.

3.2 Contradictions Within Activities

Kaptelinin and Nardi [36] indicate that activities are virtually always in the process of working through contradictions and that these contradictions are the sources of development. These contradictions have formed the basis of several studies within the Information Systems (IS) domain and as indicated by Hasan et al. [30] in reference to past work by Kuutti and Virkkunen [41] they have mostly focused on Quaternary contradictions between different activities. This focus may well relate to the typical relationship between the two activities/practices of software development and user/client. Hasan et al. [30] indicate that in the Information systems HCI domain the focus has been on Secondary contradictions within an activity between the subject and tools/techniques nodes.

Regards the occurrence of Tertiary contradictions Mursu et al. (2007) provide a description of contradictions within the information systems function which they indicate is between the object and motive of the "dominant form of the central activity" and the object and motive of a "culturally more advanced form of the central activity". They indicate that these Tertiary contradictions occur when work practices are re-organised and the old mode of operation is rebelling against the newer one (Mursu et al. 2007). This is of particular relevance to this study as it is asserted that the "dominant form of the central activity" can be regarded as a repeated software development activity and the "culturally more advanced form" could be a more mature/ improved/more agile form of the software development practice and would involve a significant change to the practice. It may be argued that perceived higher levels of agile maturity are exactly what a "culturally more advanced form of the central activity" would look like. The following section outlines the research conducted and focuses on the identification of these contradictions, their frequency of occurrence and their correlation with similar events within the literature.

4 Research Conducted

A mixed methods approach has been adopted which is underpinned by a pragmatic research philosophy [10]. This fits well with the Activity Theory framework which can aid analysis of both qualitative and quantitative data [20]. The intention is to identify occurrences of frictions and hindrances which could then be mapped to different levels of contradictions. Empirical research was conducted with five interviews with Agile professionals who were - a consultant agile coach, a portfolio & programme manager at a large public sector organisation, two scrum masters at a software supplier and a web developer at an educational institute. This was followed up by a questionnaire survey of 45 attendees at a Project and Programme Management Conference. The questions were open-ended and aimed to identify the difficulties & problems that respondents had with adopting and developing agile development practices. Collected data was transcribed and the text was analyzed for tensions among components of the activity system which were then grouped into the different levels of contradictions.

The first set of contradictions to be experienced are likely to be Primary contradictions within the **Project Delivery Team** and the **Tool/Techniques/Resources** nodes as the project delivery team acquaint themselves and grapple with new approach/tools/techniques. A combined analysis of the interviews transcripts and survey results identified a total of 57 references to contradictions. Figure 4 below indicates some typical primary contradictions within the nodes that were identified. Primary contradictions were the most often cited (22) and relate to many of the key people challenges in implementing Agile approaches.

Within the literature, there are many examples of these types of contradictions that occur as people and technical challenges [9, 14].

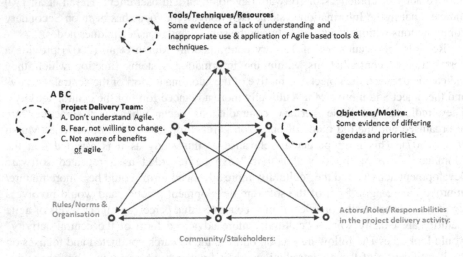

Fig. 4. Primary contradictions: within nodes – a questioning of practice

Secondary contradictions are cited almost as frequently (21) representing friction & tension between the nodes of the activity as the Project Delivery Team engaged in different behavioural norms and cultural practices, involving other stakeholders as well as adopting new roles & responsibilities.

> "And that was the way to do it and we said no we don't want the roles we just want equal team members and so basically our software engineers and a scrum master and that's it. This was only possible because we had higher support"
>
> *(Scrum master at a software supplier)*

Work by Schatz and Abdelshafi [61] and Chan and Thong [8] in their discussion of organisational characteristics and work habits has highlighted these types of issues and problems. Figure 5 below indicates the Secondary contradictions between nodes that occurred as deeper questioning and analysis took place.

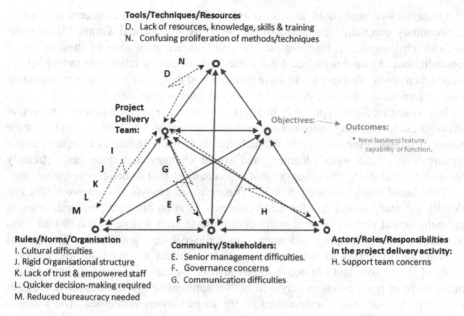

Tools/Techniques/Resources
D. Lack of resources, knowledge, skills & training
N. Confusing proliferation of methods/techniques

Project Delivery Team:

Objectives: ──►

Outcomes:
* New business feature, capability or function.

Rules/Norms/Organisation
I. Cultural difficulties
J. Rigid Organisational structure
K. Lack of trust & empowered staff
L. Quicker decision-making required
M. Reduced bureaucracy needed

Community/Stakeholders:
E. Senior management difficulties.
F. Governance concerns
G. Communication difficulties

Actors/Roles/Responsibilities in the project delivery activity:
H. Support team concerns

Fig. 5. Secondary contradictions: between nodes - involves a deeper level of analysis

As the impact of the adoption of Agile approaches gains traction within the organisation these Primary & Secondary contradictions are supplemented by Tertiary and Quaternary ones as the implications and effects of the adopted Agile practice extend beyond the project delivery team and impact on other organisational activities and practices.

Interestingly Tertiary contradictions represented the lowest (5) level of occurrences of all the contradictions. This is similar to instances in the literature where for example a study by Rauf and Al Ghafees [58] indicated that most organisations do not follow any agile method completely. They adopt a mix of agile practices and traditional approaches. This could be indicative of significant Tertiary contradiction where the "old mode of operation is rebelling against the new one" [49].

Similarly, case study analysis of agile implementations, undertaken by Rose [60] indicates that some organisations embrace agile principles without the wholesale abandonment of the already established traditional approaches. His research also noted that there was some symbolic re-labelling of some traditional elements using agile terminology. He notes that this was detrimental to moving forward with agile approaches as labelling acts as a departure point for organisational transformations and notes that "the path to innovation is not navigable when labels do not accurately reflect either the status quo or the transformed state" [60].

Such maneuverings can be viewed from a Tertiary contradiction perspective and as Rose [60] indicates there is a further opportunity for research. Of particular interest would be an understanding as to why the occurrence of Tertiary contradictions is low in comparison with the Primary & Secondary contradiction. Is it because software teams are unaware of what "culturally more advanced forms" of agile practice are?

Quaternary contradictions also occur at a fairly low level (9) compared to Primary & Secondary contradictions. Some of the work by Boehm and Turner [5] on management challenges and business process conflicts are indicative of these types of contradictions. Again it is expected that these types of contradictions are more likely to occur when project delivery teams have matured and their activities begin to impact on other organisation functions such as finance and human resources.

Implementing Agile approaches demands a much more social, cultural, behavioural and organisational change perspectives than hitherto envisioned [50]. It is not a simple matter of transplanting agile tools and techniques. In many instances it requires major organisational, behavioural, learning and social changes and these are extremely demanding (and disruptive) changes that organisations find difficulties in embracing.

This initial study has used Activity Theory as an analytical framework that can identify the many causal & influencing elements from an historical, cultural, learning and behavioural perspective that might contribute to an organisation's difficulties and problems when developing and improving agile delivery approaches. The use of Activity Theory serves to indicate the multiple elements involved and the complex levels of interactions that can occur. It may also be indicative of attempts to undertake an initiative or practice which may well not be appropriate given the specific social & environmental mix and circumstances of the organisations concerned. The research conducted so far is somewhat limited due to its high level nature and the large cross-section of participants. More detailed analysis is needed to be able to thoroughly examine the complex interactions & influences of cultural and socially constructed factors.

5 Further Research

The next steps for this research programme are detailed case study analysis of organisation's project delivery activities using a mix of observation, interview and survey methods. To date there are four participating organisations that are looking to develop and scale their agile activities and the rationale for undertaking this research is that:

- Moving up or improving an organisation's agile maturity requires collective & individual learning & development.
- The learning and development within an agile context is somewhat different as it involves organisational specific and tailored practices that "are not yet there" [18].
- This will involve individual & organisational movement along Engestrom's expansive learning cycle.
- To identify specifically how expansive learning is likely, it will be necessary to examine project delivery activity in some depth within the wider organisational, historical and cultural context.
- Identifying and resolving contradictions maybe indicative of where the hindrances are to organisational improvement and development in terms of agile maturity.

For each participating organisation detailed analysis will be undertaken of the full activity system that surrounds and impacts an organisation's project delivery capability.

Undertaking organisational and project delivery analysis from an ethnographic perspective can be a substantial task. In particular due to Activity Theory's wide–ranging and all-encompassing perspective it can be somewhat difficult to determine an appropriate approach or perspective to take. Literature that does address the application of Activity Theory is varied in terms of the elements of Activity Theory that have been selected and there is little guidance and information available on its application. An "Activity Checklist" has been suggested by Kaptelinin et al. [37] which although is based within the HCI domain, does provide a series of pointers to consider and questions to ask that can assist in direction as well as drawing attention to potential influential areas and factors to consider.

In a simplified form this analysis makes a contribution to the gap in the literature on how concepts from workplace learning could be applied to the learning processes and activities inherent in project management as indicated by Jugdev and Mathur [34]. This analysis has served to indicate an approach based on learning theory that helps with identifying and analyzing the multiple and varied factors that influence an organisation's progression towards some form of agile maturity. These learning processes and developments are likely to be different within an agile context due to the fact that the new organisation specific and tailored practices "are not yet there" [18]. Individual and collective learning will play a key part in this "maturing" process and that the use of Activity Theory is an important analytical tool to help contextualize and understand the learning processes through the identification of contradictions and tensions within the project delivery activity. A focus on contradictions, tensions and frictions within and between activities is useful as it points to obstructive elements and tensions within practice that impede & hinder improvement and development.

References

1. Argyris, C., Schon, D.: Organizational Learning: A Theory of Action Perspective. Addison-Wesley, Reading (1978)
2. Barab, S.A., Barnett, M., Yamagata-Lynch, L., Squire, K., Keating, T.: Using activity theory to understand the systemic tensions characterizing a technology-rich introductory astronomy course. Mind Cult. Act. 9(2), 76–107 (2002)
3. Barab, S.A., Evans, M.A., Baek, E.: Activity theory as a lens for characterizing the participatory unit. In: Jonassen, D.H. (ed.) Handbook of Research on Educational Communities and Technology, pp. 199–214. Lawrence Erlbaum Associates, Mahwah (2004)
4. Boehm, B.: Get ready for Agile methods with care. Computer 35(1), 64–69 (2002)
5. Boehm, B., Turner, R.: Management challenges in implementing agile processes in traditional development organisations. IEEE Softw. 22(5), 30–39 (2005)
6. Bodker, S.: Creating conditions for participation: conflicts and resources in systems development. Hum. Comput. Interact. 11(3), 215–236 (1996)
7. Barthelmess, P., Anderson, K.M.: A view of software development environments based on activity theory. Comput. Support. Coop. Work (CSCW) 11(1–2), 13–37 (2002)
8. Chan, F.K.Y., Thong, J.Y.L.: Acceptance of agile methodologies: A critical review and conceptual framework. Decis. Support Syst. 46, 803–814 (2009)
9. Conboy, K., Coyle, S., Lero, X.W., Pikkarainen, M.: People over process: key challenges in agile development. IEEE Softw. (2011)

10. Creswell, J.W.: A Concise Introduction to Mixed Methods Research. SAGE, London (2015)
11. Deming, W.E.: The New Economics. MIT Press, Cambridge (1993)
12. Dennehy, D., Conboy, K.: Going with the flow: an activity theory analysis of flow techniques in software development. J. Syst. Softw. **133**, 160–173 (2017)
13. De Souza, C.R., Redmiles, D.F.: Opportunities for extending activity theory for studying collaborative software development. In: Workshop on Applying Activity Theory to CSCW Research and Practice, in Conjunction with ECSCW (2003)
14. Dikert, K., Paasivaara, M., Lassenius, C.: Challenges and success factors for large-scale agile transformations: a systematic literature review. J. Syst. Softw. **119**, 87–108 (2016)
15. Dingsoyr, T., Nerur, S., Balijepally, V., Moe, N.B.: A decade of agile methodologies: towards explaining agile software development. J. Syst. Softw. **85**, 1213–1221 (2012)
16. Engestrom, Y.: Learning by Expanding: An Activity-Theoretical Approach to Developmental Research. Cambridge University Press, Cambridge (1987)
17. Engestrom, Y.: Activity theory as a framework for analyzing and redesigning work. Ergonomics **43**(7), 960–974 (2000)
18. Engestrom, Y.: Expansive learning at work: towards an activity theoretical reconceptualization. J. Educ. Work **14**(1), 133–156 (2001)
19. Engestrom, Y.: Expansive learning: Toward an activity-theoretical reconceptualization. In: Illeris, K. (Ed.) Contemporary Theories of Learning: Learning Theorists… in their Own Words, pp. 53–74. Routledge, London (2009)
20. Engestrom, T., Miettinen, R., Punamaki, R.L. (eds.) Perspectives on Activity Theory. Cambridge University Press. Cambridge (1999)
21. Fontana, R.M., Fontana, I.M., Garbuio, P.A., Reinehr, S., Malucelli, A.: Process versus people: how should agile software development maturity be defined? J. Syst. Softw. **1**(97), 140–155 (2014)
22. Fontana, R.M., Reinehr, S., Malucelli, A.: Agile compass: a tool for identifying maturity in agile software-development teams. IEEE Softw. **32**(6), 20–23 (2015)
23. Fritzsche, M., Keil, P.: Agile methods and CMMI: compatibility or conflict? e-Inform. Softw. Eng. J. **1**(1) (2007)
24. Gandomani, T.J., Nafchi, M.Z.: an empirically-developed framework for agile transition and adoption: a grounded theory approach. J. Syst. Softw. **107**, 204–219 (2015)
25. Ganesh, N., Thangasamy, S.: Lessons learned in transforming from traditional to agile development. J. Comput. Sci. **8**(3), 389–392 (2012)
26. Gherardi, S.: From organizational learning to practice-based knowing. Hum. Relat. **54**, 131–139 (2001)
27. Gherardi, S.: Knowing and learning in practice-based studies: an introduction. Learn. Organ. **16**(5), 352–359 (2009)
28. Gren, L., Torkar, R., Feldt, R.: The prospects of a quantitative measurement of agility: A validation study on an agile maturity model. J. Syst. Softw. **107**, 38–49 (2015)
29. Hammer, M.: The process audit. Harvard Bus. Rev. **85**(4), 111–119 (2007)
30. Hasan, H., Smith, S., Finnegan, P.: An activity theoretic analysis of the mediating role of information systems in tackling climate change adaptation. Inf. Syst. J. **27**, 271–308 (2017)
31. Heidenberg, J., Matinlassi, M., Pikkarainen, M., Hirkman, P., Partanen, J.: Systematic piloting of agile methods in the large: two cases in embedded systems development. In: Ali Babar, M., Vierimaa, M., Oivo, M. (eds.) PROFES 2010. LNCS, vol. 6156, pp. 47–61. Springer, Heidelberg (2010). https://doi.org/10.1007/978-3-642-13792-1_6
32. Henriques, V., Tanner, M.: A systematic literature review of agile and maturity model research. Interdisc. J. Inf. Knowl. Manage. **12**, 53–73 (2017)
33. Jacobsen, I., Ng, P.-W., Spence, I.: Enough of Processes: Let's Do Practices. Dr. Dobbs J. **32**(5) (2007)

34. Jugdev, K., Mathur, G.: Bridging situated learning theory to the resource based view of project management. Int. J. Project Manage. 6(4), 633–653 (2013)
35. Kahkonen, T.: Agile methods for large organisations - building communities of practice. In: Proceedings of the Agile Development Conference, pp. 2–10 (2004)
36. Kaptelinin, V., Nardi, B.A.: Acting with Technology: Activity Theory and Interaction Design. MIT Press, Cambridge (2006)
37. Kaptelinin, V., Nardi, B., Macaulay, C.: The activity checklist: a tool for representing the "space" of context. Interactions (1999)
38. Karanasios, S., Allen, D.: Mobile technology in mobile work: contradictions and congruences in activity systems. Eur. J. Inf. Syst. 23(5), 529–542 (2014)
39. Korpela, M., Mursu, A., Soriyan, H.A.: Information systems development as an activity. CSCW 11, 111–128 (2002)
40. Korsaa, M., Johansen, J., Schweigert, T. Vohwinkel, D., Messnarz, R., Nevalainen, R., Biro, M.: The people aspects in modern process improvement management approaches. Softw. Evol. Process (2013)
41. Kuutti, K., Virkkunen, J.: Organisational memory and learning network organisation: the case of Finnish labour protection inspectors. In: Proceedings of the Twenty-Eighth Hawaii International Conference on Systems Science, vol. 4, pp. 313–322. IEEE (1995)
42. Lave, J., Wenger, E.: Situated Learning: Legitimate Peripheral Participation. Cambridge University Press, Cambridge (1991)
43. Leont'ev, A.N.: Activity, Consciousness and Personality. Prentice-Hall, Englewood Cliffs (1978)
44. Leppanen, M.: A comparative analysis of agile maturity models. Inf. Syst. Dev. 329–343 (2013)
45. Lukasiewicz, K., Miler, J.: Improving agility and discipline of software development with the Scrum and CMMI. IET Softw. 6(5), 416–422 (2012)
46. Maier, A.M., Moultrie, J., Clarkson, P.J.: Assessing organizational capabilities: reviewing and guiding the development of maturity grids. IEEE Trans. Eng. Manag. 59(1), 138–159 (2012)
47. Meyer, B.: Agile!: The Good, the Hype and the Ugly. Springer, Heidelberg (2014). https://doi.org/10.1007/978-3-319-05155-0
48. Misra, S.C., Kumar, V., Kumar, U.: Important success factors in adopting agile software development practices. J. Syst. Softw. 82, 1869–1890 (2009)
49. Mursu, A., Luukkonen, I., Toivanen, M., Korpela, M.: Activity theory in information systems research and practice: theoretical underpinnings for an information systems development model. Inf. Res. Int. Electron. J. 12(3) (2007)
50. Nerur, S., Mahapatra, R., Mangalaraj, G.: Challenges of migrating to agile methodologies. Commun. ACM 48(5), 73–78 (2005)
51. Nerur, S., Balijepally, V.: Theoretical reflections on agile development methodologies: the traditional goal of optimisation and control is making way for learning and innovation. Commun. ACM 50(3), 79–83 (2007)
52. Newell, S., David, G.: Learning in IT projects-the importance of situated practice as well as formal project methodologies. In: OLKC Conference at University of Warwick (2006)
53. Paasivaara, M., Lassenius, C.: Agile coaching for global software development. J. Soft. Evol. Process. 26, 404–418 (2014a)
54. Paasivaara, M., Lassenius, C.: Communities of practice in a large distributed agile software development organisation – case ericsson. Inf. Softw. Technol. 56, 1556–1577 (2014b)
55. Packlick, J.: The agility maturity map – a goal oriented approach to agile improvement. In: Agile Conference (2007)

56. Patel, C., Ramachandran, M.: Agile Maturity Model (AMM): a software process improvement framework for agile software development practices. Int. J. Softw. Eng. **2**(1), 3–28 (2009)
57. Paulk, M.: Using the Software CMM with Good Judgement. Research Showcase @CMU. Carnegie Mellon University (1999)
58. Rauf, A., AlGhafees, M.: Gap analysis between state of practice & state of art practices in agile software development. In: Agile Conference (2015)
59. Rejab, M.M., Noble, J., Allan, G.: Distributing expertise in agile software projects. In: Agile Conference (2014)
60. Rose, D.: Symbolic innovation in agile transformation. In: Agile Conference (2015)
61. Schatz, B., Abdelshafi, I.: Primavera gets agile: a successful transition to agile development. IEEE Softw. **22**(3), 26–42 (2005)
62. Sheffield, J., Lemetayer, J.: Factors associated with the software development agility of successful projects. Int. J. Project Manage. **31**, 459–472 (2013)
63. Sidky, A., Arthur, J., Bohner, S.: A disciplined approach to the adopting agile practice: the agile adoption framework. Innovations Syst. Softw. Eng. **3**(3), 203–216 (2007)
64. Silva, F.S., Soares, F.S.F., Peres, A.L., de Azevedo, I.M., Vasconcelos, A.P.L.F., Kamei, F. K., Meira, S.R.L.: Using CMMI together with agile software development: a systematic review. Inf. Softw. Technol. **58**, 20–43 (2015)
65. Version One: The 11th Annual State of Agile Report Version One (2017)
66. Vijayasarathy, L., Turk, D.: Drivers of agile software development use: dialectic interplay between benefits and hindrances. Inf. Softw. Technol. **54**, 137–148 (2012)
67. Vygotsky, L.S.: Mind in Society: The Development of Higher Psychological Processes. Harvard University Press, Cambridge (1978)
68. Wenger, E., McDermott, R., Snyder, W.M.: Cultivating Communities of Practice. Harvard Business Review Press, Cambridge (2002)

Scaling Agile

Do Agile Methods Work for Large Software Projects?

Magne Jørgensen[✉]

Simula Research Laboratory, 1364 Fornebu, Norway
magnej@simula.no

Abstract. Is it true that agile methods do not scale well and are mainly useful for smaller software projects? Or is it rather the case that it is particularly in the context of larger, typically more complex software projects that the use of agile methods is likely to make the difference between success and failure? To find out more about this, we conducted a questionnaire-based survey analyzing information about 101 Norwegian software projects. Project success was measured as the combined performance of the project regarding delivered client benefits, cost control, and time control. We found that that projects using agile methods performed on average much better than those using non-agile methods for medium and large software projects, but not so much for smaller projects. This result gives support for the claim that agile methods are more rather than less successful compared to traditional methods when project size increases. There may consequently be more reasons to be concerned about how non-agile, rather than how agile methods, scale.

Keywords: Agile development methods · Project size · Project success

1 Introduction

Much has been written about the extent to which agile methods are suitable for large software projects. An early attempt to summarize what we know about agile methods and their success when used in large software projects, authored by Dybå and Dingsøyr [1], concludes: "The evidence […] suggests that agile methods not necessarily are the best choice for large projects." Similarly, the review published by Jalali and Wohlin [2] finds: "[…] there is not sufficient evidence to conclude that Agile is efficiently applicable in large distributed projects." More recent reviews, see for example [3, 4], emphasize challenges related to the use of agile methods for large software projects and, similarly to the previous reviews, report little or no evidence to support the use of agile methods for large software projects. Not only is much of the research literature sceptical about the use of agile methods for large software projects, but several software professionals also seem to think that agile methods are mainly for smaller software projects.[1] It is, in addition, not difficult to find examples of failed, large-scale agile

---

[1] For an example of an opinion-based argumentation of why agile is not useful for large projects, see blog. inf.ed.ac.uk/sapm/2014/02/14/agile-methodologies-in-large-scale-projects-a-recipe-for-disaster/. This blog post concludes that *"Large-scale development projects are serious business: agile development has no place here."*

© The Author(s) 2018
J. Garbajosa et al. (Eds.): XP 2018, LNBIP 314, pp. 179–190, 2018.
https://doi.org/10.1007/978-3-319-91602-6_12

software projects.[2] A comprehensive review of experience reports and case studies on the challenges and success factors regarding the introduction of agile in large-scale software development can be found in [5].

There are also reported cases where agile methods have been successfully used for large software projects, see for example [6], and reports where agile methods are claimed to have had a positive impact on the outcome of large software projects, see for example [7, 8]. Finally, there are guidelines on how to succeed with large-scale agile projects, such as [9], which claim to be based on the successful completion of large software projects using agile methods.

These diverging results and opinions on the use of agile on large software project may appear to be confusing. There are, however, several reasons why we should not expect consistent results and opinions about the effect of using agile methods on larger software projects:

- *We do not have a clear, commonly agreed upon understanding of what it means to work agile.* Agile is not a well-defined method, but rather a set of values, principles, and practices. There are consequently many good and bad ways of implementing and using agile methods. There may, in addition, be external factors that complicate the use of good agile, such as the use of fixed price contracts or insufficient involvement by the client [10]. The same problems are present for non-agile methods, which may include an even larger variety of practices. There are good and bad ways of using most software development methods and it is frequently not clear when it is the inexperience and lack of skill in using a method and when it is inherent flaws in a method that contribute to software project failures.
- *The development method is only one of many factors affecting the success of a software project.* Other factors, especially the level of provider and client competence, may be even more important to explain the outcome of large software projects.
- *We do not agree on what a large software project is.* A large software project may be defined relatively to those that an organization is used to completing or with absolute measures such as budget size, number of developers, complexity, or number of development teams [11]. In addition, the difference between a large project (e.g., a project consisting of two teams and costing 10 million Euros) and a mega-large project (e.g., a project consisting of ten teams and costing 100 million Euros) may be substantial.
- *We see it when we believe it (confirmation bias).* People are good at summarizing experience in a way that defends their beliefs. As documented in [12], those who believe in the benefits of agile will tend to find evidence supporting the use of agile even in random project data without any true patterns connecting development method and project success. One example of how to confirm a strong belief in agile

(or other) development methods is to categorize a software project as non-agile, or at least not using agile methods properly, if it fails, i.e., if it works it is agile, if it fails it is not true agile.

Despite the above methodological problems we may be able to find out more about the scalability of agile methods by systematically collecting empirical evidence. If large software projects using agile methods typically perform better than projects using other methods, then this supports the claim that agile methods do scale to larger projects. It may give this information even if we do not know exactly how agile was implemented and used by the projects, are unable to use a commonly accepted and good definition of what a large project is, and there are other factors that also matter for success. Many companies may have adopted agile methods just recently, which means that if we find that agile software projects perform worse, but perhaps not much worse, than non-agile as the project size increases, we may not be able to conclude that agile methods will not work on larger software projects. It may then improve as their competence in using the methods improves.

In this paper we empirically compare agile and non-agile software development projects by surveying a set of projects, collecting information about their size (as measured by their budget), their use of development methods, and their degree of success. The research question of our study is:

> How is the relationship between project size, as measured by its budget, and success affected by the development method?

As indicated earlier in this section, there are many studies on the use of agile methods on large-scale software projects, and there are many strong opinions about which method is the better to use on large projects. In spite of this, we have been unable to find peer-reviewed research articles empirically analysing size-dependent differences in success of projects using agile and non-agile development methods. A non-peer reviewed study by the Standish Group from 2016[3] reports that projects using agile development methods performed better than those using waterfall-based methods for small, medium, and large project sizes, and particularly the largest projects. For the largest projects, the failure rate was 42% for waterfall projects and 23% for agile projects. For the smallest project, the difference is smaller, with an 11% failure rate for waterfall and a 4% failure rate for agile projects. This study indicates that agile methods is not only well suited for large projects, but also increasingly more suited as the project size increases. This is, to our knowledge, the only related work we can compare our results with.

---

[3] There are reasons to be sceptical about the results published by the Standish Group; see our comments on their survey methods on a previous survey in [13]. In its 2016 report the Standish Group (www.standishgroup.com), improved the definition of success to include not only being on time, on cost, and with the specified functionality, but also that the project delivers satisfactory results (blog.standishgroup.com/post/23). Satisfactory results include, they claim, client value. This improvement, given that it is properly integrated in their survey and that they have improved their sampling of projects, may make their recent results more valid and useful.

The remaining article is organized as follows. Section 2 describes the survey design, limitations, and results. Section 3 briefly discusses the results and concludes.

2 The Survey

2.1 Survey Design

The respondents of the survey were participants at a seminar on management of software development projects in Oslo, Norway, March 2015.[4] All participants were asked to provide information about their last project, including:

- The respondent's role in the project.
- The project's outcome in terms of client benefits, cost control, and time control.
- The project's budget.
- The project's use of agile practices, and the respondent's assessment of how agile the project had been.

We received information about 108 projects. An examination of the responses showed that seven of them did not include the required information regarding one or more of the variables used in our analysis. Removing these left 101 valid responses in the data set.

Characteristics of the respondents and their projects include:

- *Role*: 56% of the respondents were from the client side and 44% from the provider side.
- *Client benefits*: 35% were categorized as "successful," 55% as "acceptable," and 10% as "unsuccessful" or "failed."
- *Cost control*: 30% were categorized as "successful," 32% as "acceptable," and 38% as "unsuccessful" or "failed."
- *Time control*: 37% were categorized as "successful," 32% as "acceptable," and 31% as "unsuccessful" or "failed."
- *Budget*: 48% of the projects had a budget less than 1 million Euros, 25% between 1 and 10 million Euros, and 27% more than 10 million Euros.[5]
- *Agile practices*: When asked to rank their project with respect to how agile it was from 1 (very agile) to 5 (not agile at all), 17% responded with 1, 25% with 2, 40% with 3, 14% with 4, and 4% with 5.

The participants were asked to name the agile practices they had used in their last project. Comparing those descriptions, emphasizing the use of product backlogs, frequent/continuous delivery to client, the use of scrum or similar management processes, autonomous teams, and the use of velocity to track progress, with responses regarding the degree of agility of the project using the scale from 1 to 5, we found it

---

[4] Results from this survey have not been published earlier, but the design and project performance measures are similar to those in the survey published in [14].

[5] The original survey was in Norwegian and used Norwegian Kroner (NOK) as currency. The Euro-values are the approximate values corresponding to the NOK-values.

reasonable to cluster the projects as "agile" if the response was 1 or 2, "partly agile" if the response was 3, and "not agile" if the response was 4 or 5. There were, however, no simple connection between the self-assessed degree of agility (using the scale from 1 to 5) and the implemented agile practices. This makes the development category boundaries, especially the boundary between agile and partly agile, to some extent fuzzy and subjective. While this may limit the strength of the analysis, it is clear from the analysis that those categorized as agile on average have more agile practices than those categorized as partly agile. While we believe that this is sufficient for meaningful analyses, it is important to be aware of that degree of agility in our study is based on the respondents subjective assessment.[6]

Our measure of a project's level of success used a combination of three success dimensions: client benefits, cost control, and time control. To be categorized as "acceptable", we require a score of at least "acceptable" on all three dimensions. Fifty-four percent of the projects were categorized as acceptable using this definition. Notice that the inverse of "acceptable" (46% = 100% − 54%) is the set of projects assessed to have a non-acceptable outcome on at least one of the success dimensions, i.e., the set of "problematic" projects. To be categorized as "successful," we require that all three dimensions should be assessed as "successful." Only 12% of the projects belonged to that category.

2.2 Limitations

The survey has a number of limitations that it is important to be aware of when interpreting the results, including:

- *Representativeness*. Our sample consists only of Norwegian software projects and is a convenience sample based on input from people visiting a seminar on software project management. The common use of agile methods in our data set suggests that many of the companies represented by the participants had (possibly much) experience in the use of agile methods. From more in-depth studies of software projects in similar contexts, see [10], and common sense we know that companies tend to have more problems in the initial phase when they introduce agile methods compared to subsequent projects. The level of agile maturity and other largely unknown sample characteristics, may affect how valid it is to extrapolate our results to other context.

- *Perception, not measurement*: Several of the survey questions, particularly those related to project outcome, are based on the respondents' perceptions, not measured data. This has some drawbacks, for example, different people may have different viewpoints regarding the same project. It may also have some advantages. The degree of success in time control, for example, may be more meaningfully assessed subjectively. In one context, a 10% time overrun may point to a time control failure, while in another context, the same overrun may be acceptable.

---

[6] The set of agile practises, combined with the project's own assessment of degree of agility, of a project and other project data used in the analyses will be sent to interested readers upon request to the author.

- *Role bias*. We decided to join the responses of those on the client and the provider side, even though there may have been systematic differences in their responses. For example, those in the client role seem to have been less critical than those in the provider role when assessing the outcome of the projects. Using our measure of acceptable outcomes, those on the client side found 66% of the projects to be acceptable, while the figure was 46% when assessed by those on the provider side. Those on the client and the provider side gave however approximately the same average score regarding client benefits, i.e., 37% of the projects assessed by the clients were successful regarding client benefits, while the figure was 32% when assessed by the providers. If the role bias is not dependent on the degree of use of agile methods, which we believe is the case, joining the responses of the two roles will not affect the direction of the interaction effect reported later in this paper.
- *Correlation vs. causation*. There may be systematic differences in the non-measured characteristics of the agile and the non-agile software projects. In particular, it may be that the client and/or provider competence was higher for those using one type of development method, e.g., providers and clients using agile methods may have been more competent than those using non-agile methods. This will exaggerate the effect of a development method if the most competent clients and providers are more likely to choose the better development method. As with role bias, the direction of the interaction effects from project size is less likely to be affected by such differences.
- *Few observations*. There are few projects for several combinations of development method and project size category, in particular for the non-agile projects. The low statistical power means that tests of the statistical significance of the interaction effect on the development method are not feasible. It also implies that there are limitations regarding the robustness of our results and that small to medium large differences in success rates are caused by random variance in outcomes. Our results should consequently be understood as initial, exploratory results to be followed up with more empirical research.
- *Size vs. complexity*. We categorize project size based on the project's budget. While the budget is likely to reflect the amount of effort spent, it does not necessarily reflect the complexity of the project. There may consequently be relevant differences between large and simple, and large and complex software projects that our analysis is unable to identify.

2.3 Results

The results section emphasizes key takeaways from our study, especially those related to the connection between project size, development method and project outcome.

Table 1 gives the proportion of observations per budget and development method category. It shows that agile and partly agile methods are frequently used even for the largest projects. They are used in 33% and 56% of the largest projects, respectively. While this does not say anything about the usefulness or harm of using agile methods as project size increases, it documents that many of the software professionals involved considered agile and partly agile development methods to be useful for larger projects. Notice the increase in use of partly agile as the project size increases from medium to large. This may suggest that some software professionals believe less in working fully agile when projects get large.

Table 1. Proportion use of development method per budget size category

Budget size	Agile	Partly agile	Not agile	# projects
Small	37% (18)	42% (20)	21% (10)	48
Medium	58% (15)	19% (5)	23% (6)	26
Large	33% (9)	56% (15)	11% (3)	27
# projects	42	40	19	101

Table 2 and Figs. 1, 2, 3, 4 and 5 show the interacting effect of development methods on the connection between project size and:

(i)   Proportion of acceptable projects (Fig. 1)
(ii) Proportion of successful projects (Fig. 2)
(iii) Mean score for client benefits (Fig. 3)
(iv) Mean score for cost control (Fig. 4)
(v)   Mean score for time control (Fig. 5)

The scores of the success dimensions are coded with 4 for successful, 3 for acceptable, 2 for unsuccessful, and 1 for failed projects. This scale is, according to measurement theory, an ordinal scale. We believe, nevertheless, that the mean scores (which strictly speaking require at least an interval scale) give a good indication of the typical outcome regarding client benefits, cost control, and time control.

Our results do not support the claim that projects using agile or partly agile methods do worse than non-agile methods on larger projects. Quite the opposite, the data indicates that large projects using agile or partly agile methods were more likely to be assessed as acceptable than medium large projects using these methods. The non-agile projects performed reasonably well for the smallest projects, just a little worse than the agile and partly agile projects, but very badly on the medium and large software projects. In fact, among the non-agile projects of medium and large size, there were no projects in our data set that met the criterion of being perceived acceptable or better on all success criteria. Although consisting of a small sample, only nine projects used non-agile methods for medium and large projects; this weakly indicates that it is non-agile rather than agile methods that have most problems with larger software projects. This result—i.e., that non-agile methods score relatively poorly compared to agile projects and that the performance difference increases as the project size increases—is similar to that reported in the Standish Group's Chaos Report for 2016.

For most of the measures, there were not much difference in the assessed outcome for projects using agile and only partly agile. The most notable exceptions were projects assessed to be successful in all three dimensions (Fig. 2), wherein agile performed better than partly agile for large, but worse for medium large projects.

Table 2. Success with use of development method per budget size category

Budget size	Agile	Partly agile	Not agile
Total success (% acceptable)			
Small	72%	60%	60%
Medium	46%	40%	0%
Large	67%	60%	0%
Total success (% successful)			
Small	28%	10%	10%
Medium	7%	20%	0%
Large	11%	7%	0%
Client benefits (mean score)			
Small	3.5	3.1	3.1
Medium	3.3	3.4	3.0
Large	3.4	2.8	2.3
Cost control (mean score)			
Small	3.2	2.9	2.9
Medium	3.5	2.8	1.8
Large	3.4	2.9	1.0
Time control (mean score)			
Small	3.3	3.3	2.8
Medium	2.9	2.6	1.7
Large	2.8	2.9	2.5

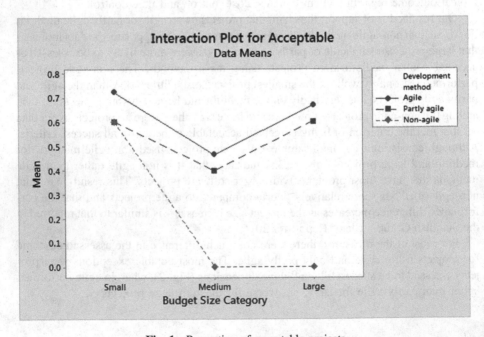

Fig. 1. Proportion of acceptable projects

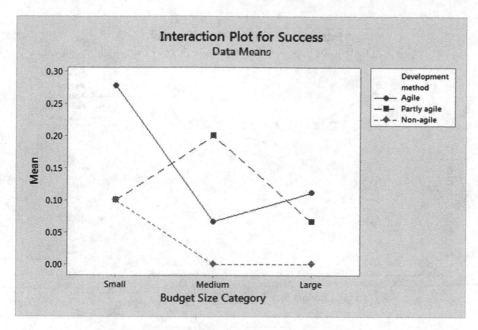

Fig. 2. Proportion of successful projects

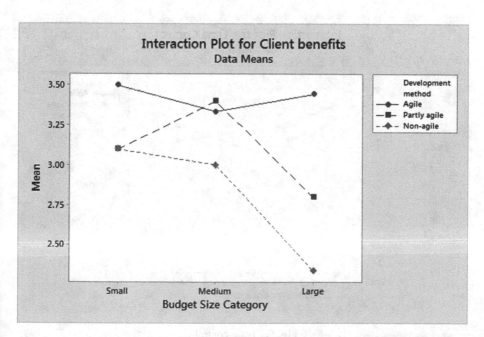

Fig. 3. Client benefits

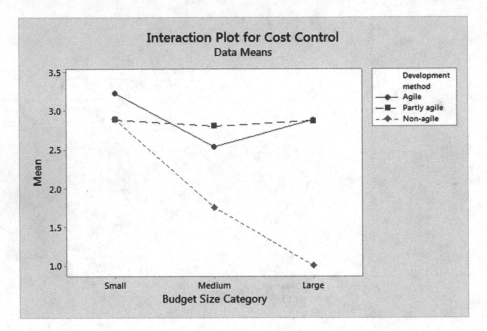

Fig. 4. Cost control

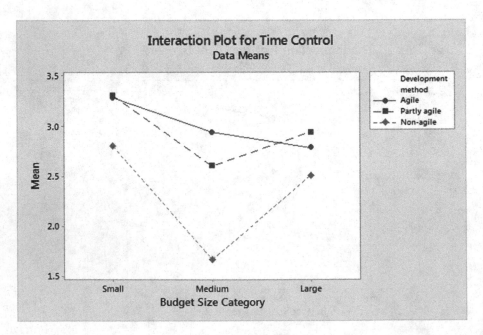

Fig. 5. Time control

3 Discussion and Conclusion

There are reasonable arguments both in favour and against good performance of agile methods on large projects. An example of an argument in favour of their use is that it is increasingly more unlikely that requirements will remain stable as the size of the software project increases. The understanding of needs is likely to change during the course of the project, and there will most likely be external changes leading to requirement changes. Agile development methods, implementing a process where change is a more integrated part, may consequently be better able to deal with the high requirement volatility of many large projects [10, 14]. An example of an argument sometimes used against the use of agile methods on large software projects is that the lack of upfront planning and architectural thinking, make projects more risky with increasing size.[7] Consequently, it is possible to analytically argue in favour of both agile and more plan-driven, non-agile software development methods. To find out which argumentation in practice is the stronger, and whether agile methods typically are good for large projects, requires empirical evidence.

The results from this study do this and provide evidence about how projects with agile practices perform on important success criteria. As pointed out in Sect. 2.2 there are several threats to the validity of our results, but the results do give some evidence in support of that the typical medium and large software projects using agile practices perform acceptably on essential success criteria. This was not the case for typical software projects using non-agile methods in our data set. Consequently, our data suggests that the question is not so much whether agile methods work well for large software projects, but rather how well non-agile software development methods work for such projects. Large projects are inherently risky, and our data suggests that the failure risk is reduced rather than increased with the use of agile methods instead of non-agile methods.

References

1. Dybå, T., Dingsøyr, T.: Empirical studies of agile software development: a systematic review. Inf. Softw. Technol. **50**(9), 833–859 (2008)
2. Jalali, S., Wohlin, C.: Global software engineering and agile practices: a systematic review. J. Softw. Evol. Process **24**(6), 643–659 (2012)
3. Khalid, H., et al.: Systematic literature review of agile scalability for large scale projects. Int. J. Adv. Comput. Sci. Appl. (IJACSA) **6**(9), 63–75 (2015)
4. Turk, D., France, R., Rumpe, B.: Limitations of agile software processes. arXiv preprint arXiv:1409.6600 (2014)
5. Dikert, K., Paasivaara, M., Lassenius, C.: Challenges and success factors for large-scale agile transformations: a systematic literature review. J. Syst. Softw. **119**, 87–108 (2016)

---

[7] See for example: www.6point6.co.uk/an-agile-agenda, which predicts that UK is wasting 37 billion GBP annually on failed agile projects. This number is based on a survey of CIOs, suggesting a 12% complete failure rate of agile projects. They did not calculate the waste on failed non-agile projects.

6. Dingsøyr, T., et al.: Exploring software development at the very large-scale: a revelatory case study and research agenda for agile method adaptation. Empir. Softw. Eng. **23**, 490–520 (2016)
7. Lagerberg, L., et al.: The impact of agile principles and practices on large-scale software development projects: a multiple-case study of two projects at ericsson. In: ESEM 2013. IEEE, Baltimore (2013)
8. Ebert, C., Paasivaara, M.: Scaling agile. IEEE Softw. **34**(6), 98–103 (2017)
9. Elshamy, A., Elssamadisy, A.: Applying agile to large projects: new agile software development practices for large projects. In: Concas, G., Damiani, E., Scotto, M., Succi, G. (eds.) XP 2007. LNCS, vol. 4536, pp. 46–53. Springer, Heidelberg (2007). https://doi.org/10.1007/978-3-540-73101-6_7
10. Jørgensen, M., Mohagheghi, P., Grimstad, S.: Direct and indirect connections between type of contract and software project outcome. Int. J. Proj. Manag. **35**(8), 1573–1586 (2017)
11. Dingsøyr, T., Fægri, T.E., Itkonen, J.: What Is large in large-scale? *A taxonomy of scale for agile software development*. In: Jedlitschka, A., Kuvaja, P., Kuhrmann, M., Männistö, T., Münch, J., Raatikainen, M. (eds.) PROFES 2014. LNCS, vol. 8892, pp. 273–276. Springer, Cham (2014). https://doi.org/10.1007/978-3-319-13835-0_20
12. Jørgensen, M.: Myths and over-simplifications in software engineering. Lect. Notes Softw. Eng. **1**(1), 7–11 (2013)
13. Jørgensen, M., Moløkken-Østvold, K.: How large are software cost overruns? A review of the 1994 CHAOS report. Inf. Softw. Technol. **48**(4), 297–301 (2006)
14. Jørgensen, M.: A survey on the characteristics of projects with success in delivering client benefits. Inf. Softw. Technol. **78**, 83–94 (2016)

Learning in the Large - An Exploratory Study of Retrospectives in Large-Scale Agile Development

Torgeir Dingsøyr[1,3(✉)], Marius Mikalsen[1], Anniken Solem[2], and Kathrine Vestues[3]

[1] Department of Software Engineering, Safety and Security, SINTEF, 7465 Trondheim, Norway
{torgeir.dingsoyr,marius.mikaelsen}@sintef.no
[2] SINTEF Technology and Society, SINTEF, 7465 Trondheim, Norway
anniken.solem@sintef.no
[3] Department of Computer and Information Science, Norwegian University of Science and Technology, Trondheim, Norway
kathrine.vestues@ntnu.no

Abstract. Many see retrospectives as the most important practice of agile software development. Previous studies of retrospectives have focused on process and outcome at team level. In this article, we study how a large-scale agile development project uses retrospectives through an analysis of retrospective reports identifying a total of 109 issues and 36 action items as a part of a longitudinal case study. We find that most of the issues identified relate to team-level learning and improvement, and discuss these findings in relation to current advice to improve learning outcome in large-scale agile development.

Keywords: Agile software development · Software engineering
Teamwork · Team performance · Post mortem review · Reflection
Learning · Process improvement

1 Introduction

Retrospective meetings are extremely important in agile methods. The Agile Practice Guide describes them as *"the single most important practice in agile development"* [1] and in his much read book on Scrum and XP, Kniberg states that retrospectives are the *"number-one-most-important thing in Scrum"* [2]. According to the 11th State of Agile report [3], the retrospective is the third most used agile practice. We find many suggestions on how to conduct retrospectives in the agile practitioner literature such as [4, 5] and online[1].

The purpose of retrospectives is to explore the work results of a team in an iteration or a phase in order to *"learn about, improve, and adapt its process"* [1]. The advice offered in the agile community has mainly focused on learning and improvement for

---

[1] See for example https://plans-for-retrospectives.com/en/?id=32-64-113-13-67 and http://www.funretrospectives.com/ and https://labs.spotify.com/2017/12/15/spotify-retro-kit/.

© The Author(s) 2018
J. Garbajosa et al. (Eds.): XP 2018, LNBIP 314, pp. 191–198, 2018.
https://doi.org/10.1007/978-3-319-91602-6_13

the team, while such practices also have a potential to provide learning both on the individual level and for a larger project or organization.

In this article, we focus on the practice of learning and improving through retrospectives in large-scale agile development. The research agenda for large-scale agile development has identified knowledge-sharing as an important topic [6]. This is a particularly challenging area of work, as such projects consists of several development teams with dependencies between teams and typically involve complex integration with existing ICT systems in projects that are critical for companies or societies [7].

We structure this article as follows: First, we provide background on studies of retrospective practices and prior studies on analysing content and effect of retrospectives and formulate research questions. Second, we present an exploratory case study and method for analysis of retrospectives. Third, we discuss what the retrospectives have addressed and what could be done to improve the learning outcome of retrospectives in the large and suggest directions for future research.

2 Background

Given the importance of retrospectives in agile development, the topic has received relatively little attention in scientific studies. A review of previous studies on IT retrospectives finds a multitude of definitions of retrospectives, descriptions of a number of outcomes, different practices described, and *"no project retrospective measurements given to confirm [...] whether outcomes have been successfully achieved"* [8].

Kniberg [2] describes a retrospective practice as a team exercise lasting 1–3 h where a team identifies what has been «good», what «could have been better» and «improvements», and suggest voting on the improvements to focus on in the next iteration. The practices described in the research literature [8] typically involve additional steps, for example including root cause analysis in order to analyse topics identified before deciding on action items to include in the next iteration.

In a study of retrospective practices at team level, Lethinen et al. [9] found that most discussions were related to topics close to and controllable by the team, but that topics that could not be resolved at the team level due to their complexity nevertheless recurred over time.

Many previous studies have seen retrospectives as an arena for reflection to enable learning and process improvement [10]. Andryiani et al. [11] studied retrospectives with a framework describing stages of reflection as reporting, responding, relating, reasoning and reconstructing. A finding is that agile teams may not achieve all levels of reflection simply by performing retrospective meetings. The study found that *"important aspects discussed in retrospective meetings include identifying and discussing obstacles, discussing feelings, analysing previous action points, identifying background reasons, identifying future action points and generating a plan"* [11].

We have not been able to identify studies of retrospectives in large-scale development, but a blog post describes how Spotify conducted large-scale retrospectives[2]

---

[2] https://labs.spotify.com/2015/11/05/large-scale-retros/.

in «one big room» in a format similar to world café [12]. Advice in one of the large-scale development frameworks, Large-Scale Scrum (LeSS),[3] is to hold an «overall retrospective» after team retrospectives, to discuss cross-team and system-wide issues, and to create improvement experiments.

We do not know of studies investigating the learning effect of retrospectives, but a summary of relevant theories of learning such as Argyris and Schön's theory of learning and Wenger's communities of practice can be found in one overview article [13], which discusses learning on individual-, team-, and organizational level. Argyris and Schön distinguish between smaller improvement («single loop learning») and more thorough learning («double loop learning»).

In this explorative study, we ask the following research questions: *1. How are retrospectives used in a large-scale agile development project? 2. What could be done to improve the learning outcome of retrospectives in large-scale agile projects?*

3   Method

We are currently conducting a longitudinal case study [14] of a large-scale development project. The case was selected as it is one of the largest development projects in Scandinavia, and is operating in a complex environment with heavy integration with other ICT systems.

The customer organization has 19 000 employees, and close to 300 ICT systems. A new solution will require changes to 26 other systems. The project uses a stage-gate delivery model with 4 stages (analysis of needs, solution description, construction, and approval, similar to a previous project described in [15]). We followed the first release, with 37 developers in four development teams. Teams had a Scrum-master, one or two application architects, one or two testers, and up to ten developers. The project uses the Scrum-method, with three-week iterations, starting with a planning meeting and ending with a demo and retrospective.

The project has three main releases, and this article is based on an analysis of minutes of meetings from 10 retrospectives in the first release. The minutes include iterations 3 to 9, with an exception of iteration 6, when no retrospective was held due to summer holidays. The minutes cover a 5-month period.

We have limited the study to an analysis of retrospective minutes from two of the four teams. The minutes describe who were present in the face-to-face meeting, a list of issues that went well, a list of issues that could be improved and most often a list of action items. The length of the minutes varied from half a page to two pages. The minutes were posted in the project wiki.

We all read three minutes individually, and then jointly established a set of categories, taken from the Scrum guide[4], which describes the purpose of the sprint retrospective as an arena for inspecting how the last sprint went with regards to the categories «people», «relationships» (merged with people), «process», and «tools».

---

[3] https://less.works/less/framework/index.html.

[4] http://www.scrumguides.org/.

We added the categories «project» and «other teams» to specifically address the large-scale level. These categories were used to code issues and action items.

4   Results

The analysis of minutes from retrospectives in Table 1 shows the issues recorded by the teams during the seven iterations. Most issues were related to «process» (41) and «people and relationships» (30). In the following, we describe issues that emerged in selected categories, and then present the resulting action items as recorded in the minutes.

Table 1. Issues that went well and issues that could be better. In total 109 issues were recorded during seven iterations for two teams. Roughly 40% of issues were statements on issues that went well and 60% about issues that could be improved.

	Iteration 3	Iteration 4	Iteration 5	Iteration 6	Iteration 8	Iteration 9	Iteration 10	Sum
Process	7	3	7	8	5	7	4	41
People & relationships	1	1	13	5	4	6	0	30
Other topics	1	2	3	0	2	2	2	12
Project	0	0	4	0	1	3	2	10
Tools	1	0	3	1	1	1	2	9
Other teams	2	0	1	2	2	0	0	7

Due to space limitations, the following results describe the issues we found relating to the categories that shed most light on how large-scale agile development influences the teams. These are «process» (41 reported issues), «project» (10 reported issues) and «other teams» (7 reported issues).

In terms of *process*, there were issues such as that the build breaks too often, design takes too much capacity from the team, that they would like more consistent use of branching in Git (tool for version control and code sharing), and that frequent check-ins makes it difficult to terminate feature-branches. The following excerpt illustrates how process issues manifest: "*A lot of red in Jenkins [a continuous integration tool], which makes it difficult to branch from «develop»*". Other issues were concerned with quality control and routines in the team, such as the need for better control and routines for branching of the code, need for more code reviews, too many and messy Jira (issue tracker) tasks, and architects have limited time to follow up on development. Issues concerning lack of structure for bug reporting were reported as such: "*Structure concerning tests, bugs are reported in all possible ways – Mails – Skype – face to face, very difficult to follow up and have continuity in test/bugfix etc.*"

Project issues are related to the overall organisation of the project as a whole. Such issues were far less frequently reported, and those we found included having updated requirements for user stories when entering sprints, that solutions designs should be more detailed, product backlog elements should be ready before sprint start, and addressing how developers move between teams. The following illustrates how one team reports the need for more technical meetings between teams on a project level: *"Review of code/project, all meetings are about organisation, but it should be one meeting about how our code/setup/project looks from a technical perspective"*.

Finally, for the category *other teams*, i.e. how teams interact in a multi-team setting, we found how there were issues with regard to how teams "takes instructions" from several different parties, and how there was challenges in detecting dependencies in the code before you develop and test. The following excerpt from the retrospective minutes illustrates how one team is not involved sufficiently in the planning of refactoring: *"We want to be notified in advance when there are big refactorings or other significant changes in the codebase, before it happens"*.

The retrospective minutes also contains actions decided on by the teams. In total, the two teams identified 36 action items, where most were related to «process» and to «other topics». We show the distribution and provide examples of action items in Table 2.

Table 2. Action items from retrospective minutes according to topic.

Topic	Number	Example action items
Process	13	"Review and assign quality assurance tasks during daily stand-up."
Other topics	7	"We need a course on the «react» technology."
Tools	5	"More memory on the application development image."
People and relationships	5	"Organise an introduction round for new team members."
Project	4	"Have backlog items ready before an iteration starts."
Other teams	2	"Be more aware of dependencies when assigning tasks, make sure that other teams we depend on really give priority to these tasks."

5 Discussion

We return to discuss our two research questions, starting with *how are retrospectives used in a large-scale agile development project?*

We found that retrospectives were used at team level, where short meetings were facilitated by the scrum master and reported in minutes on the project wiki. Minutes were available to everyone in the project, including customer representatives.

Our analysis of topics addressed in the retrospectives shows that most of the issues identified as either «working well» or «could be improved» related to *process*, followed by *people and relationships*. In the «large-scale» categories *project* and *other teams* we found in total 17 issues of the total 109. However, as shown in the results, many of the issues described as *process* were related to the scale of the project, such as identifying challenges with the merging of code or detailing of specifications before development would start. We find, however, that teams mainly deal with team-internal issues in retrospectives.

The analysis of the action items shows that 6 of the 36 action items identified during the work on the release were in the «large-scale» categories. However, we see that some of the action items in the other categories are related to scale. One example is the item "organizing an introduction round for new team members" in the category *people and relations*, which describes an action item which would not be necessary on a single-team project. However, our impression is also here that most action items concern issues at the team level.

We have not been able to conduct an analysis of the effect of retrospectives at team level. We consider that such meetings give room to develop a common understanding of development process, tasks and what knowledge people in the team possess, what in organizational psychology is referred to as *shared mental models* [13] and have been shown to relate to team performance. A common critique of retrospectives is that teams meet and talk, but little of what is talked about is acted upon. We have not been able to assess how many of the 36 identified action items were acted upon, but found in one minute that "all action items suggested to the project management has been implemented". The 36 action items identified can be considered small improvement actions. Given the short time spent on retrospectives, they do not seem to facilitate «deep» learning («double loop» learning in Argyris and Schön's framework). Having minutes public could also lead to critique being toned down or removed completely.

This leads us to discussing our second research question - w*hat could be done to improve the learning outcome of retrospectives in large-scale agile projects?*

In the background we pinpointed particular challenges of large-scale agile development such as dealing with a high number of people and many dependencies [7]. A retrospective can be used for a number of purposes. Prior studies in organizational psychology suggest that in projects with many teams, the coordination between teams are more important than coordination within teams [16]. It is reason to believe it would be beneficial to focus attention on inter-team issues in large projects. The LeSS framework suggests organizing inter-team retrospectives directly after the team retrospectives. Alternatively, teams can be encouraged to particularly focus on inter-team issues as part of the team retrospectives. A challenge in the project studied is that the contract model used may hinder changes, for example the contract model specifies handover phases between companies involved in the *analysis of needs* phase and the *solution description* and *development phase*. However, given the limitations, it is important that the project adjusts work practice also on inter-team level to optimize use of limited resources.

This exploratory study has several limitations, where one is that we have only analysed minutes available on the project wiki from two of four teams.

6   Conclusion

Many in the agile community regard retrospectives as the single most important practice in agile development. It is therefore interesting to know more about how retrospectives are practiced in large-scale development where there is a dire need to learn and improve as many participants are new to the project, the customer organization, and to the development domain. We found that short retrospectives were conducted at team level and mostly addressed issues at the team-level. The action items mainly addressed team level issues. Most actions also seem to relate to smaller improvements, what Argyris and Schön call «single-loop learning».

A large-scale project will benefit from learning and improvement on the project level, and this would be strengthened by following the advice from LeSS by facilitating retrospectives at the project level. Further, to shift learning effects towards «double-loop learning», we suggest that more time is devoted to the retrospectives.

In the future, we would like to initiate retrospectives at the inter-team level, explore the types of issues that are raised, and also gain more knowledge about perceptions of retrospectives by interviewing project participants.

Acknowledgement. This work was conducted in the project Agile 2.0 supported by the Research Council of Norway through grant 236759 and by the companies Kantega, Kongsberg Defence & Aerospace, Sopra Steria, Statoil and Sticos.

References

1. Project Management Institute and Agile Allience: Agile Practice Guide: Project Management Institute (2017)
2. Kniberg, H.: Scrum and XP from the Trenches, 2nd edn. InfoQ (2015)
3. Version One: 11th State of Agile Report (2016)
4. Derby, E., Larsen, D.: Agile Retrospectives: Making Good Teams Great. The Pragmatic Bookshelf (2006)
5. Kua, P.: The Retrospective Handbook (2013). E-book available at: https://leanpub.com/the-retrospective-handbook
6. Moe, N.B., Dingsøyr, T.: Emerging research themes and updated research agenda for large-scale agile development: a summary of the 5th international workshop at XP 2017. Presented at the Proceedings of the XP 2017 Scientific Workshops, Cologne, Germany (2017)
7. Rolland, K.H., Fitzgerald, B., Dingsøyr, T., Stol, K.-J.: Problematizing agile in the large: alternative assumptions for large-scale agile development. In: International Conference on Information Systems, Dublin, Ireland (2016)
8. Skinner, R., Land, L., Chin, W., Nelson, R.R.: Reviewing the Past for a Better Future: Reevaluating the IT Project Retrospective (2015)
9. Lehtinen, T.O., Itkonen, J., Lassenius, C.: Recurring opinions or productive improvements—what agile teams actually discuss in retrospectives. Empirical Softw. Eng. **22**, 2409–2452 (2017)
10. Babb, J., Hoda, R., Norbjerg, J.: Embedding reflection and learning into agile software development. IEEE Softw. **31**, 51–57 (2014)
11. Andriyani, Y.: knowledge management and reflective practice in daily stand-up and retrospective meetings. In: Baumeister, H., Lichter, H., Riebisch, M. (eds.) XP 2017. LNBIP, vol. 283, pp. 285–291. Springer, Cham (2017). https://doi.org/10.1007/978-3-319-57633-6_21
12. Brown, J., Isaacs, D.: The world cafe: Shaping our futures through conversations that matter. Berrett-Koehler Publishers Inc., San Francisco (2005)
13. Dingsøyr, T.: Postmortem reviews: purpose and approaches in software engineering. Inf. Softw. Technol. **47**, 293–303 (2005)

14. Runeson, P., Höst, M.: Guidelines for conducting and reporting case study research in software engineering. Empirical Softw. Eng. **14**, 131–164 (2009)
15. Dingsøyr, T., Moe, N.B., Fægri, T.E., Seim, E.A.: Exploring software development at the very large-scale: a revelatory case study and research agenda for agile method adaptation. Empirical Softw. Eng. **22**, 1–31 (2017)
16. Marks, M.A., Dechurch, L.A., Mathieu, J.E., Panzer, F.J., Alonso, A.: Teamwork in multiteam systems. J. Appl. Psychol. **90**, 964 (2005)

Reporting in Agile Portfolio Management: Routines, Metrics and Artefacts to Maintain an Effective Oversight

Christoph Johann Stettina[1,2,3(✉)] and Lennard Schoemaker[2]

[1] Centre for Innovation The Hague, Leiden University,
Schouwburgstraat 2, 2511 VA The Hague, Netherlands
c.j.stettina@fgga.leidenuniv.nl
[2] Leiden Institute of Advanced Computer Science, Leiden University,
Niels Bohrweg 1, 2333 CA Leiden, Netherlands
lennardschoemaker@gmail.com
[3] Accenture B.V., Liquid Studio,
Orteliuslaan 1000, 3528 BD Utrecht, Netherlands

Abstract. In a world where the speed of change is faster than ever, a growing number of organisations adopts Agile Portfolio Management (APM) to connect their agile teams to business strategy. A domain which has been little explored in literature and professional frameworks. Based on 14 interviews conducted in 10 large European organisations, in this paper we report the preliminary results of our study on reporting routines, artefacts and metrics in Agile Portfolio Management. In our findings we discuss the three generic domains of reporting responsibility and the novel types of reporting routines found in practice. Further, we use the concept of boundary objects to recommend which types of artefacts are effective for which reporting routines.

Keywords: Agile portfolio management · Agile reporting
PPM reporting

1 Introduction

In a world of ever-faster emerging societal and technological advancements, companies need to timely adjust their portfolio of products and services - to adapt to rapidly changing market demand, and to cope with an increasingly entrepreneurial competition [1]. Agile Portfolio Management (APM), as a potential solution, defines the heartbeat in connecting strategy to operations through the selection, prioritisation and review of initiatives an organisation executes. Still, for large organisations with strong product and service development capabilities with 50 to 500 teams, managing and keeping a meaningful overview of their ventures is a challenging task.

© The Author(s) 2018
J. Garbajosa et al. (Eds.): XP 2018, LNBIP 314, pp. 199–215, 2018.
https://doi.org/10.1007/978-3-319-91602-6_14

Agile portfolio management is associated with the capability for a swift change of priorities across initiatives based on the faster delivery of intermediate outcomes and a better collaboration in and across teams [1]. Comparing to traditional project management approaches, agile methods put a focus on understanding the value created in context and rely heavily on direct communication and frequent reviews of intermediate results with users. It follows the ethos of the Agile Manifesto *'Working software is the primary measure of progress.'* [2].

To provide the right amount of oversight and select the right reporting approach is crucial for a successful and 'agile' connection of strategy to operations, especially due to the focus on the value delivered. Authors like Müller et al. [3] point out how project and programme reporting influences the performance of portfolio management. Yet, current literature pays little attention to creating and managing oversight in portfolios in such dynamic environments [4]. Furthermore, while the origins of portfolio management lie in managing portfolios of financial assets, project selection and reporting often still follows predominantly ad hoc or financial metrics [5], or considers projects in isolation [4]. How to maintain a meaningful oversight effectively when the knowledge expands towards the boundaries of a dozen teams remains a question.

In this paper we present the findings of our study on reporting approaches, artefacts and metrics in large organisations applying agile methods within their portfolios. The remainder of the paper is organised as follows: First, we discuss the gap in existing literature and formulate our question. Second, we describe our approach and descriptive results. Then, we reflect on our findings in light of existing literature.

2   Related Work

In the following subsections, we will provide an overview of the existing literature on Portfolio Management (PPM) and Agile Portfolio Management (APM) along with the reporting of portfolio management, and include an evaluation of the current gap in the literature.

2.1   Connecting Organisational Strategy to IT Development Initiatives Through Agile Portfolio Management

Portfolio management deals with the question which initiatives an organisation should pursue and how to connect those to strategic goals. Cooper et al. [5] define the goals of portfolio management as follows: (1) to maximise return on R&D and technology; (2) To maintain the business's competitive position; (3) to properly allocate scarce resources; (4) to forge the link between project selection and business strategy; (5) to achieve a stronger focus; (6) To yield the right balance of projects and investments; (7) to communicate project priorities both vertically and horizontally within the organisation; (8) to provide greater objectivity in project selection.

Agile Portfolio Management differs from traditional Project Portfolio management as it succeeds agile software development frameworks, while traditional Project Portfolio Management (PPM) is based on principles to manage financial portfolios. Agile methods such as Scrum challenge portfolio and programme reporting in existing, especially large, organisations due to a faster and more frequent delivery of intermediate results, different roles, and a different mindset [1]. The increased delivery of intermediate results requires faster feedback loops in domains outside individual projects, such as portfolio management [1,6]. This challenges the traditional view on project portfolio management which, once selected, focuses on managing projects in isolation [4].

In a first cross-case study comparing the application of agile portfolio management in 14 large organisations to existing literature and professional frameworks, Stettina and Hörz [1] point at the characteristics of agile portfolio management as (1) transparency of resources and work items, improving trust, decision-making, and resource allocation; (2) collaboration, close collaboration based on routinised interaction and artefacts enabling frequent feedback-loops across the domains; (3) commitment to strategically managed portfolios; (4) team orientation, removing unrest in resource allocation and building capabilities in teams.

While there is an extensive body of knowledge on Project Portfolio Management, existing literature pays little attention to portfolios of initiatives in agile and dynamic environments [4]. The origins of PPM in financial models can be still traced to a dominance of financial metrics and indices in portfolio decision-making [7]. Cooper et al. [5] found that the use of financial models alone yields poorer portfolio results. They advise the application of strategic methods and scoring approaches compared to financial and quantitative indicators only. Cooper et al. [8] describe two main approaches to project portfolio review in new product development: a (1) 'gates dominate', and a (2) 'portfolio dominates' approach. In a 'gate-dominated' project portfolio management approach, senior management will evaluate individual projects within a portfolio and will make Go/Kill decisions at these gates. In a portfolio review dominated approach, the projects within a portfolio are competing with each other.

2.2 Maintaining a Meaningful and Effective Oversight Practice Across Initiatives Pursued Throughout a Portfolio of Agile Teams

Reporting is considered to be one of the main process areas in portfolio management and is positively associated with portfolio success [3].

Empirical literature on reporting in agile portfolio management is scarce. Existing contributions discuss reporting as providing visibility across projects [9]. Oversight [10] and metrics [11] are frequently mentioned as two of the domains affected by implementing agile portfolio management. Characteristics associated with the practice include transparency of resources and work items and close collaboration based on routinised interaction and artefacts enabling frequent feedback-loops [1,6]

Metrics are generally considered to be an integral part of reporting, contributing to the success of the entire portfolio. Vähäniitty [6] points out that performance metrics and incentives should not encourage local optimisation within a portfolio. In practitioner literature, Leffingwell [12] and Krebs [13] provide practical recommendations for different metric types. In his book, Krebs [13] describes three types of metrics as (1) progress, (2) team morale, and (3) quality (compare [13] p. 67). Leffingwell [12] describes (1) employee engagement, (2) customer satisfaction, (3) productivity, (4) agility, (5) time to market, (6) quality, (7) partner health (compare [12] p. 308). While existing literature points at possible metrics and artefacts to embed those, empirical evidence is lacking.

Project Management Offices (PMO), or Project Portfolio Management Offices (PPMO), traditionally serve as a supporting function, providing oversight across the pursued initiatives across the portfolio, e.g. by collecting project information and updates from respective teams and preparing it for management. Tengshe and Noble [11] describe the changing role of a PMO when adopting agile methods, by providing means of continuous improvement, training and coaching across projects and portfolios. Rautiainen et al. [9] describe their case of setting up a portfolio of agile teams with the help of a PMO to provide transparency, helping to reduce duplicate projects and aligning projects to strategy.

More recently, software tooling is proposed to support automated reports across agile teams in programmes and portfolios [6]. However, an empirical perspective beyond individual cases on what reporting practices are applied in practice and the interaction of practices with reporting artefacts and metrics is missing.

2.3   Taking the Perspective of Knowledge Boundaries to Understand Effective Reporting in Agile Portfolio Management

Reporting practices can be, analogously to documentation, considered as a knowledge conversion practice [14]. While there is little academic literature on reporting in agile portfolio management, there is a growing number of contributions on documentation and knowledge transfer across agile teams (compare [15,16]).

Project reporting and reviewing relies on knowledge transfer across different teams and different functions such as finance, product development or portfolio management. To convey knowledge across different domains or boundaries, agile methods rely heavily on frequent feedback loops based on direct face-to-face communication, but they also require the right artefacts in context to support a sustainable and effective knowledge transfer [15]. Similar to project handovers [16] or documentation practices [15], reporting relies on man-made artefacts such as marketing reports, financial status, portfolio updates, or retrospective reports. Such artefacts crossing different boundaries of knowledge, such as portfolio management, product management or software development, are considered 'boundary objects' [17].

Knowledge boundaries are both "a source of and a barrier to innovation" [18]. Innovation often happens on the boundaries of knowledge as stated by Leonard [19]. In order to create new products and service, agile teams need to effectively cross knowledge boundaries. Agile methods such as Scrum are based on cross-functional teams, which effectively cross knowledge boundaries through direct, face-to-face communication. However, when embedding agile teams in a wider organisational context, such as a portfolio management process, such teams effectively create new knowledge boundaries which need to be bridged effectively.

Carlile [18] describes knowledge boundaries in new product development, such as in Agile Software Development, and three distinct approaches move knowledge across boundaries: (1) the syntactic; (2) the semantic; and (3) the pragmatic approaches.

The *syntactic* approach deals with establishing a shared and stable syntax to enable accurate communication between sender and receiver [18]. Once a syntax is established, crossing the boundary becomes a knowledge transfer problem. Examples for boundary objects crossing the syntactic boundary are repositories storing the information using a previously agreed syntax. In the context of portfolio management, such repositories might be tools documenting a team's development progress, or the status of schedules and budgets collected over time.

The *semantic* approach acknowledges that despite a shared language or syntax, different interpretations can occur. Different worlds of thought and areas of interest exist across different functions and teams within an organisation. For example, a software development team is interested in a high-quality and bug-free software, while product and portfolio managers are interested in a product that is commercially viable. Examples of boundary objects to cross a semantic boundary are standardised forms and methods. Using a User Story template, for example, allows to translate and store user requirements in a template understandable to business. Especially, when compared to traditional requirements documentation which often use a very technical language.

At the *pragmatic* knowledge boundary the parties involved need to be willing to understand, negotiate and alternate their knowledge [17]. Product and portfolio management, for example, needs to be willing to alternate their plans based on new technical possibilities given by the development team. Teams need to be willing to (re)align their work to new strategic priorities for new and existing product lines, or communicate and negotiate work based on discovered interdependencies with other teams. Example of a pragmatic boundary object is a Program Board used in SAFe [12].

The interaction of reporting practices, the involved artefacts crossing boundaries of knowledge, and the concrete metrics applied, can thus be considered important when studying reporting in agile portfolio management.

2.4   Gap in the Literature and Research Question

Following the state of art reviewed in the previous subsection, we would now like to reflect on the gap in the literature and the resulting objectives for this study.

To summarise, the existing literature points out that: Firstly, project portfolio management is associated with overall success on R&D organisations [8], and reporting is positively associated with portfolio success [3]. Secondly, findings from organisations employing agile practices imply that higher frequency of interaction, thus also reporting, is required in agile portfolio management [1]. And thirdly, the interplay of routines and artefacts is important for a good and sustainable agile practice [15].

In light of the existing literature we would like to pose the following research question to guide our study: *What are reporting routines, metrics and artefacts applied in Agile Portfolio Management?*

3 Method

Considering the limitations of the available literature, it was felt that an explorative study would best be suited to this new topic. As is common in the study of management practices in real-world contexts, we chose the design of our casestudy research the model proposed by Yin [20]. The data collection for the case studies was carried out by conducting semi-structured interviews with professionals working in large organisations that have agile portfolio management or are in the process of moving towards an agile portfolio management process. We chose a multiple case-study protocol with the aim of drawing more robust and generic findings which would have an impact on building a theory [20]. In the following subsection we will elaborate our case study protocol.

Case Selection. Interviews for this study were conducted with professionals working in organisations that complied with our case selection criteria and which were part of the portfolio management process. In order to find suitable organisations matching our criteria we used our own network, referrals and online reports. After identifying suitable organisations, we used own network, referrals as well as LinkedIn Premium to identify the candidates. The following case selection criteria were applied: (1) The organisation has at least 250 full-time employees (FTE). (2) The organisation uses agile methods with stable Scrum or Kanban teams (3) The organisation has a portfolio/programme management process with at least one portfolio. (4) The organisation has a portfolio reporting process. (5) The organisation has at least three teams working with agile methods. (6) The interviewee is directly involved in the portfolio management process of the organisation.

Data Collection: Semi-structured Active Interviews. The interviews took place between July 2016 and December 2016, each taking between 40 and 80 min. Most interviews were conducted face-to-face at the organisation. The interview guide consisted of the following main sections: (1) General Information regarding interviewee and organisation; (2) Project Management, Portfolio Management, Agile Portfolio Management; (3) Project Portfolio Management Office; and (4) Reporting. Example questions were: *What are some of the common methods that you use within your organisation on portfolio level? What does your reporting process look like at initiative/project level? How does your reporting process* *look like at portfolio level? Could you write down a step-by-step guide to your reporting process? On a scale of 1 to 5, how satisfied are you with your portfolio reporting process? Which reporting activities and artefacts do you consider to be agile? Do you have a PMO? What are the functions of your PMO?*

Data Analysis. All interviews were digitally recorded and transcribed with the consent of the interviewees. The analysis started by creating a case description of each organisation and an overview of all case characteristics. After creating case summaries we tabulated the data on artefacts and metrics to allow for cross-case comparison. The data from the process-related questions on project and initiative level was organised into narrative fragments and translated into process diagrams. The analysis of the data took place in close discussions with the two authors in the period between February and October 2017.

4   Results

For this study, a total of 14 people were interviewed from different organisations across multiple sectors, sizes and countries. This chapter provides an overview of all gathered data and any additional observations that were made.

Overview Cases. An overview of case organisations is presented in Table 1. The majority of our cases were large organisations with thousands of employees and a large IT portfolio, predominantly in the private sector. A large majority use a monthly reporting practice, based on Gates-driven reporting.

All case organisations reported applying Scrum as their main delivery method, partially supported by Kanban and Lean practices. Case organisations use different *agile at large* models connecting Scrum in the organisational setting. Two out of the 10 case organisations, case B, and E, mentioned that they used SAFe as the starting point for defining their agile portfolio management process. There were several participants who also mentioned SAFe as a framework that they would use in the future. Half of the case organisations in this study mentioned that they to some extent use PRINCE2. Case organisation B is somewhat of an exception when it comes to applying PRINCE2. The reason for this is that two people were interviewed from two different parts of the organisation.

We applied the agile transformation maturity model, with the stages *Beginner, Novice, Fluent, Advanced and World-class*, as proposed by Laanti [21] to determine portfolio maturity.

Reporting Practices. After creating process diagrams for each case organisations (see Fig. 1) we identified three distinct reporting approaches linked to the size and agile maturity of an organisation. Across our cases we found (1) Cadence-driven, (2) Tool-driven, and (3) PMO driven reporting approaches.

Organisations with a Cadence-driven reporting approach employ reporting activities that revolve around their development cadence and method, such as

Table 1. Case organisations and descriptive variables. (Scale for satisfaction with reporting process: 1 = Not at all satisfied, 2 = Slightly satisfied, 3 = Moderately satisfied, 4 = Very satisfied, 5 = Extremely satisfied)

#	Industry	Size (FTE)	PPM type	Review frequency	Actors	PPM maturity	Satisf. PPM reporting	Method
A	Telco	350	Gates	Bi-weekly	Management Team	Beginner	3/1	Scrum and SoS
B	Electronics	4500	PPM	Quarterly	PPM	Fluent	4/3	Scrum & SAFe
C	Telco	26000	Gates	Monthly	Board of Directors	Beginner	3	Scrum & MoP
D	Finance	650	Gates	Monthly	Steerco	Beginner	2	Scrum
E	Government	30000	PPM	Bi-weekly	Portfolio Board	Fluent	4	Scrum & SAFe
F	Aviation	2000	Gates	Monthly	CIO	Beginner	4	Scrum & Custom
G	IT Service	13000	Gates	Tri-weekly	Steerco	Beginner	2/4	Scrum & Spotify
H	Public Transport	30000	Gates	Bi-weekly	Portfolio Board	Beginner	1	Kanban & MoP
I	Logistics	11000	Gates	Monthly	Steerco/CIO	Beginner	1/4	Scrum & PMI
J	E-commerce	1100	PPM	Trimesterly	Management Team	Fluent	4	Scrum & Spotify

the bi-weekly Sprints in Scrum, or the Program Increments (PI) in SAFe [12]. In our cases, we found this mostly be Scrum, which in practice means a two-weekly reporting cadence based on a two-weekly Scrum sprint, and the 4 + 1 two-sprint cadence in SAFe.

Organisations with a PMO-driven reporting approach employ reporting activities that revolve around templates provided by project management frameworks like PRINCE2. In most case organisations this meant the manual creation of reports in the form of documents or spreadsheets. Cloud-based office suites like Microsoft OneDrive or Google Drive, or network drives are often used to store and share such reporting artefacts.

Organisations with a Tool-driven reporting approach employ reporting activities that are mostly high-level or on an ad hoc basis. In our case organisations, we found that day-to-day reporting activities are mostly automated with Tools like JIRA or CA Agile Central.

Artefacts. In the cross-case results we identified three types of reporting artefacts in practice[1] as follows:

1. *Tool-based artefacts.* Are reporting artefacts that live within a tool. Examples identified among the case organisations include collaboration software, automated test reports or dashboards. Examples are the tool based Portfolio board reports in org. E.

---

[1] While there are more artefacts involved in the software delivery cycle, (compare [16]), for the sake of focus in this study we only relate to artefacts related to the reporting process.

Case B

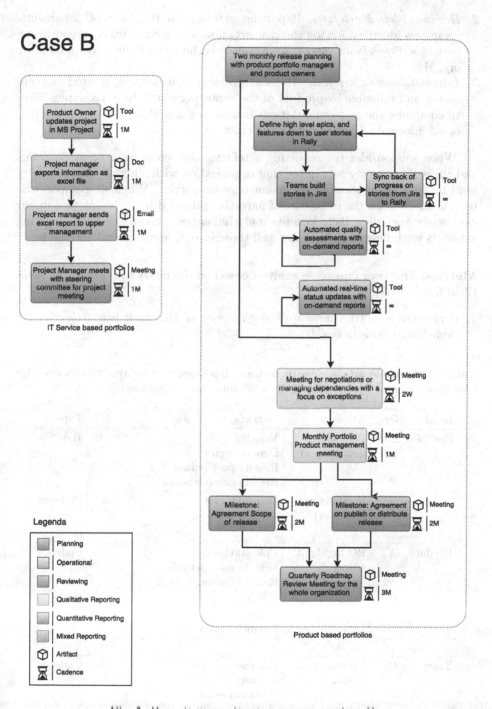

Fig. 1. Reporting practice in case organisation B

2. *Document-based artefacts.* Reporting artefacts in the form of documents. Examples identified among the case organisations include excel spreadsheets, text-files, PowerPoint sheets. An example is the project sheet maintained by org. H.
3. *Interaction-based artefacts.* Report artefacts that are not created but are rather an intangible by-product of the reporting interaction. Examples identified among the case organisations include insights shared during a meeting or an informal ad hoc update using chat.

When we consider the reporting artefacts, the reporting process diagrams and the agile maturity we can see that organisation with a higher agile maturity tend to limit the amount of document-based reporting. When we compare the used artefacts with the fragments of narrative provided by the employees in our case study regarding their benefits and challenges, we can see that reporting artefacts work best when they are well thought out, are used and add value.

Metrics. From our cross-case analysis based on the metrics in Table 2 we identified 5 metric types:

1. Performance metrics measure the efficiency of the work (e.g. velocity and cycle time trends in org. B)

Table 2. Example artefacts, with metrics, reporting routine type and knowledge boundaries crossed ($\leftrightarrow$ = syntactic; $\Leftrightarrow$ = semantic; ∞ = pragmatic)

Level	Org.	Artefact	Metric(s)	KB	Type
Portfolio	E	Portfolio board report	Velocity Dependencies Results past period Results coming period	$\Leftrightarrow$	Tool
	G	Portfolio wall (physical)	Dependencies	∞	Cadence
..	..	..	..	..	..
Product	A	PO highlight report	Epic status Results past period Results coming period	$\Leftrightarrow$	Cadence
	I	Project report	Milestones Progress Financial data	$\Leftrightarrow$	PMO
..	..	..	..	..	..
Team	G	Retrospective report	Forecast Velocity Work capacity % impediments Team happiness	$\Leftrightarrow$	Cadence
..	..	..	..	..	..

2. Quality metrics, measure the quality of the work (e.g. exceptions in org. B & D)
3. Progress metrics measure how far along you are with the work (e.g. velocity planned and realised in org. A)
4. Status metrics measure the current state of work (e.g. budget, resources)
5. Contextual metrics provide measurements and information on the work (e.g. project highlights in orgs. C, D and F, context descriptions)

5 Analysis and Discussion

Based on our data from the case organisations we will now discuss our findings in light of the existing literature.

5.1 Three Domains of Knowledge Responsibility: Product, Development and Process

Across our case organisations we identified three main domains of knowledge practice involved: (1) Product and portfolio responsibility, (2) Development, and (3) Process. We have depicted the three domains and their reporting relations in Fig. 2. As a product manager in Org. A. elaborated: *"..So it is mainly the demos, the happiness of the team members and the happiness of the stakeholders..".*

This reporting configuration fundamentally differs from other project management frameworks like PRINCE2, as the role of the traditional project manager is split up into a content, process and team responsibility in the roles of the Product Owner and Scrum Master. In the majority of our case organisations,

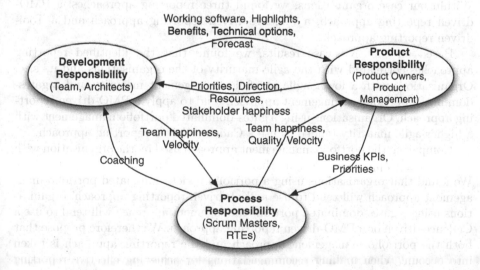

Fig. 2. Domains of reporting responsibility in Agile Portfolio Management

the team directly and frequently 'reports' to the business, demoing working software and other intermediate results at the end of each development cycle, rather than relying on ad hoc presentations, escalation meetings and intermediaries (e.g. PMO). For example as hinted by the Vice President of a product unit at Org. B.: *"..we had them [PMOs] but we got rid of them. We wanted the people in the teams to feel linked and part of the project. So we did not want the people to feel like they were a generic team, they had to feel product ownership. So we distributed the PMOs in the product teams. So every product team has a release management team, we work according to SAFe."*

Product and portfolio managers are concerned about how well the complete product performs from a business perspective, when they can expect a product to be released, and what technical options for future development there are. Product and Portfolio management needs to provide strategic vision, guidance, product priorities and resources to the team.

Development teams and software architects are concerned about the quality of the software they produce, dependencies with other teams, and the directions for a product line. Development teams are providing product demos and technical options.

Scrum masters and Release Train Engineers are concerned about the quality of the process, teamwork and the happiness of the teams involved in order to produce a good product or service. Those responsible for the process, such as Scrum Masters and release teams, guide the teams to allow for effective work and remove impediments.

5.2   Three Types of Reporting Routines: Cadence-, Tool-, and PMO-Driven

Within our case organisations, we found three reporting approaches: a PMO-driven reporting approach, a Cadence-driven reporting approach and a Tool-driven reporting approach.

Based on the cross-case results, we found that the identified reporting approaches correlated with the agile maturity of the organisations and its size. Organisations with a lower agile portfolio management maturity and a gates-dominated portfolio management approach tend to apply a PMO-driven reporting approach. Organisations using a gates-dominated portfolio management with a higher agile maturity tended to use a Cadence-driven reporting approach.

Comparing the portfolio management approach used by the organisation with the reporting approach shows us that there is a connection between the two. We found that organisations using a portfolio review-dominated portfolio management approach will tend to use a Tool-driven reporting approach. organisations using a gates-dominated portfolio management approach will tend to use a Cadence-driven or a PMO-driven reporting approach. We therefore propose that both the portfolio management approach and the reporting approach is taken into account when making recommendations for achieving effective reporting (Table 3).

Table 3. Identified portfolio reporting approaches and their characteristics

	PMO-driven	Cadence-driven	Tool-driven
Org. Size	Large	Medium to large	Large
Driving element	PMO	Cadence	Tooling
Predominant PPM approach	Phase-gates	Portfolio review	Portfolio review
Metrics	Qualitative & quantitative	Predominantly qualitative	Predominantly quantitative
Agile maturity	Low	Low to medium	Medium to high

5.3 Using Characteristics of Boundary Objects to Understand Requirements for Effective Reporting in Agile Portfolio Management

In the following subsections we will apply the notion of boundary objects to understand the requirements for effective reporting encountered in our case organisations. We will first elaborate on quantitative metrics and qualitative information used for reporting across our cases. Then, we will discuss manual and automated reporting routines. Lastly, we will elaborate why specific arte-facts and metrics, as boundary objects, are better suited for specific parts of the reporting process.

Qualitative vs Quantitative Reporting. One of the biggest differentiators for effective reporting we have found in our case organisations was a clear pres-ence of both qualitative reporting as well as quantitative reporting. We found that *qualitative reporting* allows organisations to explore opportunities, share knowledge, provide context and provide strategic insights. We found that *quan-titative reporting* allows organisations to quantify initiatives and their progress, verify goals, validate the value and provide quick tactical insights. In Table 4 we provide an overview of qualitative and quantitative reporting.

Qualitative and quantitative reporting in the case organisations with a rela-tive high agile portfolio management maturity (see B, E and J) had defined and measurable goals. Within these case organisations, virtually all initiatives are expected to be quantifiable. Qualitative reporting in these organisations, on the other hand, is more loosely defined and is more often used at a higher level, or done on an ad hoc basis. Qualitative and quantitative reporting in case organisa-tions with a medium to low agile portfolio management maturity (A and I) had fewer measurable goals. We found that case organisations with the Tool-driven reporting approach tend to have reporting processes in place that made a clear distinction between qualitative reporting and quantitative reporting. In organi-sations with a PMO- or Cadence-driven reporting approach, this distinction was less evident.

Table 4. Qualitative and quantitative reporting in our case organisations, respective types of knowledge boundaries, and examples of effective boundary objects

	Quantitative	Qualitative	
	Syntactic (effective transfer)	Semantic (effect. translation)	Pragmatic (effect. negotiation)
Product & portfolio responsibility	Business metrics Stakeholder happiness	User Stories Epic status Milestones	Portfolio wall Strategic benefits
Development responsibility	Velocity Test results Sprint Burndown	Highlights	Working software Dependencies map
Process responsibility	Team happiness % Impediments	Team radar*	Retrospectives Work agreement*

Manual vs Automated Reporting. Regardless of the scale of the organisation, manual reporting plays an important role in reporting due to the qualitative, contextual knowledge and information. While qualitative reporting information might be automated with approaches like machine learning in the future, our case organisations all employed a manual reporting process for qualitative information. From analysing the interviews, process diagrams and the literature, we found that the positive impact of automatic reporting on the effectiveness increases by contributing to more consistent and valid reporting, and more up-to-date reporting. Participant B1 stated the following when asked about what worked well in the reporting process of his organisation: *"Anything that is automatically produced. What doesn't work well is when the team needs to spend hours at night making reports using Excel and PowerPoint and all that nonsense. It's very sensitive to creative manipulation and is always out of date."*

Effective Boundary Objects for Qualitative and Quantitative Reporting in Agile Portfolio Management. We will now elaborate on the boundary objects identified across the three domains of Product, Development and team responsibility, and how they relate to the identified reporting approaches as depicted in Table 4.

We will use Carlile's [18] three types of knowledge boundaries to understand the boundary objects. Following Carlile, at a syntactic boundary, an effective boundary object *"establishes a shared syntax or language for individuals to represent their knowledge"*. At a semantic boundary, an effective boundary object *"provides a concrete means for individuals to specify and learn about their differences and dependencies across a given boundary"*. At a pragmatic boundary, an effective boundary object *"facilitates a process where individuals can jointly transform their knowledge"* [18].

Quantitative reporting is mainly associated with the syntactic boundary across our cases. Most metrics are traditional metrics such as time, budget and scope, but also more recent metrics like Velocity. In our case organisations, especially the more mature ones like B, E and J, such quantitative metrics are automated in software tools. According to Carlile [18], the syntactic boundaries resemble a knowledge transfer problem which requires a shared and sufficient syntax across the boundaries, e.g. team members and Product Owners agree on Velocity and how it is measured as a quantifiable measure of the rate at which Scrum teams consistently deliver software. Once a shared syntax has been established, repositories such as the project management tools applied by our participants (e.g. CA Agile Central/Rally or JIRA) are an effective boundary object.

Qualitative reporting is predominantly associated with semantic and pragmatic boundaries [18]. It depends if qualitative information is used by participants to translate their knowledge across boundaries, or if the boundary objects need to support a process of negotiation and transformation of knowledge - thus, if a semantic or a pragmatic boundary needs to be crossed. User Stories, for example, are effective boundary objects for analysis and communication of requirements as the template allows for the translation and understanding of requirements across different functions (e.g. system users, developers, UI designers). User Stories alone are not an effective boundary object for reporting the progress of a project. A working software artefact is an effective boundary object to support the software development process as it allows the team to communicate progress, to collect feedback of users, and negotiate next priorities e.g. with Product Owners.

According to Carlile [17], crossing a pragmatic knowledge boundary is only possible when embedded in a feedback loop, a dialogue allowing for negotiation. Crossing the pragmatic boundary requires boundary objects such a demos embedded in sprint reviews, or other forms of synchronous face-to-face communication. Cadence-driven reporting such as the one present in organisations A, E or G allows for such.

Limitations. While we employed a rigorous method and payed attention in selecting our case organisations, there are limitations to our study. The main limitation lies in the limited amount of cases. The second limitation lies in the beginning maturity of our cases.

6 Conclusions

In this paper we present the preliminary findings of our study on reporting in agile portfolio management. Based on 14 interviews in 10 organisations applying agile methods in their portfolios of IT initiatives, we present a perspective on the practice in use for the first time.

There are four main contributions discussed in this article: (1) we identify three domains of knowledge and responsibility in agile portfolio management, (2) we identify three types of reporting routines, (3) we use the concept of 'boundary objects' to understand requirements for effective reporting across the identified domains, and lastly (4) we provide examples of effective boundary objects identified across our cases.

Across our case organisations we observed three distinct types of reporting routines: Cadence-, Tool- and PMO-driven reporting. With those approaches we observe two trends: The use of software tooling to automate reporting of quantitative metrics across agile teams, and socialisation of knowledge through frequent face-to-face review meetings in teams and at the portfolio level. As an organisation grows the automation of reporting plays an increasingly important role in achieving effectiveness. We found that large-scale organisations that have automation within their reporting process were able to transfer quantitative reporting information with more consistency, validity and efficiency. Regardless of the size of the organisation, qualitative reporting and reviews remain a key part of understanding the full portfolio context. To maintain effectiveness the primary focus of qualitative reports was to translate, to transform knowledge, and to make automated reporting actionable. Our findings suggest that organisations that strongly embed both qualitative and quantitative reporting felt that their reporting helped increase their performance, and were more satisfied with their reporting process.

We may conclude that reporting in agile portfolio management is characterized by a balance of qualitative reviews and quantitative metrics to enable a transparent connection of strategy to operations in context. Agile methods have an impact on the portfolio management process as they focus on the value under development and by doing it with a much higher frequency. The notion of knowledge boundaries and boundary objects can help to understand communication requirements and shape effective reporting routines to allow for such a higher degree of interaction.

Acknowledgment. We thank all interview participants for generously contributing to this study.

References

1. Stettina, C.J., Hörz, J.: Agile portfolio management: an empirical perspective on the practice in use. Int. J. Proj. Manag. **33**(1), 140–152 (2015)
2. Williams, L.: What agile teams think of agile principles. Commun. ACM **55**(4), 71–76 (2012)
3. Müller, R., Martinsuo, M., Blomquist, T.: Project portfolio control and portfolio management performance in different contexts. Proj. Manag. J. **39**(3), 28–42 (2008)
4. Petit, Y.: Project portfolios in dynamic environments: organizing for uncertainty. Int. J. Proj. Manag. **30**(5), 539–553 (2012)
5. Cooper, R.G., Edgett, S.J., Kleinschmidt, E.J.: New product portfolio management: practices and performance. J. Prod. Innov. Manag. **16**(4), 333–351 (1999)
6. Vähäniitty, J., et al.: Towards agile product and portfolio management (2012)
7. Jeffery, M., Leliveld, I.: Best practices in it portfolio management. MIT Sloan Manag. Rev. **45**(3), 41 (2004)

8. Cooper, R.G., Edgett, S.J., Kleinschmidt, E.J.: New problems, new solutions: making portfolio management more effective. Res. Technol. Manag. **43**(2), 18–33 (2000)
9. Rautiainen, K., von Schantz, J., Vahaniitty, J.: Supporting scaling agile with portfolio management: case paf. com. In: 2011 44th Hawaii International Conference on System Sciences (HICSS), pp. 1–10. IEEE (2011)
10. Thomas, J.C., Baker, S.W.: Establishing an agile portfolio to align it investments with business needs. In: Agile Conference, AGILE 2008, pp. 252–258. IEEE (2008)
11. Tengshe, A., Noble, S.: Establishing the agile PMO: managing variability across projects and portfolios. In: Agile Conference (AGILE), pp. 188–193. IEEE (2007)
12. Leffingwell, D.: Safe Reference Guide. Scale Agile Inc. (2017)
13. Krebs, J.: Agile Portfolio Management. Microsoft Press (2008)
14. Nonaka, I., Toyama, R., Nagata, A.: A firm as a knowledge-creating entity: a new perspective on the theory of the firm. Ind. Corp. Change **9**(1), 1–20 (2000)
15. Stettina, C.J., Heijstek, W., Fægri, T.E.: Documentation work in agile teams: the role of documentation formalism in achieving a sustainable practice. In: AGILE 2012, pp. 31–40. IEEE, Washington, DC (2012)
16. Stettina, C.J., Kroon, E.: Is there an agile handover? An empirical study of documentation and project handover practices across agile software teams. In: 2013 International Conference on Engineering, Technology and Innovation (ICE) & IEEE International Technology Management Conference, pp. 1–12. IEEE (2013)
17. Carlile, P.R.: Transferring, translating, and transforming: an integrative framework for managing knowledge across boundaries. Organ. Sci. **15**(5), 555–568 (2004)
18. Carlile, P.R.: A pragmatic view of knowledge and boundaries: boundary objects in new product development. Organ. Sci. **13**(4), 442–455 (2002)
19. Leonard-Barton, D.: Wellsprings of Knowledge: Building and Sustaining the Sources of Innovation. Harvard Business School Press, Boston (1995)
20. Yin, R.K.: Case Study Research: Design and Methods. Sage publications, Thousand Oaks (2013)
21. Laanti, M.: Agile transformation model for large software development organizations. In: Proceedings of the XP2017 Scientific Workshops, p. 19. ACM (2017)

Inter-team Coordination in Large-Scale Agile Development: A Case Study of Three Enabling Mechanisms

Finn Olav Bjørnson[1], Julia Wijnmaalen[2], Christoph Johann Stettina[2],
and Torgeir Dingsøyr[1,3(✉)]

[1] Department of Computer and Information Science,
Norwegian University of Science and Technology,
Sem Sælandsvei 9, 7491 Trondheim, Norway
[2] Centre for Innovation, The Hague, Leiden University,
Schouwburgstraat 2, 2511 VA The Hague, The Netherlands
[3] Department of Software Engineering, Safety and Security,
SINTEF, 7465 Trondheim, Norway
torgeird@sintef.no

Abstract. Agile methods are increasingly used in large development projects, with multiple development teams. A central question is then what is needed to coordinate feature teams efficiently. This study examines three mechanisms for coordination: Shared mental models, communication and trust in a large-scale development project with 12 feature teams running over a four-year period. We analyse the findings in relation to suggested frameworks for large-scale agile development and a theory on coordination, and provide new recommendations for practice and theory.

Keywords: Large-scale agile software development
Multiteam systems · Inter-team coordination · SAFe · LeSS
Project management · Portfolio management

1 Introduction

Agile software development methods are increasingly used in large-scale software development. These projects typically involve multiple teams responsible for the development of numerous features of a solution, and often develop systems that are critical to companies or societies. A study investigating fundamental assumptions within large-scale agile development [1] characterises such projects as having complex knowledge boundaries within them, as well as an interactive complexity and tight coupling with technologies and processes outside the project. A key change from small- to large-scale is that work across boundaries becomes at least as important as work within teams. The topic of inter-team coordination, which has also been included in the research agenda on large-scale agile development [2], is critical in large projects and development programmes.

J. Garbajosa et al. (Eds.): XP 2018, LNBIP 314, pp. 216–231, 2018.
https://doi.org/10.1007/978-3-319-91602-6_15

Coordination is often defined as *managing interdependencies* [3]. While there is a growing body of literature on coordination in management science [4,5], in this paper we draw on multiteam system research to increase our understanding of team processes in agile development. Specifically, we refer to three coordinating mechanisms in teamwork proposed by Salas et al. [6]. In line with Scheerer et al. [7] we believe prior work in this field can inform practice in software development, and have therefore chosen this as our theoretical model and for example not theory on coordination modes from sociology [8], or works on agile development such as the model for coordination in co-located development projects [9] or previous empirical studies on agile inter-team coordination [10].

Our findings are based on material from one of the largest software development programmes in Norway, which is described in an exploratory case study [11]. We explore coordination by using three mechanisms proposed by Salas et al. [6], namely Shared Mental Models, Closed-loop Communication and Trust, and by identifying practices that supported the mechanisms in our case. We contrast our findings from the theory and case with the current frameworks for large-scale agile development in order to provide feedback on the current recommendations for practice. We investigate the following research question: *How can knowledge about multiteam systems explain inter-team coordination in a large development programme, and how can this knowledge inform recommendations to practice as expressed in current large-scale development methods?*

The paper starts with outlining present theoretical knowledge on large-scale agile development and coordination. We provide a brief description of research methods, present the findings and discussion structured after the three coordination mechanisms before concluding and providing suggestions for further work.

2   Large-Scale Development and Coordination

Large-scale agile development can be found in practice in at least two distinct forms: (1) in the case of large-scale software development project or program [11] as part of a temporal organisation, and (2) as part of a standing organisation where an IT department engages in ongoing software development embedded in a portfolio management approach [12]. In the following we use the first understanding of large-scale:

2.1   Large-Scale Agile Development: Studies and Practitioner Frameworks

A 15 million-dollar project lasting 28 months to develop a web-based customer booking engine for an American cruise company [13] was one of the first large-scale agile projects studied. The project was distributed and combined Scrum with the Project Management Body of Knowledge Framework. Customers were available but did not work together with developers on a daily basis. Some of the challenges identified in the study were due to the size and involvement of a high number of internal business sponsors, users, project managers, analysts, and external developers from the UK and India. The communications were mainly formal, and formal documents were needed for changes. However, the project was considered a success, and the study describes the balance between traditional and agile methods as essential in achieving both project control and agility.

Since this study, a small body of studies of large-scale agile development efforts have been published. A transition from traditional plan-based development to agile development is reported by Petersen and Wohlin [14], following a case with three large subsystem components developed by 117 people. Another study shows how Ericsson used communities of practice to support process improvement and knowledge transfer in a large development programme with 40 teams [15]. A third study describes chains of Scrum teams in case organisations with 150, 34 and 5 teams [16]. Further, Bass [17] investigates method tailoring in large-scale offshore development and Dingsøyr et al. [11] describe architectural work, customer involvement and inter-team coordination in a large development program. Scheerer et al. [7] describe large-scale agile development as a multiteam system, and discuss theoretically how coordination can be achieved in this domain.

Implementations of large-scale agile development are often supported by practitioner frameworks, most prominently Scaled Agile Framework (SAFe) or Large-Scale Scrum (LeSS). The Scaled Agile Framework (SAFe) [18] was designed by Dean Leffingwell, based in part on his experiences with the Nokia transformation [19]. The framework is based on the idea of an enterprise model dividing a software development organisation into three parts: Team, Program, and Portfolio. While sometimes criticised as too prescriptive, SAFe is the most applied practitioner framework specifically designed for agile methods at large [20]. The Large-Scale Scrum (LeSS) [21] model was predominantly created by Bas Vodde and Craig Larman to scale the original Scrum framework outside of individual Scrum teams. Similarly to SAFe, LeSS proposes an organisational structure based on teams, accompanied by specific practices and principles. Although coordination is mentioned as a challenge, both frameworks address this only parenthetically.

Coordination is crucial in large-scale development. Begel et al. [22] report on how Microsoft engineers coordinate, finding that coordination is mostly focused on scheduling and features. They further point out that *'more communication and personal contact worked better to make interactions between teams go more smoothly'*. Email was the most used tool to keep track of dependencies on other teams, for developers, testers and also program managers. The study emphasised that *'creating and maintaining personal relationships between individuals on teams that coordinate is indicated by many respondents as a way to successfully collaborate with colleagues'* and finally that *'respondents would like more effective and efficient communication between teams to ease their daily work burden'*. A recent study explains ineffective coordination in large-scale development as resulting from a lack of dependency awareness, due to *'misaligned planning activities of specification, prioritization, estimation and allocation between agile team and traditional inter-team levels'* [23].

2.2   Coordinating Multiple Teams

In 2001 Mathieu, Marks and Zaccaro introduced the term 'multiteam system' to indicate '..two or more teams that interface directly and interdependently in response to environmental contingencies toward the accomplishment of collective goals. Multiteam system boundaries are defined by virtue of the fact that all teams within the system, while pursuing different proximal goals, share at least one common distal goal; and in doing so exhibit input, process and outcome interdependence with at least one other team in the system' [24, p. 290].

Unlike a traditional team, a multiteam system is too large and specialised to effectively employ direct mutual adjustment among each and every member of the system [25]. An empirical study by Marks and colleagues [26] points out that coordination 'involves synchronising the efforts of multiple teams in a joint endeavour to handle situational demands' [26, p. 965]. Hence, cross-team processes appear to predict multiteam performance more than within-team processes [26]. The study by Dingsøyr et al. [11] describes practices for inter-team coordination and found that the case program established far more arenas for coordination than what is recommended in agile frameworks, that these arenas changed over time, and that program participants emphasised the importance of an open-office landscape.

The term coordination has been used for a variety of phenomena. Triggered by the impracticality of the variety of definitions, Salas et al. [6] reviewed existing literature and introduced the 'Big Five' in teamwork. The Big Five in teamwork consists of five components and three coordinating mechanisms. The components are found in almost all teamwork taxonomies: *team leadership, mutual performance monitoring, backup behaviour, adaptability, and team orientation.* While the five components have been previously used to understand teamwork in agile teams elsewhere [27,28], in this paper we will focus on the coordination mechanisms. According to Salas et al. [6], the coordinating mechanisms fuse the values of the five components. The Big Five framework is equally relevant inter-team processes in multiteam systems [29,30].

The three coordinating mechanisms are:

Shared Mental Models are crucial for coordinated effective action [31]. *'For teams to effectively work together, teams must have a clear understanding of the work process, the tasks, and of other teams capabilities'* [6, p. 565]. It is important that all teams share the same mental model so they can interpret contextual cues in a similar manner and make compatible decisions regarding their common goal [32,33]. A shared mental model is even more important in times of stress or in a fast-changing environment as the amount of explicit communication decreases in such situations [6]. Moreover, misaligned mental models can cause conflicts and misunderstandings [34, p. 299] [35, p. 99].

Closed-loop Communication is more than merely developing and sending messages; it also has to do with creating a shared meaning [36, p. 178]. Communication is the simple exchange of information whereas closed-loop communication adds a feedback loop: Was the information received and interpreted correctly [6, p. 568]? This extra feedback loop is pivotal for successful communication between multiple teams [37, p. 25]. Communication both between and within teams is needed to share information, synchronise actions and keep the shared mental model updated. Also it avoids the noise generated by teams merely focusing on their own tasks [26,36]. Although communication might be hindered by team boundaries through distrust [34].

Trust is defined as the shared belief that teams will perform their roles and protect the interests of their co-workers. [6, p. 561]. Mutual trust is the teams confidence in the character, integrity, strength and abilities of another team [38, p. 106] or group. Trust moderates the relationship between team performance and various other variables [39,40]. Trust is a crucial team process, however it does not develop easily across group boundaries [34,41].

3   Method

The empirical data in this study was gathered in a previous study, described in detail by Dingsøyr et al. [11]. The case was chosen since it was characterised as the most successful large-scale programme in Norway at the time, with extensive use of agile methods. The research question, *how agile methods are adapted at a very large-scale*, was investigated in an interpretative embedded exploratory case study. A case study approach was chosen as it achieves 'the most advanced form of understanding' [42, p. 236].

In the original study, data was collected from two sources, group interviews [43] and documents. The original study had three focus areas: Customer involvement, software architecture, and inter-team coordination. Three two-hour group interviews were organized with 24 particpants from the programme. The data from the interviews was transcribed, and the transcriptions along with project documents were imported into a tool for qualitative analysis.

A descriptive and holistic coding [44] was then performed on the topic of inter-team coordination. The results were discussed and presented back to the participants which provided input that led to some small revisions of the first findings.

Our findings in this paper are based on the original transcriptions of the inter-team coordination focus area, as well as on all material coded with 'organisation of the programme'. The material was re-analysed with a starting point in the original coding, but with respect to the coordination mechanisms. In particular we looked for description of practices of shared mental models, closed-loop communication and trust at the inter-team level.

4   Case

In this paper we refer to our case as the Perform programme, which was a programme led by a public department, the Norwegian Public Service Pension Fund, further called 'Pension Fund', which required a new office automation system. The programme ran for four years, from January 2008 to March 2012.

4.1 Context

The Pension Fund is a department with about 380 employees who provide 950,000 customers with several types of services. It integrates heavily with another public department. The Pension Fund initiated Perform due to public reform that required new functionality in their existing office automation system. The content of the reform was not known when the programme started, which was one of the main reasons for choosing agile development practices for the project. The goal of the programme was to enable the Pension Fund to provide timely and accurate services and to ensure a cost-effective implementation of the reform.

At the time, Perform was one of the largest IT programmes in Norway, with a final budget of EUR 140 million. It involved 175 people, 100 of whom were external consultants from five companies. In total the programme used about 800,000 person-hours to develop 300 epics, divided into 2500 user stories. The epics were released through 12 releases, from late 2008 to early 2012. The whole program was co-located on one floor in an open-office landscape, with team members seated together. The programme was considered a success in that it delivered the necessary functionality within time and on budget. In the following sections we focus on the period from around 2011 when the programme organisation was large and had time to adjust its work practices.

4.2 Structure and Organisation

Perform was managed as a matrix programme, with four main projects intersecting, mainly through personnel from the feature teams in the development project. The programme was led by a director, focusing mainly on external relations, and a programme manager who focused on operations. Four main projects had their own project manager: Business, architecture, development and test projects.

The *business project* was responsible for analysing needs, and defining and prioritising epics and user stories. Product owners could be found in this project along with employees from the line organisation in the department and technical architects from the development teams who contributed on a partial basis.

The *architecture project* was responsible for defining the overall architecture. This project was staffed by a lead architect as well as staffed on a part-time basis by technical architects from the development teams.

The *test project* was responsible for testing procedures and approving deliverables. The project had a lead tester and part-time testers from the development teams.

The *development project* was itself split into three sub-projects. One was lead by the Pension Fund, consisting of six teams. The other two were led by consulting companies Accenture and Sopra Steria respectively, each with three teams. These development teams worked according to Scrum with three-week iterations, delivering on a common demonstration day. Each team was staffed with a Scrum master, a technical architect, a functional architect, a test responsible, and 4–5 pure developers, a mixture between junior and senior levels.

The development process was influenced by a national contract standard with four phases: analysis, description, construction and approval. The process was staged and continuous so the programme worked on approving the previous phase while constructing the current phase and analysing and describing features in the coming phase.

4.3 Inter-team Coordination

In the following section, we show how coordination mechanisms were influenced by the practices of the programme, and how they developed over time. We only focus on practices at the inter-team level:

Shared Mental Models is observed in the solution descriptions where technical and functional architects worked together to specify on a wiki what was to be made in more in-depth detail than epics or user stories. As the project matured, these descriptions decreased in size, leading to a more effective use of resources in the business project. This is an indication that participants in the programme started to get a shared mental model of the solution, so less text was needed for specification.

Several practices can be seen as contributing to establishing this shared mental model. We have focused on practices relating to a shared understanding of the *work process*, the *tasks* to be done and the shared awareness of *who knew what*.

The *work process* was established early on in the project, and contributed to a homogenous view on the work practices and a shared mental model. Many developers had previous experience working with Scrum and together with the matrix organisation, the specialised roles and iterative four-phase development process that many developers had used before, a common understanding of how work was to be done emerged. In the beginning, formal arenas were used for communication, coordination and learning, but as time went on, more emphasis was placed on informal channels. This could indicate that a shared mental model had emerged so people knew who to contact directly instead of going through the more formal channels. In total we identified 14 arenas for coordination.

Concerning the *tasks*, there were several practices that contributed to a shared mental model. One of the most important practices was the specialised roles within those teams which were shared with other projects. In several cases, the team rotated the employee responsible for the solution description in each iteration. This lead to an overall increase in domain knowledge, and a shared mental model between the development project and the business project, which enabled more efficient collaboration. *'As the contractor starts to understand more about the context, the customers real problem is more visible, and this means we can find a solution together. Fast.'* The project also provided opportunities for people to listen in on other teams, through stand-up meetings. This was particularly useful for the leaders of the architecture and testing teams, who needed to know what was going on in other teams.

The final part of building and maintaining a shared mental model is knowing *who knows what*. Several practices contributed here. As the project was evolving, coordination increasingly took place directly between different teams. Getting to the point of knowing who knew what was a combination of formal arenas in the beginning and a willingness to experiment with those arenas and change them as the needs changed. *'Having enough coordination arenas to know that "Oh, we need to talk" and "This is what we need to talk about in detail". The combination of the semi-structured meetings and those that just happened were the most important in my opinion. But then you need enough of the places where you are informed on what is happening so you actually go and talk to the ones you need to talk to.'* In addition to the arenas where people got to know each other, the specialists in the feature team played key roles in knowing who knew what, since they often had a better overview of other parts of the project.

Closed-Loop Communication at the inter-team level was observed between several teams, but a prominent example was the introduction of mini demos, shared between feature teams and the business project. Early on, common demos were held at the end of every iteration so everyone could provide direct feedback on the implemented solution. This delayed feedback as iteration length was three weeks, and teams introduced the concept of mini-demos during iterations where they received rapid feedback from the customer in the business project to ensure they had understood the requirements correctly. The fact that the Pension Fund was able to provide upwards of 30 of their best line operatives to man the business team of the project was a great benefit to the developers who could ask directly for clarifications on user stories.

Many emphasised the importance of informal coordination arenas enabled by the co-location and open landscape when it came to the efficient (close-loop) communication in the programme. Even though there were many official coordination arenas, like the daily stand-up, a Scrum of Scrum between teams in the sub-projects and a meta-scrum covering the entire programme, a lot of the coordination happened directly between members of different teams who had to make sure the information they passed through the formal arenas was received and interpreted correctly.

The formal arenas were necessary, however, as a project manager expressed it: *'Having processes to work with dependencies is important for the maturation of the work, to get an improved understanding. But you need frequent local control and cooperation to really figure it out.'* The formal arenas seemed most important in the beginning as an enabler of later informal communication, as expressed by an architect: *'I imagine these arenas are most important in the beginning, but the importance decreases as you get to know each other. You get used to just walking over to the person you know can fix this thing for you and talking to him directly.'*

There seemed to be a widespread belief from all participants that informal direct communication would improve or enable better communication between teams in the programme. The program sought to improve the informal communication by physically moving teams around in the landscape. *'And then we had some conscious choices to cover the informal communication. A Pension Fund-team that started working with the GUI-part far into the work-flow, they were moved over there and we switched the placement of those two teams [demonstrates on whiteboard]. We wanted that team and that team to work closer together. That was a conscious choice from the Pension Fund and us.'*

Trust. An example came early in the programme, when there was a delay in delivery. Some in the management in the Pension Fund wanted to monitor the programme more closely. But the director of the Pension Fund stated: *'Let the people who know how to work, work!'* A project manager states the outcome of this decision: *'We had a delivery which we missed, and it was touch and go if we should be allowed to continue. [..] The fact that we were allowed to mature was important. I feel the suppliers learned from each other and used the others to grow.'*

There are several other examples in the material illustrating that trust was given between teams. For example, the manager team trusted the feature teams to take the right actions. *'They [feature team] told us [manager team] that they exchanged tasks, more like a checkup that if you don't mind, we've done so and so, because its better. -OK Go!'* This was also a result of a shared mental model: The teams identified each other as better suited to their respective tasks. In another example, the feature teams trusted the other teams to respect their need for shielding during hectic periods. *'You know that my team needs to be shielded for a time, and then you just walk over to (sub-project manager) and tell him.'*

Some of the trust seems to be built on the informal coordination that was enabled through the more formal arenas, as we have described previously. The matrix structure and specialised roles in the feature teams also contributed. The feature teams had to trust the business team to deliver enough work for an iteration and the business team had to trust the feature teams to swap tasks if they identified that other teams were more suited. There was much openness between teams and between suppliers who were otherwise competitors. The open workspace and common lunch area also seem to have contributed to the relaxed and trusting atmosphere between the teams. The mix of informal and formal arenas provided developers from different teams the opportunity to discuss problems and suggest solutions informally as they cropped up, but the final decision to implement was made in a formal arena. This practice allowed developers to handle problems autonomously, and made sure that there was a proper way to disseminate the solution to other teams.

5 Discussion

We return to our research question: *How can knowledge about multiteam systems explain inter-team coordination in a large development programme, and how can this knowledge inform recommendations to practice as expressed in current large-scale development methods?*

Rentsch and Staniewisz [45, p. 226] hypothesise that 'coordination mechanisms need to function at the team, inter-team and system levels in order for the multiteam system to utilise their available capacity fully'. As a program delivering on time and cost, we know that the Perform program utilised their capacity well, and we also know that the program continuously worked on improving work practice, which led to changes in coordination practices. The feature teams followed Scrum with practices such as iteration planning, daily meetings, demonstrations and retrospectives on team level. In the following section, we discuss our two research questions for each of the coordination mechanisms:

5.1 Shared Mental Model

A Shared Mental Model includes a clear understanding of the work process, the tasks, and of other teams capabilities [6, p. 565]. In the results, we showed how the solution descriptions were reduced in size, which is an indication of a shared mental model.

We believe the Scrum development method can be seen as a powerful shared mental model, as it is easy to understand with few roles, work practices and artefacts. The programme added new roles and projects on top of this, building on the contract model which was widely known amongst participants. All teams demonstrated developed functionality every three weeks. Adding more roles, work practices and artefacts risks limiting the function of a development method as a shared mental model. With the new frameworks SAFe and LeSS, we believe LeSS is closest to the model used in the Perform case. SAFe is a more complex model, and we believe this model will require more effort to function as a shared mental model. Building on a lightweight framework such as Scrum could help develop a shared mental model.

The fact that all the teams in the project are located on the same floor means that project members walk by the progress boards of other teams and this aids the formation of a shared mental model. The matrix model meant that projects such as business and development worked together to develop a shared understanding of tasks prior to actual development. Furthermore, joint responsibility from the development and testing projects led to a shared understanding of quality requirements on the codebase. Placing a team together physically is common advice in the agile practitioner literature, but having a matrix organisation is more controversial. Scrum describes only the role of a facilitator and team members for a development team. Our case suggests that adding roles on the teams and organising the programme in a matrix structure is important to develop a shared mental model. Additional roles could help develop a shared mental model of tasks.

The open-office landscape led to overall insight in the work across teams as the progress boards were visible, and it was easy to see which teams were having discussions after daily stand-up meetings. We also described the number of meetings in the beginning of the programme as something that established knowledge of who knows what. Developing a shared mental model of who knows what requires extra effort in projects with people new to a domain and the project organisation.

5.2   Closed-Loop Communication

Agile development methods have led to shorter feedback loops in development projects. In the Perform program, the iteration length was three weeks. *Closed-loop communication* is addressed by the frequent review and coordination practices in and across teams through planning, demonstrations or product backlog refinement, as well as through frequent discussions with the teams and relevant stakeholders in the preparation and review of partial results. This is also described in the SAFe and LeSS frameworks. Perform introduced the new practice of mini-demos to improve the closed loop communication between the development and business projects.

We believe that closed-loop communication was enhanced in the Perform case by frequent feedback as prescribed by agile practices, by the physical proximity of teams situated together on one floor, and by the tailored work methods to improve communication such as with the new practice of 'mini-demos'.

5.3   Trust

In the theory section we stated that closed-loop communication can be hindered by team boundaries through distrust. The Perform program involved a number of companies with their own work cultures, yet participants seem to have developed trust (as explained in our results section) both from top to bottom (as illustrated by the Programme Director's *"Let the people who know how to work, work!"*, and trust between teams as described in understanding that teams needed to be shielded during an iteration. Agile methods with focus on transparency and feedback loops are well suited to develop trust.

Other practices such as common work spaces and shared lunches also created a form of identity and stimulated contact, both of which increased the level of inter-team trust. The amount of open and informal communication and decision-making has been shown to be indicators of how trust develops [46]. Additionally, trust literature shows that trust develops if there is more interpersonal contact [47]. There is a negative relationship between team size and interpersonal contact. This relation between team size and trust might explain why the agile methods seem to work better in smaller organisations compared to larger ones.

However, relationships within teams and the context around teams are not static. Hence the static nature of the practical models does not align with the reality of how relations develop in multiteam systems.

Reflective sessions such as retrospectives used in Perform and described in both SAFe and LeSS will likely influence the amount of *trust*. Practices, artefacts and roles facilitate and stimulate coordination, yet one very influential factor hardly receives attention: the human. For example, literature on trust tells us that it does not develop easily across team boundaries [34] and that it influences the amount of communication [36]. Trust is critical in large-scale development and is challenging to develop. Co-location and the agile practices of frequent delivery seem to develop trust.

5.4 Limitations

The main limitations of this study were that the group interviews were performed after the programme was completed, and that we were not able to follow the case over time. Second, the data collection was not particularly targeted at the mechanisms identified in the multiteam systems literature, but rather structured around broad questions of how the programme organised inter-team coordination. See [11] for further discussion of the limitations of our study.

6 Conclusion

In this paper we used current multiteam systems literature to help understand inter-team coordination processes in large-scale agile project teams. In particular, we use the three coordinating mechanisms proposed by Salas et al. [6] to understand inter-team coordination in practice.

Our results indicate that using the multiteam systems perspective on large-scale agile teams is useful as it provides reasons for practices that are described in agile development frameworks. A shared mental model, closed-loop communication and trust have been identified as important coordination mechanisms in teamwork in multiteams. The findings from our case show the relevance of these three coordinating mechanisms for large-scale agile development and underline the importance of inter-team coordinating mechanisms compared to intra-team coordination.

The three mechanisms are interrelated and their combined effect influences the project's success. The practices suggested in large-scale frameworks indicate that many practices contribute to or influence more than one coordination mechanism at the same time. From the discussion, the following conclusions follow on the coordination mechanisms:

- Building on a lightweight framework such as Scrum helps develop a shared mental model of the development process.
- Additional roles could help develop a shared mental model of tasks.
- Developing a shared mental model of who knows what requires extra effort in projects with people new to a domain and the project organisation.
- Closed-loop communication was developed due to a combination of (1) frequent feedback as prescribed by agile practices, (2) co-location on one floor, and (3) tailoring of work methods to improve communication such as the practice of 'mini-demos'.
- Trust is critical in large-scale development and more challenging to develop than in small-scale scenarios.
- Co-location and the agile practices of frequent delivery seem to develop trust.

There is a growing number of studies on multiteam systems which we believe are relevant for practitioners and researchers in large-scale agile development. In particular it would be interesting for future research to further explore how human aspects influence coordination, following up on Begel et al. [22] who found that creating and maintaining personal relationships was critical to good coordination. In the future, researchers should draw further on findings in the multiteam systems field to provide better advice on how these aspects can be fostered in development methods.

Acknowledgement. This work was in partial supported by strategic internal projects at SINTEF on large-scale agile development and the project Agile 2.0 supported by the Research council of Norway through grant 236759 and by the companies Kantega, Kongsberg Defence & Aerospace, Statoil, Sopra Steria, and Sticos.

References

1. Rolland, K.H., Fitzgerald, B., Dingsøyr, T., Stool, K.J.: Problematizing agile in the large: alternative assumptions for large-scale agile development. In: International Conference on Information Systems (2016)
2. Dingsøyr, T., Moe, N.B.: Towards principles of large-scale agile development. In: Dingsøyr, T., Moe, N.B., Tonelli, R., Counsell, S., Gencel, C., Petersen, K. (eds.) XP 2014. LNBIP, vol. 199, pp. 1–8. Springer, Cham (2014). https://doi.org/10.1007/978-3-319-14358-3_1
3. Malone, T.W., Crowston, K.: The interdisciplinary study of coordination. ACM Comput. Surv. (CSUR) **26**(1), 87–119 (1994)
4. Mintzberg, H.: Mintzberg on Management: Inside Our Strange World of Organizations. Simon and Schuster (1989)
5. Jarzabkowski, P.A., Le, J.K., Feldman, M.S.: Toward a theory of coordinating: creating coordinating mechanisms in practice. Organ. Sci. **23**(4), 907–927 (2012)
6. Salas, E., Sims, D.E., Burke, C.S.: Is there a big five in teamwork? Small Group Res. **36**(5), 555–599 (2005)
7. Scheerer, A., Hildenbrand, T., Kude, T.: Coordination in large-scale agile software development: a multiteam systems perspective. In: 2014 47th Hawaii International Conference on System Sciences, pp. 4780–4788. IEEE (2014)
8. Dingsøyr, T., Brede Moe, N., Amdahl Seim, E.: Coordinating Knowledge Work in Multi-Team Programs: Findings from a Large-Scale Agile Development Program. ArXiv e-prints, January 2018
9. Strode, D.E., Huff, S.L., Hope, B.G., Link, S.: Coordination in co-located agile software development projects. J. Syst. Softw. **85**(6), 1222–1238 (2012)
10. Sharp, H., Robinson, H.: Three CS of agile practice: collaboration, co-ordination and communication. In: Dingsøyr, T., Dybå, T., Moe, N. (eds.) Agile Software Development, pp. 61–85. Springer, Heidelberg (2010). https://doi.org/10.1007/978-3-642-12575-1_4
11. Dingsøyr, T., Moe, N.B., Fægri, T.E., Seim, E.A.: Exploring software development at the very large-scale: a revelatory case study and research agenda for agile method adaptation. Empirical Softw. Eng. **23**(1), 490–520 (2018)
12. Stettina, C.J., Hörz, J.: Agile portfolio management: an empirical perspective on the practice in use. Int. J. Project Manage. **33**(1), 140–152 (2015)

13. Batra, D., Xia, W., VanderMeer, D., Dutta, K.: Balancing agile and structured development approaches to successfully manage large distributed software projects: a case study from the cruise line industry. Commun. Assoc. Inf. Syst. **27**(1), 21 (2010)
14. Petersen, K., Wohlin, C.: The effect of moving from a plan-driven to an incremental software development approach with agile practices. Empirical Softw. Eng. **15**(6), 654–693 (2010). ISI Document Delivery No.: 653OB Times Cited: 2 Cited Reference Count: 46 Petersen, Kai Wohlin, Claes. Springer, Dordrecht
15. Paasivaara, M., Lassenius, C.: Communities of practice in a large distributed agile software development organization - case ericsson. Inf. Softw. Technol. **56**(12), 1556–1577 (2014)
16. Vlietland, J., van Vliet, H.: Towards a governance framework for chains of scrum teams. Inf. Softw. Technol. **57**, 52–65 (2015)
17. Bass, J.M.: How product owner teams scale agile methods to large distributed enterprises. Empirical Softw. Eng. **20**(6), 1525–1557 (2015)
18. Leffingwell, D.: SAFe 4.0 Reference Guide: Scaled Agile Framework for Lean Software and Systems Engineering. Addison-Wesley Professional (2016)
19. Laanti, M., Salo, O., Abrahamsson, P.: Agile methods rapidly replacing traditional methods at nokia: a survey of opinions on agile transformation. Inf. Softw. Technol. **53**(3), 276–290 (2011)
20. VersionOne: 11th annual survey. the state of agile (2016)
21. Larman, C., Vodde, B.: Large-Scale Scrum: More with LeSS. Addison-Wesley Professional, Boston (2016)
22. Begel, A., Nagappan, N., Poile, C., Layman, L.: Coordination in large-scale software teams. In: Proceedings of the 2009 ICSE Workshop on Cooperative and Human Aspects on Software Engineering, pp. 1–7. IEEE Computer Society (2009)
23. Bick, S., Spohrer, K., Hoda, R., Scheerer, A., Heinzl, A.: Coordination challenges in large-scale software development: a case study of planning misalignment in hybrid settings. IEEE Trans. Softw. Eng. (2017)
24. Mathieu, J., Marks, M.A., Zaccaro, S.J.: Multi-team systems. Int. Handb. Work Organ. Psychol. **2**, 289–313 (2001)
25. Davison, R., Hollenbeck, J.: Boundary spanning in the domain of multiteam systems. In: Multiteam systems. An Organization Form for Dynamic and Complex Environments, pp. 323–362. Routledge (2012)
26. Marks, M.A., DeChurch, L.A., Mathieu, J.E., Panzer, F.J., Alonso, A.: Teamwork in multiteam systems. J. Appl. Psychol. **90**(5), 964 (2005)
27. Moe, N.B., Dingsøyr, T.: Scrum and team effectiveness: theory and practice. In: Abrahamsson, P., Baskerville, R., Conboy, K., Fitzgerald, B., Morgan, L., Wang, X. (eds.) XP 2008. LNBIP, vol. 9, pp. 11–20. Springer, Heidelberg (2008). https://doi.org/10.1007/978-3-540-68255-4_2
28. Stettina, C.J., Heijstek, W.: Five agile factors: helping self-management to self-reflect. In: O'Connor, R.V., Pries-Heje, J., Messnarz, R. (eds.) EuroSPI 2011. CCIS, vol. 172, pp. 84–96. Springer, Heidelberg (2011). https://doi.org/10.1007/978-3-642-22206-1_8
29. Shuffler, M.L., Rico, R., Salas, E.: Pushing the boundaries of multiteam systems in research and practice: an introduction. In: Pushing the Boundaries: Multiteam Systems in Research and Practice, pp. 3–16. Emerald Group Publishing Limited (2014)
30. Wijnmaalen, J., Voordijk, H., Rietjens, B.: MTS coordination in practice: micro level insights to increase MTS performance. Team Perform. Manage. Int. J. **24**(1/2), 64–83 (2017)

31. Zaccaro, S.J., Rittman, A.L., Marks, M.A.: Team leadership. Leadership Q. **12**(4), 451–483 (2002)
32. Cooke, N.J., Salas, E., Cannon-Bowers, J.A., Stout, R.J.: Measuring team knowledge. Hum. Fact. J. Hum. Fact. Ergon. Soc. **42**(1), 151–173 (2000)
33. Mathieu, J.: Reflections on the evolution of the multiteam systems concept and a look to the future. In: Multiteam Systems: An Organization Form for Dynamic and Complex Environments, pp. 511–544 (2012)
34. Hinsz, V.B., Betts, K.R.: Conflict multiteam situations. In: Multiteam Systems: An Organization Form for Dynamic and Complex Environments, pp. 289–322 (2012)
35. DiazGranados, D., Dow, A.W., Perry, S.J., Palesis, J.A.: Understanding patient care as a multiteam system. In: Pushing the Boundaries: Multiteam Systems in Research and Practice, pp. 95–113. Emerald Group Publishing Limited (2014)
36. Keyton, J., Ford, D.J., Smith, F.L., Zacarro, S., Marks, M., DeChurch, L.: Communication, collaboration, and identification as facilitators and constraints of multiteamsystems. In: Multiteam Systems: An Organization Form for Dynamic and Complex Environments, pp. 173–190 (2012)
37. McIntyre, R.M., Salas, E.: Measuring and managing for team performance: emerging principles from complex environments. In: Team Effectiveness and Decision Making in Organizations, pp. 9–45 (1995)
38. Earley, P.C., Gibson, C.B.: Multinational Work Teams: A New Perspective. Routledge, Mahwah (2002)
39. Costa, A.C., Roe, R.A., Taillieu, T.: Trust within teams: the relation with performance effectiveness. Eur. J. Work Organ. Psychol. **10**(3), 225–244 (2001)
40. Dirks, K.T.: The effects of interpersonal trust on work group performance. J. Appl. Psychol. **84**(3), 445 (1999)
41. Williams, M.: In whom we trust: group membership as an affective context for trust development. Acad. Manag. Rev. **26**(3), 377–396 (2001)
42. Flyvbjerg, B.: Five misunderstandings about case-study research. Qual. Inq. **12**(2), 219–245 (2006)
43. Myers, M.D., Newman, M.: The qualitative interview in is research: examining the craft. Inf. Organ. **17**(1), 2–26 (2007)
44. Saldaña, J.: The Coding Manual for Qualitative Researchers. Sage (2015)
45. Rentsch, J.R., Staniewicz, M.J.: Cognitive similarity configurations in multiteam systems. In: Multiteam Systems: An Organizational Form for Dynamic and Complex Environments, pp. 225–253 (2012)
46. Currall, S.C., Judge, T.A.: Measuring trust between organizational boundary role persons. Organ. Behav. Hum. Decis. Process. **64**(2), 151–170 (1995)
47. Mayer, R.C., Davis, J.H., Schoorman, F.D.: An integrative model of organizational trust. Acad. Manag. Rev. **20**(3), 709–734 (1995)

Supporting Large-Scale Agile Development with Domain-Driven Design

Ömer Uludağ[1](✉), Matheus Hauder[2], Martin Kleehaus[1](✉),
Christina Schimpfle[2], and Florian Matthes[1](✉)

[1] Technische Universität München (TUM),
85748 Garching bei München, Germany
{oemer.uludag,martin.kleehaus,matthes}@tum.de
[2] Allianz Deutschland AG, 85774 Unterföhring, Germany
{matheus.hauder,christina.schimpfle}@allianz.de

Abstract. An increasing number of large organizations are adopting agile and lean methods at larger scale for building complex software systems. One major critique of agile development and in particular of large-scale agile development is the neglect of proper architecting assistance in such development efforts. On the one hand, emergent architecture design may require excessive redesign efforts in large systems, while on the other hand, big upfront architecture delays the starting point of implementation. Domain-driven Design (DDD) addresses this problem by providing means for evolving the architecture of complex systems in an agile way. We describe how DDD can support large-scale agile development based on a conducted case study in a large insurance company with three agile teams. Furthermore, we present a lightweight framework that can be used by agile teams as guidance for architecting in large-scale agile development programs. The presented framework is largely based on Large-Scale Scrum and incorporates strategic and tactical DDD.

Keywords: Large-scale agile software development
Domain-driven design · Scaling agile frameworks

1 Introduction

Over the past two decades, agile methods have transformed and brought unprecedented changes to software development practice by strongly emphasizing change tolerance, continuous delivery, and customer involvement [1]. The success of agile methods for small, co-located teams has inspired enterprises to increasingly apply agile practices to large-scale endeavors [2]. One major critique of agile development and in particular of large-scale agile development is the lack of assistance for building and managing architecture in such development endeavors [2,3]. On the one hand, agile teams naïvely hope that a suitable architecture will gradually emerge out of weekly refactorings [4]. However, the practice of this design is effective at team level, but insufficient when developing complex systems. It requires

J. Garbajosa et al. (Eds.): XP 2018, LNBIP 314, pp. 232–247, 2018.
https://doi.org/10.1007/978-3-319-91602-6_16

excessive redesign efforts, architectural divergence, and functional redundancy increasing the complexity of the system's architecture [5,6]. On the other hand, large "big design upfront" efforts delay the starting point of implementation [7]. The planned architecture might not be contemporary after it meets the "real world" [5].

Large-Scale Scrum (LeSS), Scaled Agile Framework (SAFe), and Disciplined Agile Framework 2.0 (DA 2.0) [8], suggest to apply Domain-driven Design (DDD) to architect in an agile way. However, so far, no real-world example exists which describes how to combine and implement scaling agile frameworks with DDD. The main objective of this paper is to explore how DDD can be utilized in order to support large-scale agile development. Based on this objective our three research questions are:

- *Research Question 1: Which scaling agile frameworks reference DDD?*
- *Research Question 2: How can DDD be adopted in a large organization with several agile development teams?*
- *Research Question 3: Which roles, processes, artifacts, and tools are required to support a large-scale agile development endeavor with DDD?*

The remainder of this paper is structured as follows. In Sect. 2, we motivate the need of architecting in large-scale agile development and provide an overview of related works. In Sect. 3, we present the research approach of this paper. Section 4 describes the case study on the adoption of DDD in the insurance company. Section 5 presents the evaluation results of the proposed framework. We discuss the main findings in Sect. 6 before concluding the paper with a summary of our results and remarks on future research in Sect. 7.

2   Background and Related Work

Agile methods such as Scrum, Extreme Programming (XP), and Crystal Clear, which more or less adhere to the values of the Agile Manifesto[1] [9], share common characteristics, such as iterative and incremental development life cycles, focusing on small releases, collocated teams, and a planning strategy based on a release plan or feature backlog [10] where architectural design issues are not very important [11]. For instance, the incremental design practice of XP claims that architecture can emerge in daily design (emergent design) [12], which implies that architecture emerges from the system rather being imposed by some direct structuring force [11]. Apart from verbal discussions related to design decisions and overall architecture, also Scrum does not place any emphasis on architecture related practices. In Scrum, the architecture of one-project application can always be re-factored and repackaged for a higher level of reuse [11]. While *"refactoring, for its part, has emerged as an important software engineering technique, it is not a replacement for sound upfront design; if an architecture is decent you can improve it, but re-factored junk is still junk"* [13]

---

[1] http://agilemanifesto.org/, last accessed on: 2018-01-18.

However, the role of architecture in agile endeavors has changed and it is now gaining more attraction by agilists [14]. This phenomenon is also reinforced by the increasing number of *"agility and architecture can coexist"* advocates cf. [3,4], or [15]. For building complex and large-scale systems, some amount of architectural planning and governance becomes even more important [16]. Nord et al. [4] argue that for large-scale software development endeavors, agility is enabled by architecture, and vice versa. They highlight some benefits of architecture in large-scale agile efforts such as providing a common vocabulary and culture, a systematic way to control dependencies, a way to keep technical debts in check, and a guide for release planning and configuration management [4].

Some architectural tactics or models to support rapid and agile stability in large-scale agile endeavors have been proposed by academics such as aligning feature-based development and system decomposition, creating an architectural runway, using matrix teams, or the zipper model [15–17]. Also, practitioners are grappling with the issue of marrying agile approaches with architectural practices for building complex systems such as Cockburn and his walking skeleton [18], Leffingwell and his colleagues' SAFe [19], or Ambler and his colleagues' DA 2.0 [20]. Recognizing the importance of architecting in large-scale agile endeavors, we have investigated the role of architects based on a structured literature review with an excerpt in Table 1 [8].

Table 1. Excerpt of scaling agile frameworks maturity and architecture [8].

	Maturity						Architecture					
	Contributions	Cases	Documentation	Training Courses and Certifications	Community, Forum or Blog	Rating	Enterprise Architect	Software Architect	Solution Architect	Information Architect	Domain-Driven Design	Architecure Design
Large Scale Scrum	29	22	Yes	Yes	Yes	●	-	-	-	-	X	emergent
Scaled Agile Framework	35	35	Yes	Yes	Yes	●	X	X	X	X	X	emergent & intentional
Disciplined Agile 2.0	27	4	Yes	Yes	Yes	●	X	X	X	-	X	emergent & intentional

Given that architecting should be an iterative activity, we found that mature scaling agile frameworks [8] suggest DDD as a light-weight approach for large-scale agile efforts. DDD facilitates an iterative process of collaboration to explore a model and develop a ubiquitous language between agile teams and domain experts. Although, DDD has been proposed by these frameworks, to the best of our knowledge, there is no other work that describes the adoption of DDD in real large-scale agile development program.

3   Case Study Design

A case study is a suitable research methodology for software engineering research since it studies contemporary phenomena in its natural context [21]. It is a valuable research method in situations where a researcher aims to understand phenomena in a complex, real life context [22,23]. We followed the guidelines described by Runeson and Höst [21] for the research process.

Case study design: Main objective of this paper is to explore how DDD can be utilized in order to support large-scale agile development. Based on this objective, we defined three research questions (see Sect. 1). Our study is a single-case study and the case was purposefully selected, because the studied company had been experimenting with agile approaches for the last two years and is now transitioning from planned-driven methodology to large-scale agile development. Our case is exploratory as we are looking into an unexplored phenomenon [21]. Our unit of analysis is the large-scale agile development endeavor at the large insurance company.

Preparation for data collection: We used a "mixed methods" approach with three levels of data collection techniques according to [24]:

1. As direct methods, we made observations with high degree of interactions [21] in several event storming workshops [25] and conducted structured interviews. The workshops helped us to develop a deep understanding of the overall structure of the development endeavor with its roles, process, artifacts, and tools. We interviewed nine stakeholders involved in the development effort with different roles in order to enable the triangulation of data sources [26]. The structured interviews helped us to evaluate our framework and incorporate feedback into the final version of it.
2. In the issue tracking tool Jira[2], agile teams assigned user stories to domains and subdomains. This user story assignment provided us quantitative data for determining in which subdomains the different teams on the program are working on.
3. The collaboration tool Confluence[3] provided us wikis with detailed information on logical architecture models and documentations. We used it as a complementary source of information.

Analysis of collected data: The quantitative data of the user story assignment was analyzed by using descriptive statistics. The Likert-scale data of the structured interviews were coded, which then were used to calculate the mean for each question per stakeholder group. Workshop protocols and wikis were analyzed and information was clustered utilizing open coding [27]. After the initial coding, we looked at groups of code phrases and merged them into concepts. Subsequently, we related the concepts to our formulated research questions. Finally, the main findings were incorporated in a framework.

---

[2] https://www.atlassian.com/software/jira, last accessed on: 2018-01-18.
[3] https://www.atlassian.com/software/confluence, last accessed on: 2018-01-18.

4 Applying Domain-Driven Design in Large-Scale Agile Development

4.1 Case Description

This paper comprises the result of a case study conducted 2017 in a large insurance company. The involved interview partners form a unit with three agile teams with two to eight developers developing with other teams an integrated sales platform for several distribution channels. The agile teams are cross-functional including employees from the IT department as well as from business domains and coexist next to many other teams that use waterfall methodologies for software development. This agile unit primarily focuses on the development of its particular product, without being distracted by other external tasks. For that reason, they are co-located at another location of the company. As agile methodologies were not commonly used in the company before, the agile teams received training concerning agile methodologies before the program begins and during the development process. The agile based product development has started two years ago and is not finished yet.

It is required that all teams adopt the same lean and agile based methodology which is basically LeSS extended by some XP practices. This methodology tailored for the insurance company was created with assistance of the company Pivotal that provided know-how on lean startup and agile principles [28]. The most essential feature added to the Scrum methodology is the development and release of Minimum Viable Products (MVP). Prototypes are used to validate proof of concepts. An MVP already represents a finished product that includes only minimal features. An MVP is released very early in the development process in order to incorporate and adapt customer feedback [29]. After having released a first MVP after 100 days, the team extends the MVP gradually with further functions.

4.2 Framework

In the following, we will describe the large-scale agile development endeavor of the insurance organization along the tiers, roles, processes, artifacts, and tools of our proposed framework (see Fig. 1).

Strategic Domain-driven Design: Determines in which subdomains the different teams work. This is achieved by assigning all user stories of all teams to the subdomain they belong to. An overview of all domains and their subdomains was created by an enterprise architect (EA) before applying the defined framework. However, the overview of the domains can be adapted in the course of the process, e.g., in case completely new features are implemented. The assignment is conducted by the teams themselves and is continuously evaluated through an enterprise architecture management (EAM). The results support decisions of program managers (PM) and product owners (PO), e.g., to determine whether the teams have overlapping requirements. Ideally, there is little overlap between the domains and subdomains to reduce dependencies across the teams.

Large-scale agile development process: It is the central part of the framework, which is the main process of all teams. It is enriched by DDD practices. During the development process, all teams provide input to the DDD processes. Based on their inputs teams can also profit from the results of the incorporated DDD approaches. The development process in the framework incorporates many elements as defined by LeSS. LeSS is considered to fit best in those challenges where the number of teams is still manageable, but likely to increase in the near future. LeSS incorporates agile modeling approaches which can be easily connected to DDD. Additionally, LeSS suggests to have a single PO and a single product backlog for all teams. This is crucial for product quality and dealing with overarching functions.

Tactical Domain-driven Design: It describes how agile teams can use the DDD approach to contribute to their own development process. The central element of tactical DDD is the domain model which serves as ubiquitous language in each team individually. All input for the domain model comes from the respective team, while the EA mainly provide methodological guidance, e.g., as facilitator. The domain models are continuously improved throughout within entire development process. For evolving the domain model, agile modeling techniques, such as event storming workshops, are used. Each agile team defines, uses, and evolves its own domain model.

Roles: Our framework proposes program managers (PM) and enterprise architects (EA) in addition to developers, a scrum master (SM), and a single PO. The developers are organized in three agile teams. The teams are self-managing, co-located and long-lived. The teams clarify, implement, and test user stories. The role of the SM is not depicted explicitly in our framework, as the SM role correspondents to the SM role in Scrum. Each team has an own SM who has no specified inter-team responsibilities. Within our framework, one PO is responsible for all agile teams. The PO manages the single product backlog. This especially includes prioritization of user stories and assignment of them in cooperation with representatives from all teams to the most suitable team. The PO acts as a connector between teams, customers, and higher-level management being in continuous exchange with the PMs. The PO communicates with all teams continuously and is aware of team dependencies. The PO advises the PM concerning organizational structures and suggests to reorganize teams. The PM mostly use the input from strategic DDD for strategic decisions, e.g., determining the organizational structure and deciding if additional teams are necessary for the overall program. PM only take part in strategic DDD and participate in higher level workshops in order to detect overarching functions which are to be implemented within the program. The EA provides methodological guidance to teams. On a strategic level, the EA gives an overview of domains and subdomains to the team. This includes a first draft of the overview as well as coaching the team on how to use this artifact. The EA evolves the domain overview considering the input from the teams and is responsible that the overview is adapted accordingly in all tools. The EA supports teams with the continuous user story assignment and presents its results comprehensively to the PO and PMs.

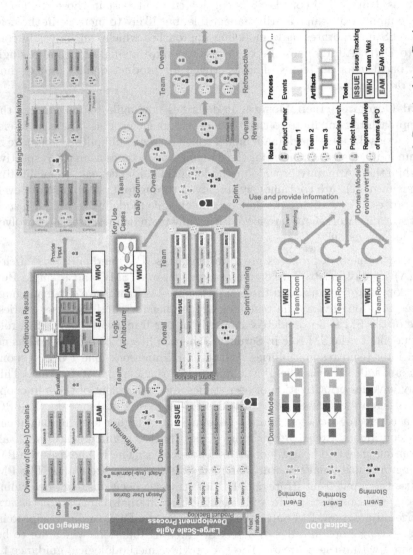

Fig. 1. Overall framework for supporting large-scale agile development with Domain-driven Design.

The EA has no decision-making authority, but provides input to decisions. On a tactical level, the EA introduces the method of event storming as well as domain modeling to the teams. The EA is the moderator in all event storming workshops and teaches the teams how the event storming approach works and how they can incorporate the domain model in their development process in a way that provides value to the teams in terms of reaching a common understanding and defining an own ubiquitous language. The EA optionally participates in team backlog refinements or team retrospectives to help with keeping the domain model up-to-date. Also, the EA supports teams with their continuous domain modeling.

Events: They consist of four types: traditional Scrum events, large-scale agile events, DDD events, and the Sprint itself. The traditional Scrum events comprises the intra-team events, namely sprint planning, backlog refinement, daily Scrum, and retrospective. The large-scale agile events consist of overall sprint planning, backlog refinement, daily scrum, retrospective, and review events. The PO and representatives from all teams participate in all inter-team events. This allows the PO in the framework to communicate with all teams continuously and in parallel. These meetings especially allow discussions about dependencies and responsibilities of the teams. The DDD events include the continuous user story assignment and evaluation, and strategic decision making on the strategic DDD level. The event storming workshops takes place on the tactical DDD level. The continuous user story assignment and evaluation serves to determine a suitable organizational structure in line with the DDD approach. The goal is to have teams that are working in one bounded context within one subdomain. The strategic decision making in the framework is done by the PO and PMs. Here, they are mostly concerned about the organizational structure of the teams. This comprises not only potentially restructuring of existing teams, but also deciding about the responsibilities as soon a new team is added. The event storming workshop supports exploration of complex business domains with domain models starting with domain events as their most crucial part. It allows to come up with a comprehensive model of the business flow in a domain by bringing domain experts and developers together in a room to build a model collaboratively. The approach is in line with DDD, as it helps to determine bounded contexts and aggregates quickly. It has a very easy and intuitive notation that all participants can understand. The event storming workshops create an atmosphere for discussions about the business logic. In the case study, event storming is regarded as a first step towards defining a domain model with the central concept of events.

LeSS suggests to synchronize the sprints for all teams. This means the same sprint length as well as sprint start and end. Here a sprint length of one to two weeks is suggested.

Artifacts: Essential to the framework are different artifacts which are used and created in the process. While on the strategic DDD level, the overview of the subdomain as well as the results of the user story assignment are essential, on the tactical DDD level the domain models are the central artifacts. User stories, product and sprint backlog are very essential in the strategic DDD as well as in the development process. It makes sense for the teams to define key use cases and to document the logic architecture. The logic architecture models provides a rough sketch of the entire system. Key use cases can be used to understand what a typical user expects from a system, how a user interacts with the systems and benefits from it.

Tools: The agile teams use Jira to manage the product backlog. In order to document which domain and subdomains are affected by a user story, a new field called "Affected Domain" has been added to Jira (see Fig. 2).

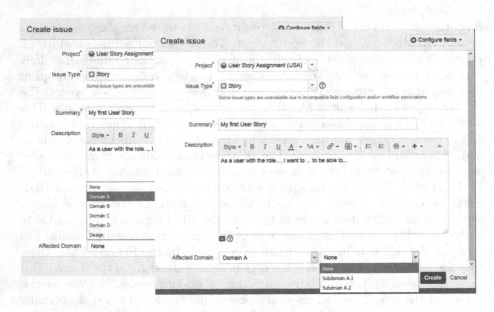

Fig. 2. Example of assigning domains and subdomains to user stories.

Further application of the framework requires a team collaboration software and a wiki. In the case study, the agile teams utilize Confluence as a knowledge base for collaboration and documentations. All teams have established a wiki for their documentations. Each team has its own wiki space. An overarching wiki space is also present. The overarching space includes among others documentation on strategic and tactical DDD as well as documentation of the overview of domains and subdomains. Most importantly, on one page the event storming method is explained and a picture of the current domain for the corresponding team is included. All former versions of the domain model are included to document its development over time. Additionally, an Enterprise Architecture Management (EAM) tool is necessary to be able to automate the evaluation of the user story assignment. The EA uses the EAM tool Iteraplan. It facilitates the automation of the evaluation of the user story assignment. The user stories with assigned domains and subdomains can be imported from Jira in order to build figures, e.g., nesting cluster graphics, which visualize subdomains and teams working on them with (sub-)domains colored depending on their total number of user stories. PM can use Iteraplan's figures for strategic decision making.

5   Evaluation

In order to evaluate the defined framework, we conducted interviews with nine persons in the insurance company of which four are part of an agile team. The other interview partners work in roles that frequently interact with agile teams. The interviewees were two PM (PM1, PM2), one scrum master (SM), two business analysts (BA1, BA2), one PO, one department head of sales processes and applications (DH), one lead EA, and one domain architect (DA). Interview partners were not only asked if they agree or disagree to a statement, but also for the reasons for their choice. Figure 3 shows the statements and the respective degree of agreement by the interviewees.

Strategic Domain-driven Design: The evaluation of the Strategic DDD component includes the user story assignment and interview results. In total, 425 stories were assigned by three teams. User stories purely concerned with UI design and technical issues - around 35% - have not been assigned as they do not belong to any business subdomain. Nearly 58% were assigned unambiguously to a business subdomain. Only 3% of user stories were either very difficult to assign meaning that no suitable subdomain was defined yet. 4% of the user stories were assigned to more than one subdomain which is caused by a very broad scope of user stories. This can be prevented by dividing the respective stories focusing on functional requirements of only one subdomain. According to the interview results, the agile teams themselves have not profited extensively from the user story assignment so far. However, the architects, PMs, and PO evaluated the assignment of user stories as more beneficial. The PO considered that the result of the user story assignment proved correct about the overarching subdomains his team works in. DH, PM1 and PM2 confirmed that the results show the core focus of each team as well as overarching functions that need to be discussed with different teams. Further, they state that results can be a valid basis to restructure teams and their responsibilities. The SM stated that making benefits of such a method clearer to agile team members help them to profit from the user story assignment in the future. This could include providing the results continuously on a wiki page accessible by all involved persons.

Tactical Domain-driven Design: Evolving own domains models for each team starting with event storming workshops reveals a very high agreement among all interview partners. The model helps the teams to reach a common understanding of the business logic in its domain and serves as a shared language for all team members - developers and business experts (DA, PO, EA). SM regarded domain models as very helpful to detect which functionality could be added next and as a tool to discuss how the logic changes. DA mentioned that in the future this domain model has to be found in the code as a representation of the

242   Ö. Uludağ et al.

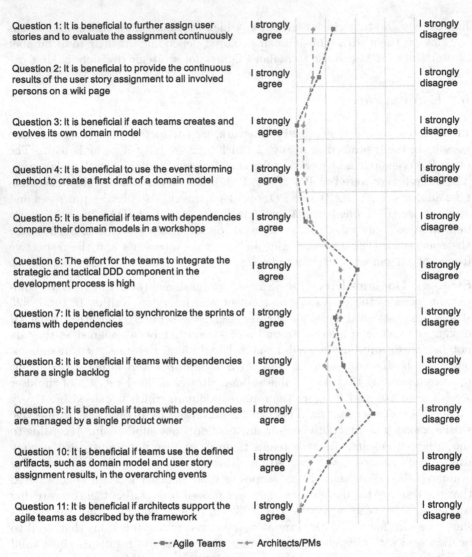

Fig. 3. Evaluation results of the proposed framework.

business logic. However, PM1 mentioned that this might make more sense in the future when the teams are structured based on subdomains. In general, the team members who participated in the event storming workshops were convinced that the method is helpful. Advantages of the method are that it is very simple (PO, AM), that it creates a good atmosphere for open discussions (BA2, EA), that its focus is on business events and logic (BA2) and helps to find aggregates and (sub-)domain boundaries (PM1). According to DA, focusing on business logic before addressing technical issues is helpful. Comparing domain models between teams is considered beneficial to determine boundaries of each teams work (BA2), to reach a common understanding of the business logic and where interfaces between the applications are required as well as to define a published language (DH). However, this approach can increase the need for cross-team coordination and communication (EA, BA1). Further, this might not be desired by the teams as they are supposed to reach their own goals and therefore their interests in common goals and overall architecture might not be given (AM). According to DA, the EA's responsibility is to compare domain models and to detect challenges that might occur. An EA could contact the affected teams and bring them together to discuss and decide on the detected issues. These results were also observed in the event storming workshops.

Large-Scale Agile Development Process: The effort for the integration of the strategic and tactical DDD components was assessed neither as low nor high. Team members who participated in the assignment and the workshops assessed efforts higher. As this component of the framework has not been operationalized yet, further questions concerned the development process in general. The opinions differ if synchronizing sprints, sharing a single backlog and a single PO is beneficial. Some interviewees argued that actually no dependencies should exist and continuous delivery and integration would make such means unnecessary (PM2, BA2, DA). However, other interviewees stated that with similar complexity, using components of scaling agile frameworks could enhance transparency and focus on common goals (EA, PM1). A single PO supports overarching prioritization of user stories (AM, EA), but if the agile teams are inexperienced it might be too much work for one person (PO, DH, PM2).

Concluding, the use of the defined artifacts, such as domain models and user story assignment results, was considered as helpful and especially support of agile teams by architects has been seen as very beneficial by all interview partners. According to DH, architects play a central role for making overarching strategic considerations, e.g., concerning team structure (PO, BA1, BA2). Others considered architects also as coaches for new methodologies, such as DDD and event storming (PM1, AM, BA2).

6 Discussion

Key findings: After working independently from all architectural governance, the agile teams and PM conceived that without any form of architectural guidance large agile programs can hardly be successful. Therefore, one of the key findings is that agile teams, as soon as there are several of them on a program, need to be supported by EA having an overview of the teams and the applications they develop. Many challenges arise which cannot be addressed by single teams, but need to be addressed with overarching methods driven by overarching roles within the organization. Especially, combining large-scale agile practices and DDD can address various challenges. While scaling agile frameworks support cross-team coordination and communication, they lack detailed advice on how to do architecting in large scale agile programs. DDD provides basic concepts for the architecture that can be beneficial not only to the agile teams, but the program overall. Architectural activities in agile programs earlier were not accepted by agile teams who wanted to work independently. However, if architects are capable of providing apparent value to the agile teams, they appreciate architectural support. The same applies for PM and other decision makers. To be able to demonstrate value quickly to both decision makers and agile teams, we recommend starting with both strategic and tactical DDD at the same time. Decision makers will profit soon from the strategic DDD, while agile teams profit mostly from the tactical component. The framework shows how to combine large-scale agile development and DDD in a light-weight manner.

Threats to validity: We discuss potential threats to validity using Runeson and Höst's [21] criteria for assessing the validity of case studies. The first criterion is **construct validity**. It reflects to what extent the operational measures that are studied really represent what the researcher has in mind, and what is investigated according to the research questions. To address this aspect, we interviewed multiple persons with different roles and attended various event storming workshops. The interviews and workshop protocols were coded and analyzed. We also applied a "mixed methods" approach as we gathered data through direct observations, structured interviews, and various software tools. Another potential concern is that of **internal validity**, which is not relevant, as this research was neither explanatory nor causal [21]. A third criterion is **external validity**, i.e. to what extent it is possible to generalize the findings. We focus on analytical generalization [21] by providing a thorough description of the case. Particularly, our case study provides empirical insights that allow for a profound understanding of this insurance organization's large-scale agile development endeavor. The presented findings should be viewed as valuable insights for other organizations interested in supporting large-scale agile development efforts with DDD. Runeson and Höst's [21] last criterion is **reliability**. It is concerned with to what extent the data and the analysis are dependent on the specific researcher. To mitigate this threat, the study has been designed so that data was collected from different sources.

7   Conclusion and Future Work

The success of agile methods for small, co-located teams has inspired organizations to increasingly apply agile practices to large-scale endeavors [2]. However, large organizations face challenges when scaling agility such as inter-team coordination, dependencies on other programs, and lack of clearly defined requirements [30]. Especially, a lacking definition of architecture causes problems when adopting agile methods. Agile methods do not provide guidance on architecture, but assume that it emerges with each iteration and continuous re-factoring. This can be problematic as soon as complex systems are built by many teams. Some governance and architectural planning is required to define work coordination and to develop reliable and scalable systems [2,16]. DDD encourages an iterative and collaborative process for evolving architecture in an agile way.

Our case study provides a detailed description of how DDD can support large-scale agile development. The findings indicate that it is easier to gain traction of decision makers and agile teams at first by demonstrating the value of DDD. Our findings show that agile teams need some form of architectural guidance and support by EA having a holistic overview of the teams and the applications they develop. Stakeholders involved in the large-scale agile program appreciate that architects not only coach the teams concerning new methods, but also support them in application and exploitation. Our proposed approach fostered the acceptance of architectural thinking of agile teams. It helped them to realize the benefits of architecting, thus, encouraging their intrinsic motivation. Our study contributes to the growing knowledge base on supporting large-scale agile software development with EA.

We will continue to study the case organization as the large-scale agile development effort becomes more mature and the presented framework will be further operationalized. In addition, we plan to study the collaboration between EA and agile teams in other large organizations that are pursuing large-scale agile development endeavors. Also, we are interested in identifying recurring stakeholder concerns and beneficial practices.

References

1. Dingsøyr, T., Nerur, S., Balijepally, V., Moe, N.B.: A decade of agile methodologies: towards explaining agile software development (2012)
2. Dingsøyr, T., Moe, N.B.: Towards principles of large-scale agile development. In: Dingsøyr, T., Moe, N.B., Tonelli, R., Counsell, S., Gencel, C., Petersen, K. (eds.) XP 2014. LNBIP, vol. 199, pp. 1–8. Springer, Cham (2014). https://doi.org/10. 1007/978-3-319-14358-3_1
3. Rost, D., Weitzel, B., Naab, M., Lenhart, T., Schmitt, H.: Distilling best practices for agile development from architecture methodology. In: Weyns, D., Mirandola, R., Crnkovic, I. (eds.) ECSA 2015. LNCS, vol. 9278, pp. 259–267. Springer, Cham (2015). https://doi.org/10.1007/978-3-319-23727-5_21
4. Nord, R.L., Ozkaya, I., Kruchten, P.: Agile in distress: architecture to the rescue. In: Dingsøyr, T., Moe, N.B., Tonelli, R., Counsell, S., Gencel, C., Petersen, K. (eds.) XP 2014. LNBIP, vol. 199, pp. 43–57. Springer, Cham (2014). https://doi. org/10.1007/978-3-319-14358-3_5
5. Agile architecture. http://www.scaledagileframework.com/agile-architecture/. Accessed 22 Nov 2017
6. Mocker, M.: What is complex about 273 applications? untangling application architecture complexity in a case of European investment banking. In: 2009 42nd Hawaii International Conference on System Sciences HICSS 2009, pp. 1–14. IEEE (2009)
7. Nord, R.L., Ozkaya, I., Sangwan, R.S.: Making architecture visible to improve flow management in lean software development. IEEE Softw. 29(5), 33–39 (2012)
8. Uludağ, Ö., Kleehaus, M., Xu, X., Matthes, F.: Investigating the role of architects in scaling agile frameworks. In: 2017 IEEE 21st International Enterprise Distributed Object Computing Conference (EDOC), pp. 123–132. IEEE (2017)
9. Abrahamsson, P., Babar, M.A., Kruchten, P.: Agility and architecture: can they coexist? IEEE Softw. 27(2), 16–22 (2010)

10. Augustine, S.: Managing Agile Projects. Prentice Hall PTR, Upper Saddle River (2005)
11. Babar, M.A.: An exploratory study of architectural practices and challenges in using agile software development approaches. In: 2009 Joint Working IEEE/IFIP Conference on Software Architecture & European Conference on Software Architecture WICSA/ECSA 2009, pp. 81–90. IEEE (2009)
12. Beck, K.: Extreme Programming Explained: Embrace Change. Addison-Wesley Professional, Boston (2000)
13. Meyer, B.: Agile!: The Good, the Hype and the Ugly. Springer, Switzerland (2014). https://doi.org/10.1007/978-3-319-05155-0
14. Freudenberg, S., Sharp, H.: The.top 10 burning research questions from practitioners. IEEE Softw. 27(5), 8–9 (2010)
15. Bellomo, S., Kruchten, P., Nord, R.L., Ozkaya, I.: How to agilely architect an agile architecture. Cutter IT J. 27(2), 12–17 (2014)
16. Leffingwell, D., Martens, R., Zamora, M.: Principles of agile architecture. LLC. and Rally Software Development Corp., Leffingwell (2008)
17. Buchmann, F., Nord, R.L., Ozakaya, I.: Architectural tactics to support rapid and agile stability. Carnegie-Mellon Univ Pittsburgh PA Software Engineering Inst., Technical Report (2012)
18. Cockburn, A.: Crystal Clear: A Human-powered Methodology for Small Teams. Pearson Education, Upper Saddle River (2004)
19. Scaled agile framework. http://www.scaledagileframework.com/. Accessed 05 Dec 2017
20. The disciplined agile (DA) framework. http://www.disciplinedagiledelivery.com/. Accessed 05 Dec 2017
21. Runeson, P., Höst, M.: Guidelines for conducting and reporting case study research in software engineering. Empir. Softw. Eng. 14(2), 131 (2008). https://doi.org/10.1007/s10664-008-9102-8
22. Benbasat, I., Goldstein, D.K., Mead, M.: The case research strategy in studies of information systems. MIS Q. 11(3), 369–386 (1987)
23. Yin, R.K.: Case Study Research: Design and Methods. Sage Publications, Thousand Oaks (2013)
24. Lethbridge, T.C., Sim, S.E., Singer, J.: Studying software engineers: data collection techniques for software field studies. Empir. Softw. Eng. 10(3), 311–341 (2005)
25. Brandolini, A.: Introducing EventStorming: An act of Deliberate Collective Learning. Leanpub (2017)
26. Stake, R.E.: The Art of Case Study Research. Sage, Thousand Oaks (1995)
27. Miles, M.B., Huberman, A.M., Saldana, J.: Qualitative Data Analysis: A Methods Sourcebook. Sage Publications Ltd., Thousand Oaks (2014)
28. Pivotal Software: Pivotal labs (2017). https://pivotal.io/labs
29. Moogk, D.R.: Minimum viable product and the importance of experimentation in technology startups (2012). http://timreview.ca/article/535
30. Paasivaara, M., Lassenius, C.: Scaling scrum in a large globally distributed organization: a case study. In: 2016 IEEE 11th International Conference on Global Software Engineering (ICGSE), pp. 74–83, August 2016

Towards Agile Scalability Engineering

Gunnar Brataas[1(✉)], Geir Kjetil Hanssen[1], and Georg Ræder[2]

[1] SINTEF Digital, Trondheim, Norway
{Gunnar.Brataas,Geir.K.Hanssen}@sintef.no
[2] EVRY Norway AS, Fornebu, Norway
Georg.Raeder@evry.com

Abstract. Scalability engineering is currently not well integrated into agile development techniques. This paper extends agile development techniques so that scalability can be handled in an incremental and iterative development process. By scalability we mean the ability of a system to handle increasing workload. We propose the ScrumScale Method which includes scalability engineering in Scrum. This extension should also be applicable to other agile techniques. For scalability testing, we indicate how quality thresholds should be scaled up or down according to the degree of completeness of the product, test hardware, test software, test data and test workload. Using action research, we have conducted three pilots in three Norwegian software organizations. These three pilots have different architectures and operate in different markets yet have in common scalability challenges.

Keywords: Scrum · Software performance engineering (SPE)
Action research

1 Introduction

A scalable system can handle increasing workloads by utilizing more hardware or software resources [4, 6]. A system with poor scalability is unable to extend its capacity if demanded by unexpected workloads. A costly and time-consuming redesign is required. Despite careful planning and design, scalability is still a "fragile" property that can easily be jeopardized by carelessness or problems in inter-connected systems. Hence, scalability is a pervasive property of a system.

Agile methods address a similar challenge. Agile methods target development projects where requirements are not fully known in advance. Using agile methods, software projects deliver parts of the solution with the intention of quickly validating whether the deliverables meet user expectations. Many software organizations are continuously challenged to reduce time to market for new solutions. Agile methods help them to scope delivered solutions so that they can rapidly adjust to unpredictable market needs.

At present, we lack conceptually sound approaches to incorporating scalability engineering into agile software development. Many software organizations are faced with a difficult balancing act when trying to accommodate both. Scalability is a

J. Garbajosa et al. (Eds.): XP 2018, LNBIP 314, pp. 248–255, 2018.
https://doi.org/10.1007/978-3-319-91602-6_17

property of a system that accentuates the tensions between planning and agility to a new level. Both scalability and agility seek to accommodate uncertainty. Both scalability and agility are important to meeting the needs for software organizations' competitiveness. It is therefore imperative that we find solutions to how scalability and agility can be combined.

Babar et al. advocate a middle ground between agile development and incorporating elements of up-front planning [1]. We seek to develop more powerful concepts for dealing with scalability to assist stakeholders and practitioners in their collaboration on scalability engineering. In particular, we think that a more effective language for scalability will assist in enabling collaboration among product owners, architects, developers and testers on the construction of sound scalability requirements. Scalability testing can be put to use in a more agile working practice where it contributes to produce continuous feedback.

We are in the middle of the ScrumScale project that seeks to resolve this challenge. The main objective of the ScrumScale project is to reduce the cost of handling scalability using agile development practices. This cost may be reduced in three ways: (1) Using care when developing software so that costly and time-consuming redesign is reduced. (2) Less gold-plating of subsystems that scale "too well," to reduce development costs. (3) Reduced consumption of hardware (CPUs, disks, networks) and software resources (with license and cloud service fees) as a result of improved scalability.

The main result of ScrumScale will be an extension of agile techniques to accommodate scalability. We have started with Scrum, but these extensions should also be applicable to other agile techniques. The main contribution of this paper is a Scrum-based process for how to handle scalability in Sect. 2. For scalability testing, we indicate how quality thresholds should be scaled up or down according to the degree of completeness of the product, test hardware, test software, test data and test workload. In Sect. 3, conclusions and further work are outlined.

ScrumScale adopts the action research paradigm where researchers and practitioners seek to solve problems in collaboration using cycles of the steps diagnosis, planning, intervention, evaluation and reflection [5]. In addition to the research partner SINTEF, ScrumScale has the three industrial partners EVRY, Powel and Altinn. EVRY delivers financial services solutions, Powel energy and public software solutions with related services, while Altinn is the largest Norwegian public portal.

We have completed the first pilot phase with one pilot for each industrial partner. These pilots differ both in scope, domain as well as duration. Common to all these three pilots were anticipated scalability challenges. The initial diagnosis before starting these three pilots showed that the root cause of problematic scalability was vague scalability requirements [2]. Clarifying scalability requirements has therefore been the focus in the first pilot phase. Scalability testing has also been done. Monitoring during operations is not handled yet. Apart from participating in the three pilots, we have arranged retrospectives and conducted structured interviews with main stakeholders in all three organizations.

2   The ScrumScale Method

With the ScrumScale Method, we seek to combine scalability concerns with agility, and so we work with scalability earlier in the development cycle than what is normally the case, as illustrated in Fig. 1.

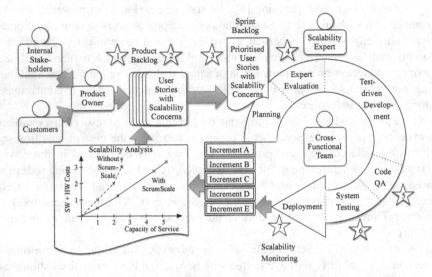

Fig. 1. ScrumScale vision

The ScrumScale Method has the following seven steps for each new product:

1. Scalability triage with a rough, intuitive expert evaluation and feedback
2. Extract business-related scalability requirements to get feedback on them
3. Derive testable scalability requirements to get feedback on them
4. Expert evaluation to get feedback on solution suggestions
5. Code review to get feedback on implementation
6. Scalability testing to get feedback on solution
7. Exploit monitoring data to improve the solution but also to get feedback on the actual workload

In all these steps, we get feedback, so they are applied iteratively and lend themselves to integration in an agile development process, such as Scrum. In fact, this integration is driven by both sides: Modern, agile practice calls for scalability to be handled likewise, but scalability also will benefit from a more light-weight, iterative approach.

The product backlog is set up initially where the product owner in collaboration with customers and other stakeholders defines and prioritizes user stories. Some user stories may be associated with scalability concerns. In between each iteration, the product owner may revisit the product backlog to add or change user stories based on the outcome and new knowledge from the previous sprint. If needed, the product owner should include a scalability expert (champion) to evaluate whether a new or changed story will impact the scalability of the solution. This evaluation may be supported by scalability testing and monitoring of the solution as it is so far. Likewise, a scalability expert may also assist the team that creates code to implement user stories. Sprints are short and time-boxed work periods, typically 2–4 weeks, where scalability is evaluated as part of the sprint review and the planning of the next sprint.

For code review (step 5) and monitoring (step 7) we build on existing practices. The other five steps are described in more detail below.

2.1 Scalability Triage

This is a fast and informal step where scalability experts try to answer the question: Are there scalability risks associated with the product? Work, load, and quality thresholds are not analyzed explicitly. Therefore, this step requires extensive experience. Features dealing with GUI or adding small details to an otherwise large computation will probably not pose a threat to scalability. Only for features where there may be a threat to scalability will we go further in the ScrumScale Method, where we start by working with the scalability requirements. For the remainder of the features, we simply stop here. This is important, since the remainder of the steps, even though they are light-weight, involve some effort.

2.2 Extract Business-Related Requirements

Like other product requirements, scalability requirements originate from business goals: What is the ambition and planned roadmap for the product? The first step in scalability requirements elicitation is therefore, to engage product management and ask questions such as:

- What is the total number of users we want to support?
- What types of users (roles) are there: the public, administrators, specialists, etc.
- What is the total number of objects the system should be able to handle (such as the number of books in an on-line book store)?
- What are good quality metrics? Is a 90-percentile response time metric useful?
- What are expected magnitudes of quality thresholds –0.1 s, 1 s, 10 s, 1 min, 1 h, 1 day, etc.?
- What is the time horizon for the scalability requirements? Is there a planned ramp-up of user load or objects handled? A time horizon larger than five years is probably too much, but shorter than two years probably too small.

Product owners may also have an idea of the expected operating cost of the system in terms of hardware and software license cost per user, per transaction, or similar. If this is clear, it is recorded at this stage, but it cannot be validated until fairly late in the process when resource demands become understood [2].

The requirements gathered at this stage are often imprecise, and not always consistent or even relevant, but they capture the stakeholders' expectations in a language that they are comfortable with. The next step is to analyze this input and derive precise, useful and testable scalability requirements.

2.3   Derive Testable Scalability Requirements

To derive systematic, testable requirements, we build on the conceptual model in [4] which is used to understand scalability requirements in [3]. The *system boundaries* define which services are included when measuring quality metrics. An *operation* defines a unique and relatively similar way of interacting with a service. A *quality metric* defines how we measure a certain quality and is a key part of an SLA (service-level agreement). At an overall level, response times and throughput are traditional scalability quality metrics, but more details are required. Is it average or 90 percentile response times? *Quality thresholds (QTs)* describe the border between acceptable and non-acceptable quality for each operation and is connected to a particular quality metric. With the 90-percentile response time quality metric some operations may have a 0.1 s quality thresholds, while the threshold is 10 s for other operations.

Load is how often an operation is invoked. In a closed system, load is specified by the number of users (N) and the think time (Z). Since no users enter or leave the system, the number of users is constant. Think time is the average time to compose operation invocations to the system. For an open system, we use arrival rate (λ), measured in operations per time unit, for example 100 transactions per second. In the context of scalability, we are interested in the highest load, i.e. the load during the busiest hour, week, month, and year in our planning horizon.

Work characterizes the amount of data to be processed, stored or communicated when invoking one operation. Ultimately, work describes the amount of hardware and software resources consumed when invoking one operation. The set of operations is of course an important part of work characterization, but so are also key data objects, like documents and accounts. When considering scalability, we are interested in how the work for one operation varies. This is connected to sizes of objects, e.g. number of documents and the average size of these documents. Such parameters are *work parameters*. For scalability, we focus on the highest values of the work parameters. Whereas load typically go up and down during the day, week, and month, work parameters typically only increase.

Together, work multiplied by load becomes *workload*. The highest workload fulfilling quality thresholds is the *capacity* of a system.

The *critical operations* are the operations where the product of load and work poses a risk of not fulfilling the quality thresholds. Of course, it would be beneficial to establish the critical operations early, but this set is also a result of the analysis. Therefore, iterations, a strong point in agile methods, are required.

As more knowledge is gained, the granularity may increase or decrease, when operations are split or merged, more work parameters are introduced, or the quality thresholds are defined for each individual operation instead of the same threshold for several operations [2]. The system boundary may also change. However, as we learn more, we see what we can simplify and leave out. This is a typical modeling experience where the granularity (size) of the model increases because of increased understanding before it decreases, when we understand what really matters.

At this step, it is useful to get information on the technical approach: system type (e.g. three-tier web application or batch application) and platform (e.g. cloud).

2.4   Expert Evaluation

The most important outcome of this light-weight expert evaluation is advice on good design decisions and the identification of problem areas when systems are built step by step. This will be part of the planning process and also give input to defining testable scalability requirements, and it will only be performed for high-risk projects. Performance patterns and anti-patterns are explicit and well-documented examples of this knowledge [7], but experts have "silent" knowledge much beyond this. The experts will try to answer the question "Will the product of work and load pose a threat to the quality thresholds?" This can have two outcomes: (1) No risk. (2) Potential risk so that more investigation is required.

Scalability experts (champions) will be a limited resource in all organizations. Therefore, one scalability expert will assist several teams and in this way transfer experience across many different projects and technologies.

2.5   Scalability Testing

During scalability testing, we have partial information across many dimensions:

- Solution: Only some increments are completed.
- Test hardware: May not be as powerful as the production hardware.
- Test software: The versions may not resemble the production environment.
- Test data: Synthetic test data may not represent the details which make scalability hard. Real data may be used, after obfuscation.
- Test workload: It may be hard to anticipate all strange usage patterns for real users.
- Time to do scalability testing: It is clearly a trade-off between how extensive scalability testing can be performed with frequent iterations. A full, frequent scalability test will simply not be feasible. It is an open question how many scalability requirement violations can be detected by a simple automated test.
- Partial competence because of less-than perfect knowledge exchange between scalability tester, architects and developer. To participate in the same Scrum team will of course help. Moreover, selecting optimal configuration parameters for software and hardware is challenging.

As a result, we should also scale the scalability requirements. When only parts of the solution are completed, it cannot consume *the complete* quality thresholds. We do not use models for unfinished parts of the system, but some kind of implicit modelling is required to scale the requirements up or down, according to the degree of completeness of the other dimensions. We may, for example, assume that the basic platform takes half of the time, whereas each of ten features share the rest. A system with two features should then consume approximately 60% of the resources compared to a complete product. Moreover, if the database server resembles the production environment, while the application servers and the network are weaker compared to the production environment, it becomes harder.

3 Conclusion

Half-way into the ScrumScale project, we see the contours of a profitable fusion of scalability engineering and agile practices. To lay the foundation for such an approach, we have described a series of method steps that can be applied in an iterative manner, allowing an agile approach to scalability engineering.

ScrumScale extends Scrum by connecting functional requirements with scalability requirements to enable evaluation of scalability after each sprint, supported by monitoring and testing. When new sprints are planned detailed design is evaluated with respect to scalability. ScrumScale also adds a new role, the scalability expert, or champion, that supports the team in making the right decisions.

We are developing these artefacts iteratively through trials on real pilots in three partner companies. We will continue with more pilots, making the ScrumScale Method a practical tool for agile scalability engineering.

Acknowledgements. The research leading to these results has received funding from the Norwegian Research Council under grant #256669 (ScrumScale). Tor Erlend Fægri, then in SINTEF Digital, contributed with early ideas for this paper. EVRY, Powel and Altinn contributed with pilots.

References

1. Babar, M.A., Brown, A.W., Mistrík, I.: Agile Software Architecture: Aligning Agile Processes and Software Architectures. Newnes, Oxford (2013)
2. Becker, S., Brataas, G., Lehrig, S.: Engineering Scalable, Elastic, and Cost-Efficient Cloud Computing Applications: The CloudScale Method. Springer, Cham (2017). https://doi.org/10.1007/978-3-319-54286-7
3. Brataas, G., Fægri, T.E.: Agile scalability requirements. In: Proceedings of the 8th ACM/SPEC on International Conference on Performance Engineering. ACM (2017)
4. Brataas, G., Herbst, N., Ivansek, S., Polutnik, J.: Scalability analysis of cloud software services. In: 2017 IEEE International Conference on Autonomic Computing (ICAC). IEEE (2017)
5. Davison, R.M., Martinsons, M.G., Kock, N.: Principles of canonical action research. Inf. Syst. J. **14**(1), 65–86 (2004)
6. Herbst, N.R., Kounev, S., Reussner, R.H.: Elasticity in cloud computing: what it is, and what it is not. In: ICAC (2013)
7. Smith, C.U., Williams, L.G.: Performance Solutions: A Practical Guide to Creating Responsive, Scalable Software. Addison-Wesley, Boston (2001)

Human-Centric Agile

Stress in Agile Software Development: Practices and Outcomes

Andreas Meier[1], Martin Kropp[2], Craig Anslow[3], and Robert Biddle[4(✉)]

[1] Zurich University of Applied Sciences, Winterthur, Switzerland
meea@fhnw.ch
[2] University of Applied Sciences Northwestern Switzerland, Windisch, Switzerland
martin.kropp@fhnw.ch
[3] Victoria University of Wellington, Wellington, New Zealand
craig.anslow@ecs.vuw.ac.nz
[4] Carleton University, Ottawa, Canada
robert.biddle@carleton.ca

Abstract. Stress is an important workplace issue, affecting both the health of individuals, and the health of organizations. Early advocacy for Agile Software Development suggested it might help avoid stress, with practices that emphasize a sustainable pace, and self-organizing teams. Our analysis of a 2014 survey, however, suggested that stress might still be commonplace in Agile teams, especially for those with less experience. We also noticed that newcomers to Agile emphasized technical, rather than collaborative, practices, and speculated this might explain the stress. We explored this in our analysis of a follow-up survey conducted in 2016, and report our findings in this paper. We show that there are a variety of factors involved, and that avoiding stress is associated with both collaborative and technical practices, and a range of outcomes.

Keywords: Stress · Agile · Software development

1 Introduction

Occupational stress is an important workplace issue, affecting both the health of individuals, both physical and mental, and the health of organizations, from turnover, poor productivity, and poor collaboration [1]. Since its inception, Agile software development has emphasized elements that should prevent stress. For example, Extreme Programming (XP) specified a "sustainable pace", and both XP and Scrum emphasized the importance of self-organizing teams. In analysis of the 2014 Swiss Agile Survey [3], however, we were surprised to see that stress appeared to be an issue, especially for practitioners new to Agile. In this paper, we explore the possible reasons for this phenomenon, using data from the 2016 Swiss Agile survey [4].

In the earlier study [5], we asked professionals to identify characteristics that reflected their perception of working in an Agile software development environment. In particular, we explored differences reported by those new to Agile,

© The Author(s) 2018
J. Garbajosa et al. (Eds.): XP 2018, LNBIP 314, pp. 259–266, 2018.
https://doi.org/10.1007/978-3-319-91602-6_18

those with some experience, and those with more extensive experience. One of the themes in our analysis of the 2014 survey was collaboration, and we showed that Agile experience typically began emphasizing technical practices, but that collaborative practices increased in importance with experience. We therefore speculated that stress in Agile might relate to an under-adoption of collaborative practices. The 2016 Swiss Agile Study gave us an opportunity to explore this. Our overall questions were: how do professionals rate how Agile has influenced their stress; how is their stress related to the level of agility in their process; and how is their stress related to their team practices and to the influences they see resulting from their process.

The rest of this paper is structured as follows. In Sect. 2 we outline related research on stress in software engineering processes, and in Sect. 3 we describe our study method. We then present our results in Sect. 4, showing how stress was related to aspects of the software engineering process. In Sect. 5 we discuss these findings and offer our conclusions.

2   Related Work

The paper we cite in the introduction [1] marked a recognition of the way that stress has a negative effect on both individual and organization, and much research has followed. We focus here on research specifically relating to software engineering.

Sonnetag et al. [10] found that stress was related to the "burnout" phenomenon in software development, in particular stress stemming from lack of control, high task requirements, and poor interaction within teams. Mannaro et al. [7], studied factors affecting satisfaction in software teams, and specifically looked at the relationship between stress and the software process being used, finding that (then new) Agile methods were associated with less stress. Rajeswari and Anantharaman [8] studied software professionals in India, and found major stress factors were fear of obsolescence and unhelpful interactions within the team and with clients. A general review of research on teamwork and stress [9] addressed teamwork in a range of industry work, including software development, finding that the quality of interactions within the team to be a key issue. Laanti studied wellbeing and stress in Agile teams within a large organization [6], and found empowerment to be the major factor for healthy teams, but also found that teams perceived as performing poorly experienced stress. Overall, this body of work suggested to us that issues relating to collaborative practices might indeed be related to stress.

3   Study Setup

Our study was a nationwide online survey conducted by us in Switzerland [4]. The study is about the usage of development methods and practices in the IT industry, and about the influence of applying Agile methods on projects. The study addressed both Agile and plan-driven companies as well as both Agile and plan-driven IT professionals. The study was executed as two independent online surveys; one for companies, and one for IT professionals. The survey questions were identical for both groups. The company survey was completed by high-level managers on behalf of their organization. In this paper, therefore, we focus only on the professional survey, where individuals answered describing their own personal situation.

We emailed IT professionals with an anonymous link to the survey. The addresses of the professionals were collected from the participating national IT associations, as well as from our own institutional databases. We distributed the link to the anonymous survey also through professional social media like LinkedIn and XING. 185 IT professionals filled out the complete survey.

The responding IT professionals were typically Senior Software Developers (17%), Software Developers (12%), Project Managers (13%), Team Leader (10%), and Designer/Architects (10%). We had a high number of "Others" (17%), which include roles like Scrum Masters, Agile Coaches and Product Owners. In our analysis, we sometimes isolate the two main categories respondent: "managers", meaning coaches, project managers, and the like, and "developers", meaning those directly engaged in technical work.

We used an input-output model to address project aspects: We were asking about the application of common development practices, especially in Agile software development. We also asked about *influences* of Agile software development, meaning how the process influenced outcomes, especially about business influences, team influences and the influence on software quality. We also added questions about experience, self-ratings and the personal situation and company background. The main basis for our questions were earlier surveys [3,12], and our own experience with industry.

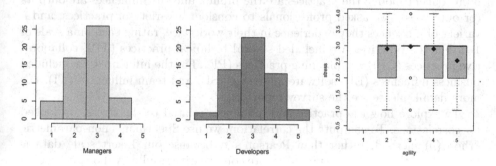

Fig. 1. Left and Centre: Reported stress by managers and developers, on a scale from 1 (unstressed) to 5 (very stressed). Right: Stress reported by Level of Agility; the boxplots show the medians as heavy black lines, inner quartiles as coloured boxes, outer quartiles as whiskers, and the means as diamonds. (Color figure online)

4   Findings

In our survey we asked how Agile software development had influenced their stress at work. They answered on a scale from 1 (significantly less stressed) to 5 (significantly more stressed). Figure 1 (left and centre) shows histograms of the results. As we can see there is a range of answers, with most developers reporting a neutral level, and most "managers" reporting somewhat less. Although these results are not extreme, they do suggest some reason for concern, with sizeable numbers reporting they are more stressed or significantly more stressed (levels 4 and 5).

Our next question relates to the role of Agile development. In our survey, we asked professionals to report the "level of agility" on a scale of 1–5, where 1 was "Mostly Plan-Driven", and 5 was "Mostly Agile". We show the results as a set of boxplots in Fig. 1 (right). These show that at each level of agility, there is a range of stress reported, but the ranges are remarkably similar at all levels. For example, the distribution, median, and mean are the same for agility levels 2 (14%) and 4 (36%). Level 3 (36%) and Level 5 (15%) show tighter and lower ranges, but they have the same median as levels 2 and 4. We found this interesting, because it suggests that the level of agility is not particularly related to the stress reported. We also explored the relationship between stress and experience with Agile methods, and again found little evidence. We do note, however, that we had fewer professionals with little experience in Agile than in our 2014 survey: we speculate this is simply because of the increasingly widespread adoption of Agile methods.

Our survey was designed to explore various aspects of the software development experience, and in particular we wanted to identify the practices in use, and the influences that were perceived as resulting. This is the basis of our input-output model: the practices are the inputs, and the influences are outputs (or outcomes). We asked professionals to consider a variety of practices, and a variety of influences they experience in their workplace, rating each on a scale of 1–5. For the practices, we included several technical practices (TP), collaborative practices (CP), and planning practices (PP). For the influences, we included business influences (BI), software influences (SI), and team influences (TI). For more detail, please see the survey report [4].

To explore how the practice and influences related to the stress, we looked for correlations. To compute the correlation, we use Spearman's non-parametric "rho" (ρ) method, rather than Pearson's r, because our Likert scale data is ordinal, and this approach supports more conservative results. A rho approaching 1 is an extremely close match, approaching -1 is a strong inverse match, and rho approaching 0 is a very poor match.

Our speculation was a relationship between collaborative processes overall, and stress. We therefore calculated a composite score based on all collaborative practices, and compared it with the stress data. We did not find a strong connection: $\rho = -0.16, p = .05$.

We then explored each of the practices, and each of the influences, calculating the correlation of each individually with stress. We modified p-levels with the Bonferroni correction for multiple tests, and used an alpha level of 0.05. For practices, we found the *only* practice with a significant effect was the "Self-Organizing Team" collaborative practice showing $\rho = -0.27, p = 0.02$ (Bonferroni corrected). On further inspection, we found this relationship was strongest with managers, with $\rho = -0.54$.

Exploring influences, we found a more diverse picture. Table 1 shows the top 10 correlations, ranked by $|\rho|$. The p-levels again reflect Bonferroni correction for multiple tests, and we omit any results above an alpha level of 0.05.

As can be seen, the influences that play a role are varied, with software, business, and team influences all involved. Perhaps most notably, several software influences (SI) rate highly: lower defect levels, good software architecture, and overall software quality are all associated with lower stress. The business influences (BI) also relate to good process outcomes, such as requirements management and ability to manage changing priorities. Team influences (TI) reflect a positive environment, such as good morale, an engaged customer, and effective meetings. Looking at differences between managers and developers, we found most of the influence relationships concerned managers, but it was developers who most highly rated low defect rates, ability to manage changing priorities, and morale as most related to reduced stress.

Table 1. Stress correlations for practices.

	Question	rho	p.value
1	SI Defect rate	−0.439	<.001
2	TI Team morale motivation	−0.413	<.001
3	SI Software architecture	−0.374	<.001
4	SI Software quality	−0.362	<.001
5	BI Requirements management	−0.353	0.001
6	SI Engineering discipline	−0.337	0.001
7	SI Software maintainability	−0.335	0.001
8	TI Engagement of customer product owner	−0.333	0.001
9	BI Ability to manage changing priorities	−0.323	0.002
10	TI Effectiveness of meetings	−0.321	0.002

Although the correlation tables are helpful, we know that various factors are involved in understanding stress and we suspected some were more important than others. To explore this further, we applied recursive partitioning to create regression trees [2, 11]. This approach begins with the whole data set, and determines which independent variable, and at what point, best distinctly divides the dependent variable: stress in our case. We thus obtain two coherent sets, one with lower satisfaction, and one with higher, and so on recursively; we stop at 10% of the sample. We show two trees in Fig. 2, one each for practices and influences. The top number at each node shows the stress value mean for the subtree.

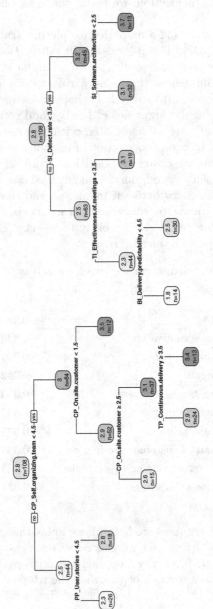

Fig. 2. Recursive partitioning: stress factors in practices and influences.

Looking at practices, we see again that the Self-Organizing Team is the single most important factor. People who rate their experience of that practice as 4 or lower are more stressed. Those without an on-site customer are worse still. Alternatively, those who strongly use user stories are least stressed. For influences, low defect rate dominates. Those who rate that outcome as less than 3.4 are more stressed. Those who rate software architecture as poor are even more stressed. Alternatively, those who achieve effective meetings and predictable delivery are least stressed.

5 Discussion and Conclusions

In this paper we set out to explore a speculation based on earlier work: that in Agile development it appears that stress was still a factor in professional experience. We suspected a lack of collaborative practices might be the cause. Using data from a new study, we found a somewhat more complex picture. First, while a number of participants reported more stress, a similar number reported less stress, and the dominant level was neutral. Second, neither the level of agility claimed, nor Agile experience, was much related to the level of stress reported.

When we explored the practices related to avoiding stress, we found collaborative practices in general were only weakly related to reduced stress, but the effect of Self-Organizing Teams was stronger, especially among those with a leadership role. Lower stress was also linked to many software quality outcomes, such as low defect rate and good software architecture. Looking for the dominating effects, for practices we again found self-organizing teams were most helpful, and story mapping; for developers it was again technical outcomes that were linked to lower stress. The result is not quite what we expected, but indicates a complex structure of stress in software development, and in particular the practices and influences most related to low stress environments.

We acknowledge a number of threats to validity. Our data was self-reported, and from a single country, Switzerland, so local organizational culture might influence the results. There was little evidence for our initial idea about the origin of stress, so our exploration was post-hoc. We therefore need to conduct more research, which will also allow us to take more care in clarifying the key constructs, and to better explore causality.

Acknowledgements. We thank the study participants, the anonymous referees of this paper, and the Swiss IT organizations swissICT and SWEN for funding the study.

References

1. Beehr, T.A., Newman, J.E.: Job stress, employee health, and organizational effectiveness: a facet analysis, model, and literature review. Pers. Psychol. **31**(4), 665–699 (1978)
2. Breiman, L., Friedman, J., Stone, C.J., Olshen, R.A.: Classification and Regression Trees. CRC Press, Boca Raton (1984)

3. Kropp, M., Meier, A.: Swiss agile study 2014. Technical report, Swiss Agile Study (2014). ISSN 2296–2476, http://www.swissagilestudy.ch/files/2015/05/SwissAgileStudy2014.pdf

4. Kropp, M., Meier, A.: Swiss agile study 2016. Technical report, Swiss Agile Study (2017, unpublished). http://www.swissagilestudy.ch

5. Kropp, M., Meier, A., Biddle, R.: Agile practices, collaboration and experience: an empirical study about the effect of experience in agile software development. In: Abrahamsson, P., Jedlitschka, A., Nguyen Duc, A., Felderer, M., Amasaki, S., Mikkonen, T. (eds.) PROFES 2016. LNCS, vol. 10027, pp. 416–431. Springer, Cham (2016). https://doi.org/10.1007/978-3-319-49094-6_28

6. Laanti, M.: Agile and wellbeing-stress, empowerment, and performance in Scrum and Kanban teams. In: 2013 46th Hawaii International Conference on System Sciences (HICSS), pp. 4761–4770. IEEE (2013)

7. Mannaro, K., Melis, M., Marchesi, M.: Empirical analysis on the satisfaction of IT employees comparing XP practices with other software development methodologies. In: Eckstein, J., Baumeister, H. (eds.) XP 2004. LNCS, vol. 3092, pp. 166–174. Springer, Heidelberg (2004). https://doi.org/10.1007/978-3-540-24853-8_19

8. Rajeswari, K., Anantharaman, R.: Development of an instrument to measure stress among software professionals: factor analytic study. In: Proceedings of the 2003 SIGMIS Conference on Computer Personnel Research: Freedom in Philadelphia-Leveraging Differences and Diversity in the IT Workforce, pp. 34–43. ACM (2003)

9. Rasmussen, T.H., Jeppesen, H.J.: Teamwork and associated psychological factors: a review. Work Stress **20**(2), 105–128 (2006)

10. Sonnentag, S., Brodbeck, F.C., Heinbokel, T., Stolte, W.: Stressor-burnout relationship in software development teams. J. Occup. Organ. Psychol. **67**(4), 327–341 (1994)

11. Therneau, T.M., Atkinson, E.J., et al.: An introduction to recursive partitioning using the RPART routines. Technical report, Mayo Foundation for Medical Education and Research, Rochester, Minnesota, USA (1997)

12. VersionOne: 11th state of agile survey. Technical report, VersionOne, Inc. (2017)

Teamwork Quality and Team Performance: Exploring Differences Between Small and Large Agile Projects

Yngve Lindsjørn[1]([⊠]), Gunnar R. Bergersen[1], Torgeir Dingsøyr[2,3],
and Dag I. K. Sjøberg[1]

[1] University of Oslo, Oslo, Norway
{ynglin, gunnab, dagsj}@ifi.uio.no
[2] SINTEF, 7465 Trondheim, Norway
torgeird@sintef.no
[3] Department of Computer and Information Science,
Norwegian University of Science and Technology, Trondheim, Norway

Abstract. Agile principles were originally developed for small projects but are now widely used in larger projects with hundreds of developers. Teamwork quality is essential in any development work, but how does teamwork quality differ in small and large agile projects? We report from an explorative survey with 64 agile teams and 320 team members and team leaders, from 31 teams in small projects and 33 teams in large projects. For small projects, teamwork quality was considered by both team members and team leaders to primarily affect product quality. For large projects, the effect of teamwork quality on product quality was positive when it was rated by team members but was negative when rated by team leaders. At a finer granularity, the six dimensions of teamwork quality that we investigated affected team performance differently in small and large projects. These findings question to what extent findings from previous studies on teamwork in agile development in small projects apply to large projects.

Keywords: Agile software development · Team performance
Software engineering · Teamwork · Teamwork quality

1 Introduction

Agile software development methods have become mainstream [1]. Originally aimed at development in small teams, agile methods are now used also in large software projects [6]. Teamwork is central in agile development [2, 3]. There are a growing number of studies on large-scale agile development that focus on topics such as how product owners are involved in development and how to achieve inter-team coordination [6, 7]. This paper explores differences between small and large-scale projects with respect to teamwork quality and its effect on team performance. We state the following research question: *How does the effect of teamwork quality on team performance differ between small and large projects?*

J. Garbajosa et al. (Eds.): XP 2018, LNBIP 314, pp. 267–274, 2018.
https://doi.org/10.1007/978-3-319-91602-6_19

The teamwork quality aspects defined in Sect. 2 describe both aspects of interaction (communication, coordination, and mutual support) and motivation (effort, balance of member contribution, and cohesion) within a team. Hoegl et al. [4] suggest that with less task uncertainty and complexity in settings with fewer teams, that is, smaller projects, the motivational aspects are relatively more important and interactions aspects less important than in larger projects. We investigated whether the same findings would be confirmed in our study.

Teams that use the most popular agile development method, Scrum, focus mainly on managing internal relations during an iteration through daily meetings [5]. External relations are managed by the team and through the collaboration between the product owner and the customer and other stakeholders, and through demonstrating the product to stakeholders at the end of an iteration.

One important difference between small-scale and large-scale development is the number of relations that have to be managed. Large projects are characterized by complex knowledge boundaries among team members, more complex interplay with a larger number of technologies involved, and a larger set of stakeholders [6]. The first version of Scrum suggests handling interdependencies between teams in a new forum, the "Scrum of Scrums". This forum has shown to be challenging when the number of teams are high [7].

2 Background

The Teamwork Quality (TWQ) constructs of this paper are based on Hoegl and Gemuenden [8], and also used in Lindsjørn et al. [2]. The six subconstructs of *communication*, *coordination*, *balance of member contribution*, *mutual support*, *effort*, and *cohesion* cover performance-relevant measures of internal interaction in teams. A brief description of the TWQ subconstructs is given below:

- *Communication* may be classified as to whether the communication is (1) internal versus external, (2) formal versus informal, and (3) written versus oral [10]. In agile teams, the team members are often placed closely together in open-plan offices to stimulate informal and open communication.
- *Coordination* may be described as managing dependencies between activities [11]. Common understanding when working on parallel subtasks, and agreement on common work-down structures, schedules, budgets, and deliverables are important aspects.
- *Balance of member contribution* refers to the ability to exploit all team members' skills and expertise in such a way that it benefits the team [8].
- *Mutual support* refers to the team members' ability and willingness to give assistance to other team members when needed [12].
- *Effort* refers to how much workload team members spend on the team's tasks [8].
- *Cohesion* may be described as the tendency for a group to stick together in order to achieve its goals and objectives [13].

Team performance may be defined as the extent to which a team is able to meet established *product quality* requirements, as well as cost and time objectives, which are included in *project quality*. A more detailed description of the team performance concept is given in [2, 9]. This paper reports a study on the extent to which the effect of teamwork quality on team performance is moderated by the size of development projects.

With respect to the teamwork quality constructs, the main differences between small and large projects concern communication and coordination. Due to communication bottlenecks, large projects need more external, formal, and written communication than do small projects. Coordination in large projects is more challenging due to many development teams and dependencies between tasks among different teams.

3   Method

To operationalize the concepts of teamwork quality and team performance, we used a questionnaire reported in [8]. We define a small project to consist of one or two teams and a large project to consist of 10 or more teams. We collected data from 31 teams in small projects and 33 teams in two large projects. The data from the small projects was also used in a previously published study [2]. This data set also includes 11 teams in one large project used in this study. In total, the responses from 231 respondents are included. Another data set with 22 teams (89 respondents) was collected from an ongoing large project in a company that we collaborate with. All teams in the study used Scrum as the agile methodology. There are two rater categories in this study: team members and team leaders. All the team leaders were scrum masters; none of them were product owners or managers.

The respondents indicated their agreement with the items on a Likert scale from 1 (strongly disagree) to 5 (strongly agree). The questionnaire was previously found to have acceptable reliability, as measured by Cronbach's alpha [13].

The value of a variable for a respondent is calculated as the mean of each of the questions that form that variable (i.e., similar to using the sum-score in internal consistency reliability estimates such as Cronbach's alpha). The unit of analysis is the team itself, rather than the individuals in the team. When two or more team members (or two team leaders) respond from the same team, the results are aggregated using the mean. Although such aggregations can be problematic (e.g., when faced with strongly non-normal distributions), the number of responses per team in the available data is also too low to determine whether the distribution is non-normal. Thus, the aggregation procedure used in this study is a target for improvement in the future. Only team members rate teamwork quality (the independent variable). Both team members and team leaders rate team performance (the dependent variable).

The analysis was conducted using R [14]. The correlations are illustrated using the qgraph package [15]. The saturation of lines (edges) between the variables (nodes) shows the strength of the correlations, which are green for positive correlations and red for negative correlations. The placements of the nodes are calculated using the "spring" function of qgraph; highly correlated nodes are placed in close proximity and nodes with little or no shared variance with other nodes are placed distant from other nodes. Also, nodes with many strong relations to other nodes are centrally placed.

The placement of nodes is averaged for project size so that differences in (Pearson and partial) correlations for small and large projects is more clearly displayed.

Responses to a few of the questions for some team members and team leaders were missing. For the six variables rated by team members, no variable had more than 0.4% missing data. However, product quality as rated by team leaders had 7.4% missing data (project quality had 1.1%). To not discard otherwise usable data, we imputed the missing data using the mice package [16] in R before aggregating each of the six variables that comprise teamwork quality and each of the two variables that comprise team performance.

4   Results

Table 1 shows the descriptive statistics of the analyzed variables for the small (S) and large (L) projects. All variables are normally distributed according to the Shapiro-Wilk test of normality, except three of the variables for large projects: Communication ($p = 0.03$), Mutual support ($p = 0.04$) and Product quality for team leaders ($p = 0.01$). Product and project quality data for team leaders was not available for 10 of the teams in one of the large projects, reducing n to 23. Only small differences in the mean values were detected for the two groups of project; the largest difference was that product and project quality was rated higher by team leaders in the large projects than in the small projects. Variability (SD) in ratings given by team members was higher for both product and project quality than for the six teamwork quality variables; variability was even higher for ratings given by team leaders.

Table 1. Descriptive statistics of the investigated variables.

Variable	Rater	Size	n	mean	SD
Communication	TM	S	31	3.93	0.29
		L	33	3.95	0.38
Coordination	TM	S	31	3.76	0.28
		L	33	3.76	0.36
Mutual support	TM	S	31	4.01	0.33
		L	33	4.09	0.35
Effort	TM	S	31	3.93	0.34
		L	33	4.03	0.38
Cohesion	TM	S	31	3.82	0.30
		L	33	3.89	0.33
Balance of member contribution	TM	S	31	3.91	0.30
		L	33	4.03	0.34
Product quality	TM	S	31	3.78	0.37
		L	33	3.93	0.32
Project quality	TM	S	31	3.57	0.42
		L	33	3.53	0.41
Product quality	TL	S	31	3.82	0.46
		L	23	4.16	0.48
Project quality	TL	S	31	3.54	0.60
		L	23	3.75	0.60

Note. TM = Team members, TL = team leaders, S = small projects and L = large projects.

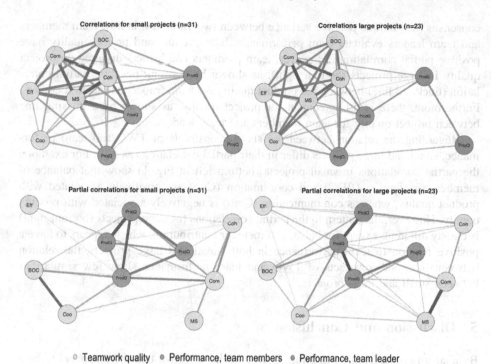

○ Teamwork quality   ● Performance, team members   ● Performance, team leader

Note. Com = Communication, Coo = Coordination, MS = Mutual support, Eff = Effort, Coh = Cohesion, BOC = Balance of member contribution, ProdQ = Product quality and ProjQ = project Quality.

Fig. 1. Pearson and partial correlations for small and large projects (Color figure online)

The top part of Fig. 1 shows the correlations between teamwork quality (grey) and team performance (blue and red). In small projects (top left), product quality (ProdQ) is more strongly correlated with the teamwork quality for both team members (blue) and team leaders (red) than is project quality (ProjQ). Product quality is, further, more centrally placed closer to teamwork quality. Project quality (for both team members and leaders) is more distantly placed with weaker correlations with the teamwork quality variables.

In large projects (top right of Fig. 1), the relation between teamwork quality and team performance is similar to that found in small projects when team performance is evaluated by the team members. However, for team leaders, product quality is negatively correlated with several teamwork quality variables as well as product quality as evaluated by the team members. In small projects, the correlations between product quality and teamwork quality as rated by team leaders are between 0.29 and 0.50, whereas they in large projects are either negative or zero (−0.47 to 0.02).

When a set of variables, such as those that form teamwork quality, are highly correlated, it is difficult to determine the unique contribution of each variable. The partial correlation explains what is uniquely shared between two variables that cannot be explained through the correlations with other available. The bottom part of Fig. 1 shows the partial correlations. For small projects (bottom left) there appears to be consensus (i.e., unique positive variance between two variables) in how team members and team leaders evaluate team performance; both product and project quality have positive partial correlations. However, team members and leaders disagree on project quality in large projects (bottom right), as shown by a strong negative partial correlation (thick red line) between the product quality for team leaders and team members. Furthermore, there is no agreement for project quality, as shown by a missing line between project quality for team members and team leaders.

Regarding the relation between the six subconstructs of TWQ and team performance, small and large projects differ in their partial correlations as well. For example, the partial correlations in small projects (bottom left in Fig. 1) show that balance of member contribution (BOC) and coordination (Coo) are positively associated with product quality, whereas communication (Com) is negatively associated with product quality. However, the pattern in the partial correlations for large projects (bottom right) is clearly different: except for balance of member contribution, which appears to have a positive relation to team performance in both small and large projects, the relation between other subconstructs of TWQ and team performance show few similarities between small and large projects.

5 Discussion and Conclusion

By analyzing data from 64 software teams, we have shown that there appears to be a disagreement between team members and team leaders in the evaluation of team performance for large projects. We have also shown that the effect of different teamwork quality variables (subconstructs) appears to influence team performance in small and large projects differently.

One possible reason why teamwork quality seems to affect product quality more than project quality in small projects is that team members and team leaders are working closely in small projects, and, therefore, there is little need for following a plan, updating documents and controlling the project by specific means; the progress of the team is apparent anyway. Effort is tailored towards the product.

Regarding large projects, a possible reason for the stronger relationship between teamwork quality and project quality when team performance was evaluated by team leaders is that project management, which is a primary concern of leaders, is more important in large projects. Interdependencies between development teams and various stakeholders, and interdependencies between tasks in different teams, need stronger mechanisms to control cost and time schedules. Such control is primarily the responsibility of team leaders.

Prior studies suggest that coordination is more important to team performance in large projects [4]. Our results show that coordination has some impact on project quality when evaluated by team members but is negatively correlated with product quality for both team members and team leaders. We would also have expected that the three motivation teamwork aspects (effort, cohesion and balance of member contribution) would have more impact in small projects, while the three interaction aspects (communication, coordination and mutual support) would have more impact on large projects. Our results show, however, that balance of member contribution and coordination were central to team performance in both small and large projects. Further, effort, mutual support, communication, and cohesion appear to show a common theme. This calls for further investigation.

The main limitation of this study concerns sample size. Although we had responses from more than three hundred team members and leaders, "large projects" in this paper is only represented by two projects and their respective organizations. The available data indicates that the values of the investigated variables differ between small and large projects, but the small sample for large projects means that caution should be made when generalizing the findings. Another limitation is that the analysed variables are ordinal (Likert-scale) which, ideally, should be analysed using non-parametric statistics (e.g., Spearman correlations and median values). However, we found no substantially different results when using Spearman correlations for the investigated variables.

In conclusion, this study suggests that prior findings on teamwork in agile development in small projects may not apply to large projects. Future studies should investigate the quality of interactions between teams to better adopt agile methods in large projects, and in particular pay attention to difference among different stakeholder in the rating of team performance.

Acknowledgement. We thank the anonymous reviewers for valuable comments. This work was partly funded by the Research Council of Norway through the projects TeamIT (grant 193236) and Agile 2.0 (grant 236759).

References

1. Dingsøyr, T., Nerur, S., Balijepally, V., Moe, N.B.: A decade of agile methodologies: towards explaining agile software development. J. Syst. Softw. **85**, 1213–1221 (2012)
2. Lindsjørn, Y., Sjøberg, D.I.K., Dingsøyr, T., Bergersen, G.R., Dybå, T.: Teamwork quality and project success in software development: a survey of agile development teams. J. Syst. Softw. **122**, 274–286 (2016)
3. Dingsøyr, T., Fægri, T.E., Dybå, T., Haugset, B., Lindsjørn, Y.: Team performance in software development: research results versus agile principles. IEEE Softw. **33**, 106–110 (2016)
4. Hoegl, M., Weinkauf, K., Gemuenden, H.G.: Interteam coordination, project commitment, and teamwork in multiteam R&D projects: a longitudinal study. Organ. Sci. **15**, 38–55 (2004)
5. Stray, V., Sjøberg, D.I.K., Dybå, T.: The daily stand-up meeting: a grounded theory study. J. Syst. Softw. **114**, 101–124 (2016)
6. Rolland, K.H., Fitzgerald, B., Dingsøyr, T., Stool, K.-J.: Problematizing agile in the large: alternative assumptions for large-scale agile development. In: International Conference on Information Systems, Dublin, Ireland (2016)
7. Paasivaara, M., Lassenius, C., Heikkila, V.T.: Inter-team coordination in large-scale globally distributed scrum: do scrum-of-scrums really work? In: Proceedings of the ACM-IEEE ESEM, pp. 235–238. IEEE, New York (2012)
8. Hoegl, M., Gemuenden, H.G.: Teamwork quality and the success of innovative projects: a theoretical concept and empirical evidence. Organ. Sci. **12**(4), 435–449 (2001)

9. Pinto, M.B., Pinto, J.K.: Project team communication and cross functional cooperation in new program development. J. Prod. Innov. Manag. **7**(3), 200–212 (1990)
10. Malone, T.W., Crowston, K.: The interdisciplinary study of coordination. ACM Comput. Surv. **26**(1), 87–119 (1994)
11. Tjosvold, D.: "Cooperative and competitive goal approach to conflict": accomplishments and challenges. Appl. Psychol. **47**(3), 285-34 (1998)
12. Mudrack, P.E.: Defining group cohesiveness. A legacy of confusion. Small Group Res. **20**(1), 37–49 (1989)
13. Nunnally, J.C., Bernstein, I.H.: Psychometric Theory, 3rd edn. McGraw-Hill, New York (1994)
14. R Core Team: R: A language and environment for statistical computing. R Foundation for Statistical Computing, Vienna, Austria (2016)
15. Epskamp, S., Cramer, A.O.J., Waldorp, L.J., Schmittmann, V.D., Borsboom, D.: qgraph: network visualizations of relationships in psychometric data. J. Stat. Softw. **48**(4), 1–18 (2012)
16. van Buuren, S., Groothuis-Oudshoorn, K.: mice: multivariate imputation by chained equations in R. J. Stat. Softw. **45**(3), 1–67 (2011)

Continuous Experimentation

Challenges and Strategies for Undertaking Continuous Experimentation to Embedded Systems: Industry and Research Perspectives

David Issa Mattos[1]([✉]) [iD], Jan Bosch[1] [iD],
and Helena Holmström Olsson[2] [iD]

[1] Department of Computer Science and Engineering,
Chalmers University of Technology,
Hörselgången 11, 412 96 Göteborg, Sweden
{davidis,jan.bosch}@chalmers.se
[2] Department of Computer Science and Media Technology,
Malmö University, Nordenskiöldsgatan, 211 19 Malmö, Sweden
helena.holmstrom.olsson@mah.se

Abstract. Context: Continuous experimentation is frequently used in web-facing companies and it is starting to gain the attention of embedded systems companies. However, embedded systems companies have different challenges and requirements to run experiments in their systems. **Objective**: This paper explores the challenges during the adoption of continuous experimentation in embedded systems from both industry practice and academic research. It presents strategies, guidelines, and solutions to overcome each of the identified challenges. **Method**: This research was conducted in two parts. The first part is a literature review with the aim to analyze the challenges in adopting continuous experimentation from the research perspective. The second part is a multiple case study based on interviews and workshop sessions with five companies to understand the challenges from the industry perspective and how they are working to overcome them. **Results**: This study found a set of twelve challenges divided into three areas; technical, business, and organizational challenges and strategies grouped into three categories, architecture, data handling and development processes. **Conclusions**: The set of identified challenges are presented with a set of strategies, guidelines, and solutions. To the knowledge of the authors, this paper is the first to provide an extensive list of challenges and strategies for continuous experimentation in embedded systems. Moreover, this research points out open challenges and the need for new tools and novel solutions for the further development of experimentation in embedded systems.

Keywords: Continuous experimentation · Data-driven development
Controlled experiments · Embedded systems

1 Introduction

Traditional embedded systems companies continuously rely on software to be a differentiator on their products. As the software size of the products increases, these companies are moving from being mechanical producers to software companies.

© The Author(s) 2018
J. Garbajosa et al. (Eds.): XP 2018, LNBIP 314, pp. 277–292, 2018.
https://doi.org/10.1007/978-3-319-91602-6_20

In their development process, these companies traditionally make use of up-front requirements and rigid methodologies to ensure quality or safety attributes in their products. Nevertheless, the requirements of several parts of their systems are not clear or cannot be defined in advance [1]. In this context, developers either negotiate with requirement teams or they make implicit assumptions about the requirements [2].

Even during the requirement specification, several requirements are written based on assumptions and does not necessarily deliver value to the company or the customers. Often, research and development effort is spent on features that are never or rarely used [3] by the users of the product. To minimize the full development of features that do not deliver value, companies make use of post-deployment data of current products to iterate in future software releases or in even in new products. In the web domain, companies provide empirical evidence of the use of continuous experimentation in their development, decision-making and feature prioritization process [4–6].

As software becomes the key differentiator for many embedded systems companies, these companies started to adopt continuous development practices, such as continuous integration, deployment, and experimentation to develop faster, better and more cost-effective products. A typical pattern that companies follow is shown in the "Stairway to Heaven" model [7]. When these companies start to move to move to continuous deployment scenarios, they see opportunities to run their first experiments as well.

Although the research in continuous experimentation in web systems is continually growing, there are few examples of works investigating the use of continuous experimentation in embedded systems.

This paper identifies and analyzes the different challenges that embedded systems companies face when adopting continuous experimentation in their development processes. Moreover, it also presents strategies, guidelines, and potential solutions to overcome each of the identified challenges.

The scope of this research is captured with the following research question.

RQ: How can embedded systems industry adopt continuous experimentation in their development process?

This research question is further developed in terms of the following sub-questions:

RQ1: What are the recognized challenges towards continuous experimentation faced by the embedded systems industry?

RQ2: What are the recommended strategies to facilitate the use of continuous experimentation in the embedded systems domain?

The contribution of this paper is twofold. First, it identifies the key challenges faced by embedded systems companies when adopting continuous experimentation. These challenges are identified from both the industry perspective, through a multi-company case study, and the academic perspective, through a literature review. Second, this paper proposes different strategies and guidelines to overcome the identified challenges. This paper, to the knowledge of the authors, is the first to present an extensive set of challenges and strategies that embedded systems companies face when adopting continuous experimentation. Moreover, the analysis of the challenges points out the need for new tools and novel solutions for the further development of experimentation in embedded systems.

The rest of the paper is organized as follows. Section 2 provides a background review in continuous experimentation. Section 3 presents the research method. Section 4 presents and discusses the results in the form of identified challenges and suggested strategies. Section 5 discusses the validity threats of this research. Section 6 concludes and discusses research challenges and future works.

2 Background

Continuous experimentation refers to the research and application of controlled experimentation to drive software development, for reliably evaluate and prioritize development activities [4].

Studies show that the prioritization of features is traditionally driven by past experiences, beliefs, and organizational role [6, 8]. The decision to invest development resources in a full feature can result in inefficiency and opportunity cost if the feature does not have a confirmed value [9]. Companies traditionally rely on customers interviews and qualitative studies to derive requirements for the system in the early stages of the development [10]. However, customers usually are not good in predicting what they want or they are not aware of other potential solutions [1].

In the post-deployment stage, companies usually collect customer and product data. Most software companies, from both the embedded and web systems domains collects and logs usage and operational data [10]. In embedded systems, these log data are mostly used for troubleshooting and improving subsequent products. However, over the last decade, software companies are showing an increasing interest in using the collected data to improve not only future products but also to improve the current products.

Recent technological trends focus on not only identifying and solve technical problems but also delivering value to their customers and users [11]. The Lean Startup methodology proposes the cycle build-measure-learn [12]. In this methodology, the collected post-deployment data is also used in the improvement of the current product. The HYPEX model [9] presents an approach to shorten the feedback loop between companies and customers. The model uses hypotheses, customer feedback and the minimum viable product (MVP) to continuously decide upon the full development or abandonment of a feature.

Web-facing companies continuously report the use of post-deployment data and controlled experiments to develop and continuously improve their systems. The uncertainty raised by the environment, interaction with humans and other agents impact in the system behavior in unknown and unpredictable ways. Controlled experiments help companies to establish the causal relationship between a variation in their system and the observed behavior [6].

In software development, A/B test is the simplest version of a controlled experiment. "A" stands for the control variation and "B" stands for the treatment variation. The treatment (variation "B") represents any point in the system that you want to modify and compare to the control (variation "A"). Both variations are deployed to randomized users, to avoid bias, and the analyzed behavior is the measured in both cases. Statistical analysis helps to determine if there is a causal difference between the observed behavior and the variations. Other experimentation techniques are described in [6].

Kohavi et al. [6] provides a guide on how to run controlled experiments in web systems. The paper discusses the important ingredients, limitations of experimentation, architectures for experimentation systems, how to analyze and how to design controlled experiments for the web. Kohavi et al. [13], presents some rules of thumb and common pitfalls when running experimentation, such as iterating in the experiment design, the impact of speed and performance, number of users and how experiments impact key metrics.

Fagerholm et al. [11] provides a general infrastructure for running continuous experimentation systematically. The RIGHT framework describes how to design and manage experiments, and how different stakeholders (business analyst, product owner, data scientists, developers, and DevOps engineers) interact with an experimentation infrastructure.

Fabijan et al. [4] describes the Experimentation Evolution Model, based on experimentation at Microsoft. This model analyzes how teams scale their experimentation from a few experiments to a data-driven organization. The model divides this evolution into four steps: crawl (teams are running and setting their first experiments), walk (teams already run a few experiments and determining metrics and experimentation platforms), run (the teams run several experiments and iterate quickly to identify effects of experiments on the business) and fly (experiments are the norm for every change to any product). Each of these phases is discussed in three different perspectives, the technical, the organizational, and the business perspectives.

One of the challenges in controlled experiments is defining an Overall Evaluation Metric (OEC) [4, 6, 14]. The OEC is a quantitative measure of the experiment's objective. It provides a balance between short and long-term effects considering the business objectives. Olsson and Bosch [14], present a systematic approach to model the value of experiments. This approach allows companies that are starting to run the first experiments to understand and improve their own OEC metrics.

To the knowledge of the authors, the first research discussing the experiments in embedded systems appeared in 2012 [15]. This paper discusses experimentation in the context of Innovation Experiment Systems. It identifies some challenges with experimentation in embedded systems, such as experimentation in safety systems, managing multiple stakeholders and hardware limitations. It also presents an initial infrastructure to run experiments in embedded systems.

Giaimo and Berger [16], discuss continuous experimentation in the context of self-driving vehicles. The paper presents functional (such as instrumentation, logging, data feedback to a remote server) and non-functional (separation of concerns, safety, short cycle to deployment) requirements to achieve continuous software evolution. Bosch and Olsson [17], extended the concept of experimentation towards automated experimentation. Automated experimentation aims to leverage the number of experiments by letting the system own and control the experiments, opposed to the R&D organization. Mattos et al. [18, 19], identified a set of architectural qualities to support automated experimentation that was implemented in a research mobile autonomous vehicle.

3 Research Method

The research process used in this study combines a literature review with multiple case study. This research method aims to strengthen the evidence of the challenges and strategies found in a multiple case-study with others found in the research literature. Research in continuous experimentation generally utilizes the case study as the research method, combining results from both approaches reinforce the empirical evidence of the findings.

The method is composed of two parts. The first part consists of a literature review in the continuous experimentation domain. This literature review collects challenges and strategies to overcome them from academic research. The second part consists of semi-structured interviews with software companies in the embedded systems domain. It aims to be exploratory, collect and confirm challenges and strategies from the embedded systems industry. Below, the research method is described in details. The results of both parts were aggregated and described in Sect. 4. Table 1 summarizes the research process used in this paper.

Table 1. Summary of the research method. LR stands for the literature review part and CS for the multiple case study part.

Step	Description
1	Search definition and execution (LR)
2	Papers review (LR)
3	Identification of literature challenges and strategies (LR)
4	Data selection: Contact with companies (CS)
5	Semi-structured interview protocol definition (CS)
6	Data collection: Interviews and workshop (CS)
7	Data analysis: thematic coding and categorization (CS)
8	Case study report (CS)

3.1 Literature Review

The first part of the research method consists of a literature review in continuous experimentation. Although most of the studies in continuous experimentation focus on web-facing companies, the experiences from this domain, sometimes, can be extrapolated to the embedded systems domain. In this literature review, the authors identified challenges recognized in academic collaboration with industry, regardless of the industry domain. The identified challenges were discussed with the embedded systems companies to see if the literature challenges were also relevant in this domain.

Relevant works in the literature covering continuous experimentation were identified by searching the Scopus digital indexing library, by keywords, title and abstract. The used search phrase was "((continuous experimentation) OR (field experiments) OR (innovation experiment systems)) AND (software engineering)". This search query was restricted to the fields of engineering and computer science and limited from 2000 to 2017. This search phrase resulted in 534 articles. Positioning papers and papers with less than 5 pages were excluded. From this subset of articles, the results were filtered based on the abstract. After the first screening process, the papers were read in their integrity. Continuous experimentation is also largely studied from the statistical/algorithmic side. Research papers that focused solely on improving or evaluating algorithms without industry evaluation or application were excluded.

After this screening process, the authors identified 30 articles with relevance to this study. An additional set of 12 articles were included using a snowballing [20] process, where new references were added according to the references mentioned in the other articles. Thematic coding was used to [21] identify the challenges from the literature. These challenges were categorized according to the three different categories of the Experimentation Evolution Model [4] discussed in Sect. 2, the technical, the organizational and the business perspective. The identified set of challenges were also used as input for the semi-structured interviews as discussed in Sect. 3.2. The strategies are categorized in three groups: changes in the development process, changes in the system's architecture and changes in how the experiment and organizational data is handled and analyzed.

The complete set of papers can be found at the following link: https://github.com/davidissamattos/public_documents/blob/master/LR-XP18.png.

This part of the research process allowed the identification of challenges that served as input for the multiple case study and confirmation of identified challenges inside the company.

3.2 Multiple Case Study

The second part of the research method consists of a multiple case study [21] with semi-structured interviews conducted with software companies in the embedded systems domain. This study was conducted from December 2016 to October 2017 with five companies in the embedded systems domain. The empirical data consists of interviews and a workshops transcripts and notes. There were 8 individual semi-structured interviews with an average of one hour each, three in *Company A*, two in *Company B*, one in *Company C*, one in *Company D* and 2 in *Company E*. The workshop session was conducted with 8 people from *Company A* lasting 3 h. The analysis of the empirical data consisted of thematic coding of [21] interviews transcriptions and notes to identify and categorize the challenges and solutions. Additionally, during the interviews challenges identified in the literature were clarified to the interviews and asked if the current company relates to the challenge partially or not.

The empirical data were aggregated together with the identified challenges and strategies from the literature review. The current published research already provides guidelines and solutions for the challenges that were also identified in the literature review phase. Other guidelines and solutions were suggested by practitioners during the interviews. Challenges identified in the literature that was not confirmed neither through a previous case study nor by the case study companies are not shown.

Due to confidentiality reasons, only a short description of each company and their domain is provided:

Company A is a multinational conglomerate company that manufactures embedded systems and electronics and provides software solutions for both consumers and professionals. This study was conducted with two teams, one providing mobile communications solutions and the other providing business-to-business products. In recent years, the company started to adopt experimentation in their software solutions and is looking for data-driven strategies in their embedded systems products. The interviewees were developers, managers and data analysts.

Company B is a multinational company that provides telecommunication and networking systems. The company is adopting continuous development practices and is looking for new strategies to deliver more value to their customers by optimizing their products. The interviewees were managers.

Company C is a global automotive manufacturer and supplier of transport solutions. As the company's products are continuously growing in complexity and software size, the company is looking for strategies to prioritize their R&D effort and deliver more value to their customers. As some employees have experience in web and pure software-systems development, experimentation is getting attention in some development teams. Challenges in experimentation arise since the company is subjected to several regulations and certification procedures. The interviewee was a senior engineer.

Company D is a global software company that develops and provides embedded systems software solutions related to autonomous driving technology for the automotive industry. Autonomous driving is an emerging and fast-moving technology and the company is looking to deliver competitive solutions faster by adopting continuous development practices. However, as it interfaces with the highly regulated automotive domain its software is also subjected to regulation and certification. The interviewee was a manager.

Company E is a global software company that develops both software and hardware solutions for home consumers. The company already has experience running continuous experimentation in their web systems and is starting to run experiments in their hardware solutions. The interviewees were senior data analysts working in experimentation in their embedded systems.

4   Challenges and Proposed Strategies

This section presents results obtained from the research process. The challenges are grouped in the three different perspectives as discussed in the Experimentation Evolution Model [4]: the technical challenges, the business challenges and the organizational challenges. The technical challenges refer to challenges related to the system architecture, experimentation tooling and development processes. The business challenges refer to challenges faced in the business side, such as evaluation metrics, business models and privacy concerns. The organizational challenges refer to challenges faced by the cultural aspect of the R&D organization.

All the strategies identified in this study are used, suggested by companies, or supported by strategies identified in previous literature case studies. The strategies are categorized in three groups: (1) changes in the development process. This refers to how companies organize their development activities. (2) changes in the system's architecture. Often restrictions in the running experiments comes from limitations in the system's architecture, that does not support data collection, or does not allow parametrization of features for experiments. (3) changes in how the experiment and organizational data is handled and analyzed. This refers to how the company stores data, comply to data regulations or use data analysis tools. The challenges are not presented in any specific order as they might reflect different challenges the companies are facing.

Figure 1 represents a summary of the identified challenges and strategies. In Fig. 1, it is possible to see the relation of how each strategy relates to the different challenges, as some of them are part of the strategy of one or more challenge. This figure was obtained using the thematic codes generated in the analysis of the interviews. It maps the identified challenges within their groups with the obtained strategies groups. The rest of this section discusses each challenge individually and presents strategies to overcome them.

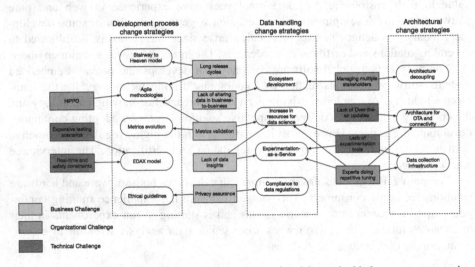

Fig. 1. Summary of the challenges and the strategies faced by embedded systems companies adopting continuous experimentation.

4.1   Technical Challenges

Lack of over the air (OTA) updates and data collection

Continuous experimentation requires over-the-air (OTA) post-deployment data collection and updates. When testing a different hypothesis, the system needs to have the ability to measure the specific behavior under investigation and to update the system with the new variants as well. It is possible to run experiments without OTA, however, several experiments pitfalls can be identified in the first hours and be corrected [6]. Moreover, experiments for optimization are looking in practical significance as low as 1–2% in their metrics [6, 13]. If OTA updates and data collection are not available the cost of the experiment and the practical significance level are high and the optimization process might not be worth it.

Strategies: At the moment of this study, embedded system companies are not looking into experimentation in low level systems, but in computing systems that already support modern operating systems with connectivity and the necessary infrastructure for OTA updates. OTA updates and post-deployment data collection should be part of the functional requirements of the system when designing the hardware. Mobile companies already provide such functionality in their operating systems. Car manufacturers are also introducing continuous delivery of new software to their vehicles in the context of autonomous vehicles (Tesla Motor's Model S, Volvo Drive Me and the Volvo XC90).

Lack of experimentation tools that integrate with their existing tooling
Continuous experimentation started in web-facing companies. Today several experimentation tools, both commercial and open source, are available on the website and mobile applications domains. However, in the embedded systems domain, companies lack tools that integrate with their development process. Setting up an infrastructure to run experiments from scratch increases the cost of running the first experiments while hindering the benefits.

Strategies: Several tools available for websites are open source or have open source SDKs. Although not ideal, some of these tools can be modified to support experimentation problems. Experimentation-as-a-Service (EaaS) is a business model that provides a working platform for continuous experimentation. EaaS have the benefit of avoiding the cost and pitfalls of development of an experimentation platform from scratch. EaaS platforms also provide SDKs that can be incorporated in the product [22]. However, the system under experimentation should support data collection so it can be integrated with EaaS tools.

Expensive testing environments
Software-intensive embedded systems are extensively tested before release. One of the challenges faced by embedded systems companies is to include experimentation as part of the verification and validation process. In some cases, such as in the development of a new vehicle, the testing environment is expensive and not all experiment hypotheses are allowed to go to a physical testing platform. This high cost also increases minimum level necessary to reach practical significance and demotivates teams to formulate hypothesis beyond the basic requirements of the system.

Strategies: The development of experiments in the embedded systems domain require additional steps from the hypothesis to the final user. The development of a feature in embedded systems follows a testing procedure, beginning with integration and going to simulation, test beds, internal deployment until user deployment. The experimentation procedure should follow similar testing procedure, to identify early pitfalls, and even improve the system behavior during each testing phase.

The practical significance level to implement a new hypothesis increases with the associated costs of such testing procedure. The EDAX model [17] describes how experimentation and automated experimentation is incorporated in this process.

Automated experimentation [18] also suggests that it can reduce the experimentation costs and therefore the practical significance level.

Experimentation constraints in real-time and safety-critical systems
Embedded systems are employed in several real-time and safety-critical systems. These products have subsystems that are constrained to regulations and certification. Experimenting with these systems in the field might not be allowed by regulation or might impact substantially the performance of the system.

Strategies: Embedded systems companies are starting to run their first experiments. Safety-critical or real-time systems provide additional challenges, as it is subjected to legislation and certification. The initial recommendation in all case study companies is not to run experimentations in these subsystems. However, these safety-critical subsystems can run experiments in the earlier phases prior to the deployment, as discussed in the EDAX model [17].

4.2 Business Challenges

Determining good experimentation metrics and metrics validation
One of the biggest challenge faced by companies is to determine good business metrics to understand and compare different experiments, and validate that the current metrics are aligned with the company strategy

Strategies: Web companies traditionally rely on conversion metrics such as Click-Through-Rate in the beginning of their experimentation process. As their experimentation teams and the number of experiments increase the metrics start to become more tailored to the business and stable [4]. Embedded systems companies can have very different and complex metrics, depending on the product. However, team level optimization experiments can use customized metrics. Olsson and Bosch [14] presents a systematic approach to determine metrics and value functions for experiments. This is an iterative process that should be refined with usage and aligned with the business strategies and goals. As the metrics become complex, companies allocate of resources for the evolution and ensuring that the experiment metrics are aligned with the company's main KPIs.

Privacy concerns regarding user data
Continuous experimentation relies on the collection and analysis of post-deployed software. However, some issues arise when collecting data, such as the legal and contractual issues or user consent and data sharing.

Strategies: Data sensitivity and the use of data vary largely between different organizations and countries. Data collection should be aligned with the legal requirements for utilization and consent of the users. Data regulations such as the European GDPR (https://www.eugdpr.org/) create restrictions that might imply in technology and process modifications for compliance. Additionally, some ethical questions regarding the experiment must be evaluated, such as: How are participants guaranteed that their data, which was collected for use in the study, will not be used for some other purpose?

What data may be published more broadly, and does that introduce any additional risk to the participants? Web companies, besides compliance with regulations also create ethical checklists to ensure that the experiments follow the companies' policies [23]

Lack of sharing user data in business-to-business (B2B) solutions

Several embedded systems companies operate in a business-to-business domain. In this scenario, there is a difference between user and customer data. Experiments with users might not be possible, they might require deeper involvement between the companies, or there might be a mismatch between the customer and the user value [1].

Strategies: Ecosystems refers to companies co-opting third parties to build and leverage their products and services in such a way that they have more utility value to their customers [24]. In this sense, companies might agree on implementing and sharing data collected inside the ecosystem. Some mobile operating systems (e.g. iOS and Android) collect data and usage statistics to share with app developers. Although most of its use is connected to crash reports, similar strategies can be used to share user data in business-to-business products.

Lack of insights obtained from the collected data

Companies are continuously collecting data from their deployed software. The collected data is mainly used for troubleshooting purposes. However, little insight is provided by the collected data [14]. In the Experimentation Evolution Model [4], web companies evolve from centralized data science teams to small data science teams presented in each product teams. The interviewed embedded systems companies don't have data science teams incorporated in the product development.

Strategies: If the experimentation benefits are not clear, the extra cost of involving data scientists in the product development might be a large step. Different companies started to provided experimentation and data analysis services. Experimentation tools usually incorporate basic statistical analysis, such as statistical significance testing, power analysis, A/A tests and more. Using experimentation and data analysis services to generate basic insights can be used as a short-term solution. Once the benefits of experimentation are clear to the company, investments such as integrating data scientists in the product development or acquiring a complex tool are easier to justify.

Long release cycles

Traditionally, embedded systems have a long software release cycle based on upfront defined requirements. Sometimes the software is deployed only once and last for several years [1, 15]. This happens due to several reasons, from both the organizational (structure and decision-making) and business (engineering effort in every cycle, requirements definition and products updates) to the technical perspective (architecture, functionalities available and support for over-the-air updates).

Strategies: From the organizational and business perspective, continuous experimentation aligns with the organizational transition to agile methodologies and the Lean Startup methodology [12]. Continuous experimentation makes use of extreme programming practices such as continuous integration, delivery and deployment to deliver experiments and new software aligned with customer behavior. The Stairway to

Heaven [7] conceptual model helps companies to evolve their practices towards continuous deployment of software.

4.3 Organizational Challenges

Managing multiple stakeholders in the experiment design
One of the challenges embedded systems companies face is the involvement of multiple stakeholders in an experimental design. Experimentation in embedded systems requires that the involved stakeholders understand the implications of continuous practices in their systems.

Strategies: Embedded systems require the interaction with multiple stakeholders, such as software developers, systems architects, electrical and mechanical engineers, suppliers and subcontractors. Continuous experimentation requires that these stakeholders are aware of the implications in the system design. To overcome some of these challenges, it is prosed a decoupling of the application and the underlying software and also a decoupling in time (software is not integrated at the manufacturing time) [15]. Additionally, if the interaction of the stakeholders happens in a business ecosystems perspective the experiment can be designed to benefit multiple parts [24].

Highest Paid Person Opinion - HiPPO
Some companies are organized in vertical structures, where lower rank developers have fewer possibilities to influence and address customer's needs. Several requirements and architecture specifications are based and determined by higher paid ranks inside the company.

Strategies: This challenge is persistent in several domains and it is not restricted to the embedded systems industries. This challenge is discussed extensively in [6] among other publications. The traditional adopted strategy is to run the first experiments. Usually, experiments continuously disprove beliefs and opinions adopted by the higher paid ranks [6]. However, this requires changes in the organizational and cultural aspect of the company.

Tuning experiments is repetitive and requires highly qualified engineers
One of the interviewed companies runs experiments for parameter optimization. The experiments rely on the system response instead of the customer response. However, running these experiments for tuning and optimization is a repetitive task that consumes R&D time and requires highly qualified engineers to perform them.

Strategies: Existing algorithms in search-based optimization, reinforcement learning and others artificial intelligence algorithms support this kind of optimization strategies. However, both the complexity of these algorithms as well as the introduced technical debt in the existing systems [25] prevent embedded systems companies to use such strategies. Experimentation-as-a-Service solutions allow companies to test Machine Learning algorithms in their system for optimization purposes. Although still in early phases, automated experimentation [18] solutions can help companies to optimize their systems through field experiments.

5 Validity Threats

The first threat to the validity of this study refers to the scope of the literature review. The search query was applied to the Scopus indexing library. Both the choice of the search string and the indexing library could miss other research work that can contribute to the literature review. To mitigate this threat the authors performed a backward and forward snowballing [20] process. The snowballing process allowed the authors to identify other cited work in the same area that was not identified by the search query.

An external validity to this is study is the generalization of the challenges to the entire population of embedded systems companies. To mitigate this threat, the authors sample companies producing different products in embedded systems. The authors sampled contacted multiple companies explaining the research goal, and selected only companies that are adopting/running controlled experiments in their development process were included. During the data analysis part, we reviewed all challenges only challenges that had correspondence in more than one company or that could be triangulated with the literature review were included. Challenges that could not be triangulated with other source, and that could be specific to current situation of the company, were not included in this study.

The companies that participated in this study are adopting their first steps towards continuous experimentation and are running their first experiments or trying to scale experimentation practices from a few development teams to the organization. Therefore, most of the presented challenges are faced in these first steps and cannot be generalized to companies or teams that are running experimentation at scale. As the companies evolve their experimentation practices, new challenges will arise from all three perspectives.

6 Conclusion

This paper addresses the question of how embedded systems companies can adopt continuous experimentation in their software development process. This question can be divided in two parts: first, the identification of problems and challenges that limit the adoption of continuous experimentation, and second selected strategies adopted by companies to overcome these challenges.

This paper identified twelve key challenges faced by embedded systems and them grouped in three perspectives, the business, the technical and the organizational. The challenges are also presented with suggested strategies to overcome them. The set of strategies can be grouped in three categories, changes that need to take place in how the company handles and analyze the post-deployment collected data, changes in the company development process and changes in the product architecture. The relation between the different strategies and the challenges is seen in Fig. 1. The paper used a combination of literature review and a multiple company case study to provide a stronger empirical evidence.

Further research is needed to understanding how the system can be architected to support continuous experimentation as a first-class citizen in the development process while still guaranteeing safety and real-time requirements as well as intermittent connectivity. Additionally, continuous experimentation changes how the development process takes place, as it emphasizes in an outcome-driven development and this scenario might lead to impactful organizational changes. For future works, the authors are investigating where is the perceived highest return on investment that companies see and plan to invest to overcome the identified challenges and further support of continuous experimentation in their products.

Acknowledgments. This work was partially supported by the Wallenberg Autonomous Systems and Software Program (WASP) and the Software Center.

References

1. Lindgren, E., Münch, J.: Raising the odds of success: the current state of experimentation in product development. Inf. Softw. Technol. **77**, 80–91 (2016)
2. Eliasson, U., Heldal, R., Knauss, E., Pelliccione, P.: The need of complementing plan-driven requirements engineering with emerging communication: experiences from Volvo Car Group. In: Proceedings of 2015 IEEE 23rd International Requirements Engineering Conference RE 2015, pp. 372–381 (2015)
3. Olsson, H.H., Bosch, J.: From opinions to data-driven software R&D: a multi-case study on how to close the 'open loop' problem. In: Proceedings of 40th Euromicro Conference Series on Software Engineering and Advanced Applications SEAA 2014, pp. 9–16 (2014)
4. Fabijan, A., Dmitriev, P., Olsson, H.H., Bosch, J.: The evolution of continuous experimentation in software product development. In: Proceedings of the 39th International Conference on Software Engineering ICSE 2017 (2017)
5. Tang, D., Agarwal, A., O'Brien, D., Meyer, M.: Overlapping experiment infrastructure. In: Proceedings of the 16th ACM SIGKDD International Conference on Knowledge Discovery and Data Mining-KDD 2010, p. 17 (2010)
6. Kohavi, R., Longbotham, R., Sommerfield, D., Henne, R.M.: Controlled experiments on the web: survey and practical guide. Data Min. Knowl. Discov. **18**(1), 140–181 (2009)
7. Olsson, H.H., Bosch, J.: Climbing the "Stairway to Heaven": evolving from agile development to continuous deployment of software. In: Bosch, J. (ed.) Continuous Software Engineering, pp. 15–27. Springer, Cham (2014). https://doi.org/10.1007/978-3-319-11283-1_2
8. Bosch, J.: Building products as innovation experiment systems. In: Cusumano, M.A., Iyer, B., Venkatraman, N. (eds.) ICSOB 2012. LNBIP, vol. 114, pp. 27–39. Springer, Heidelberg (2012). https://doi.org/10.1007/978-3-642-30746-1_3
9. Olsson, H.H., Bosch, J.: The HYPEX model: from opinions to data-driven software development. In: Bosch, J. (ed.) Continuous Software Engineering, pp. 1–226. Springer, Cham (2014). https://doi.org/10.1007/978-3-319-11283-1_13
10. Fabijan, A., Olsson, H.H., Bosch, J.: The lack of sharing of customer data in large software organizations: challenges and implications. In: Sharp, H., Hall, T. (eds.) XP 2016. LNBIP, vol. 251, pp. 39–52. Springer, Cham (2016). https://doi.org/10.1007/978-3-319-33515-5_4
11. Fagerholm, F., Sanchez Guinea, A., Mäenpää, H., Münch, J.: The RIGHT model for continuous experimentation. J. Syst. Softw. **123**, 292–305 (2017)
12. Ries, E.: The Lean Startup: How Today's Entrepreneurs Use Continuous Innovation to Create Radically Successful Businesses, 1st edn. Crown Publishing Group, New York (2011)

13. Kohavi, R., Deng, A., Longbotham, R., Xu, Y.: Seven rules of thumb for web site experimenters. In: Proceedings of the 20th ACM SIGKDD International Conference on Knowledge Discovery and Data Mining-KDD 2014, pp. 1857–1866 (2014)
14. Olsson, H.H., Bosch, J.: So much data ; so little value : a multi-case study on improving the impact of data-driven development practices. In: Proceedings of the Ibero American Conference on Software Engineering (ClbSE), 22nd–23rd May, Buenos Aires, Argentina (2017)
15. Bosch, J., Eklund, U.: Eternal embedded software: towards innovation experiment systems. In: Margaria, T., Steffen, B. (eds.) ISoLA 2012. LNCS, vol. 7609, pp. 19–31. Springer, Heidelberg (2012). https://doi.org/10.1007/978-3-642-34026-0_3
16. Giaimo, F., Berger, C.: Design criteria to architect continuous experimentation for self-driving vehicles. In: 2017 IEEE International Conference on Software Architecture (ICSA), pp. 203–210 (2017)
17. Bosch, J., Olsson, H.H.: Data-driven continuous evolution of smart systems. In: Proceedings of the 11th International Workshop on Software Engineering for Adaptive and Self-Managing Systems-SEAMS 2016, pp. 28–34 (2016)
18. Mattos, D.I., Bosch, J., Olsson, H.H.: Your system gets better every day you use it: towards automated continuous experimentation. In: Proceedings of the 43th Euromicro Conference on Software Engineering and Advanced Applications (SEAA) (2017)
19. Mattos, D.I., Bosch, J., Holmström Olsson, H.: More for less: automated experimentation in software-intensive systems. In: Felderer, M., Méndez Fernández, D., Turhan, B., Kalinowski, M., Sarro, F., Winkler, D. (eds.) PROFES 2017. LNCS, vol. 10611, pp. 146–161. Springer, Cham (2017). https://doi.org/10.1007/978-3-319-69926-4_12
20. Wohlin, C., Runeson, P., Höst, M., Ohlsson, M.C., Regnell, B., Wesslén, A.: Experimentation in Software Engineering, vol. 1. Springer, Heidelberg (2012). https://doi.org/10.1007/978-3-642-29044-2
21. Runeson, P., Höst, M.: Guidelines for conducting and reporting case study research in software engineering. Empir. Softw. Eng. **14**(2), 131–164 (2009)
22. Optimizely, "Optimizely." https://www.optimizely.com/. Accessed 28 June 2017
23. Zhang, B.: Privacy Concerns in Online Recommender Systems: Influences of Control and User Data Input, pp. 159–173 (2014)
24. Holmström Olsson, H., Bosch, J.: From ad hoc to strategic ecosystem management: the Three-Layer Ecosystem Strategy Model? (TeLESM). J. Softw. Evol. Process **29**, e1876 (2017)
25. Sculley, D., Holt, G., Golovin, D., Davydov, E., Phillips, T., Ebner, D., Chaudhary, V., Young, M., Dennison, D.: Hidden Technical debt in machine learning systems. In: NIPS, pp. 2494–2502 (2015)

ICOs Overview: Should Investors Choose an ICO Developed with the Lean Startup Methodology?

Simona Ibba[1]([⊠]), Andrea Pinna[1], Gavina Baralla[1], and Michele Marchesi[2]

[1] Department of Electric and Electronic Engineering,
University of Cagliari, Cagliari, Italy
{simona.ibba,a.pinna,gavina.baralla}@diee.unica.it
[2] Department of Mathematics and Computer Science,
University of Cagliari, Cagliari, Italy
marchesi@unica.it

Abstract. An Initial Coin Offering (ICO) is an innovative way to raise funds and launch a startup. It is also an opportunity to take part in a project, or in a DAO (Decentralized Autonomous Organization). The use of ICO is a global phenomenon that involves many nations and several business categories: ICOs collected over 5.2 billion dollars only in 2017. The success of an ICO is based on the credibility and innovativeness of project proposals. This fund-raising tool contains however some critical issues, such as the use of tokens that have no intrinsic value and do not generate direct liquidity, and the role of investors in the management of the startup. We analyzed if the Lean Startup methodology is helpful to face this critical aspects and we examined some ICOs in which the proposing team states explicitly that a lean startup approach is used.

Keywords: ICO · ICOs overview · Lean software startup · Blockchain

1 Introduction

ICOs are the new trend in the cryptocurrencies field. The technology to create a new cryptocurrency is cheap: in a short time and without large investments any company can present itself to the market with its fundraising and the related token. With these premises, an ICO is the most innovative solution to finance themselves outside the traditional channels, especially for startups.

In fact, a good source of funding is essential to launch a startup. At first, it is possible to apply for local or international institutional funding, that generally does not provide for the repayment of the grant, but which also involves very long waiting times and a very complex bureaucracy. Even traditional funding operations that involve venture capitalists (VCs) or business angels have long waiting times. The risk is also that a traditional VC could acquire a high percentage of shares and become prevailing in the key decisions of the company.

© The Author(s) 2018
J. Garbajosa et al. (Eds.): XP 2018, LNBIP 314, pp. 293–308, 2018.
https://doi.org/10.1007/978-3-319-91602-6_21

On the other hand, a typical fundraiser needs a good marketing campaign, with many supporters participating with small amounts of money. Even a financial partner can be very risky, especially if the partner is a very experienced person who want to steal the business idea. The creation of an ICO therefore represents a valid way to collect initial capital for startups.

The success of an ICO is fundamentally based on three key elements: reliability of team members, evaluation of the project and of its white paper, and comments from other investors. Analyzing these three factors, investors should be able to answer two simple questions: "What novelty and what value does this project bring to the world?" And consequently: "Does it make sense to invest in this project?" The questions arising from this premise are therefore the following: "Can an investor monitor the evolution of the startup based on an ICO and actively collaborate on the success of this startup?" In this paper we evaluate the lean startup approach as a methodology for the implementation of an ICO based on the collaboration between all the stakeholders involved and founded on a continuous iteration process that allows investors to be an integral part in the startup's development and therefore to interact continuously with the executive team and product development team. The paper is structured as follows. Section 2 presents the related works. Section 3 proposes an ICOs overview which includes phenomenon statistics, a taxonomy, and a description of critical aspects. In Sect. 4 we show ICOs as Lean Startups and discuss about some study cases. Finally, in Sect. 5 we present the conclusions.

2   Related Work

This paper presents an overview of ICOs initiatives, pinpointing the opportunity for early stage lean startups to raise funds in an innovative and fast way.

To date, because of its novelty, literature hardly addresses this topic. In October 2017 Flool et al. [2], analyzing the history of the blockchain technology and of cryptocurrencies, presented the ICO phenomenon as a realization of an anarcho-capitalists system, made trusty by the underlying technology. Authors reported results of their studies related to key elements which make *good* an ICO, stating that the *crucial element* is trust (generated by the technology and by the ICO features). The initial coin offering process has also been studied by Kaal et al. [4] in November 2017. They described ICOs and the related environment. In addition, they underline the similarities and differences between ICOs and the IPOs of the stocks market, focusing the attention on risks and bad practices which could compromise investments and the general trust in the ICO system. Trust creation can not ignore the legal aspects of the ICO funding mechanism. Barsen [1] gave particular attention to this aspect. He highlights regulator organisms are well equipped to apply existing regulation to virtual currencies and ICOs. He also provides a legal classification of ICOs, distinguishing the currency-like tokens from the security-like ones. In order to evaluate risks and actual value of an ICO, Venegas [7] proposed an empirical approach based on the correlation analysis of the network activity. Adhami et al. [8] too focused the attention on empirical evaluation of ICOs, classifying them in accomplished and failed. Very recently, Fenu et al. analyzed 1387 ICOs, assessing the factors that were critical to theirs success [5] using a statistical analysis, whereas Hartmann et al. analysed 28 ICO websites to reveal the state of the practice in terms of ICO evaluation [6].

ICOs are a startup funding method that has similarity with the crowdfunding. In 2014, Mollick presented results of his empirical analyses on the dynamics of crowdfunding [11] and factors that influence the performances. Recently, Wang et al. studied the effects of the interaction between creators and backers on crowdfunding success [12], basing on the sentiment analysis of the comments. On the other hand, several works focused the attention on the lean startup development and their funding opportunity. Poppendieck et al. described lean startup concept and its key elements in their tutorial [9] in 2012. In 2013, Bosch et al. proposed a early stage startup development framework [10] in which all stages which a startup team have to accomplish during the first phases of their business initiative, starting from the idea generation to the validation of the Minimum Viable Product (MVP), are described.

3   ICOs: Overview

We can describe an ICO both as a way, not regulated by an authority, to raise funds and launch a startup, and as an opportunity to take part in a project, in a DAO or even in an economic system.

3.1   The Main Characteristics of ICOs

The idea of ICO is very similar to the well-known concept of Initial Public Offering (IPO), where a company decides to place its shares on the stock exchange, to open its capital to new shareholders. In this way, new listed companies enter the stock market and consequently increase their capital. We can therefore define ICOs as investments that provide "crypto objects" to investors. These are commonly named *tokens*. Tokens are also considered to be coins offered during an ICO, and as such they can be considered equivalent to the shares purchased under an IPO. Note also that the vast majority of ICOs issue tokens in exchange for cryptocurrencies convertible into real money; this allows investors to access the functionality of a particular project. Moreover, ICOs in general remain open for a period of a few weeks, up to a maximum of one or two months. In the following we indicate the main features of an ICO.

- ICO prices are set by the creators of the startup or by the person who designed the project;
- the investor who owns the tokens issued by a startup in the phase of capital raising does not always have the right to express an opinion or to be part of decisions about the project, even if it remains one of the available options;

- the first investors will probably have greater advantages included in their tokens as incentives. The creators of a startup, to thank investors and to improve their loyalty, often offers them a variable bonus percentage that is proportional to the amount of cryptocurrency that the investor chooses to put in that token, and then in that startup;
- after the conclusion of an ICO, its tokens are traded on some cryptocurrency exchange, which is a website where digital currencies can be traded against each others, and against legal money, so that they can be traded very soon with respect to other kinds of startup financing;
- the startups that collect capital through ICOs are not subject to taxation (at least by now).

3.2   How Does an ICO Works?

A startup initiates the ICO process by establishing, first of all, three aspects: the blockchain [3] underlying the system, its protocols and rules. Subsequently the ICO's creators define and make available the tokens that will be sold. In addition, in order to evoke the greatest possible interest, startups announce their ICO in several ways. The most used are represented by social media and ICO websites in which ICO's creators describe their business project.

The new token issued during the ICO will also need to be traded in an exchange, in a similar way of trading in the stock exchange after an Initial Public Offering (IPO). ICOs active or about to be activated can be traced through different websites, whereas the sale of tokens against cryptocurrencies is performed through selected exchange platforms (the most famous being Bittrex, Kraken, Poloniex, Livecoin, SpaceBTC and Bitlish). In order to buy tokens, the investors must possess a virtual wallet holding the needed cryptocurrencies, that can in turn be bought in an exchange using traditional money. Investors can buy ICO tokens very easily and directly, starting from the startup website. So, investors eager to invest in promising startups through their ICOs have to explore thoroughly the various exchange platforms and the social media dealing with ICOs. In this way, they find and evaluate the active and forthcoming ICOs, and can make their choice, buying the chosen tokens.

3.3   Overview of ICOs Phenomenon Statistics

In this section, in order to figure out the dimension of the ICO phenomenon, we provide some statistics. We analyzed from the 1th of December up to the 12th January 2017 specialized websites[1] which collect ICOs and their details.

---

[1] ICO data are extracted from the following websites:
http://www.icobench.com,
http://www.coinschedule.com,
http://www.icowatchlist.com,
http://www.coingecko.com,
http://www.icoalert.com,
http://www.icostats.com,
http://www.icodrops.com.

We can state that 2017 was the year of ICOs. According with icowatchlist.com data, during that year ICO raised over 3.3 billion dollars. By comparison, in 2016 ICOs raised a total of 106 million dollars[2]. Exploring ICOs we realize that they represent a global phenomenon. In particular, 88 nations presented at least one ICO. Despite this reality, it must be said that four countries raised over the 54% of the total. They are Switzerland (21%), United States (19.1%), Israel (7.6%) and Singapore (6.7%). As regards the number of ICOs per nation, USA, Russia, UK and Singapore are the most active nations. Table 1, summarizes the first ten nations per total raised amount.

Table 1. The first ten nation involved in the ICO phenomenon spread

Country	Total raised	% of Total	ICO projects
Switzerland	463,775,825	21.02%	51
United States	421,402,100	19.10%	248
Israel	167,370,000	7.59%	15
Singapore	148,780,000	6.74%	79
Russian Federation	81,174,361	3.68%	202
France	78,050,000	3.54%	15
United Kingdom	61,050,000	2.77%	106
Serbia	53,070,000	2.41%	4
Gibraltar	27,480,000	1.25%	14
Spain	26,660,000	1.21%	10

By the end of 2017 the icobench.com website listed 1259 ICOs, referring to a heterogeneous set of projects. About 50% of ICO projects are ICOs already ended. 33% are ongoing ICO and the remaining 17% are upcoming ICOs.

In order to understand the ICO trend we decided to categorize them by industrial sector. In this regard, we pinpointed all relevant data from the aforementioned ICO websites. However, each website presents information by considering different criteria and perspective, and only a few of them propose a classification. In general, an ICO is described by: name, logo, token, start date, end date, description, website, white paper, social links, accepted cryptocurrency, development platform, ICO price, min and max target amount to raise, country, upcoming, ongoing, ended, and so on.

Merging and cross-referencing the analyzed data, we built the taxonomy shown in Table 2. To identify the taxonomy dimensions, we made a list of categories already identified by the various websites, using as labels the most used ones. In some cases we joined some of them. In total, we identified 24 dimensions which represent the category of industrial ICO sectors. Afterward, we populated the taxonomy considering both the number of projects developed and the amount

---

[2] https://www.coindesk.com/2016-ico-blockchain-replace-traditional-vc/.

Table 2. An industrial sector taxonomy of ICOs

Category	% Projects per category	% Fund raised per category
Blockchain Platform & Services	20,00%	25,00%
Finance	12,00%	7,00%
Trading & Investing	10,00%	8,50%
Commerce/Retail	8,00%	3,00%
Payments/Wallets/Cryptocurrency	8,00%	9,00%
Gaming/VR	6,00%	4,00%
Funding/VC	5,00%	1,20%
Network/Communication/Storage	5,00%	20,00%
Betting/Gambling	3,00%	2,00%
Data/Artificial Intelligence/Machine Learning	3,00%	2,00%
Media/Content	3,00%	0,50%
Healthcare	2,00%	7,00%
Real estate	2,00%	0,80%
Security/Identity	2,00%	2,00%
Social Network	2,00%	3,00%
Energy/Utilities	1,50%	0,40%
Education	1,00%	0,01%
Industry/Logistics	1,00%	0,20%
Insurance	1,00%	0,20%
Mining	1,00%	0,30%
Transportation	0,70%	0,20%
Tourism	0,40%	0,10%
Legal	0,05%	0,40%
Other	2,35%	3,19%

of funds raised in each specific sector. In this way, we were able to understand the ICO sector trend and the investors interest towards projects. We represent results in percentage terms. Table 2 shows that projects in *Blockchain Platform & Services* are the most popular: 20% of projects has been launched in this sector. We can also see that these projects are the most heavily funded, having received 25% of the total raised amount. The second most funded category is *Network/Communication/Storage* with 20% of funds raised. Therefore, we notice that nearly half of all investors are interested in the two above mentioned categories.

Since ICO funding is an ever changing phenomenon, the proposed classification should not be considered as definitive, but as a starting point on a path toward a more exhaustive categorization.

Table 3. The ten most important ICOs of 2017

Name	Total raised (USD M.)	Category	Start date	Duration	Team (Advisors)	Nation
HDAC	258	BC Platform & Services	27/11/17	25	17 (7)	Switzerland
FileCoin	257	Network/Communication/ Storage	10/08/17	31	13 (0)	USA
Tezos	232	BC Platform & Services	01/07/17	12	11 (3)	USA
EOS	185	BC Platform & Services	11/06/17	15	4 (0)	USA
Paragon Coin	183	BC Platform & Services	15/09/17	30	12 (0)	Russia
Sirin Lab	158	Commerce/Retail	12/12/17	14	42 (7)	Switzerland
Bancor	153	BC Platform & Services	12/06/17	31	8 (10+5)	Israel
Polkadot	145	BC Platform & Services	15/10/17	12	NA	Singapore
QASH	105	Trading & Investing	606/11/17	02	9 (9)	Singapore
Status	102	Other	20/06/17	31	7 (0)	Switzerland

We show in Table 3 the ten most funded ICOs in 2017, reporting also their category, according to the taxonomy shown in Table 2.

ICO Dataset. The dataset has been populated using the API provided by icobench.com website[3]. On date 16 January 2018, we updated the ICO dataset, holding on that date information regarding 1542 ICOs. In particular, we used the POST request

$$https://icobench.com/api/v1/ico/\{id\}$$

where {id} is a progressive number that uniquely identifies an ICO. This request provided comprehensive information about each ICO stored in the website database. The data were extracted using a script written in R language, which includes the *httr*[4] library developed by Wickham.

In order to analyze a temporally homogeneous set of ICOs, we selected the ICOs started and ended during 2017. This set includes 690 ICOs. The sum of the raised amounts by these ICOs during 2017 is about 5.20 billion dollars. Considering only ICOs with non-zero raised amount, the average value of these amounts is about 17.21 million dollars, whereas the median is 7.30 million dollars. To focus the attention on the magnitude of the raised amounts, we considered the raised amount in log_{10} scale. This value is included in the range 2–9. In addition, to describe each ended ICO, we extracted four static key features from the dataset: the ICO Duration in days, the Rate (a rating score provided by icobench.com that summarize the overall quality of the ICO), the total Team size, the number of advisors, and the total raised amount. We then excluded 119 ICOs having zero team members or whose total raised amount was not-available.

---

[3] https://github.com/ICObench/data-api for references.
[4] https://cran.r-project.org/web/packages/httr/httr.pdf.

We investigated if and how key features influence the final raised amount computing, at first, the correlation factor between each key element and the raised amount for each ICO. In Table 4 we summarize the four key features and their values. It is interesting to note that the ICO duration and the raised amount have a negative correlation. We focused the attention on the team size, considering all people registered in the dataset, including developers, advisors and supporters of the ICO. The average number of team members is 10.9, with a standard deviation equal to 7.1. In Fig. 1 the distribution of the team size is provided.

Table 4. Summary of the four key elements selected to investigate how they affect the total raised amount in terms of correlation coefficient.

	Duration	Team size	Advisors	Rating
Max value	112 days	58	17	4.9
Average	29.65 days	10.87	2.17	3.18
Standard Deviation	18.09	7.05	3.37	0.80
Correlation	−0.28	0.32	0.22	0.34

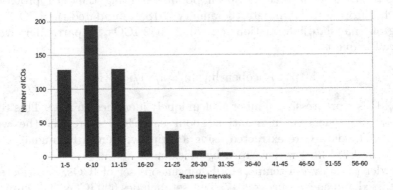

Fig. 1. Team size distribution

The correlation between the time size and the raised amount of the ICO in log_{10} scale is equal to 0.32. To investigate the relation between team size and ICO success, we computed the average raised amount per team size (AR), and the minimum raised amount per team size (MR). Results show that both these data are more correlated with the team size than the original data. The AR and the team size have a correlation coefficient equal to 0.51, whereas MR and team size have a correlation coefficient equal to 0.76. To describe the proportionality of these results with the team size, we computed the linear regression $y = m(x) + q$, where and x is the team size and y is the log_{10} of the amount. The AR function has parameters m = 0.017 (with standard error 0.11) and q = 6.67 (with standard error 0.12). The MR function has parameters m = 0.064 (with standard error 0.009) and q = 4.88 (with standard error 0.23) Fig. 2 shows these two functions. Blue diamond dots represent the linear regression function of the minimum raised amount per team size. Red squared dots represent the linear regression function of the average raised amount per team size.

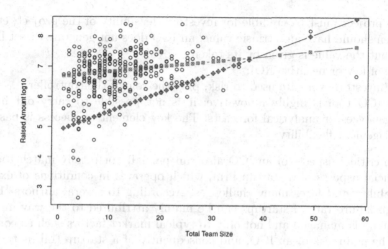

Fig. 2. Raised amount per team size.

3.4   ICOs' Critical Aspects

An ICO is based on the assumption that investors will buy the ICO token in order to obtain a future return on investment (ROI). In particular, an investor will buy the token at the ICO selling price with the aim of selling it after ICO ends, at a higher price. For this reason, an ICO must be organized to be attractive to investors. In short, an ICO must first of all be credible. ICO general information, the product information, the team composition, and the vision of the proposing startup, are key elements in the eyes of investors during the evaluation of investment opportunity.

In traditional VC rounds, investors acquire an ownership percentage, after a business evaluation. Conversely, ICO investors do not enter in the business ownership. Investors aim to obtain a profit on what they are buying, i.e. the token. Actually, token are something that will allow the access to some services after the startup idea will be realized. Investors wish to buy tokens whose value will increase after the startup business will launch its product. The first investment performance indicator is the ROI. As of writing, the vast majority of closed ICOs are characterized by a positive ROI, and several cases present a very high increase of the token value (see for instance the ROI of Stratis and NEO, characterized by a return on January 2018, greater than one thousand percent!). In few cases, investors lost theirs money, as in the case of Paragon ICO, one of the ICOs which raised most money, that currently has a negative ROI (−44%). Another important aspect is that ICO investment can be liquidated just by selling the bought tokens (the equivalent of the exit operation in venture capital). Tokens, however, are not directly payable in fiat currency. They have to be sold in specialized exchange websites, at the market price. This price is typically highly volatile, thus presenting a high risk. Summarizing, critical aspects of ICOs are:

- ICO project must be credible for investors (feasibility of the project, etc.);
- Token should have an intrinsic value: an ICO does not generate direct liquidity, but the value is given by its token;
- Risk of low or negative ROI;
- The investors, who are used to risk, play the role of the controller.
- The ICO tool is highly innovative: it is not possible to carry out historical analyzes or analytical forecasts. The key element of success is based on management flexibility.

The critical aspects of an ICO also can partially or totally match the typical crucial aspects of a startup firm, which operates in conditions of extreme vulnerability and faces many challenges. According to several authors [13,14], the high failure rate of startups can be mainly attributed to the way in which the startup is managed and not only to typical market factors such as competition. The main risk of an ICO, and consequently of a startup [14], is therefore to spend time, money and energy in the development of a service or a product which people are not interested in.

What Would be Needed to Reduce the Identified Problems?

After highlighting the limitations of an ICO and the challenges that a startup faces, in the followings we point out what are the elements that can contribute to the success of an ICO.

- Investor involvement not only in the fundraising phase, but also in the subsequent phases. Business risk is therefore shared, and investors are called upon to invest only in projects they really believe in and where they can make a significant contribution also in terms of ideas. In this way, the risk of speculation is limited.
- The design idea must be manageable through a token.
- The business model must be feasible and therefore concrete, sufficiently detailed, but at the same time must be flexible.
- A complex project can be divided into phases: the first steps, if the startup project is innovative, are the most critical.
- It is good to test the project idea right away by analyzing feedback from a small number of users.

The elements highlighted above, designed to increase the probability of success of a startup, are supported by numerous studies [15–18], and are typical of lean startup methodology in which the focus is on the customer, the decision-making process is based on the facts and pivoting and agile/lean thinking is fundamental.

4 ICOs as Lean Startups

According to [19], in order to create a successful ICO it could be helpful the use of The Lean methodology and Value Proposition Canvas. These strategies in fact can be used to ensure that the market of designed product actually exists and that the idea can be considered good. In the context of an ICO, moreover, the activities can not be exclusively focused on reaching a solution, but it is necessary to examine the problem in detail before proceeding with any elaboration [20]. At the start of an ICO, in fact, both the problem and the solution are not generally well understood by investors and often also by the development team. In this context of uncertainty, the typical elements of lean startup methodology such as prototyping, execution of experiments [22], validation of initial business hypotheses and continuous learning can be easily applied as elements of greater security [15,21]. We outline below some aspects of this methodology that can be easily applied to the management of an ICO.

1. **The Pivot**. It is a change of direction during the development of the project. All changes are based on what is learnt in the previous stages. If you reduce the time between the pivots you increase chances of success and you spend less money. The pivot is connected to the concept of feedback cycle formed by the three phases Build-Measure-Learn (BML) and to the Minimum Viable Product (MVP). A chance of success is proportional to the minimum time it takes to get through the BML loop, and then to the minimum time between pivots. With this approach, you start with an idea of product or startup, and the end result can be something else. The direct feedback and the tests by potential users of the product could therefore induce to change market segment, customer type, costs, partners, strategies, while maintaining the same vision of the startup. In an ICO, given that initial investors back the team more than the idea, the pivoting should not be a problem.

2. **Validated learning**. This process should apply to an ICO that works in an area of extreme uncertainty in order to verify the progress of the project [14]. A positive marker of an ICO in fact cannot be just the revenue. An iterative validated learning process allows an evaluation of the hypothesis (that could be valid or invalid) by running experiments and by the analysis of information that leads to the formulation of new ideas. Identifying a very clear use case that requires the decentralized approach typical of blockchain technology could be the first step of this process.

3. **Testing**. The Lean startup methodology highlights the importance of test cycles. It allows to verify concretely if the need really exists, if it is perceived by the identified target, and if it is strong enough to be satisfied. Testing speeds up learning and create a competitive value. When a stakeholder analyses an ICO, one of the most relevant questions is if the idea and the team are good in that specific context. According to Lean Startup methodology, the success of an ICO could be connected to testing the product in each phase, to verify the need and the use of the product. In accordance with the decentralized nature of the blockchain, the use of tests applied in a decentralized way can be useful.

4.1   Three Different Case Studies

In our work, we aim to analyze the ICO phenomenon based on the lean startup methodology. We examined those ICOs in which the proposer team states explicitly that a lean startup approach is used. We examined three different case studies, each with a different application of this methodology. The first ICO uses the principles of modularity, simplicity and scalability typical of lean startup methodology to develop a platform to build decentralized applications; the second, according to lean startup methodology, focuses its attention on feedback from users. Finally, the third ICO designs a platform that, using the lean startup methodology, aims to address the problem of lack of interaction between investors and development team of ICOs.

Lisk - Blockchain Application Platform. Lisk[5] is one of the oldest ICOs and is a lean startup. It was registered in Switzerland by Max Kordek, Oliver Beddows and Guido Schmitz-Krummacher on 22 February 2016 and raised money in bitcoins. The platform was born from a fork of Crypti's blockchain and its price, as well as that of most tokens, peaked in 2017. At present, Lisk is one of the most solid startups financed by an ICO. Lisk has raised over 14,000 Bitcoins or about $ 9 million at the time of the campaign, and has now a market cap of more than one $ billion. Every month, on the ICO website a monthly report is published on the activities of the startup and on its financial evolution. Lisk spends around 76,000 CHF for its running costs per month. The daily volume traded on exchanges is of several tens of million CHF. Lisk is based on the principles of modularity, simplicity and scalability typical of lean startup methodology, and provides a platform for the construction and distribution of decentralized apps. Developers have the ability to build decentralized applications (DApp) with some mainstream programming languages such as JavaScript and Node.js. Therefore, developers do not need to learn the Solidity language, as in the Ethereum blockchain. Unlike what happens to the DApp on Ethereum, the applications developed on Lisk will be built on a parallel blockchain (sidechain), so as not to create problems for the main blockchain, especially in the case of bugs. A modular SDK allows developers to take advantage of a series of libraries, modules, algorithms and third-party tools that make the development environment user-friendly and customizable, and therefore suitable for creating blockchain applications.

Galactikka - A Social Networking Project. Galactikka[6] is another ICO in which the proposing team declares to use the lean startup methodology. Galactikka is an innovative social network that allows authors to promote their original content and to earn money with their posts, photos and video materials when they are published and shared. The platform integrates a community, blogs and a system for Q&A. The goal of Galactikka is therefore to help amateur authors to make themselves known and to profit from their creativity. Galactikka was designed in Russia, so its the main language is Russian. Galactikka uses the

---

[5] https://lisk.io/.
[6] http://galactikka.com/.

approach of phases and interactions typical of the Lean Startup methodology, giving great value to the feedback provided by the users. For this reason, in the first instance, the team prefers to use only the Russian language, because it is the language best known to them. In the first phase also the contents inserted by the users will have to be in Russian language. According to the lean startup method, it is in fact convenient to test the application on a small group of users. In this way, the development team intends to concentrate initially on a limited user target, whose language is fully understood, in order to avoid wasting energy and resources on a global audience that is too large. In this way, it is possible to increase the speed of development of the project.

doGood - Blockchain-Fueled Social Platform for Lean Startup. doGood[7] aims to get through one of the main limitations of an ICO: the lack of tools that can allow investors to provide feedback during the development phases of the project idea related to a startup. With a lean startup approach, doGood wants to offer funders the opportunity to monitor the team's progress and to provide direct guidance at all stages of the project. The lean startup methodology is needed, given the uncertainty in the evolution of the project, and in order to ensure that the proponent team provides the promised results, thus determining an increase in the value of the token. Using the lean startup methodology, the doGood ICO seeks to improve interactions between the team and other stakeholders. Smart contracts help decision making and reduce the cost and the time-to-market. In this way, it is possible to increase token value and reduce the risks involved in these ventures. doGood is therefore a web platform that stems from the idea that it is necessary to improve interaction between people by proposing a democratic method to solve complex problems based on open innovation principles, design thinking and especially on lean startup philosophies. Every person involved in the project, and therefore also every investor, in a decentralized way and from any part of the world can indeed perform a series of activities and be totally protagonist of the success of the startup. Incentives and governance system are based on the Ethereum blockchain, aiming to a better identification of solutions to problems, and to the ability of proposing arrangements in a decentralized and large-scale manner. The system is designed with the hybrid use of two architectural paradigms: a client-server architecture (centralized), and a client-server architecture based on blockchain technology (decentralized). This ICO merges the use of smart contracts with the lean startup methodology, gaining a double advantage for investors – they have greater visibility within the project and the related startup, and can provide relevant and appropriate information on the construction of the system. The token is called just GOOD. A smart contract system, in application of the lean startup methodology, is connected to the various decision-making milestones of the project's evolution. A GOOD token is assigned to a project in exchange for the VOTE tokens. VOTE-type tokens are used by investors, proportional to the amount of GOOD Token hold, to be able to cast their votes in the decision-making stages of the project. In this way, the Product Development Team can understand unequivocally, as a

---

[7] https://dogood.io/.

result of a democratic operation, what are the wishes of the investors. The use of the blockchain is useful for its intrinsic properties that guarantee authenticity and security of the vote of the stakeholders.

5 Conclusions

In our work we analyzed the new and complex phenomenon of ICOs, an alternative means of financing startups based on the concept of token and on a decentralized blockchain approach. Startups based on a ICO are playing a fundamental role in creating the market of blockchain applications. ICOs provide a pre-sale of tokens what will be used to pay for a service to be launched on the market, or even the launch of a new cryptocurrency. In most cases, the same investors become consumers or users of the same service. All this allows investors to buy crypto tokens at a discounted price, even if in reality their value will be dictated by the mechanism of supply and demand only after being placed on the market. An ICO can be a valuable tool for those teams that want to quickly obtain financing, but it also has several limitations, due essentially to the immaturity of the technological system and to the risk of financial speculation.

In this work, we analyzed the ICO phenomenon starting from the available data provided by ICO datasets, performing various statistical computations to understand what affects the ICO success. Then, we tried to understand if the Lean startup approach can be useful to solve some of ICO issues. The tokenization nature of an ICO proposal needs a form of sustainable and regulated token sale event, that can be built on an MVP. The concepts of *pivot* and *validated learning* can be very useful, but also the investors' goals must be taken into account. They can be directed exclusively to immediate gain and not to company growth, strategic planning or operational work. A Lean startup methodology could be useful in order to respond to a tokenization that gives rise to new business models and new products or services that must effectively address customer needs. Many iterations and the direct involvement of all the stakeholders can further improve and help to market the original idea.

Acknowledgments. The work presented in this paper has been partially funded by Regione Autonoma della Sardegna, under project AIND - POR FESR Sardegna 2013. The authors thank icobench.com for permission to use their API.

References

1. Barsan, I.: Legal Challenges of Initial Coin Offerings (ICP). Social Science Research Network (2017)
2. Flood, J., Robb, L.: Trust, Anarcho-Capitalism, Blockchain and Initial Coin Offerings. Social Science Research Network (2017)
3. Porru, S., Pinna, A., Marchesi, M., Tonelli, R.: Blockchain-oriented software engineering: challenges and new directions. In: Proceedings of the 39th International Conference on Software Engineering Companion, pp. 169–171. IEEE, May 2017

4. Kaal, W., Dell'Erba, M.: Initial Coin Offerings: Emerging Practices, Risk Factors, and Red Flags. Social Science Research Network (2017)
5. Fenu, G., Marchesi, L., Marchesi, M., Tonelli, R.: The ICO phenomenon and its relationships with ethereum smart contract environment. In: Proceedings of the SANER 2018 Conference, IWBOSE (2018)
6. Hartmann, F., Wang, X., Lunesu, M.I.: Evaluation of initial cryptoasset offering: the state of the practice. In: Proceedings of the SANER 2018 Conference (2018)
7. Venegas, P.: Initial Coin Offering (ICO) Risk, Value and Cost in Blockchain Trust-less Crypto Markets. Social Science Research Network (2017)
8. Adhami, S., Giudici, G., Martinazzi, S.: Why do businesses go crypto? An empirical analysis of Initial Coin Offerings. Social Science Research Network (2017)
9. Poppendieck, M., Cusumano, M.A.: Lean software development: a tutorial. IEEE Softw. **29**(5), 26–32 (2012)
10. Bosch, J., Holmström Olsson, H., Björk, J., Ljungblad, J.: The early stage software startup development model: a framework for operationalizing lean principles in software startups. In: Fitzgerald, B., Conboy, K., Power, K., Valerdi, R., Morgan, L., Stol, K.J. (eds.) Lean Enterprise Software and Systems. Lecture Notes in Business Information Processing, vol. 167, pp. 1–15. Springer, Heidelberg (2013). https://doi.org/10.1007/978-3-642-44930-7_1
11. Mollick, E.: The dynamics of crowdfunding: an exploratory study. J. Bus. Ventur. **29**(1), 1–16 (2014)
12. Wang, N., Li, Q., Liang, H., Ye, T., Ge, S.: Understanding the importance of interaction between creators and backers in crowdfunding success. Electron. Commer. Res. Appl. **27**, 106–117 (2018)
13. Blank, S.: The Four Steps to the Epiphany: Successful Strategies for Products that Win. BookBaby, Cork (2013)
14. Ries, E.: The Lean Start-up: How Constant Innovation Creates Radically Successful Business. Portfolio Penguin, Londres (2011)
15. Björk, J., Ljungblad, J., Bosch, J.: Lean product development in early stage startups. In: IW-LCSP@ ICSOB, pp. 19–32, June 2013
16. Mueller, R.M., Thoring, K.: Design thinking vs. lean startup: a comparison of two user-driven innovation strategies. In: Leading Through Design, p. 151 (2012)
17. Silva, S.E., Calado, R.D., Silva, M.B., Nascimento, M.A.: Lean Startup applied in Healthcare: A viable methodology for continuous improvement in the development of new products and services. IFAC Proc. **46**(24), 295–299 (2013)
18. Miski, A.: Development of a mobile application using the lean startup methodology. Int. J. Sci. Eng. Res. **5**(1), 1743–1748 (2014)
19. Initial Coin Offerings (ICOs): What They Are and How to Market Them. https://blog.ladder.io/ico-marketing-strategy. Accessed 10 Jan 2018
20. Mullins, J.W., Komisar, R.: Getting to Plan B: Breaking Through to a Better Business Model. Harvard Business Press, Boston (2009)
21. Hart, M.A.: The Lean Startup: How Today's Entrepreneurs Use Continuous Innovation to Create Radically Successful Businesses Eric Ries, 2011, 320 pp. Crown Business, New York (2012)
22. Moogk, D.R.: Minimum viable product and the importance of experimentation in technology startups. Technol. Innov. Manage. Rev. **2**(3), 23 (2012)

Author Index

Anslow, Craig 259

Baralla, Gavina 293
Barroca, Leonor 131
Bergersen, Gunnar R. 267
Biddle, Robert 259
Bjørnson, Finn Olav 216
Bosch, Jan 277
Brataas, Gunnar 248

Chita, Pritam 160
Choma, Joelma 68

da Silva, João Pablo S. 3
da Silva, Tiago Silva 68
Diebold, Philipp 123
Dingsøyr, Torgeir 191, 216, 267
Dominguez-Mayo, F. J. 19
dos Santos, Ernani César 104

Ecar, Miguel 3

Florea, Raluca 54
Fontdevila, Diego 146

Gainey, Fernando 146
Grini, Mari 86
Guerra, Eduardo M. 68

Hanssen, Geir Kjetil 248
Hauder, Matheus 232

Ibba, Simona 293

Jørgensen, Magne 179

Karvonen, Teemu 131
Kepler, Fabio 3
Kleehaus, Martin 232
Kropp, Martin 259

Lindsjørn, Yngve 267

Marchesi, Michele 293
Matthes, Florian 232
Mattos, David Issa 277
Meier, Andreas 259
Mikalsen, Marius 191
Milosheska, Bisera 86

Oliveros, Alejandro 146
Olsson, Helena Holmström 277
Oyetoyan, Tosin Daniel 86

Paez, Nicolás 146
Pinna, Andrea 293

Ræder, Georg 248
Rivero, José Matias 19
Rossi, Gustavo 19

Schimpfle, Christina 232
Schoemaker, Lennard 199
Sharp, Helen 131
Sjøberg, Dag I. K. 267
Soares Cruzes, Daniela 86
Solem, Anniken 191
Stettina, Christoph Johann 199, 216
Stray, Viktoria 54

Theobald, Sven 123
Torres, Nahime 19

Uludağ, Ömer 232
Urbieta, Matias 19

Vestues, Kathrine 191
Vilain, Patrícia 104

Wagner, Stefan 37
Wang, Yang 37
Wijnmaalen, Julia 216

Author Index

Printed in the United States
by Bookmasters

Printed in the United States
By Bookmasters